THE GREAT RAILWAY

The National Dream
and *The Last Spike*

PIERRE BERTON

THE GREAT RAILWAY

Abridged by the author from

The National Dream
and *The Last Spike*

M&S

Canadian Cataloguing in Publication Data

Berton, Pierre, 1920–
  The great railway

Contents: The national dream — The last spike.
Includes index.
ISBN 0–7710–1335–3

1. Canadian Pacific Railway — History.   2. Canada — History —
1867–1914.   3. Railroads and state — Canada.
I. Title.   II. Title: The national dream.   III. Title: The last spike.

HE2810.C2B4   1992   385′.0971   C92–093249–5

Printed and bound in Canada

McClelland & Stewart Inc.
The Canadian Publishers
481 University Avenue
Toronto, Ontario   M5G 2E9

Contents

Maps

Drawn by Courtney C. J. Bond

Books by Pierre Berton

The Royal Family
The Mysterious North (1956), (1989)
Klondike (1958), (1972)
Just Add Water and Stir
Adventures of a Columnist
Fast, Fast, Fast Relief
The Big Sell
The Comfortable Pew
The Cool, Crazy, Committed World of the Sixties
The Smug Minority
The National Dream
The Last Spike
Drifting Home
Hollywood's Canada
My Country
The Dionne Years
The Wild Frontier
The Invasion of Canada
Flames Across the Border
Why We Act Like Canadians
The Promised Land
Vimy
Starting Out
The Arctic Grail
The Great Depression

Picture Books
The New City (with Henri Rossier)
Remember Yesterday
The Great Railway
The Klondike Quest

Anthologies
Great Canadians
Pierre and Janet Berton's Canadian Food Guide
Historic Headlines

For Younger Readers
The Golden Trail
The Secret World of Og
The Capture of Detroit
The Death of Isaac Brock
Revenge of the Tribes
Canada Under Siege
Bonanza Gold
The Klondike Stampede

Fiction
Masquerade (pseudonym Lisa Kroniuk)

Preface to the Abridged Edition

This book contains about half the material appearing in the original editions of *The National Dream* and its sequel, *The Last Spike*. In the present work I have concentrated on the main story of the building of the railroad and have dispensed with many side issues, which, though interesting as social history, are not essential to the tale. In pruning the original volumes from more than four hundred thousand words to a manageable two hundred thousand, I have also cut the number of examples and anecdotes, often letting one do the work of two. Scholars will find complete reference notes in the hardcover editions.

Kleinburg, Ontario
November, 1973

THE
NATIONAL
DREAM

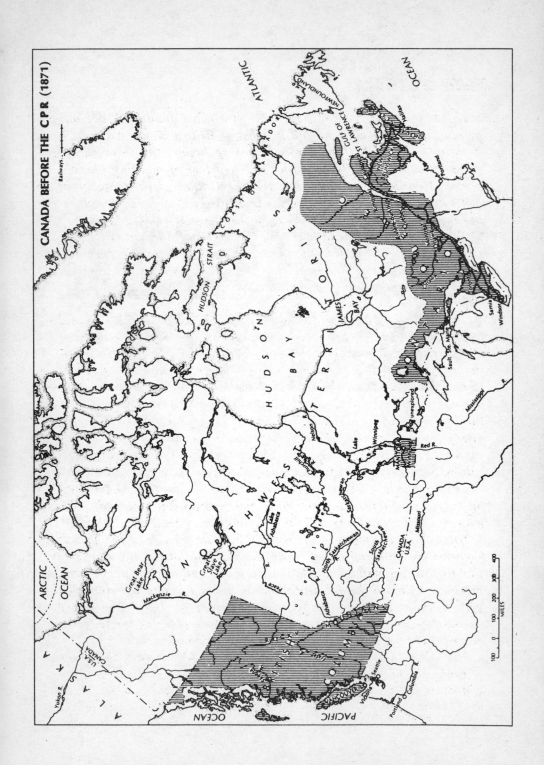

CANADA BEFORE THE CPR (1871)

FROM SEA TO SEA

It is New Year's Day, 1871, the year in which Canada will become a transcontinental nation, and in most of British North America it is bitterly cold. In Ottawa, where it is 18 below, the snow, gritty as sand, squeaks eerily beneath the felted feet of morning church-goers. A cutting wind, blowing off Lake Ontario, is heaping great drifts against the square logs of the Upper Canadian barns, smother-ing the snake fences and frustrating the Grand Trunk's Montreal-Toronto passenger schedule. On the St. Lawrence, in front of Quebec City, that annual phenomenon, the ice bridge, is taking form. In the harbour of Saint John, the rime hangs thickly upon the rigging, turning schooners and barquentines into ghost ships.

Only at the colonial extremities is New Year's Day a green one. In the English gardens of Victoria, British Columbia, the occasional yellow wallflower still blooms shyly, and in the verdant colony of Prince Edward Island the fields are free of frost. The editorial com-ments are as salubrious as the climate. The potato farmers of Souris and Summerside read their Saturday Islander with approval: "In our cosy little Island we have scarcely experienced anything but the blessings of Providence," it says. "It is probable that never at any previous period of our existence were we as rich a commun-ity as we are at the moment." There is cause for rejoicing: the colony is eagerly awaiting new proposals from Canada calculated to entice it into Confederation; the rumours say that these will be far more liberal than the ones that have been rejected. And why not? After all, British Columbia has been promised a railway!

Three thousand miles to the west, the steam presses of the British Colonist are pumping out a New Year's salutation for the morrow. For British Columbia, the editor writes, the outlook has never been brighter: "Clad in bridal attire, she is about to unite her destinies with a country which is prepared to do much for her." The paper carries a reprint from a Tory journal back east, praising the Govern-ment for the nuptial present it is about to bestow.

The world is in its customary turmoil – the Germans at the gates of Paris, the insurrectionists bedevilling Cuba – but in Canada there is nothing but good humour. Even George Brown, the caustic editor of the Globe, is in a mellow mood. One can almost surmise a half-smile lighting up those long, Scottish features as he scribbles an unusually

15

*benign editorial in his Toronto office. "Peace and plenty prevail,"
he writes, "and there is nothing for us but hope and encouragement
as we welcome the advent of another year."*

*It is the Lord's Day and all across settled Canada the curtains
are drawn and the church bells are sounding. Only an eccentric would
resist their summons. Because of the Sabbath, all the elegant and
sometimes lusty New Year's rituals of the Canadian social classes
have been postponed for a day. The brass and rosewood, the sterling
and cut glass have all been polished to a high gloss by an army
of servants, making ready for Monday's "calling." Then will the
gentlemen of the towns, frock-coated and convivial, trudge unsteadily
from threshold to threshold, to be greeted by well-bustled matrons
with puckered lips and full decanters. The temperance movement
is crying out against such debauchery. In Montreal, it is reported,
some of the ladies have been persuaded to serve coffee. That city,
a correspondent notes, has already given the New Year "a sober
and orderly welcome."*

*Far off beyond the sombre desert of the Canadian Shield, at Fort
Garry in the new province of Manitoba, the welcome is not so orderly.
Fiddles screech, pipes skirl, and the settlers caper like souls possessed
to an endless succession of Red River reels, while nearby tables groan
with smoking joints of venison and buffalo. The great Scottish feast
of Hogmanay – New Year's Eve – is far more important than
Christmas.*

*For one Scotsman, there is a special reason to celebrate. Donald
A. Smith, late of Labrador, has just won a federal seat in his adopted
province's first election. It is a significant victory. The events set
in motion by the decisions of 1871 will change the current of Smith's
life and enshrine his likeness in the history books of a later century,
linking him forever with a symbolic railway spike in a distant mountain
pass.*

*That pass is one thousand miles to the west of the Red River and
for all that thousand miles scarcely a light flickers or a soul moves.
Awesome in its vastness and its isolation, the newly acquired North
West – the heart of the new Canada – sleeps beneath its blanket
of snow. Walled off from the Pacific by the vertebrae of the Cordilleras
and from the settled East by a granite Precambrian wasteland, the
great central plain is like an unconquered island.*

*The North West! The name is beginning to take on overtones of
romance. In the winter, when the blizzard strikes and the heavens
are blotted out, it can be a white hell; in the summer, by all accounts,
it is an enchanted realm. Once can travel for days, they say, along
the ruts of the Carlton Trail between Fort Garry and Fort Edmonton
without encountering human kind – only ridge after ridge of untram-*

melled park land rolling on towards the high arch of the sky. Out there, they say, the eye can feast upon acres and acres of tiger lilies and bluebells, stretching to the horizon "as if a vast Oriental carpet had been thrown across the plains." The prairie chickens, they say, are so numerous that they mask the sun, while the passenger pigeons roost so thickly on the oaks that the very branches snap beneath their weight. And there are exquisite lakes, speckled with geese and swans, broad meadows where the whooping cranes stalk about in pairs, and everywhere the ultimate spectacle of the buffalo, moving in dark rivers through a tawny ocean of waist-high grass. Only a privileged few have gazed upon these marvels; the events of 1871 will ensure that they will soon be just a memory.

How many white men inhabit this empty realm? Perhaps twenty-five hundred. Nobody knows for certain because there has never been an accurate census. The North West is a scattered archipelago of human islets, each isolated from the others by vast distances and contrasting life-styles – Scottish farmers, Métis buffalo hunters, Yankee whiskey traders, French missionaries, British and Canadian fur merchants. In the lonely prairie between these human enclaves the nomadic and warlike Indian bands roam freely.

For all of the decade, this wild, misunderstood domain will be the subject of endless speculation, curiosity, political manoeuvre and debate. There are few Canadians yet who care greatly about it; most provincial politicians, indeed, are "either indifferent or hostile to its acquisition." Yet by the fact of its acquisition, the young Dominion has set itself upon a new course. The Conservative prime minister, Sir John A. Macdonald, has just promised British Columbia a great railway across the North West to Pacific tidewater. Once that decision is confirmed, as it must be in this pivotal year of 1871, nothing can ever again be the same.

Chapter
One

THE
GREAT
LONE
LAND

1

Its political opponents pretended to believe that the Macdonald government had gone mad. "Insane" was the word the Liberal leader, Alexander Mackenzie, used, time and again for most of the decade of the seventies, to describe the pledge to build a railway to the Pacific. It was, he said in the House that spring of 1871, "an act of insane recklessness," and there were a good many Canadians, including some of John A. Macdonald's own supporters, who thought he was right.

Here was a country of only three and a half million people, not yet four years old, pledged to construct the greatest of all railways. It would be longer than any line yet built – almost one thousand miles longer than the first American road to the Pacific, which the United States, with a population of almost forty million, had only just managed to complete.

The Americans had more money, shorter mileage, and fewer obstacles; for one thing, they knew where they were going – there were established cities on their Pacific coastline. But the only settlement of account on the Canadian Pacific coast was on an island; the indentations in the mainland were uncharted, the valleys were unexplored, and the passes were unsurveyed.

For another thing, the United States was not faced with any barrier as implacable as that of the Precambrian Shield. If the railway followed an all-Canadian route, its builders would have to blast their way across seven hundred miles of this granite wasteland. There were ridges there that would consume three tons of dynamite a day for months on end; and, where the ridges ended, there was another three hundred miles of muskegs, which could (and would) swallow a locomotive at a single gulp. This was land incapable of cultivation. There were many who held with Alexander Mackenzie that to build a railway across it was "one of the most foolish things that could be imagined."

After the Shield was breached, the road was to lead across the North West – a tenantless empire of waving grass (which many thought to be unproductive desert) bordered by the thinly forested valley of the North Saskatchewan River. Every sliver of timber – railroad ties, bridge supports, construction materials – would have to be hauled, league after league, across this desolate land where, it seemed, the wind never ceased.

At the far limit of the plains the way was blocked by a notched wall of naked rock, eight thousand feet high. Beyond that wall lay a second wall and beyond that wall a third. At the end of that sea of mountains lay the unknown coastline, tattered like a coat beyond repair. George Etienne Cartier, acting for his ailing leader, had promised British Columbia that the railway would reach that coastline, ready to operate, within ten years. To Edward Blake, the intellectual giant of the opposing Liberal (or Reform) Party, it was "a preposterous proposition." Many of Macdonald's own followers agreed with him.

The Government had promised the railway to British Columbia in order to lure that colony into the new confederation of Ontario, Quebec, New Brunswick, Nova Scotia, and Manitoba. Macdonald's vision of Canada did not stop at the Great Lakes; his dream was of a transcontinental British nation in North America – a workable alternative to the United States. To achieve this dream and stitch the scattered provinces and empty territories of the West together, the Prime Minister insisted, the railway was a necessity. But there were also more pragmatic reasons. Macdonald needed the diversion of the railway to maintain himself in office. If he succeeded in fulfilling his pledge, the Conservative Party could probably look forward to a generation of power.

If the sceptics had considerable logic on their side, Macdonald had emotion. Could a country of three and a half million people afford an expenditure of one hundred million dollars at a time when a labourer's wage was a dollar a day? Perhaps not; but Macdonald meant to persuade the country that it could not do without a railway if it wanted to be a nation in the true sense of the word. Besides, the Government insisted, the railway would not bring any rise in taxes: it could be paid for with land from the North West.

Why the fixed date of ten years? As Macdonald's opponent Mackenzie said, most of the railway would run through an uninhabitable wilderness: "It wouldn't be necessary to construct the greater portion of the line for another thirty years." That was also perfectly true; but Macdonald's attitude was that there might be no nation in thirty years without a railway. If the land remained empty, the Americans would move in to fill the vacuum. Besides, he had the assurance of the chief British Columbia delegate, Joseph Trutch, that the ten-year clause was not a "cast iron contract"; the province would not hold the Canadian government to the letter of the wording.

It was the apparent insistence on an all-Canadian line that brought the harshest criticism. Few Canadians really believed that any railway builder would be foolhardy enough to hurdle the desert of rock between Lake Nipissing and the Red River. Macdonald's opponents were all for diverting the line south through United States territory, and then into Manitoba from Duluth. If North America had been one nation that would have been the sensible way to go. But Macdonald did not believe that Canada could call herself a nation if she did not have geographical control of her own rail line. What if Canada were at war? Could soldiers be moved over foreign soil? In the half-breed uprising of 1869, the troops sent to the Red River had taken ninety-six days to negotiate the forty-seven portages across the Canadian Shield. A railway could rush several regiments to the North West in less than a week.

The Prime Minister's nationalism had two sides. On the positive side he was pro-Canadian which, in those days, was much the same as being pro-British. On the negative side he was almost paranoiac in his anti-Americanism. The Americans, to Macdonald, were "Yankees," and he put into that term all the disdain that was then implied by its use. Macdonald's opponents might feel that the price of holding the newly acquired North West was too high, but he himself was well aware that some Americans, especially those in Minnesota, saw it as a ripe plum ready to fall into their hands. He believed, in fact, that the United States government "are resolved to do all they can, short of war, to get possession of the western territory." That being so, he wrote in January, 1870, "we must take immediate and vigorous steps to counteract them. One of the first things to be done is to show unmistakeably our resolve to build the Pacific Railway."

As Macdonald well knew, there were powerful influences working in the United States to frustrate the building of any all-Canadian railway. In 1869, a United States Senate committee report declared that "the opening by us first of a Northern Pacific railroad seals the destiny of the British possessions west of the ninety-first meridian. They will become so Americanized in interests and feelings that they will be in effect severed from the new Dominion, and the question of their annexation will be but a question of time." A similar kind of peaceful penetration had led eventually to the annexation of Oregon.

It was the railwaymen who coveted the North West. "I have an awful swaller for land," the Northern Pacific's General Cass told the Grand Trunk's Edward Watkin. In 1869 the Governor of Vermont, John Gregory Smith, who also happened to be president of the Northern Pacific, determined to build that line so close to the Canadian border that it would forestall any plans for an all-Canadian railway.

By the following year, Jay Cooke, the banker who was the real power behind the Northern Pacific, was so sure of capturing the same territory as a monopoly for his railroad that he was using the idea to peddle the company's bonds. On one side of the mountains, the railway would siphon off the products of the rich farmlands; on the other side it would drain the British Columbia mining settlements.

21

"Drain" was the operative verb; it was the one the Senate committee used. As for the Minnesotans, they saw their state devouring the entire Red River Valley. Their destiny lay north of the 49th parallel, so the St. Paul *Pioneer Press* editorialized. That was "the irresistible doctrine of nature."

But it was Macdonald's intention to defy nature and fashion a nation in the process. His tool, to this end, would be the Canadian Pacific. It would be a rare example of a nation created through the construction of a railway.

In the Canada of 1871, "nationalism" was a strange new word. Patriotism was derivative, racial cleavage was deep, culture was regional, provincial animosities savage and the idea of unity ephemeral. Thousands of Canadians had already been lured south by the availability of land and the greater diversity of enterprise, which contrasted with the lack of opportunity at home. The country looked like a giant on the map; for most practical purposes, it stopped at the Great Lakes.

The six scattered provinces had yet to unite in a great national endeavour or to glimpse anything remotely resembling a Canadian dream; but both were taking shape. The endeavour would be the building of the Pacific railway; the dream would be the filling up of the empty spaces and the dawn of a new nation.

2

For almost forty years before Macdonald made his bargain with British Columbia, there had been talk about a railway to the Pacific. Most of it was nothing more than rhetoric. For most colonial Canadians at mid-century the prospect of a line of steel stretching off two thousand miles into the Pacific mists was totally unreal. As early as 1834 a Toronto journalist, Thomas Dalton, talked vaguely of an all-steam route by river, rail, and canal from Toronto to the Pacific. His friends dismissed him as a mere enthusiast, by which they probably meant he was slightly demented. Later proposals were taken more seriously, but it was not until 1851 that the first concrete move was made when a Toronto promoter, Allan Macdonell, applied to the Legislative Assembly of Canada for a charter to build a railway to the Pacific. The standing committee on railways reported that the plan was premature: the land across which Macdonell's line would run belonged to the Hudson's Bay Company.

Macdonell's scheme was viewed "as an hallucination to amuse for a moment and then to vanish," but such criticism failed to daunt him. In spite of two more rejections he persevered, organizing public meetings to denounce the Hudson's Bay monopoly. He was perfectly confident that he would get his railway charter and he had reason to be, for the climate for railway building in Canada was undergoing a dramatic change. In 1853, the country entered into an orgy of railroad building. In this euphoric period was launched the partnership between railways, promoters, politicians, and government that was to become the classic Canadian pattern for so many public works.

Profits and politics tended to become inseparable, especially among Conservatives. Most Conservative politicians were business or professional men who welcomed the idea of a partnership between big business and government to build the country. By 1871, there were fifty-two men in the House and Senate with vested interests in railroads. Thirty-seven were Conservatives.

The Liberals' opposition to Macdonald's railway policy stemmed in part from the excesses of the railway boom of the fifties. They had reason to be outraged. Between 1854 and 1857 an estimated one hundred million dollars in foreign capital was pumped into Canada for the purpose of building railways. Much of it found its way into the pockets of promoters and contractors. Thomas Keefer, a respected engineer, told of cabinet ministers who accepted fees from these men and made them "their most intimate companions, their hosts and guests, their patrons and protégés." One American contractor, he said, virtually ran the Upper Canadian government in the fifties.

In this charged atmosphere Allan Macdonell got his way. In 1858, he secured a charter to construct a railway to the North West. His board of directors included two former premiers, a chief justice, and a future lieutenant-governor. In spite of this glittering display of political muscle the scheme had collapsed by 1860.

Then, in 1862, Sandford Fleming placed before the government the first carefully worked out plan for building a railroad to the Pacific. He was only thirty-five at the time and most of his awesome accomplishments, including the invention of standard time, lay ahead of him. Typically, his outline for a "highway to the Pacific" was explicit. It was to be built in gradual stages, it would cost about one hundred million dollars, and it would take at least twenty-five years to build.

It was the cautious and meticulous plan of a cautious and meticulous Scot, for Fleming, in spite of his inventive record (he had designed the first postage stamp in Canada and founded the Canadian Institute), was nothing if not deliberate. He worked out every detail down to the last horse, cross-tie, and telegraph pole, and, of course, to the last dollar. His gradualness, he conceded, would not "satisfy the precipitate or impatient," but he included in his memorandum a reminder of Aesop's hare and tortoise, pointing out that the line of the railway extended over forty-five degrees of longitude, which was "equal to one-eighth of a circle of latitude passing entirely around the globe." After all, wrote Fleming, "half a continent has to be redeemed and parted at least from a wild state of nature."

It was an impressive memorandum and it undoubtedly did a great deal to advance Fleming's considerable ambitions. Eight years later, when Canada's pledge to British Columbia passed the Commons, the Prime Minister appointed Fleming engineer-in-chief of the Canadian Pacific Railway in addition to his previous appointment to the same capacity with the government-owned Intercolonial, then being built to link the Maritime Provinces with central Canada. Being a politician, though a Scot, Macdonald *was* both "precipitate and impatient" by Fleming's standards. George Etienne Cartier had, on his behalf, promised British Columbia that the railway would be commenced within two years and finished in ten. Certainly ten years had a more attractive ring than twenty-five; and the Prime Minister could reassure himself that he had Joseph Trutch's promise that the Pacific province would not hold him too firmly to that reckless schedule.

3

The Canada of 1871 was a pioneer nation without an accessible frontier. The Canadian Shield was uninhabitable, the North West virtually unreachable. The real frontier was the American frontier, the real West the American West. As the decade opened, a quarter of all Canadians in North America were living south of the border.

Some went for adventure; some went for greater opportunity; but most went for land. The good land ran out in Upper Canada in the 1850's and over the next generation the country began to feel a sense of limitation as farmers' sons trekked off to Iowa and Minnesota, never to return. The nation's life-blood was being drained away.

The call of the land was far stronger than the call of country, for nationalism, in the seventies, was a sickly plant. The very utterance of the phrase "Canadian Nation" was denounced in some quarters. "Canada," said the *Globe*, "except by a mere play on words, is not a nation." The whole idea of a "national sentiment," to use the phrase of the day, was under suspicion as being slightly treasonous.

If far-off fields looked greener to many Canadians, it was because life at home often seemed drab and unrewarding. The novelist Anthony Trollope confessed that in passing from the United States into Canada one moved "from a richer country into one that is poorer, from a greater country into one that is less." An Irishman who had spent

24

a brief period in Canada before succumbing to the lure of the United States set down, in 1870, his feelings about the land he had left behind: "There is no galvanizing a corpse! Canada is dead – dead church, dead commerce, dead people. A poor, priest-ridden, politician-ridden, doctor-ridden, lawyer-ridden land. No energy, no enterprise, no snap."

It was a harsh indictment but there was some truth in it. The country was controlled by the land-owning classes – the merchants, the professional people, and the farm owners. In the United States manhood suffrage was universal; in Canada, the propertyless had no vote.

The new dominion was not yet a cohesive nation but rather a bundle of isolated village communities connected by tenuous threads. Three-quarters of the population lived in comparative isolation on farms where, of necessity, most activity ceased at dusk and where, at certain times of the year, the condition of the back roads made extended travel nearly impossible. There was scarcely a city worthy of the name "metropolis." Montreal with a population of one hundred thousand was really two communities – one French speaking, one English. Toronto, with half that population, was still largely an over-sized village dominated by men of narrow views – Methodists, Tories, and Orangemen. Ottawa was beyond the pale. For a newly elected Member of Parliament, it was, in the words of George Rose, the British humorist, "simple banishment." Rose, who passed briefly through the new dominion after touring the United States, thought of Canada as "at best the Siberia of Great Britain."

The industrial worker toiled for longer hours and for lower pay than his counterpart across the border. (In Quebec the *annual* wage in industry was $185; in Ontario, $245.) But industry employed fewer than two hundred thousand people. Thus the cities provided little opportunity for those who wanted to escape the drudgery of the farms.

In those days of dawn to dusk labour, there were three major spare-time activities: politics for the land holders, religion for the women, and strong drink for the labourers. The church was a welcome respite for those women who enjoyed no real reprieve from the desolation and travail of farm life. Politics was a game played in earnest by those who enjoyed the franchise; animosities were bitter and party allegiance was generally unyielding. As for alcohol, it was both the national pastime and the national problem. Half of all the arrests in the Dominion were for offences connected with liquor. Barn raisings, picnics, and work "bees" of all kinds were lubricated with barrels of what the flourishing temperance movement was calling "demon rum." Delirium tremens was a common ailment.

The labouring classes drank the most, for drink was the only amusement that came within the reach of their pocketbooks. A newspaper cost five cents – for that price you could get a full quart of beer in a tavern. A minstrel show cost fifty cents and for *that* you could buy a gallon or two of whiskey. The link between strong drink and the grey quality of Canadian life is inescapable.

It is small wonder, then, that under these conditions many a Canadian looked with longing eyes across the border where the work opportunities were more varied, where social conditions were better, where every man had the vote, and where the way to the frontier farmland was not barred by a thousand miles of granite and swamp.

It was a strangely intense love-hate relationship that the country had with the United States. Publicly the Americans were vilified; secretly they were admired. The Yankees were thought of as go-getters and, though this propensity was publicly sneered at, many a Canadian felt his own country's business leaders lacked something of the Americans' commercial zeal.

If the Yankees were envied, they were also feared. The memory of the Fenian raids by British-hating Irish-Americans was still green in everyone's mind; the suspicion lingered that the Americans had secretly encouraged them. Canadians were still moving to the United States in disturbing numbers, but in spite of this – or perhaps because of it – any newspaper could be sure of a hearing if it launched a violent anti-American attack and any politician could secure a following by damning the Yankees.

All these attacks on the Yankees underlined the undeniable truth that they were different from the British. Canada – aside from Quebec –was still very much a British nation, with British habits, attitudes, speech, mannerisms, and loyalties. Almost all immigrants came from the British Isles, continued to think of the motherland as "home," and often returned to it. The Dominion was, indeed, more British than Canadian. Class was important; church and family traditions were often placed above money in the social scale, and the "best" families flaunted coats of arms. Titles were coveted by politician and merchant prince alike. That was the great thing about Canada in their eyes: its British background provided the climate for a merchant nobility that served as a bulwark against the creeping republicanism from south of the border, which the newspapers decried so vehemently.

The newspapers published dire warnings to those who would emigrate. American commerce was declining, they declared; prices in the U.S. were excessively high; the rates of taxation were crushing; but it is doubtful if these attacks prevented many young men from quitting the narrow concession roads of Canada for the broader highways to the south. The railways were running west and prosperity followed them. In those halcyon days the building of a railway was automatically believed to spell good times: anyone who turned his eyes south and west could see that.

But railways meant something more. Out beyond that sprawl of billion-year-old rock lay an immense frontier, of which Canadians were dimly becoming aware. It was now their land, wrested in 1869 from the great fur-trading monopoly of the Hudson's Bay Company after two centuries of isolation; but they did not have the means of exploiting it. A railway could give them access to that empty empire. Canada in 1871 was a country whose population was trapped in the prison of the St. Lawrence lowlands and the Atlantic littoral. A railway would be the means by which the captive finally broke out of its cage.

4

The North West was, in 1871, an almost totally unknown realm. Until the sixties, it had been generally considered worthless to anyone but fur traders – a Canadian Gobi, barren, ice-locked, forbidding, and unfit for settlement. In 1855 the Montreal *Transcript* wrote that it would not even produce potatoes, let alone grain. This attitude was fostered and encouraged by the Hudson's Bay Company, whose private preserve it had been for almost two centuries. The last thing the great fur-trading empire wanted was settlers pouring in. Even bridges were taboo: they might enourage colonists.

James Young, the Galt politician, in his reminiscences of those days recalled that "even the most eminent Canadians were deceived by these representations": in 1867 Cartier was strongly opposed to the acquisition of the North West and Macdonald had no idea of its value.

George Brown, editor and publisher of the *Globe* and head of the Liberal or "Reform" party until 1867, felt differently. Historically, Montreal had dominated the North West through control of the fur trade; but in the mid-fifties, Toronto – under Brown's leadership – moved to seize the initiative from its metropolitan rival. In the summer of 1856, at the height of the railway-building spree, Brown launched a campaign designed to educate his readers to the potential of the North West and to force the Hudson's Bay Company to sell out. Twelve years later the company gave in and ceded all its territories to Canada.

Macdonald's own indifference to the North West terminated abruptly in 1869 when the Red River uprising inflamed the nation and launched the tragic odyssey of Louis Riel. No other figure in Canada's frontier past has so fascinated historians and writers, not

27

to mention playwrights and even librettists. Villain or hero, martyr or madman – perhaps all four combined – Riel dominates the story of the opening of the prairies.

When he set up his independent state in the heart of North America he was just twenty-five years old, a swarthy figure with a drooping moustache and a shock of curly hair. Some scores of literary scalpels have since attempted the dissection of that perplexing personality. All agree that he was a solitary man with few confidants outside of his priest and his mother. All agree that his Roman Catholic religion was a dominant force in shaping him; at the end of his life it was interwoven into his madness. The evidence shows that he was a passionate man with a quick temper and a love of popular adulation who liked to get his own way and who could be violent when crossed; it also shows that he preferred non-violence and on more than one occasion practised it to his own detriment. He could be as compassionate as he was pious, but he was hanged for a crime which some called murder and others, execution. He was, by turns, politically pragmatic and mystically idealistic. A champion who was prepared to sacrifice himself for his people, he was also capable of taking a bribe (to quit the country) in 1871 and of asking for another (to abandon his people and his cause) in 1885.

Riel was born a westerner and a Métis, which means he was a French-speaking Roman Catholic of mixed race. His father became an eloquent tribune of his people, and Louis inherited the mantle of political agitator. His schooling in Montreal and his own prairie heritage had moulded this clever, intense, and apparently humourless youth into a racial patriot ready to champion the half-breed cause at Red River.

The Métis were in a state of turmoil when Riel arrived back at St. Boniface in 1868, because their status quo was threatened by the yeasty combination of events arising out of Confederation and the imminent sale of the Hudson's Bay lands to Canada. The settlement of the West, they knew, meant an end to their own unique society, the loss of the lands on which many of them had squatted, usually without title, and the eventual break-up of their race.

Métis society was built on the law of the buffalo hunt, a twice-yearly event, which was run with a military precision that produced generalship of a high order and led to the first stirrings of political organization among an essentially nomadic people. The Métis were not Canadians and did not think of themselves as such. Neither did the white Selkirk settlers of the Red River region or the Protestant half-breed farmers. Within this community there was a small "Canadian Party" whose orientation was white, Protestant, Orange, and Upper Canadian. This group helped to precipitate the Métis uprising, which Riel did not begin but which he did organize and shape with consummate skill.

By the end of 1869, without a single act of violence, Riel and the Métis had raised their own flag over the Red River settlement and were preparing to treat on equal diplomatic terms with Donald A. Smith, the Hudson's Bay man from Montreal and Labrador, whom the Government had hastily dispatched. Since the fur company had formally relinquished its territory and Canada had yet to take it over, Riel was in an interesting bargaining position. Soon he had the entire community behind him save for the incendiary members of the Canadian Party whom he had imprisoned. Had matters rested there, Louis Riel would undoubtedly have brought the community peacefully into Confederation on Métis terms and taken his place as a great Canadian statesman.

That was not to be. Some of the prisoners escaped and mounted a counter-movement. The Métis quickly put it down, but one of the Canadians, a sinewy Orangeman named Thomas Scott, could not be put down. When he tried to murder Riel, he was summarily court-martialled and sentenced to be shot. In this single act of violence was laid the basis for a century of bitterness and controversy. Scott's tragedy, mythologized out of recognition (as Riel's was to be), kindled an unquenchable conflagration in Orange Ontario.

The massive demand for revenge forced the government to mount, in 1870, a largely unnecessary military expedition across the portages of the Shield to relieve a fort which Riel was preparing to hand over peacefully. The expedition did have one other purpose: Macdonald, now thoroughly alive to the perils of further indifference, was not unhappy about a show of military strength in the valley of the Red River which the Minnesota expansionists clearly coveted. By January, 1870, the Prime Minister had determined that speedy construction of a railway across the new territory to the Pacific was a necessity. He was certain Washington would try to use the Riel troubles to frustrate Canada's acquisition of the North West.

Riel's own story almost exactly parallels that of the railway. Unwittingly, he helped to launch it; unwittingly again, fifteen years later, he helped to save it; he was hanged within a few days of the driving of the last spike. Forced into hiding and finally into exile in the United States, Riel was twice elected to Parliament from the riding of Provencher in the new province of Manitoba, of which he was the undisputed founder. He could not take his seat – the Ontario government had put a price of five thousand dollars on his head – but before he vanished over the border, he indulged in one last, dramatic piece of stagecraft.

The scene is Ottawa in 1874 – a snowy afternoon in January. Two muffled figures appear at a side door of the Parliament Buildings.

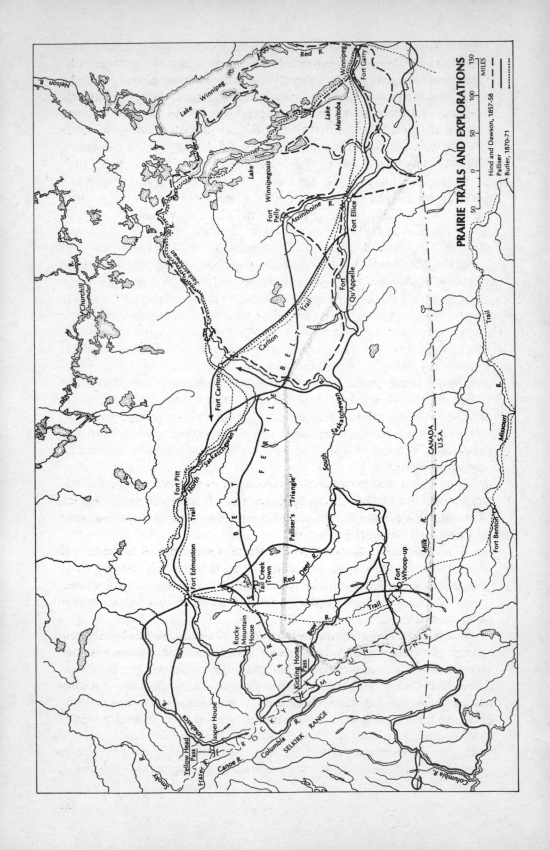

PRAIRIE TRAILS AND EXPLORATIONS

Hind and Dawson, 1857-58
Palliser
Butler, 1870-71

MILES

0   50   100   150

One tells the clerk on duty that a new member has come to sign the roll. The bored clerk hands the stranger a pen: he scratches his name and slips away. Idly, the clerk glances at it and utters a startled cry. There are the words "Louis Riel" burning themselves into the paper. The clerk looks up; but the outlaw waves sardonically and vanishes. He will not return until 1885 to play his unknowing role at the most critical moment of all in the history of the Canadian Pacific Railway.

5

By 1871, with the events from Manitoba still making headlines week after week, Canadians began to look upon their new North West with a mixture of wonder, guilt, and apprehension. *It must be wonderful to see it! Oh, if only one COULD see it, but it was so remote, so hard to reach! Something ought to be done about developing it; they said parts of it were very rich. But would you want to LIVE there – so far away from everything, in that dreadful climate? One day, of course, millions would live there – that was certain. One day . . .*

If the attitudes to the North West were vague, confused, and uncertain, part of the reason lay in the conflicting reports about it. Some said it was little more than a desert; others saw it as a verdant paradise. Even the two official government explorations of the territory launched in 1857 – one by the British, one by the Canadians – differed in their assessments.

The best-remembered of these expeditions was that of the British, mounted by a dashing Irish bachelor named John Palliser, who left his name on a triangle of supposed desert in what is now southern Alberta and Saskatchewan.

The expedition, backed by the Royal Geographical Society and the Imperial government, was asked to explore an empire from Lake Superior to the Rockies and to report on *everything* – agriculture, minerals, settlement possibilities, and, of course, possible transportation routes.

Palliser and his companions were two years in the field and their accomplishments were monumental. They explored, by a variety of routes, all of the country between Lake Superior and the Pacific coast. One of Palliser's associates, James Hector, discovered the Kicking Horse Pass and was almost buried alive as a result. His horse, stumbling in the frothing waters, dealt him a blow with its hoof which rendered him insensible. The Indians, believing him dead, popped him into a freshly dug grave and were about to shovel in the earth when the supposed corpse, conscious but unable to utter a word, managed, by a single prodigious wink of one eye, to shock the would-be burial party into less precipitate action. With Hector in great pain and his companions close to starvation, the party plunged on through the newly named pass, following the turbulent river along the line of the future CPR.

But the idea of a railway in the shadows of those rumpled peaks was far from Palliser's mind. He had been asked to judge whether or not, in the carefully non-committal prose of the Colonial Office, "the country presents such facilities for the construction of a railway as would at some period, though possibly a remote one, encourage her Majesty's government in the belief that such an undertaking between the Atlantic and Pacific Oceans will ever be accomplished."

His answer was bluntly negative. His knowledge of the country would never lead him to advocate a railway "exclusively through British territory." Across the prairies, certainly; but that armoured barrier north of Lake Superior "is *the* obstacle of the country and one, I fear, almost beyond the remedies of art." The sensible method was to go through American territory south of the lake and cut up to Manitoba through Pembina on the border, if and when the Americans built their own lines to that point.

Meanwhile the government of the united Canadas had mounted, in 1857 and 1858, two similar expeditions. The Canadian explorers were far more optimistic about an all-Canadian railway than their British colleagues. One, George Gladman, did not feel the difficulties to be "insuperable to Canadian energy and enterprise." Another, Henry Youle Hind, thought Palliser too sweeping in his condemnation of the route across the Shield. Hind, a geology professor from Toronto, agreed that the Great American Desert had its apex in the Far West, but along the wooded valley of the North Saskatchewan and some of its tributaries there was "a broad strip of fertile country." Hind wrote in his report that "it is a physical reality of the highest importance to the interest of British North America that this continuous belt can be settled and cultivated from a few miles west of the Lake of the Woods to the passes of the Rocky Mountains." In Hind's view this was the route that any railway must take to span the great central plain. He borrowed the magic name of "Fertile Belt," which Palliser had first used, and the name stuck.

Hind's enthusiasm for the Fertile Belt was to have a profound effect on the railway planners; from that point on few gave serious consideration to taking the CPR farther to the south. Hind also helped promote the North West as a land of promise. "A great future lies before the valley of the Saskatchewan," he declared. "It will become the granary of British Columbia, the vast pasture field by which the mining industry of the Rocky Mountains will be fed."

In 1871, a decade after Hind wrote those words, his vision still belonged to the future. To the men of the North West, Canada remained a foreign country; their world ran north and south. In the Far West, the mail bore United States postage, for it went out to civilization by way of Fort Benton, Montana. The Red River settlers' nearest neighbours lived in Minnesota, and the most travelled of the prairie trails was the one that ran from Fort Garry on the present site of Winnipeg to the railhead at St. Cloud, where the settlers did their shopping.

To cross the North West, in the days before the railway, was a considerable feat attempted by only a hardy few. The chief form of transportation was by Red River cart. These carts, pulled by oxen, were adapted from Scottish vehicles – light boxes, each perched on a single axle with wheels six feet high. There was one difference: they contained not a single nail or, indeed, a scrap of iron. Instead, tough strands of buffalo hide – the all-purpose "shaganappi" – were used. The axles could not be greased because the thick prairie dust would quickly immobilize the carts; as a result the wheels emitted an infernal screeching. As one traveller put it, "a den of wild beasts cannot be compared with its hideousness."

The carts generally travelled in brigades, some of them as long as railway trains, and they left deep ruts in the soft prairie turf, so deep that the wagons tended to spread out, the right wheel of one cart travelling in the wake of the left wheel of the cart ahead; thus, the prairie trails could be as much as twenty carts wide, a phenomenon that helps explain the broad streets of some of the pioneer towns.

These trails furrowed the plains like the creases on a human palm. The most famous was the Carlton Trail, winding for 1,160 miles from Fort Garry to the Yellow Head Pass in the Rockies. For half a century this was the broad highway used by every explorer, settler, trader, or adventurer who set his sights for the West. When the railway was planned, almost everybody expected it to follow the general course of the Carlton Trail. This was not to be, but a later railway did just that: it forms part of the Canadian National system today.

One man who followed the Carlton Trail and excited the imagination of the nation was an impulsive young subaltern named William Francis Butler. He was stationed in England when he learned that the Canadian government was mounting an expedition against Riel. The news could not have come at a more propitious moment. A remarkably intelligent officer, who had seen twelve years' overseas service in India, Burma, and Canada, he ought to have been promoted long before. But in those days commissions were purchased, not earned, and Butler did not have the fifteen hundred pounds it would have cost him to accept the proffered command of a company. He was positively thirsting for adventure "no matter in what climate, or under what circumstances." The news of the expeditionary force had scarcely reached England before Butler was off to the nearest telegraph office, dashing off a cable to the expedition's commander, Colonel Wolseley: *"Please remember me."* Then, without waiting for an answer, he caught the first boat for North America.

When Butler reached Canada he found to his chagrin that there was no job for him. He immediately invented one: that of an intelligence officer who, by travelling through the United States, might possibly enter Riel's stronghold from the south. Wolseley liked the idea and Butler leaped into his assignment with enthusiasm. He slipped past Riel and his men at the Red River, returned to the rebels' headquarters where he interviewed Riel himself, and then, following the old voyageur route, paddled his way east to the Lake of the Woods where he made his report.

When the troops entered Fort Garry, Butler was with them; but he found the subsequent weeks irksome. One night during a dinner at the home of Donald A. Smith, he suddenly announced that he was returning to Europe to resign his commission.

Smith had a better idea. Out along the North Saskatchewan there had been continuing disorders, which the local Hudson's Bay Company factors had been powerless to prevent. The Indians were being ravaged by smallpox and cheap whiskey. Something in the way of troops might be needed. Why not send Butler to make a thorough report?

Shortly thereafter, the Lieutenant-Governor sent for Butler, outlined Smith's plan, and suggested he think it over.

"There is no necessity, sir, to consider the matter," responded the impetuous officer. "I have already made up my mind and, if necessary, will start in half an hour."

It was typical of Butler that he made his mind up on the instant, regardless of the circumstances. He would not wait for the summer, when the trails were dry, the grouse plentiful, the shadberries plump and juicy, and the plains perfumed with briar rose. It was October 10, "and winter was already sending his breath over the yellowed grass of the prairies." With a single Métis guide, Butler set off on a cold and moonless night, the sky shafted by a brilliant aurora, prepared to travel by foot, horseback, and dog sled across four thousand miles of uninhabited wilderness.

"Behind me lay friends and news of friends, civilization, tidings of a terrible war, firesides, and houses; before me lay unknown savage tribes, long days of saddle-travel, long nights of chilling bivouac, silence, separation and space!" Butler loved every minute of it.

He acquitted himself handsomely. It was his recommendation to the government, following his return, that led to the formation of the North West Mounted Police. But it was his subsequent book, *The Great Lone Land,* with its haunting descriptions of "that great, boundless, solitary waste of verdure" that caught the public's imagination. The title went into the language of the day. For the next fifteen years no description, no reference, no journalistic report about the North West seemed complete without some mention of Butler's poetic phrase. It was as well that the CPR was built when it was; long before the phrase was rendered obsolete, it had become a cliché.

But Butler's description of what he saw and felt on that chill, solitary trek across the white face of the new Canada will never be hackneyed:

"The great ocean itself does not present more infinite variety than does this prairie ocean of which we speak. In winter, a dazzling surface of purest snow; in early summer, a vast expanse of grass and pale pink roses; in autumn, too often a wild sea of raging fire. No ocean of water in the world can vie with its gorgeous sunsets; no solitude can equal the loneliness of a night-shadowed prairie: one feels the stillness and hears the silence, the wail of the prowling wolf makes the voice of solitude audible, the stars look down through infinite silence upon a silence almost as intense. This ocean has no past – time has been nought to it; and men have come and gone, leaving behind them no track, no vestige, of their presence."

Butler's book was published in 1872. The following year another work on the North West made its appearance. It was so popular that it went into several editions and was serialized. Its title, *Ocean to Ocean,* also became part of the phraseology of the day. It was the saga of two bearded Scots, who, in one continuous passage by almost every conveyance available, travelled entirely through British territory to the Pacific Coast – a feat which captured the public's imagination.

The author of *Ocean to Ocean* was a remarkable Presbyterian minister from Halifax named George Monro Grant, who was to become one of the most distinguished educators and literary figures of his time. He was Sandford Fleming's choice for the post of secretary to the transcontinental expedition that the engineer-in-chief organized in 1872 to follow the proposed route of the new railway. The surveyor had determined to see the country for himself and discuss the progress of the field work at every point with the men on the ground.

Fleming was an impressive man, physically as well as intellectually, with a vast beard, a rugged physique, and a questing mind. He was forty-five years old at the time, and he still had half of his life ahead of him in which to complete the Intercolonial and plan the Canadian Pacific, devise a workable system of standard time, plan and promote the Pacific cable, act as an ambassador to Hawaii, publish a book of "short daily prayers for busy households," become chancellor of Queen's University, girdle the globe, and cross Canada by foot, snowshoe, dog team, horseback, raft, canoe, and finally by rail.

In Grant, Fleming had a trail-mate who was leather-tough and untroubled by adversity, a good man in the best sense, from whose bald brow there always seemed to shine the light of Christian good humour, in spite of an invalid wife and one retarded son. He himself had come through the fire, having been thrice at death's door in the very first decade of life: scalded half to death, almost drowned and given up for dead, and mangled by a haycutter, which cost him his right hand.

The expedition set out across the Great Lakes by steamer into the stony wasteland of the Shield where Fleming's surveyors were already inching their way. Not long after embarkation, Fleming's attention was attracted by the enthusiasms of an agile man who invariably leaped from the steamer the instant it touched the shoreline and began scrambling over rocks and diving into thickets, stuffing all manner of mosses, ferns, lichens, sedges, grasses, and flowers into a covered case which he carried with him.

It was only because the steamer whistled obligingly for him that he did not miss the boat. The sailors called him "the Haypicker" and treated him with an amused tolerance, but his enthusiasm was so infectious that he soon had a gaggle of passengers in his wake, scraping their shins on the Precambrian granite, as he plucked new specimens from between the rocks.

This was John Macoun, a professor of natural history, enjoying a busman's holiday in the wilds. Fleming asked him casually if he would care to come along to the Pacific, and Macoun, just as casually, accepted. Timetables in the seventies were elastic and, though the prospect of a twenty-five-hundred-mile journey across uncharted prairie, forest, mountain peak, and canyon might have deterred a lesser man, it only stimulated Macoun, in the garden of whose lively mind the images of hundreds of unknown species were already blooming.

Macoun was almost entirely self-taught. At thirteen he had quit school and departed his native Ireland to seek his future in Upper Canada. He began his new life as a farmhand, but he could not resist the lure of plants. Partly by trial and error, partly by osmosis, and partly by sheer, hard slogging he slowly made himself a naturalist of standing in both Europe and America. In 1869, he was offered a chair at Albert College, Belleville. That summer he began the series of Great Lakes vacation-studies that brought him, three years later, into the ken of Sandford Fleming.

This accidental meeting between Fleming and Macoun was immensely significant. Macoun became enamoured of the North West and ultimately helped change the course of the railway and thus, for better or for worse, the very shape of Canada.

By the time they left the steamer and headed out across the rock and muskeg towards the prairie, Macoun, Grant, and Fleming had become a close triumvirate. It makes a fascinating picture, this spectacle of the three bearded savants, all in their prime, each at the top of his field, setting off together to breast a continent. The prairie lured them on like a magnet. One night, after supper, realizing that it was only thirty-three miles away, they decided they *must* see it and pushed on through the night, in spite of a driving rain so heavy that it blotted out all signs of a trail. The three men climbed down from their wagon and, hand in hand, trudged blindly forward through the downpour until a faint light appeared far off in the murk. When, at last, they burst through the woods and onto the unbroken prairie they were too weary to gaze upon it. But the following morning the party awoke to find the irrepressible Macoun already up and about, his arms full of flowers.

"Thirty-two new species already!" he cried. "It is a perfect floral garden."

"We looked out," Grant wrote, "and saw a sea of green, sprinkled with yellow, red, lilac and white. None of us had ever seen the prairie before and behold, the half had not been told us. As you cannot know what the ocean is without having seen it, neither in imagination can you picture the prairie."

In Winnipeg, the party picked up a new companion – a strapping giant named Charles Horetzky, co-opted as official photographer for the party – and set out along the Carlton Trail. There were surprises all along the line of route. At one point they happened upon a flat plain, twelve miles wide, which was an unbroken mass of sunflowers, asters, goldenrod, and daisies – an Elysian field shining like a multi-coloured beacon out of the dun-coloured expanse of the prairie. At another they were struck by a hailstorm so strong that the very horses were flung to the ground and the carts broken.

At Edmonton the party split up. Fleming suggested that Horetzky and Macoun go north and try to get through the mountains by way of the Peace River and then head for Fort St. James and thence to the coast. He and Grant would go through the Yellow Head Pass to meet one of Fleming's survey parties. For Macoun it became a bizarre journey. It became increasingly clear, as the days wore on, that the swarthy Horetzky felt that the botanist was a drag on the expedition and had determined to get rid of him by fair means or foul – or at least that is what Macoun believed.

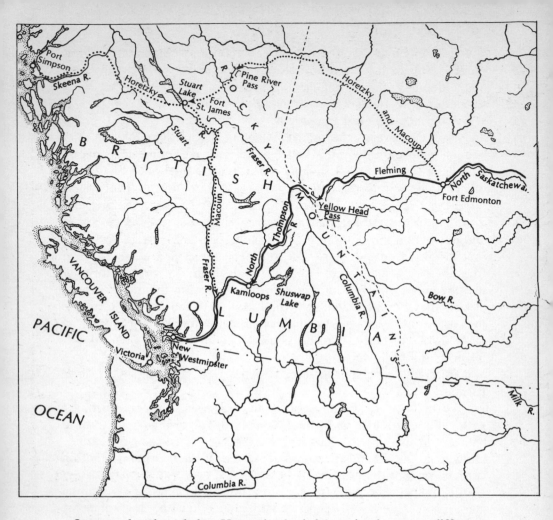

It soon developed that Horetzky had determined upon a different course from the one Fleming had proposed for the Peace River exploration. He had decided to go through the mountains by another pass, following the Pine River, a tributary of the Peace, and he did not want Macoun in the way. He tried to get the botanist to turn back, but Macoun told him, stoically, that he would rather leave his bones in the mountains than fail.

He almost did. According to Macoun's later account, Horetzky planned to lure him into the mountains, then leave him with the encumbering baggage to die or make his own way out while he, Horetzky, pressed on, lightly equipped, to new and dazzling discoveries. The photographer was now giving orders to the Indians in French, a language Macoun did not understand. But the botanist was no fool; he clung to his companion like glue. The two made a hazardous 150-mile journey through the mountains in 26 below weather, carrying their own bedding and provisions and struggling with great difficulty

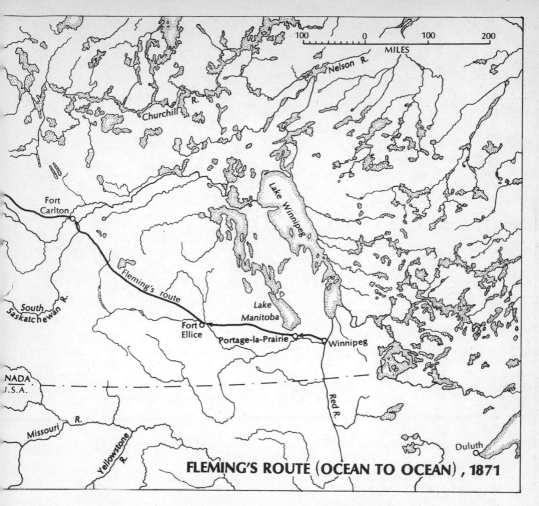

FLEMING'S ROUTE (OCEAN TO OCEAN), 1871

over half-frozen rivers and lakes. They finally reached Fort St. James, the exact centre of British Columbia, on November 14.

Horetzky was already planning to push on westward through virtually unknown country to the mouth of the Skeena, but Macoun had no intention of accompanying him. He was penniless by now, totally dependent on the charity of the Hudson's Bay Company. Accompanied by two Indian guides, he fled south, wearing snowshoes seven feet long. He had never worn snowshoes in his life and soon abandoned them, content to flounder through the drifts which reached above his knees. Eventually, on December 12, he reached Victoria where he learned that, in his absence, his wife had been delivered of a fifth child. What she thought of her husband's impetuous and extended summer vacation is not recorded.

Grant's journey with Fleming lacked the cloak-and-dagger aspects of Macoun's struggle, but it was certainly arduous. There were long swamps "covered with an underbrush . . . that slapped our faces,

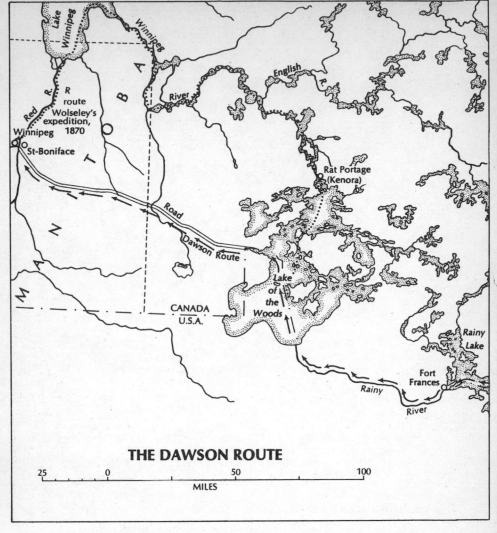

THE DAWSON ROUTE

25   0   50   100

MILES

and defiled our clothing with foul-smelling marsh mud." At times the nine-year-old trail was buried out of sight by debris. The horses' hooves sank eighteen inches into a mixture of bog and clay, but "by slipping over rocks, jumping fallen trees, breasting precipitous ascents with a rush, and recklessly dashing down hills," the crossing of the Thompson River was reached. To the one-handed clergyman, the comfortable parish of St. Matthew's in Halifax must have seemed to be on the far side of the moon.

It was, by any standard, an impressive journey that he and his companions had made. In 103 days of hard travel they had come 5,300 miles by railway, steamer, coach, wagon, canoe, rowboat, dugout, pack and saddle horse, and their own sturdy legs. They had made sixty-two camps on prairie, river bank, rock, brush, swamp, and mountainside; and they were convinced that the future railway

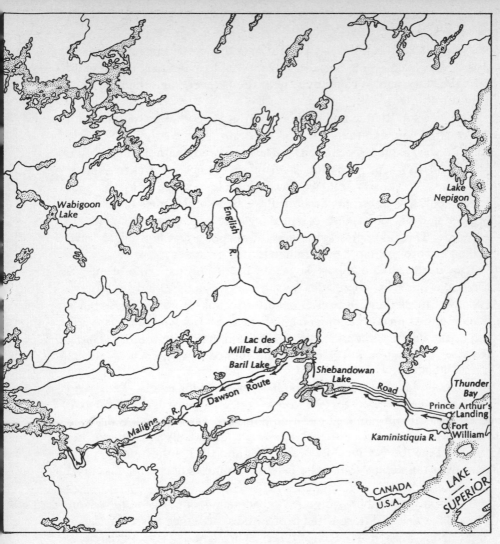

would follow their route across the Shield, up along the Fertile Belt and through the Yellow Head Pass, which was Fleming's choice from the moment he first saw it. This physical accomplishment was magnificent but its subtle concomitant was far more significant: in the most graphic and dramatic fashion, the clergyman and the surveyor had given the Canadian public a vision of a nation stretching from sea to sea.

6

It was one thing to have an itch to go west. It was quite another to get there. At the start of the decade, the would-be homesteader had a choice of two routes, both of them awkward and frustrating.

41

He could take the train to St. Paul and thence to the railhead and proceed by stagecoach, cart, and steamboat to Winnipeg; or he could take the all-Canadian route by way of the lakehead and the notorious Dawson Route.

The Dawson Route consisted of a corduroy road, interspersed with water stretches, and then a wagon road cut directly from the prairie turf. It was named for Simon J. Dawson who, with Henry Youle Hind, had been sent out by the government in the late fifties to explore the North West. Dawson, who was later to become a Member of Parliament, was known as Smooth Bore Dawson because of his even temper and his quiet way of speaking. He needed to husband his reserves. The calumnies subsequently heaped upon him might have driven a more excitable man to dangerous excesses.

As a result of the report he made following his explorations of the Lake Superior country, Dawson was commissioned in 1868 to supervise the building of a series of corduroy links from Prince Arthur's Landing to connect the long chain of ragged lakes which lie between Superior and the Lake of the Woods. From that point the Fort Garry Road would lead on to the prairie and thence to Winnipeg.

Eventually it was completed. Tugs and steamboats were placed on a dozen lakes. Dams were built to raise water levels. Tents and shanties were erected for the convenience of passengers. And two great locks, eight hundred and two hundred feet high, were planned at Fort Frances so that steamboats might eventually circumvent the rapids of the Rainy River. Between 1872 and 1873, a thousand settlers paid their ten dollars to use the Dawson Route between the lakehead and Winnipeg.

It was a formidable route. A tug or steamboat was required on every lake and a different team of horses, together with harnesses and wagons, at each of the ten portages. Throughout its brief existence, there was never a time when some section of the Dawson road was not in need of repair.

In 1874, the government determined to contract out the freight and passenger service to a private company. The contractors agreed to move passengers from the lakehead to Winnipeg in ten or twelve days and freight in fifteen to twenty. But because they were subsidized by the government to carry passengers at low fares, it was in their interest to carry as few as possible and put most of the $75,000 subsidy in their pockets.

The story is told of one luckless settler arriving in a pitiable state of exhaustion and dilapidation at the office of Donald A. Smith, M.P., in Winnipeg and proclaiming: "Well, look at me, ain't I a healthy sight? I've come by the Government water route from Thunder Bay and it's taken me twenty-five days to do it. During that time I've been half starved on victuals I wouldn't give a swampy Indian. The water used to pour into my bunk of nights, and the boat was so leaky that every bit of baggage I've got is water-logged and ruined. But that ain't all. I've broke my arm and sprained my ankle helping to carry half a dozen trunks over a dozen portages, and when I refused to take a paddle in one of the boats, an Ottawa Irishman told me to go to h—l and said that if I gave him any more of my d—d chat he'd let me get off and walk to Winnipeg."

In June and July, 1874, the pioneer newspaper of Manitoba, the *Nor'wester,* began to carry the immigrants' complaints. They considered the station-master at Fifteen Mile shanty "a brute," and the men at the Height of Land "mean and surly." At Baril Lake, the baggage was flung helter-skelter into the hold of a barge where it rested in eight inches of water. On one passage across Rainy Lake where, true to nomenclature, a cloudburst descended, male passengers compassionately took the tarpaulin off a woodpile and placed it over the heads of the women and children. This so enraged the engineer that he seized an axe and threatened to chop away at the customers unless the covering was instantly replaced. It was not, whereupon the engineer "out of sheer spite" held up the boat for five hours.

Many a passenger was on the edge of revolt as a result of conditions on the trail. Scores arrived in Winnipeg in a state of semi-starvation, their effects destroyed by leaky boats. Complaints began to pour into Ottawa. In July, 1874, an alarmed government sent Simon Dawson himself out to investigate. When the surveyor arrived at the North West Angle of the Lake of the Woods, he was nearly mobbed by a crowd of infuriated and starving passengers who were vainly awaiting transportation to Winnipeg. Dawson scrambled about and found some half-breeds with Red River carts who arranged to handle the job, but his smooth-bore temperament must have been sorely tried. That year he quit in disgust as superintendent of the route.

The road continued to operate in a desultory kind of way. The Governor General's lady went over it in 1877 and was knocked about so much she preferred to get out and walk. Another traveller, Mary Fitzgibbon, wrote that she would never forget her own trip. "It was bump, bump, bang and squash and squash, bang and bump; now up now down, now all on one side, now all on the other. Cushions, rugs, everything that could slide, slid off the seats . . . and one longed to cry out and beg to be stopped if only for a moment. . . ."

Finally the road was abandoned, and the locks at Fort Frances, on which the government had squandered three years and $289,000, were abandoned too. The days of canals and corduroy roads were over. The railway was on its way.

Chapter
Two

THE
PACIFIC
SCANDAL

1

The debate on the terms of admission of British Columbia was not yet over when the first of the entrepreneurs arrived in Ottawa. These were Alfred Waddington of Victoria, seventy-five years old and a fanatic on the subject of a Pacific railway, and his partner, a promoter of unbuilt railroads named William Kersteman. Both men were wildly overconfident and unrealistic. Though they themselves would never have believed it, there was no possibility of either or both successfully promoting the great railway to the Pacific. Historically, they were merely the means by which the sinister figure of George W. McMullen was introduced to the Pacific railway scheme.

McMullen was just twenty-seven years old, a stubby man with a pudgy face, luminous brown eyes, and a short cropped beard. He came from a prominent Conservative family in Picton, Ontario, where his mother's relatives owned the local Tory paper. His father, Daniel, who had retired early from the Wesleyan Methodist ministry because his energetic revivalism had overtaxed his strength, was "greatly esteemed for his piety." The phrase scarcely applied to the son, a hard-nosed Chicago businessman.

Interested in railways, canals, and in anything else that might make him a dollar, McMullen had an agile, inquisitive mind which, for all of his long life, intrigued him into the most curious ventures – the growing of aphrodisiacs, for example, and the development of a long-distance cannon. He had come to Ottawa in the spring of 1871 as part of a Chicago delegation seeking the enlargement of the Chicago and Huron Shipping Canal. Waddington and Kersteman were both ardent Yankeephiles. Armed with surveys, maps, pamphlets, and copies of speeches, the two enthusiasts approached McMullen, who was intrigued enough to seek further support in the United States.

By July, McMullen had brought a covey of American businessmen into the scheme: Charles Mather Smith, a Chicago banker; W. B. Ogden, an original incorporator of the Northern Pacific; General George W. Cass, heir apparent to the presidency of the Northern Pacific; and, more important, Jay Cooke, the Philadelphia banker who controlled the railroad's purse strings and who had his clear, boyish eyes focused on the Canadian North West, which he hoped would become a tributary of his railroad.

Cooke's first hope was for out-and-out annexation, which would

45

give the Northern Pacific a total monopoly west of the lakes. Failing that, Cooke and his agents intended to work for a Canadian line which would be dependent on the U.S. road for an outlet. In his dreams, Cooke visualized an international railway, running from Montreal through American territory south of Lake Superior and then cutting back into Canada by way of the Red River to proceed westward across the prairies. The railroad, and eventually the territory itself, would be totally under American control. When Ogden wrote to Cooke in June, 1871, urging him to take preliminary steps to "control this project," it was exactly the opportunity that Cooke had been seeking. Thus the first people to call on the Canadian government to offer to build the Canadian Pacific were the representatives of the very men whom the Canadian Pacific was intended to thwart.

The Americans arrived in Ottawa in mid-July about a week before the contract was signed (on July 20) with British Columbia. They came armed with a set of documents stating the terms on which they would undertake to build the railway. The Prime Minister agreed to see them "as a matter of politeness" but made it quite clear that any railway scheme, at that stage, was too premature for serious discussion. Moreover, any plan would have to be substantially Canadian. To Macdonald, the only value this patently Yankee delegation had was as a kind of lever to force Canadian capitalists to take the matter of the railway seriously. And *the* Canadian capitalist was Sir Hugh Allan, the richest man and the most powerful financier in Canada.

Allan's annual income was estimated at more than half a million dollars a year, a sum so immense that it is hard to grasp today. A dollar in 1871 was worth four or five in 1971. Since there was no income tax, his net income amounted to more than two millions annually in modern terms. It allowed him to build and maintain his baronial mansion in Montreal on which he bestowed the Gothic title of Ravenscrag. Here he had entertained Prince Arthur, a piece of hospitality which undoubtedly contributed to his knighthood in 1871.

Like so many Canadian financiers of the period, Allan was a Scot and a self-educated as well as a self-made man. His father had been a shipmaster, engaged in trade between the Clyde and Montreal, and young Allan was raised in the company of sailors. He left school at thirteen, immigrated to Montreal three years later in 1826, and shortly after went to work for a firm of commission merchants and shipbuilders. Within a dozen years, he had risen to senior partner, a driving, hard-working man who studied furiously in his spare hours to make up for his lack of schooling. Unlike most English-speaking Canadians of that time, he made a point of learning French; it was to his advantage to become fluent in the language.

If he was proud, egotistical, and single-minded he had reason to be. The penniless, half-educated Scottish boy had become head of one of the principal fleets of the world. He was president of the Merchants' Bank, which he had founded, and of fifteen other corporations; he was vice-president of half a dozen more. His interests encompassed telegraphs and railways, coal and iron, tobacco and cotton, cattle, paper, rolling mills, and elevators. Basking in the adulation of press and peer group, praised for his business acumen, his public philanthropies, and his regular church attendance, Allan could scarcely be blamed if he felt himself to be above other men. He *was* a good businessman – his habits so strict that he never acted on a question which involved the spending of money without first having the transaction reduced to writing. He *was* a good churchman – he often read the lesson or delivered a lecture from the pulpit. He was also an imperious and uncommunicative martinet who had a hearty disdain for the public, the press, and politicians. The first could be ignored, the last two purchased. He was used to making handsome loans, with vague terms, to newspapers: the Montreal *Gazette* and the influential French journal *La Minerve* were two which enjoyed his largesse. His only real politics, as one acidulous commentator remarked, were the politics of steamboats and railways. Allan undoubtedly felt himself above politics – more powerful than any politician and certainly more astute. He was a man long accustomed to getting his own way and it certainly never occurred to him, in the summer of 1871, that this very bull-headed self-confidence would frustrate his ambitions and besmirch his name.

It was to Sir Hugh Alan that Sir Francis Hincks, Macdonald's minister of finance, dropped the news, early that August, that some Americans were interested in building the Pacific railway. It was too bad, Hincks added casually, that a work of such importance should be entrusted to foreigners. Allan was immediately interested: as the country's leading shipowner he could benefit, perhaps more than anyone else, from a railway link to the Pacific. It would place him at the head of a transportation colossus and probably lead to a baronetcy. Perhaps more than anything else the Lord of Ravenscrag, as the press had informally dubbed him, wanted a genuine title.

Allan lost little time in getting in touch with the Americans whose names Hincks had obligingly supplied. In September he met McMullen and Smith in Montreal and proceeded to form a company which, though ostensibly Canadian, would be almost entirely controlled and financed by the Northern Pacific; it was planned, in fact, that it would be part of the Northern Pacific complex. Allan's reward was to be a large block of stock and a secret fund of forty to fifty thousand dollars to distribute, in McMullen's phrase, "among persons whose accession would be desirable." One such person was Sir George Etienne Cartier, Macdonald's dynamic but ailing Quebec lieutenant, who was unalterably opposed to any U.S. participation. "As long as I live," he had declared, ". . . never will a damned American company have control of the Pacific." He was prepared to resign rather than consent to it.

Nonetheless, the Americans signed a formal but secret agreement with Allan on December 23, 1871. As Jay Cooke explained, "the American agreement has to be kept dark for the present on account of the political jealousies in the Dominion, and there is no hint of the Northern Pacific connection, but the plan is to cross the Sault Ste. Marie through northern Michigan and Wisconsin to Duluth, then build from Pembina up to Fort Garry and by and by through the Saskatchewan into British Columbia."

At the same time a pretense would be made that an all-Canadian route was being constructed north of Lake Superior: "The act will provide for building a north shore road to Fort Garry merely to calm public opinion." Its actual construction, however, was to be delayed for years while the Montreal-Duluth link through the United States was put into operation, financed by Canadian Pacific bonds sold in London to investors who believed they were promoting an Imperial project.

Jay Cooke was then at the peak of his meteoric career – a big, apple-cheeked financier, boyish-looking in spite of his flowing beard, dreaming dreams of a railway empire that would devour half of Canada for America's manifest destiny. He was known throughout the financial world as the Tycoon, a name that had yet to be vulgarized by American journalism. He was nothing if not pious. On the Lord's Day he engaged in a round of church and Sunday school services; on weekdays he worked hard at manipulating newspapers, politicians, and governments, all of whom praised him to the skies.

"Manipulate" was a word that came easily to Cooke. The year before he had written to a colleague to invite his aid "in manipulating the annexation of British North America north of Duluth to our country." It could be done, he suggested, without any violation of treaties but "as a result of the quiet emigration over the border of trustworthy men and their families." Cooke was secure in the belief that "the country belongs to us naturally and should be brought over without violence or bloodshed." In this scheme, he planned to use the new Canadian Pacific railway in which he and his associates would have a fifty-five per cent interest. Among other things, Cooke believed that a union between the two railroads (for that is what he ultimately envisaged) would strengthen the Northern Pacific's chances for a loan in London.

If it ever occurred to Allan that he was engaged in a secret plot with American businessmen to deliver the Canadian North West into the hands of the United States, he was able to rationalize it magnificently. Business, after all, was business, and American investment in Canada was not only desirable but also necessary. At one point he even wrote to General Cass, who was about to become the new president of the American railroad, that "the plans I propose are in themselves the best for the interests of the Dominion, and in urging them on the public I am really doing a most patriotic action." What was good for Sir Hugh was, in his eyes, good for the country.

By the time this letter was written (with unconscious irony on July 1 – Dominion Day – 1872) Allan had for almost six months been engaging in a lavish shopping spree, using the Americans' money in an attempt to buy up politicians, newspapermen, and business opponents, such as Senator David Macpherson, who was putting together a rival company to compete for the contract. Macpherson's Interoceanic company had a directorate of prominent Toronto and Ontario capitalists. His stated object was to defeat Allan's scheme, which the Liberal press was denouncing almost daily as a front for the Northern Pacific.

It was not difficult for Macpherson or Allan to find partners for their ventures; they were clamouring to be let in. All directors of the successful company stood to make substantial profits with minimal risk, for it was planned that each director would get a proportionate share of the stock without paying for it.

Allan did his best to buy Macpherson off – or so he told his American backers on February 24 – but he did not succeed. He claimed Macpherson had insisted on a quarter-million dollars' worth of stock and threatened opposition if he did not get it.

Macpherson's subsequent account of their meeting was quite different. Allan, he said, had called upon him to join in forming the Canada Pacific Railway Company with the understanding that he, Allan, would head it. There would be eleven directors – six Canadians, including Allan and Macpherson, and five Americans, all of them directors of the Northern Pacific. Macpherson objected strenuously to the Americans' involvement; all they needed to control the company was one vote – Allan's – and if they controlled the purse strings they certainly controlled that. The naïve idea that the Americans would own the railway and yet allow the Canadians to run it was too much for Macpherson. He washed his hands of Allan and set about getting a charter for his all-Canadian company.

2

George Etienne Cartier was one of the leading architects of Canadian Confederation and, next to Macdonald, the most important politician in Canada. Before Allan could succeed he must have Cartier with him. To achieve that end he was prepared to use brutal methods.

Cartier controlled the parliamentary action of forty-five Quebec members who voted in a solid phalanx. The Government needed this Quebec vote since its majority was considerably less than forty-five. The defection of half could, on a tightly fought issue, put it out of office. If Allan could win over a slice of Cartier's following he would then control the means to manipulate their leader. The lever, he shrewdly decided, would be the Quebeckers' hunger for a railroad along the north shore of the St. Lawrence from Quebec City, through Montreal to Ottawa. He himself headed the Northern Colonization Railway which planned to build the Montreal-Ottawa link of the coveted line. Cartier, who had connections with the rival Grand Trunk Railway, could be presumed to oppose it. Allan began at once to spend the money provided by his American backers to stir up the French Canadians along the proposed route against Cartier.

He proudly reported to General Cass of the Northern Pacific the particulars of his successful campaign. He had, he said, paid several French-Canadian lawyers to write up the matter in the press. He had bought controlling stock in newspapers and subsidized others as well as their editors and proprietors. He had stumped the country through which his proposed railway would go, calling on the people, visiting the priests, making friends, sending paid agents among the more prominent citizens, and making speech after speech himself, in French, to show the habitants "where their true interests lay."

The scheme began to bear fruit. Allan won over twenty-seven of Cartier's forty-five followers and felt he could control the government. An election was in the offing for the late summer of 1872 and Cartier, to his astonishment and dismay, woke up to the truth that he had lost much of his political power. His surrender was total. On June 12, Allan wrote to McMullen: ". . . we now have the pledge of Sir G. that we will have a majority, and other things satisfactory. I have told you all along that this was the true basis of operations. . . ."

Meanwhile, Senator David Lewis Macpherson and his rival Interoceanic company were proving an embarrassment to Macdonald. Macpherson remained utterly convinced, in spite of all disclaimers, that Allan was prepared to deliver the railway into the hands of Yankee freebooters.

The Highlander Macpherson was an old friend and a staunch Conservative and his stubbornness posed a real dilemma for the Prime

Minister, who was anxious to resolve the railway problem before the election; there was no doubt it would strengthen his hand politically in a tight contest. Macdonald was faced with an impossible choice: he could choose the Toronto group and alienate French Canada, or he could choose the Allan group and alienate Ontario. Clearly an amalgamation was indicated. Macdonald genuinely believed that Allan was the only possible choice to head the venture. Only a man of his established wealth and apparent business know-how could command the confidence of the international financial community. But Macpherson continued to insist stubbornly that Allan was a tool of the American railway; he would welcome amalgamation, but not with Allan as president.

As it turned out, Macpherson was right. It ought to have been clear to Allan by this time that the government had no intention of allowing American control of the railway; and yet, while pretending publicly that his was an all-Canadian company, the imperious shipbuilder retained his secret ties with New York and Chicago. On August 7, he told General Cass that the government was obliged to stipulate that no foreigner could appear as a shareholder in the company: "The shares taken by you and our other American friends, will therefore have to stand in my name for some time." To McMullen he sent a reassuring letter: the Americans were to be excluded, but "I fancy we can get over that some way or other."

In vain Macdonald tried to effect a *rapprochement* between Macpherson and Allan. In July, with the election campaign underway, Macpherson suggested that the new directors – seven from his company and six from Allan's – elect their own president; but to this Allan would not consent. The Tory party desperately wanted to place the *fait accompli* of a strong railway company before the electors; but the principals remained deadlocked.

By this time Allan was hard at work trying to restore the political fortunes of the badly battered Cartier, who had been transformed from enemy into ally by his machinations of the previous spring. Though he did not know it then, Cartier had less than a year to live: the telltale symptons of Bright's disease – the swollen feet, the impaired judgement – had already appeared.

If Allan threw himself heart, soul, and pocketbook into the election, it was because he believed he had a pledge from the Government to give him the charter for the railway. The events of July 29 and 30, when promises were made by Cartier and Macdonald, and election funds were pledged by Allan, can only be understood against the background of the political morality and practice of the time.

Elections in post-Confederation Canada were fought with money, and often enough it was the candidate who spent the most who cornered the votes. Dollars spoke louder than ideas and out-and-out bribery was not uncommon. At the end of the decade a contemporary historian wrote that "bribery at elections was scarcely regarded as an offence; both parties resorted to it freely and almost openly." Charles Clarke, who was clerk of the Legislature of Ontario, recalled that "nearly every active politician who had experience in Canadian Parliamentary elections was aware of the existence of bribery and intimidation. So common was this experience that, although never seeing money actually exchanged for a vote, its use was as well known to me as was the existence, say, of the Queen of England, or the fact that she occupied the throne."

In those days before competing electronic pleasures, politics was *the* major pastime in city and village. The entire country was almost totally partisan, which meant that in the absence of any really burning issue it was difficult to change a man's mind unless, in the euphemism of the period, you "treated" him – to a drink, a bottle, a dinner, or a five-dollar bill. Treating was against the law, as was the practice of driving or dragging reluctant voters to the polls, but these expensive customs, as Macdonald himself admitted, were common to both parties. There was still no secret ballot in the 1872 election; it did not make its appearance until 1874. This meant that bribery was extraordinarily effective since the party agents could check on the loyalty of their paid supporters.

The election was particularly hard fought, especially in Ontario, where the Liberals were on the rise. Macdonald thought that financially the Opposition had the best of it. He himself was hard pressed for funds and was scraping up every dollar he could find from reluctant friends.

Cartier was equally desperate, and this desperation was increased by the knowledge that he faced an uphill battle in his own constituency. For him the moment of truth came at the close of July. Allan had conferred with him on several occasions, urging him to procure the amalgamation of the two companies "upon such terms as I considered would be just to myself" – in short, the presidency for Allan. On the thirtieth, he and his lawyer, J. J. C. Abbott, visited Cartier once again for a meeting that was to become memorable. Cartier had received, on July 26, a telegram scribbled by Macdonald in Kingston. The Prime Minister had been unable to change Macpherson's mind. "Under these circumstances," he wired, "I authorize you to assure Allan that the influence of the Government will be exercised to secure him the position of President. The other terms to be as agreed on between Macpherson and Abbott. The whole matter to be kept quiet until after the elections. . . ."

Four days later Cartier showed the wire to Allan. It was not quite enough for the shipping magnate. What if Macpherson continued to be stubborn? Cartier was forced to concede that, if a new amalgamated company could not be formed, then Allan's Canada Pacific company would be given the charter. But Allan wanted that promise nailed down in writing.

Cartier suggested that Abbott draw up the necessary document and return with it that afternoon. As Allan and Abbott rose to leave, Cartier asked in his abrupt way: "Are you not going to help us in our elections?" When Allan asked how much Cartier wanted, Cartier replied that it might come to one hundred thousand dollars. Allan, the model businessman, suggested he put that in writing, too.

That afternoon – the date was July 30, 1872, the day on which Fleming, Grant, and Macoun first reached the open prairie – he and Abbott were back again with two letters. One, to be signed by Cartier, promised Allan the charter; the other, also to be signed by Cartier, asked for financial help in the elections. Cartier was not satisfied with either of the letters and both were rewritten. One was to become notorious:

"The friends of the Government will expect to be assisted with funds in the pending elections, and any amount which you or your Company shall advance for that purpose shall be recouped by you. A memorandum of immediate requirements is below.

NOW WANTED

Sir John A. Macdonald	$25,000
Hon. Mr. Langevin	15,000
Sir G.E.C.	20,000
Sir J. A. (add.)	10,000
Hon. Mr. Langevin	10,000
Sir G.E.C.	30,000"

In spite of promises to recoup, Allan did not really expect to see his money again.

Meanwhile, in Kingston, Macdonald was impatiently awaiting a reply to his telegram of July 26. When it finally arrived he was appalled. He could not afford to take time off from last minute electioneering, but he wired Cartier, repudiating the letter: his original telegram of July 26 must be "the basis of the agreement." *Agreement!* The ambiguity of that word would return to haunt Macdonald.

Cartier broke the news to Allan, who gracefully withdrew the letter; but he did not withdraw his financial support. He increased it. The additional fifty thousand dollars in Cartier's original NOW WANTED memo was swiftly paid over – ten thousand to Langevin, Macdonald's portly minister of public works and Cartier's successor as the leader of the Quebec wing of the party, another ten thousand to the Prime Minister, and thirty thousand to Cartier's central election committee. That was not the end of it. Altogether he distributed more than $350,000 among Conservative candidates.

And for what? The Conservative government barely squeaked into power. In Ontario it was badly battered and in Quebec, where most of the Allan funds had been spent, it managed to capture only a bare majority. Without the West and Maritimes, Macdonald would have been ruined politically. As for Cartier, he suffered a stunning personal defeat, which had its own ironies. By some mysterious process, a large slice of Allan's money had been appropriated by the other side. On the day of the election, the open balloting revealed that man after man who had been paid in good hard cash to work for George Etienne Cartier had actually been in the secret service of the enemy all the while.

3

All that autumn, Sir John A. Macdonald was haunted by his secret promise to Allan. There was no way out of it. Senator David Macpherson, who remained utterly immovable, kept asking awkward questions: Why was the Government so committed to a man who was, in the Senator's furious phrase, the instigator of "one of the most unpatriotic conspiracies ever entered into in this Dominion . . . an audacious, insolent, unpatriotic and gigantic swindle"? Macpherson could not understand it, nor could he believe, as Macdonald tried to make him believe, that Allan, as president, would have little influence.

Macdonald realized that he must form a new company without Macpherson. Like it or not, he had to keep his promise to the man who had been the biggest contributor to the Conservative coffers. At this juncture he ought to have entertained some doubts about Allan. On October 7, he was shocked to discover that the Montrealer, in spite of all his pious proclamations, had not actually broken off relations with McMullen and the others. Was this the man who ought to be heading up the greatest national venture?

There was nothing the Prime Minister could do. He had made a promise, through Cartier – Allan kept using that awkward word "agreement" – and he would have to stick by it. Macdonald began to wonder uneasily just what the agreement consisted of; the memory of that ambiguous telegram, dispatched at the height of a fatiguing campaign, when whiskey and wine were flowing freely, began to nag at him. What actually *had* Cartier promised Allan? Macdonald realized that he himself did not know the exact details. But already there were rumours floating around Montreal about Allan's gifts to the Cartier campaign. The Liberals had got wind of it.

Macdonald, meanwhile, learned from Allan the full extent of Cartier's financial dependence upon him. The Prime Minister was horrified. Was it possible that the once astute Cartier could have been so foolish? He could not believe it and sought reassurance from his old friend, who had sailed for England to seek medical aid for his disease. Cartier's reply confirmed Macdonald's worst fears.

In Chicago, George McMullen was also experiencing twinges of uneasiness as he studied Allan's expense accounts. On September 16, 1872 (Grant and Fleming reached the summit of the Yellow Head Pass that day), Allan informed him that he had paid out the staggering sum of $343,000 and still had $13,500 to distribute. McMullen lost no time in getting to Montreal to confront Allan, who managed to mollify him. Then, on October 24, Allan, under Macdonald's goading, finally broke the news to his American associates that he would have to dump them. McMullen was shocked and furious. In a face-to-face meeting between the two men in Montreal, Allan made it clear that he was closing off all arrangements with the Americans and repudiating any obligations they might feel he was under to them.

McMullen was in a state of rage. He had squandered more than a year of his time and tens of thousands of his and his associates' dollars and now it appeared that he had had no hope of success from the outset. Allan had deceived everybody. He had deceived the government; he had deceived his friends; he had deceived his backers, and, above all, he had deceived himself – led on to greater and greater folly by what Lord Dufferin, the Governor General, was to call "the purse proud and ostentatious notion of domineering over everybody and overcoming all obstacles by the brute force of money."

The apoplectic McMullen suggested that if Allan had a scrap of honour left he would either stick to the original agreement or step out of the picture. When Allan refused, McMullen threatened to go to the Prime Minister; after all, he had in his possession all of Allan's indiscreet correspondence.

Allan remained obdurate. Perhaps he did not believe that McMullen would carry out his threat. But McMullen was not a man to shilly-shally. He wanted compensation and if he did not get that, he wanted revenge. Off he went to Ottawa with no less a purpose than to black-mail the Prime Minister of Canada. The encounter took place on New Year's Eve, while the rest of the nation was preparing jubi-lantly to usher in a year that would be the blackest in all of Macdonald's long political career.

It makes a striking picture, this pivotal meeting in the Prime Minister's office. The youthful McMullen, his round eyes coldly furious, faced a man thirty years his senior, whose languorous attitude gave no hint of his inner emotions. Physical opposites, the two antagonists had certain common qualities. Both were possessed of lively imaginations, which allowed them to glimpse future benefits in schemes others thought hare-brained. Both, as a result, enjoyed the steady nerves of committed gamblers. For Macdonald, the railway project had been an immense political risk; for McMullen, a considerable financial one. Oddly, McMullen, the apparently hard-headed businessman, was far more quixotic than the pragmatic politician who faced him across the desk. Macdonald's gambles – or visions, or dreams (all three nouns apply) – had a habit of turning out far more successfully than McMullen's astonishing series of ventures, several of which certainly *were* hare-brained.

The interview took up two hours. McMullen came armed with Allan's letters to him; he proceeded to read the Prime Minister some compromising extracts. He talked mysteriously about political payoffs of Parliament. He said he would name names in that connection – names of persons "who are very near to you." Macdonald was inwardly aghast but, at moments like this, he knew enough to maintain a poker face. He denied that Allan had bribed the Government. In that case, McMullen replied smoothly, Allan must be a swindler – he had taken almost four hundred thousand dollars from the Americans on just that pretext. He urged Macdonald either to stick to the original agreement or leave Allan out of the new company. Macdonald replied that he could do neither; if McMullen thought he was badly used, that was his problem. The Americans, said the Prime Minister, had been out of the company for some time.

Not so, replied McMullen, and he produced Allan's own correspondence in evidence. Again Macdonald was appalled, but he did not show it.

McMullen grew more threatening. He began to talk about what would happen politically if the public knew all the facts. Macdonald made no comment but asked for time to consult with Allan and his lawyer, Abbott. On that note the encounter ended.

McMullen was back in Ottawa three weeks later. This time he brought along two colleagues and more compromising correspondence. Macdonald agreed that the Americans had been badly used by Allan, who should certainly be made to refund the money. With this the atmosphere grew almost genial. McMullen offered to let Macdonald have copies of all the damaging correspondence, including some new documents nailing down Allan's dishonesty regarding the extent of the American interest in his company. These showed that on October 12, at the very time when Allan and Abbott had assured Parliament that negotiations with the Americans had been terminated, Allan was paying over American money to incorporate the railway company.

Although none of the men involved knew it at the time, this was not the full extent of Allan's duplicity. The day before he finally dumped McMullen, Allan had a long talk with Lycurgus Edgerton, one of Jay Cooke's agents, about the new company Macdonald was forming. Allan assured the Northern Pacific man that there was nothing in the charter to affect Cooke's plans. Edgerton was able to report to Cooke that there would be no all-Canadian route via the north shore of Lake Superior, if Allan remained in control. It was a "useless expenditure . . . dictated by a sentimental patriotism, and a narrow minded jealousy and prejudice." For the next five or ten years "if not for *all time,* the Canada Pacific must be subservient and tributary to the interests of the Northern Pacific."

Even without this knowledge it must have been clear by now to the Prime Minister that Allan was an unfortunate choice to head the new company. For almost a year Macdonald had been telling his colleagues, his friends, his political enemies, and the country at large (as well as himself) that Allan was the only possible choice for the job – a man of business acumen, probity, sagacity, and experience who commanded the total respect of the financial community. Now he stood revealed as a blunderer, a conniver, a liar, a double-dealer, and, perhaps worst of all, a Yankee-lover – a man whose imprudence, in Macdonald's own words, "has almost mounted to insanity." And this was the man who would shortly be setting off for London on a mission of the greatest delicacy to secure the underwriting of the world's largest railway project. Clearly, if the financial community or the public at large knew what Macdonald knew, the railway scheme would collapse like a soap bubble.

Would they find out? Worry gnawed at Macdonald as he prepared for the session of 1873. There was a bitter letter from Senator Asa B. Foster, a long-time railway contractor, regretting that he had not been included on the board of the new company. Both Cartier and Allan had promised him this plum, he claimed. For the past eighteen months, Foster revealed, he had had knowledge of Allan's dealings with the Americans and he had "seen all of the papers that were shown to you and some that were not." There was no knowing what use the disgruntled Foster would make of that information.

McMullen would have to be bought off. The Prime Minister wrote to Hincks in Montreal and Hincks sought out Abbott, the lawyer. Abbott bargained McMullen down to $37,500 for the Allan letters. He paid him twenty thousand down and placed Allan's cheque for the rest in an envelope which he gave to Henry Starnes of Allan's Merchants' Bank. McMullen then placed the offending correspondence in another envelope and gave that to Starnes. The banker's instructions were to wait until ten days after the end of the coming session and then deliver the envelope with the money to McMullen and the envelope with the correspondence to Allan. This was the best arrangement that Abbott could make to keep the story from becoming public before Allan completed his negotiations in England and while Parliament was in session.

The arrangement was concluded on the very eve of Allan's departure. In the months and years that followed, a good many pundits and politicians asked aloud or in print why Macdonald had not bought off McMullen as soon as McMullen arrived in his office on New Year's Eve. The answer surely is that in Macdonald's shrewd view, McMullen was perfectly capable of taking the money and selling the correspondence later on. The view was absolutely correct. George McMullen did not bother to collect the second envelope from Henry Starnes, the banker. He had already received a higher bid from Macdonald's political enemies.

4

The first session of the Second Parliament of Canada opened on March 6, 1873, with no hint of the storm that was gathering. To Lord Dufferin, the dapper new governor general, setting off for Parliament Hill in his four-horse state carriage, the weather was "quite divine."

He was deposited promptly at three o'clock before the main archway to the accompaniment of brass band and Royal Salute, and as he entered the Senate door, he found himself proceeding through a "double file of living millinery." The crimson chamber had been cleared of desks and the chairs were now occupied by the wives and daughters of the parliamentarians.

It was Lord Dufferin's first parliament and it was perhaps as well that he could not foresee the trials that lay before him. He had served as a diplomat at St. Petersburg, Rome, and Paris, but nothing in his past had prepared him for the political hurly-burly of the Canadian scene.

At the call of the Gentleman Usher of the Black Rod, the Members "swarmed in like a bunch of schoolboys" (there were four future prime ministers in that swarm) and the Governor General read the Speech from the Throne. One of the key paragraphs in the speech dealt with the railway: "I have caused a charter to be granted to a body of Canadian capitalists for the construction of the Pacific

Railway. The company now formed has given assurance that this great work will be vigorously prosecuted, and the favourable state of the money market in England affords every hope that satisfactory arrangements may be made for the required capital."

Macdonald was not the only member present who must have felt the hollowness of those words. By this time, the Liberal Party was in on the secret and, as the session progressed, rumours began to flit around Ottawa about a coming political earthquake. On March 31, the Opposition's intentions were revealed when, at the opening of the day's proceedings, Lucius Seth Huntington rose to give notice of a motion to appoint a committee to inquire into matters generally affecting the Canadian Pacific railway. Huntington sat down amid Opposition cries of "Hear! Hear!" and a tingle of excitement rippled through the House.

Two days later when Huntington prepared to make his motion, the corridors of the House were filled to suffocation, the galleries were crowded, the Treasury benches were full, and every Opposition seat was occupied. The Commons was silent and expectant. Seldom had any member faced such an attentive audience.

Huntington rose that evening. At forty-six, he was a man of commanding presence, big-chested and handsome, with a classic head that a sculptor might covet – aquiline nose, poetic eyes, thick shock of light, wavy hair. He was a lawyer and politician of long experience, a polished speaker, resonant and melodious, but now there was a tremor in his voice and he spoke so softly that the back-benchers had to lean forward to catch his words. He had reason to be nervous for he was putting his career on the line. If he could not prove his charges, he would certainly be forced to resign; if he *could* prove them, his name would go down in history.

His speech was astonishingly brief; it ran to no more than seven short paragraphs and was supported by no documentary evidence. Huntington charged that the Allan company was secretly financed by American capital and that the Government was aware of that fact, that Allan had advanced large sums of money, some of it paid by the Americans, to aid the Government in the elections, and that he had been offered the railway contract in return for his support. Lord Dufferin, who was a descendant of Richard Sheridan and had some of the eloquence of that great playwright, put the case more forcefully in his report to the Colonial Secretary. Huntington, he said, had charged that the Government had "trafficked with foreigners in Canada's most precious interests in order to debauch the constituencies of the Dominion with the gold obtained at the price of their treachery."

Dufferin, who had been seduced by the Prime Minister's considerable charm, did not believe a word of this. He thought the scene in the House, which he could not witness, "a very absurd one" and Huntington himself "a man of no great political capacity."

But it was not absurd, as events were to prove. Huntington called for a seven-man parliamentary committee to inquire into every circumstance connected with the railway negotiations with power to subpoena papers, records, and witnesses. Then he sat down, "full of suppressed emotion," as a historian of the day recorded.

An oppressive silence hung over the House – a silence so deathly that some who were present recalled years later the solemn ticks of the parliamentary clock falling like hammer blows. Every eye had turned to the lean, sprawled figure of Macdonald. The Prime Minister, one hand toying with a pencil, remained "inscrutable as stone." There were those who said he was stunned by the charges, but this is scarcely credible; he had been expecting them since Huntington gave his notice. More likely he was bothered by their lack of substance. Why was Huntington holding back? Why hadn't he read the evidence into the record? What was the Opposition plotting?

The silence was broken at last by the Speaker, asking for the question. The motion was lost by a majority of thirty-one – one of the largest the Government had enjoyed that session – and the House moved on to other business. Huntington's motion, unsubstantiated by any evidence, had produced no result. The Government press took the view that the motion was nothing more than a device to needle the ministry.

Macdonald, however, was having second thoughts. He had faced a rebellion from his own followers between sittings. Many felt that the Government had given the appearance of riding roughshod over its opponents and that its silence in the face of charges so serious could be taken as an admission of guilt. Accordingly, the Prime Minister rose a week later to announce the appointment of a select committee of five to investigate the Huntington charges.

Now Macdonald proceeded to set in motion a series of tactics of the kind that would eventually earn him the sobriquet – an affectionate one – of Old Tomorrow. His was to be a policy of delay. He agreed that the evidence should be taken under oath. But before the witnesses could be sworn, a bill had to be introduced into the House; that could take a month. Macdonald was reasonably confident that England, if prompted, would disallow such a bill. That would pave the way for a royal commission. From Macdonald's point of view, a royal commission composed of aging jurists of his own choosing was far preferable to a parliamentary committee with men of Edward Blake's calibre ready to tear into Sir Hugh Allan.

It was May 3 before the Oaths Bill received the Governor General's signature. On May 5, the committee met for the first time, but again Macdonald engineered a delay, using Allan's absence in England as an excuse. He had no idea what the erratic Allan might blurt out on the witness stand. Their stories must dovetail and that could not be achieved until Allan and Abbott, who was with him, returned. With the help of the Tories on the committee and his own parliamentary majority, Macdonald got the hearings postponed until July 2, and the Opposition had yet to get a shred of evidence on the record.

Delay was dangerous to the Liberal cause. Telegrams could be destroyed in the interval; originals of documents and letters could disappear, and, indeed, did. The Liberal leadership belatedly realized that it had made a tactical error in not placing some of the evidence on the record when Huntington first made his charges. It is clear that he had seen copies of the Allan-McMullen correspondence and knew where the originals were stored. The evidence was to indicate that the Liberal Party had purchased Allan's indiscreet correspondence from McMullen for twenty-five thousand dollars, using the aggrieved Senator Asa B. Foster as a go-between.

Outwardly, the Prime Minister was totally in command. Inwardly, he was sick at heart with grief, disappointment, and foreboding. In May he suffered two terrible blows. Their force was not lessened by the fact that he was braced to expect them.

By the middle of the month it was clear that Allan's mission to England had been destroyed by the whispers of scandal from across the water, and so Macdonald's railway policy lay in tatters. The settlement of the North West, the knitting together of the disunited provinces, the building of a workable, transcontinental nation, all these remained an elusive dream.

And the partnership of Macdonald and Cartier was no more. Macdonald's friend, confidant, bulwark, political comrade-in-arms and strong right hand was dead in England of the kidney disease that had ravaged him for two years. At the nadir of his career, Macdonald had no one to turn to. Politically, he stood alone – weary, overworked, tormented, dispirited. He wanted out, but his party could not let him resign; there was no one to replace him.

He was, in fact, a Canadian fixture and it was unthinkable that he should go. In those days, when politicians were not always instantly recognizable, everyone knew Macdonald. The long, rangy figure, the homely face, the absurd nose, the tight curls round the ears made him a caricaturist's delight. J. W. Bengough portrayed him week after week in *Grip* as a kind of likable rogue with matchstick legs and giant proboscis.

Likable he was, though often enough a rogue in the political sense. In those days of partisan hatreds, when one's political adversary really *was* the enemy, Macdonald's opponents found it hard to hate him. One Grit, Joseph Lister, who attacked Macdonald viciously in Parliament, confessed he was so attracted to the man's personality that he dared not trust himself in his company.

His singular lack of choler is remarkable when set against the tragedies and travails of his private life. Macdonald's first wife had been a hopeless invalid, bed-ridden for most of the fourteen years of their married life. His second baby boy had died of convulsions. His daughter Mary, the only issue of his second marriage, was mentally retarded and physically deformed. After Confederation, Macdonald's life savings were wiped out, and he found himself plunged into heavy debt, partly because he had neglected his law practice for politics and partly because of an unexpected bank failure. Never robust, always apparently on the cliff-edge of physical breakdown, he had been felled for six months in 1870 by a nightmarish attack of gallstones, which brought him to the brink of death (his obituary set in type and ready for release) and weakened him for life.

Now, in the late spring of 1873, piled on top of all these adversities, Macdonald was burdened by the loss of his closest associate, the collapse of his national dream, and the possible political destruction of himself and his party.

He turned, as he so often did in moments of stress, to the bottle; and for the next several weeks all who encountered him, from governor general to hack reporter, were treated to the spectacle of the Prime Minister of Canada reeling drunk. "Indisposed" was the euphemism usually employed by the newspapers, but the public knew exactly what *that* meant. After all, the stories about his drinking were legion: how he had once mounted a train platform so drunk and shaken that he had been seen to vomit while his opponent was speaking but had saved the day by opening his speech with the words: "Mr. Chairman and Gentlemen, I don't know how it is, but every time I hear Mr. Jones speak it turns my stomach"; how he had told a public gathering during his campaigns against the former Liberal leader and *Globe* editor: "I know enough of the feeling of this meeting to know that you would rather have John A. drunk than George Brown sober"; how, when his colleagues urged him to speak to that other great toper, D'Arcy McGee, about his alcohol problem, he had said: "Look here, McGee, this Government can't afford two drunkards and you've got to stop."

Macdonald's own drinking bouts – he would sometimes retire to bed and consume bottle after bottle of port – were to become an endearing Canadian legend; but at the time they were a source of concern to his friends and colleagues and a perplexing embarrassment to his statuesque and highly moral wife, for whom, in the first glow of courtship, he had given up the bottle. To the sympathetic Dufferin, who was more than once publicly discomfited by the presence of his tipsy Prime Minister, Macdonald suffered from an "infirmity." The prim and granite-faced leader of the Opposition, Alexander Mackenzie, was not so tolerant. To him, Macdonald was, quite simply, a "drunken debauchee."

Yet his powers of recuperation were marvellous. He had the ability to pull himself together, even after days of drinking, when there was necessary business to attend to. And at the end of June, Macdonald needed his faculties; the Oaths Bill was officially disallowed just five days before the investigating committee was due to meet. Macdonald renewed his offer of a royal commission.

A furious debate followed when the committee sat on July 3. The Government members wanted to pack up until Parliament reconvened on August 13. The Opposition wanted to dispense with the oath and examine unsworn witnesses. The Government inevitably prevailed. Once again the Opposition had been frustrated in its attempts to get the evidence before the public. It was more than three months since Huntington had raised the issue and the country was in no sense aroused. There was only one course left open: the press.

5

On the morning of July 4, the faithful readers of the Toronto *Globe* and the Montreal *Herald* opened their slim papers to the scoop of the decade. "PACIFIC RAILWAY INTRIGUES," the *Globe* headline read, and there, for column after column, was laid bare the correspondence of Sir Hugh Allan with his secret American backers. It was all in print for the country to ponder: Allan's detailed account of his victory over Cartier; Allan's long report on his coercion of the Quebec press and public; Allan's disbursements of $343,000; Allan's double game with his American associates.

These seventeen letters all but ended Sir Hugh Allan's public career. One associate declared in Montreal that he would not be seen walking the streets with Sir Hugh. For the first time the public had something it could get its teeth into and the Pacific Scandal, as it was now universally called, became the major topic of the day.

The letters, the *Globe* insisted, showed that the Government was "hopelessly involved in an infamous and corrupt conspiracy." They scarcely showed that. Macdonald's name was mentioned only three times and always innocuously. There was only one suspicious, if ambiguous, paragraph in a letter to General Cass of the Northern Pacific, in which Allan wrote that "we yesterday signed an agreement by which, on certain monetary conditions, they agreed to form the company, of which I am to be President, to suit my views, to give me and my friends a majority of the stock."

Meanwhile, a much chastened Allan, at Macdonald's urgent behest and with Abbott's legal skill, was preparing a sworn affidavit to be published on July 6 in major Government newspapers. This lengthy document was designed to get the administration off the hook, and it largely succeeded. Allan's sworn denials were explicit and positive. Though he had certainly subscribed money to aid in the election of his friends, he had done so without any understanding or condition being placed upon such funds. None of this money, he swore, had come from the Americans. It was true that he had left the door ajar for his American friends until told specifically by the Government that they must be excluded; he felt honour bound to do so. As for McMullen, he had made such financial demands on Allan that "I declined altogether to entertain them."

The statement, which bears the imprint of Abbott's sensitive legal mind, was a masterpiece of tightrope walking. "He[Abbott] has made the old gentleman acknowledge on oath that his letters were untrue," Macdonald wrote gleefully to Dufferin. "This was a bitter pill for him to swallow, but Abbott has gilded it over for him very nicely." It was not easy for Allan to wriggle out of correspondence written in his own hand but he did his best in a painfully contorted way: the letters, he said, were "written in the confidence of private intercourse in the midst of many matters engrossing my attention, and probably with less care and circumspection than might have been bestowed upon them had they been intended for publication. At the same time, while in some respects these letters are not strictly accurate, I can see that the circumstances, to a great extent, justified or excused the language used in them."

Allan, then, was cast as the villain of the piece, and though the *Globe* regurgitated the correspondence daily, it was clear that Macdonald's ministry, though bruised, was by no means broken. The weary Prime Minister felt that he could afford a short holiday at Rivière du Loup. It was while he was there, in his small cottage near the riverside, that the world crashed in on him.

The blow fell on July 17 and it was devastating. The *Globe* ran a great bank of type on the right-hand column of its front page: "THE PACIFIC SCANDAL: ASTOUNDING REVELATIONS." The revelations appeared identically and simultaneously in the *Globe*, the *Herald*, and *L'Evénement* of Quebec and they *were* astounding.

The story took the form of a historical narrative by George McMullen, who laid about him with a scythe. He claimed that Allan had lent Macdonald and Hincks $4,000 and $4,500 respectively "with very good knowledge that it was never to be repaid." He identified the newspapers that Allan told him he had paid. He said that Allan had made an additional indefinite loan of ten thousand dollars to Hincks and had promised Langevin twenty-five thousand for election purposes, "on condition of his friendly assistance."

This was strong meat, though not of itself conclusive since McMullen, branded in the public mind as a blackmailer, was himself suspect. But unlike most newspaper stories, the sting of this one was in its tail. Appended to McMullen's narrative, deep inside the newspaper, was a series of letters and telegrams which contained political dynamite. They had been buried at the end by design in an attempt to divert suspicion from the source from which they had been obtained. They had been rifled from Abbott's safe in the dark of the night, during the lawyer's absence in England, copied by his confidential secretary, George Norris, Jr., and an assistant, and sold for hard cash to the Liberal Party.

Cartier to Abbott, Montreal, August 24, 1872: "In the absence of Sir Hugh Allan, I shall be obliged by your supplying the Central Committee with a further sum of twenty thousand dollars upon the same conditions as the amount written by me at the foot of my letter to Sir Hugh Allan on the 30th ult.

George E. Cartier

"P.S. Please also send Sir John A. Macdonald ten thousand dollars more on the same terms."

Terms? Conditions? What price Allan's sworn denials now?

Memorandum signed by three members of the Central Committee, J. L. Beaudry, Henry Starnes, and P. S. Murphy: "Received from Sir Hugh Allan by the hands of J. J. C. Abbott twenty thousand dollars for General Election purposes, to be arranged hereafter according to the terms of the letter of Sir George E. Cartier, of the date of 30th of July, and in accordance with the request contained in his letter of the 24th instant."
Montreal, 26th Aug., 1872.

Again, that damning word: *terms.* It was well for the Government that poor Cartier was dead.

Telegram: Macdonald to Abbott at St. Anne's, Toronto, Aug. 26, 1872: "I must have another ten thousand; will be the last time of calling; do not fail me; answer today."

Reply: Abbott to Macdonald from Montreal, Aug. 26, 1872: "Draw on me for ten thousand dollars."

"Three more extraordinary documents than these . . . never saw the light of day," Lord Dufferin wrote to the Colonial Secretary. There was, in addition, a final clincher: a statement from the discontented Senator Asa B. Foster, commenting on the McMullen revelations and corroborating them.

The effect on the public of these revelations was incalculable. Dufferin was later to refer, in his dramatic fashion, to "the terror and shame manifested by the people at large when the possibility first dawned upon them of their most trusted statesman having been guilty of such conduct." The Pacific Scandal became the sole topic of conversation in those late July days and continued so into the fall. All other news and comment was subordinated as the newspapers now took up the great scandal with what *The Times* of London called "colonial vehemence." The carnage among the party faithful was devastating. Many a loyal Tory was transformed, during that tempestuous summer, into a working Liberal.

In all his long career nothing hit Macdonald so hard as the McMullen revelations. The news, which reached him at Rivière du Loup in a hurriedly scribbled letter from Langevin, "fairly staggered" him. It was, he later told Dufferin, "one of those overwhelming misfortunes that they say every man must meet once in his life." He had expected trouble but nothing so cataclysmic as this. He had certainly sent the telegrams; but he had never expected to be found out.

Alexander Campbell, Macdonald's old law partner and Senate leader, was in touch with his chief immediately with a call for a hurried conference with Langevin in Quebec City. The strategy was clear: a royal commission was now an absolute necessity, preferably one that included "safe" judges. The indispensable Abbott was hurriedly called upon to assist in the negotiations. He wrote "very guardedly" to Charles Dewey Day, a retired Superior Court judge, who was Chancellor of McGill University. Abbott had every confidence "in his acting judiciously." A sympathetic letter to Macdonald from the judge himself, two days later, made clear just what the cautious Abbott meant. Judge Day was squarely on Macdonald's side, disturbed by the fact that the correspondence as published in the press was "in a shape which tells against you." The judge wrote that "no time should be lost in endeavouring to change the current of public opinion." Obviously, from Macdonald's point of view, Charles Dewey Day was the proper choice to head the royal commission.

At this point, with the crisis swirling around him, Macdonald took to the bottle and vanished from sight. No member of his cabinet could reach him or learn of his plans or purpose. The press reported that he had disappeared from Rivière du Loup. His wife had no idea where he was. The frantic Governor General, in the midst of a state tour of the Maritimes, could get no answer to an urgent and confidential letter. He followed it with an equally urgent telegram; silence. On August 5, the Montreal *Daily Witness* published in its two o'clock edition a rumour that Macdonald had committed suicide by throwing himself into the St. Lawrence. The story, concocted by his political enemies, vanished from the next edition but was widely believed at the time; it seemed to confirm the Government's guilt. Suicide or no, the fact was that for several days, in a moment of grave political crisis, the Prime Minister of Canada was on a drinking bout and could not be found by anyone. Dufferin finally unravelled the mystery and put it delicately in a private letter to the Colonial Secretary: "He had stolen away, as I subsequently found, from his seaside villa and was lying perdu with a friend in the neighbourhood of Quebec."

6

The three Royal Commissioners appointed under the great seal of Canada on August 14 began to take evidence at noon, on September 4, in the railway committee room of the House of Commons.

In his choice of commissioners, Macdonald was not able to escape the shrill charge of collusion. Oddly, Judge Day was not attacked by the press, but the other two were greeted with scepticism. The *Globe* dismissed Judge Antoine Polette, ex-politician and retired Superior Court judge from Lower Canada, as "a bitter, prejudiced French Conservative." It reserved its heaviest ammunition, however, for the Honourable James Robert Gowan, a county court judge from Simcoe, Ontario, known to have been Macdonald's close friend for twenty-five years. The newspaper saw him as a hack political appointee and party follower.

The commission was unsatisfactory on several counts. There was no commission counsel to cross-examine witnesses. Huntington had been expected to assume that role, but Huntington, along with all members of the Opposition, was boycotting the entire proceedings because he believed they ought to be in the hands of a parliamentary committee. The commission had Huntington's list of witnesses but the commissioners did not really know what to ask them. Their opening query was generally vague. Apart from the three elderly judges no one else, save the Government in the person of Macdonald, was allowed the right of cross-examination. Several of the principals would not be heard from. Cartier was in his grave. McMullen ignored the subpoena. Senator Asa B. Foster found it inconvenient to attend. George Norris, the clerk who had rifled Abbott's safe, replied through his lawyer that he was too ill to appear. Of the thirty-six witnesses called, fifteen contributed nothing whatsoever to the proceedings, nor were they pressed to contributed more. They only knew, as the saying goes, what they read in the papers.

It was obvious from the beginning why Macdonald had opted for a royal commission. In Dufferin's words, "elderly judges have hardly the disembowelling powers which are rife in a young cross-examining counsel." No wonder that Macdonald had "no fear but that the report must be a satisfactory one."

Day after day, for all of September, the public was treated to the spectacle of powerful business figures and important politicians, by nature and training supposedly men of precision, fumbling about on the stand, delivering fuzzy or evasive answers, testifying to receipts that were "lost" or missing, prefacing their remarks with such phrases as "I cannot remember," or "It is not very likely . . ."

The first witness, Henry Starnes, president of Allan's Merchants' Bank and chairman of Cartier's election fund, was a mountain of uncertainty when asked about contributions to the campaign: "I cannot say how all the money came but it was deposited with me, and by what means I do not exactly know." This was the city's leading banker talking! He could not name the exact amount the committee had received, or how much of that money Allan had supplied, nor was he asked by the commission to file any account.

Sir Francis Hincks was the second witness. Because of his fierceness in debate he was known as the Hyena, but he was positively calflike on the witness stand. He professed ignorance that Allan had been "a liberal contributor to the election funds." Yet he must have known the money was coming from somewhere; he had got some himself.

When the managers of the Ottawa and Montreal telegraph companies took the stand, it developed that copies of the telegrams of the previous year had been destroyed under new rules which provided that originals could be kept for only six months. Thus all copies of telegrams for the period under investigation were gone. The ubiquitous Allan, it turned out, was also president of the telegraph company.

Hector Louis Langevin was one of several public figures who claimed to destroy most of their mail. Macdonald's minister of public works testified: "It has always been a rule with me as soon as I have finished with a letter to destroy it, unless it is an official letter to be filed in the Department . . . and I think, from what I have seen since, that I was perfectly right in this."

Langevin admitted getting election funds from Allan but, "as far as I can recollect," insisted there were no conditions attached to them. These funds amounted to $32,600. This was an enormous sum to receive from a single source; in modern terms it would be equivalent to some two hundred thousand dollars.

The tendency of the commissioners to take statements at their face value without further searching inquiry did not go unremarked. In the *Globe,* George Brown and his editorial writers pounded this point home daily. Brown had just returned from England, where he had been sent for health reasons immediately following his publication of the McMullen revelations. The Scandal had worn *him* down, too. Once across the water, Macdonald's old adversary dined with one of *The Times*'s chief editorial writers, supplied him with documents dealing with the Scandal, and then went after the lesser dailies and periodicals. "Putting the press men right," he called it. The result was that when Macdonald testified before the commission, the major British papers were ready to pounce.

It was Macdonald's testimony that the country was waiting for. The Prime Minister denied or qualified many of the statements in the McMullen account and also denied that Allan's election contributions had influenced the Government in any way. Further, he made it clear that the Government had never had any intention of allowing the Americans to control the railway. But there were two damning accusations that he could not and did not deny: he *had* asked Allan for election funds and he *had* promised Allan the presidency of the company.

Macdonald swore that he had not used one cent of Allan's money for his own election; but he was forced to make one other damaging admission: Allan's money had been spent in a manner "contrary to statute" in bringing voters to the polls and in "dinners and things of that kind." The Prime Minister's euphemisms and deliberate vagueness could not obscure in the public mind the obvious deduction that the money had been used to bribe the voters. In his second capacity of Minister of Justice, he had knowingly broken the law. Even Lord Dufferin, who had been leaning over backward on Macdonald's behalf, thought his testimony had "a very bad appearance."

The British press came down very hard on the Prime Minister. *The Times* declared that his testimony had confirmed the McMullen revelations. The *Pall Mall Gazette* asserted that "the scandal of his conduct is without precedent" and called for his removal from office forever. George Brown's spade-work had paid off for the Liberal Party.

Two days later, Allan took the stand – a chastened witness and a forgetful one. He even forgot that he had signed a supplementary contract with his American backers on March 28, 1872, in which he was authorized to accept, if necessary, a smaller land grant for the railway than that originally proposed.

"I had no recollection of this contract until the last few days," the laird of Ravenscrag declared, "and if I had been asked would have said I had never seen it." But there was no question that the contract existed and that the most astute business leader in Canada, who insisted that everything be in writing, had put his signature to it.

As for the notorious correspondence with McMullen, Smith, and Cass, they were "private letters for private information and not for publication at all," and, in Allan's view, that seemed to take care of that. He admitted that some of the statements in the letters might "appear to conflict" with his own evidence and then repeated his previously published explanation that they had been written carelessly.

In his testimony, Allan showed himself a master of double talk. McMullen had charged that a secret agreement had been made between Cartier and Allan, with Macdonald's blessing, between July 30 and August 6, 1872, by which, for certain monetary considerations, Allan was to get the charter. And there, staring at him, was Allan's own letter to General Cass of August 7, stating that "we yesterday signed an agreement by which, on certain monetary conditions, they agree to form a company of which I am to be President to suit my views, to give me and my friends a majority of the stock, and to give the company so formed the contract for building the road. . . ."

He had also used the word "agreement" in an August 6 letter to McMullen. But in Allan's curious interpretation, "yesterday" no longer meant yesterday, "signed" did not really mean signed, and an "agreement" was actually, on second thought, not an agreement at all.

The word "yesterday," Allan insisted, was used inadvertently for "recently" or "some time ago." It was "merely a slip of the pen." "Signed an agreement" was an expression "used in the hurry of the moment." And though Allan was faced with a letter in which he had written that the contract decision was ultimately in the hands of one man – Cartier – he now denied that he ever thought that an agreement with Cartier was equivalent to an agreement with the Government. Then he added that until Macdonald sent the wire refusing to accede to it he really *had* looked on it "as a kind of agreement."

Again the commissioners dealt lightly with the witness. What happened, exactly, to the money he paid to three cabinet ministers? Why, if it was a free gift freely given, did he make so much fuss about getting receipts? Was he normally in the habit of spending almost four hundred thousand dollars at election time? The commissioners did not bother to ask these questions.

By the time J. J. C. Abbott took the stand (his testimony peppered with "not likely's") interest in the Royal Commission was fast fading. Very little had emerged from the tangle of evasion, hedging, and double talk that the public did not already know. The newspapers were still publishing verbatim accounts of the proceedings, but the people were bored. When Abbott returned on September 27 to read and correct his deposition – a task that occupied two hours – one of the commissioners went into a calm sleep from which, at intervals, he would rouse himself to take snuff. Another paced the floor at the rear of the bench, pausing to help himself from the snuff box of his slumbering comrade. Only Judge Day, the chairman, managed to stay alert.

Abbott's fine tenor voice, the pride of Montreal's Christ Church Cathedral, droned on and on. The messengers nodded. The secretary of the commission read listlessly from the *Canada Monthly*. One of the three or four newspapermen present laid himself out on one of the cushioned seats that the public had abandoned and he too slept.

Thus did the proceedings of the Royal Commission grind slowly towards their close. The commissioners made no report but simply published the evidence without comment. It was left to Lord Dufferin to write its epitaph as he sent his account of the affair off to the Colonial Secretary. "A greater amount of lying and baseness," he remarked, "could not well be crammed into a smaller compass."

7

The final act was played out on Parliament Hill from October 23 to November 5 in what James Young, the parliamentarian-historian, called "one of the most remarkable and profoundly exciting debates of that period." There would be only one subject discussed in this new session of Parliament: the evidence taken before the Royal Commission.

Parliament opened on Thursday, October 23, a raw, wet day with the smell of snow already in the air. But this did not deter the crowds that congregated all along the principal streets early that morning. Tantalizing rumours were about. It was said that Macdonald was despondent over the criticisms of the British press. It was said that Macdonald was confident of a majority. It was said that Macdonald would retire into private life. In the cavernous stairwells of the Russell

House, the whispers echoed as human eddies formed and parted and circulated and formed again to exchange gossip about the scandal.

By noon a river of people was flowing towards Parliament Hill. By two, the galleries and corridors of the House were so tightly packed that it was difficult to breathe. Never before had there been such a crush within those Gothic walls. Outside, a damp wind was cutting through the thickest overcoats; inside, the temperature had become oppressive.

Once again Lord Dufferin found himself within the crimson chamber reading another man's speech in two languages – a speech that announced, among other things, that the report of the Royal Commission would be placed before the House and that the Royal Charter for the Canadian Pacific Railway would be surrendered for lack of financial backing. The House adjourned. The preliminaries were over. After the weekend, the real contest would begin.

At three that Monday afternoon the members of the Government and Opposition were in their places. Macdonald lounged at his desk to the Speaker's immediate right, presenting to the world a picture of jaunty indifference. Nearby, in Cartier's old place, squatted the rotund figure of Langevin, his new Quebec lieutenant. It was a powerful front bench: Hincks, the aging Hyena; Leonard Tilley, the handsome New Brunswicker; and, of course, Charles Tupper, the doughty "Cumberland War Horse," perhaps the best tactician in the House, all poised for the attack.

Directly across from Macdonald sat Alexander Mackenzie, whose features might have been carved out of the same granite he himself had fashioned in his days as a stonemason. His desk was piled high with references for the speech that he had been working on all weekend.

The Opposition had a formidable offensive team of its own: Mackenzie himself, caustic and dry, an expert at invective; Edward Blake, the strongest man in the Grit party, his scorn so withering that he could crush an opponent with a phrase; Richard Cartwright, known as the Rupert of Debate, a coiner of pungent, cutting phrases; the one-armed E. B. Wood, called Big Thunder because of his roaring speeches; and, of course, the eloquent, sonorous Huntington. They faced their enemies across the no-man's land of the Commons, hungry for the kill.

Both sides were confident of success. Though the Opposition had the public on its side, the Government still had the votes. At this stage of political development, party lines were not yet tightly drawn. The Opposition was a loose amalgam of Reformers and Clear Grits, working under the umbrella of the Liberal Party. Many of those who supported Macdonald called themselves Independents. Nobody knew

72

how the six members from the new province of Prince Edward Island would vote.

Part of the parliamentary struggle, therefore, took place behind the scenes, as one side struggled to hold its supporters and the other strove to capture them. Doubtful members found themselves besieged day and night with promises, cajolery, threats, and even bribes. In Ottawa the whiskey flowed as freely as the waters of the Rideau and to such an extent that certain Government supporters, known for their conviviality, were kept under lock and key lest they, in the phrase of the day, be "spirited away" and persuaded to vote contrary to their expressed intentions.

At the close of the commission's hearings, Macdonald had estimated a Tory majority of twenty-five. By Monday, October 27, the number had dropped to eighteen and then to sixteen; some thought it as low as thirteen. But if the Prime Minister could hold the debate down to three or four days and make one of his powerful speeches early in the game, he could probably win the vote.

This was not to be. Everyone wanted to speak (forty managed to do so); and everyone was on hand. Every seat seemed occupied save one: the elusive Louis Riel would not be heard from.

The battle was joined shortly after three. To the cheers of the Opposition, a grim Mackenzie rose to his feet. He spoke for almost three hours to the continual accompaniment of applause. It was a wickedly effective speech, in which Mackenzie told the House that it was being asked to vote that black was white – that Sir Hugh Allan had simply given his money as a good member of the Conservative Party, though the country had been told "very plainly by that gentleman that he had no party views at all." Mackenzie wound up with a motion of censure.

When Tupper rose to reply after the dinner recess, the galleries were jammed. The entire first row of the Speaker's Gallery was occupied by Lady Dufferin and her entourage. It was whispered that the Governor General himself was in the audience in disguise. Actually, the eager Dufferin had pleaded with Macdonald "to arrange some little closet for me in the House," but the Prime Minister was too wise to allow such a breach at this moment of crisis.

Tupper was a master of the bludgeon. The robust Nova Scotia doctor with the unblinking eyes and the pugnacious face believed in one tactic: attack with every weapon available; admit nothing; pound, hammer, swipe, thrust; if an opponent dares utter a word, batter him down.

He leaped to his feet, rejoicing that "the time has come when I and my colleagues are in a position to discuss this question in the presence of an independent Parliament." After that barefaced opening, he never let up: The country's prosperity was being affected. Canada's name was being tarnished. The real plan was to frustrate the building of the railway, nothing more. The sum Allan had contributed was "of an insignificant character." The charges were false and scandalous.

This show of bravado put the House in a spirited mood and the Cumberland War Horse had to trample his way through a thicket of catcalls. Totally undeterred, he galloped on for more than three hours and then gave way to the hero of the Opposition, Lucius Seth Huntington.

With the clock past eleven, Huntington plunged into a stalwart defence of his own position and a sardonic attack upon his adversaries, among whom Charles Tupper led all the rest.

At one point, he had the House roaring with laughter as he pounced on Allan's statement to General Cass that he had suborned twenty-seven of Cartier's phalanx of forty-five parliamentary supporters: "As a mere matter of curiosity, I should like to know who are the twenty-seven. (*Cheers and laughter.*) We have in this House a Sir Hugh Allan brigade consisting of twenty-seven members. We have it upon Sir Hugh Allan's authority that they were sent here to vote for the Government, and if any of the twenty-seven desire to stand up, I will sit down. (*Loud laughter.*)"

Huntington continued, in the same vein, to twit the Prime Minister for being on the bench, in the dock, and prosecutor all at the same time. He wound up at 1:30, with a glance at the wavering Government supporters, by declaring that "the time comes when they have to choose between fidelity to party and fidelity to country."

Thus, day after day, the debate see-sawed back and forth. On Wednesday night, the citizens awoke to find their city shrouded in the first snow of winter. But a more important question than the weather hung on every lip: What on earth was wrong with Macdonald? Why had he remained silent? His boasted majority was drifting away "like leaves in the Valley of Vallombrosa" (Dufferin's literary style again); and yet he had not joined in the debate. His friends were full of angry entreaties. He *must* speak; only he could stem the tide. Stubbornly, the Prime Minister refused.

He had started to drink again. Haggard in appearance, he was weak with fatigue and ill with strain. It was assumed by many that he did not feel himself fit to take up the cudgels in his party's defence.

But this was not the case. Macdonald was waiting for Blake to speak, for he was tolerably certain from hints in the Liberal press that the Opposition was holding some damning piece of evidence, some document of "a fatally compromising character," that Cartier had written. Or, perhaps, he himself had dispatched some damaging letter during the election; the appalling thing was that the Prime Minister could not be sure whether he had or not, he had been in his cups for so much of that period. He *must* have the last word. He could not afford to make his move and then have Blake follow him with such a *coup de grâce*.

It was only at the end of the week that the truth began to dawn upon him that, for once, he had been shamelessly outmanoeuvred. Blake was holding back on purpose, calculating that Macdonald's physical condition would deteriorate to the point where he could not speak at all. There would be no fresh revelations; the Liberals were waging a war of attrition.

It was dangerously late. James Edgar, the Liberal whip, tried to figure how a division would go. He thought he could count on ninety-nine votes with perhaps four more from the province of Prince Edward Island. That would give the Opposition 103 votes out of 206. Edgar had been working mightily, buttonholing members, talking, cajoling, and promising. His most recent trophy was David Glass, the former mayor of London, Ontario, who defected with a ringing speech. Later, Glass would be rewarded for that defection.

Macdonald resolved to enter the arena on Monday night. The preliminaries were not propitious. That very afternoon, Lord Dufferin noted that he was tipsy. And when one Liberal rose to charge that a fellow member had been offered a bribe of five thousand pounds to vote for the Government, the Prime Minister had to be dragged to his feet before he could reply. Yet in just three hours he would have to make the speech of a lifetime.

That night the corridors of the House were choked. Scores had missed their dinners in order to hold their places in the packed galleries. Even the back-benches were invaded by strangers. Hundreds more, holding useless tickets, stood outside, straining for a whisper of the proceedings within. People had poured into the capital anticipating the coming verbal duel between John A. Macdonald and Edward Blake.

In the parliamentary restaurant, a few stragglers were finishing their coffee. Suddenly the word came: "Sir John is up!" The cups scattered as the stragglers raced to the floor.

Every member, save the exiled Louis Riel, was in his seat as Macdonald rose slowly to his feet, pale, nervous, and haggard, "looking as if a feather would knock him down." Then, for the next five hours, he proceeded to electrify the House.

Those who were there would never forget it. Many felt it was the greatest speech Macdonald had ever made; some said it was the greatest they had ever heard. Even the vituperative *Globe* called it "extraordinary." Sick, dispirited, and weary he might be; but somewhere within himself this homely, errant, and strangely attractive political animal had tapped a hidden well of energy. Some claimed it was the gin, which pageboys reportedly poured into the water glasses at his elbow, but Macdonald was driven by another, more powerful stimulation. He was fighting for his career; only he could salvage it.

He began very slowly and quietly, but, bit by bit, he warmed to his audience. Gradually, tone and manner changed, the voice became more strident: Macdonald began to fight. He struck savagely at Huntington: his object was "to kill the charter." Huntington's course was governed from behind the scenes by a "foreign and alien power." The Yankee-lover sat in the House "not only by alien money but by alien railway influence." The Opposition had thieves in its employ; why, Huntington had paid McMullen seventeen thousand dollars for the famous documents.

"I challenge the Honourable gentleman to combat!" cried Huntington.

"It is very evident," said Macdonald, over the resultant hubbub, "I hit a sore spot."

The Speaker stepped in and the Prime Minister moved on to other subjects, reiterating, again and again, that there was no bargain, no contract, between his government and Allan – and that Allan's contribution was merely an election subscription.

It was past 1:30. Not a soul had left the House. Macdonald, roused now to a kind of fever pitch, intoxicated as much as the crowds and the cheers as by the glass in his hand, was reaching the climax of his address. No illegal expenditure had yet been proved before any legal tribunal against any Member of Parliament, he declared. He challenged the House, he challenged the country, he challenged the world to read the charter – to read it line by line and word by word to see if there was in it anything that derogated from the rights of Canada *(loud cheers)* or if there was in it "any preponderance of any one man of these thirteen [directors] over another" *(more cheers)*.

"Sir, I commit myself, the Government commits itself, to the hands of this House, and far beyond this House, it commits itself to the country at large. *(Loud cheers.)* . . . I have fought the battle of Confederation, the battle of Union, the battle of the Dominion of Canada. I throw myself upon this House; I throw myself upon this country; I throw myself upon posterity, and I believe that I know, that, notwithstanding the many failings in my life, I shall have the voice of this country, and this House rallying round me. *(Cheers.)* And, Sir, if I am mistaken in that, I can confidently appeal to a higher Court, the court of my own conscience, and to the court of posterity. *(Cheers.)*

"I leave it with this House with every confidence. I am equal to either fortune. I can see past the decision of this House either for or against me, but whether it be against me or for me, I know, and it is no vain boast to say so, for even my enemies will admit that I am no boaster, that there does not exist in Canada a man who has given more of his time, more of his heart, more of his wealth, or more of his intellect and power, such as it may be, for the good of this Dominion of Canada."

It was over. He sat down, utterly exhausted, while his supporters, and even some of the Opposition, cheered him to the roof. With that single speech, Macdonald solidified his hold upon the Conservative Party, a hold which had become increasingly weak and aimless. Without it he could scarcely have continued as leader.

In spite of the late hour, the House continued to sit. Now Edward Blake hoisted his big frame from his chair and stood, erect and commanding, peering sombrely through his silver-rimmed spectacles at his adversaries. To this tousled lawyer with the powerful build and strange pallor the Liberal Party had entrusted its final volley. Blake was a nemesis to many, a friend to few, and an enigma to all, a kind of political Hamlet who, seething inwardly with personal ambition, showed a strange distaste for those laurels that were dangled before him. Generally considered by his colleagues as the man most likely to succeed, he never quite succeeded. He had been Premier of Ontario for scarcely a year when he quit to enter the federal arena. He could have led the Liberal Party, instead of Mackenzie, but he declined the opportunity. All his life he would dally over similar honours.

The key to this diffidence lay in Blake's extraordinary sensitivity; an imagined slight could cause him to burst into tears in public. He once astonished the Governor General by crying in his presence over a remark Macdonald had made about him. As a brilliant lawyer he had been used to the deference of his judges and his peers. He could not accustom himself to the bitter invective that was a feature of the politics of his day. And this was singular because Blake himself, when in full voice, was perfectly capable of reducing an opponent to jelly.

The speech Blake was about to give was exactly the kind the situation called for and exactly the kind at which he excelled. It was Blake's strength that he built his speeches, brick by brick, on solid fact and hard evidence and his weakness that he generally gave his listeners too much of both. Blake took nothing for granted. He verified every statement by reference to the original documents, and long after he had proved his case conclusively he kept piling it on and on. No wonder Blake appeared pale, nervous, and exhausted. While others were relaxing in the smoking room, the Hamlet of the House was grubbing away in the parliamentary library.

The two speeches, Macdonald's and Blake's, are mirrors of the two totally disparate men who made them. Where Macdonald had been hotly emotional, Blake was icily dispassionate. Where Macdonald had been witty, Blake was earnest. Where Macdonald had been personal and subjective, Blake was aloofly analytical.

He stood now, as the cheering died, left hand sunk deep into his side pocket, totally immobile – Blake the Avenger. He had neither the time nor the inclination for humour. Instead he cut right to the bone, scooping up Macdonald's closing plea and turning it against him: "It was not to these high and elevating sentiments that the right honourable gentleman appealed during the election, it was not upon the intelligent judgement of the people he relied, but upon Sir Hugh Allan's money!" This blunt beginning, James Young recalled, galvanized the House. Blake kept on until 2:30 that morning, in his soft, resonant voice, and then for another four hours the following afternoon and evening, building his case, fact piled upon fact, every sentence deftly turned, the phrases all arranged in ringing parallels. To the faltering Members, Blake's very lack of histrionics – no arm-waving, no rising inflections – added weight to his words. And when he said "I believe that this night or tomorrow night will be the end of twenty years of corruption," there were ringing cheers. Macdonald was not present when Blake took his seat. He lay upon a couch in a committee room, half conscious, ill with fatigue.

Still the vote was in doubt. How effective had Blake been? Had he managed to cancel out the morale-building effects of Macdonald's passionate appeal? The Liberals had still not been able to force a vote; every man was in his place, waiting hour after hour for the division that would not come.

Finally it was the turn of Donald A. Smith to speak. The tough former fur trader, who was becoming a power in the Hudson's Bay Company and the Bank of Montreal, represented the riding of Selkirk, Manitoba. An independent, Smith usually supported the Government but, though he had been a member of Allan's board of directors, it was by no means certain how he would vote. Macdonald' supporters had been hesitant about approaching this frosty and imperious man who managed, throughout his career, to remain constantly in the limelight without ever appearing to seek it. Finally, the Prime Minister was himself persuaded to talk to Smith. The meeting was not a success; when the Member was taken to Macdonald's office he found him drunk and belligerent. Nonetheless the feeling in the Government ranks was that Smith was on their side.

It was one a.m. on November 5 when Smith rose to an expectant chamber. The future Lord Strathcona was not unaware of the drama. His speech was brief but he managed to squeeze from it every possible ounce of suspense. His tone was bland, his manner inoffensive: he did not consider that the first minister took Allan's money with any corrupt motive; in fact, he knew personally that Allan at one time had thought of giving up the charter. In every instance he knew the provisions were made more and more stringent against Sir Hugh.

The Government benches began to cheer. Some twenty Tories rushed to the parliamentary restaurant, prepared to drink Smith's health in champagne.

But Smith was not finished: he felt the leader of the Government was incapable of taking money from Allan for corrupt purposes. He would be most willing to vote for the Government – the cheers from the ministerial benches were now gleeful – *could he do so conscientiously* . . .

Consternation on the Conservative side! Cheers and laughter from the Opposition.

. . . It was with great regret, Smith said, that he could not do so: there was no corruption but "a very grave impropriety."

The Members skulked back to their seats as Smith sat down and with that the Speaker adjourned the House. There was a storm around Smith. He had been Macdonald's choice to deal with Riel during the Red River uprising; the Prime Minister had always admired him. Now he felt betrayed. For most of the decade the name of Donald A. Smith was anathema to the Conservatives.

It was, of course, all over. Macdonald did not wait for the ignominy of a vote. He resigned the following day and went, remarkably cheerfully, into opposition.

"Well, that's gone along with," he remarked casually to his wife that evening.

"What do you mean?" she asked.

"Why, the Government has resigned," he replied. He slipped into his dressing gown, picked up two or three books from a nearby table, and stretched out on the bed.

"It's a relief to be out of it," he said. Then he opened a volume and began to read. Characteristically, he never again alluded to the subject; it was as if, to preserve his equilibrium, he had dismissed it from his mind.

The new leaders of the country did not. For most of the decade they would, on every possible occasion, taunt their opponents with the memory of the Pacific Scandal. It would influence their policies and their actions as it would influence those of the Conservatives. When, years later, a contract was finally signed for the construction of the Canadian Pacific Railway, the terms of the agreement, the choice of the principals, and their later relations with the Government would, in some degree, be affected by the events of 1873.

When Mackenzie went to the country early in 1874, he was returned in a landslide. It was generally agreed that Macdonald was finished and that he would quickly vanish from the political scene. The railway, it seemed, had been his nemesis. It had ruined his health, stained his honour, and wrecked his career. George Ross remembered thinking that a Macdonald revival would be a greater miracle than the passage of the Israelites through the Red Sea.

From Sir Hugh Allan there was only silence in the years that followed the scandal. Taciturn and uncommunicative after his one terrible lapse, he left no memoir of his role in the affair, expressed no regret, delineated no hint of his emotions at the time. The closest he ever came to it was one night in his cavernous castle in Montreal when he was entertaining William Smith, a deputy minister of marine and fisheries. Emboldened by Allan's brandy, Smith attempted to break through the crust of Allan's reticence.

"Sir Hugh," he ventured, "between ourselves, don't you think you made rather a mistake in mixing yourself up with John A. in that Pacific Scandal business?"

The shaggy knight of Ravenscrag stared into the fire. It was some time before he delivered himself of a definitive response. Finally . . .

"Mebbe," he replied.

Chapter
Three

THE
PATHFINDERS

1

All this time, while the political hurricane was gathering force in the settled East, hundreds of men were freezing, starving, sickening, and sometimes dying in the unexplored crannies of the new Canada, as they tried to chart a route for the railway.

No life was harsher than that suffered by members of the Canadian Pacific Survey crews. None was less rewarding. Underpaid, over-worked, exiled from their families, deprived of their mail, sleeping in slime and snowdrifts, suffering from sunstroke, frostbite, scurvy, fatigue, and the tensions that always rise to the surface when weary and dispirited men are thrown together for long periods of isolation, the surveyors kept on, year after year. They explored great sections of Canada, scaling mountains that had never before been climbed, crossing lakes that had never known a white man's paddle, and fording rivers not yet on any map. They walked with a uniform stride developed through years of habit, measuring the distances as they went, checking altitudes with an aneroid barometer slung around the neck, and examining the land with a practised gaze, always seeing in the mind's eye the finished line of steel. In the first six years of the Canadian Pacific Survey, forty-six thousand miles of Canada were reconnoitred in this manner.

Twelve thousand of these miles were then laboriously charted, foot by foot, by scores of survey parties. Axemen, following the pathfinders' blazes, hacked the lines clear of brush. The chainmen who followed meticulously divided the distances into hundred-foot sections, each marked by a stake. Behind the chainmen came the transit men, calculating the angle of each bend and estimating those distances which could not be measured by a chain. Behind the transits, the rodmen and levellers worked, reckoning the altitudes and inscribing them on bench marks at half-mile intervals. By 1877 there were twenty-five thousand of these bench marks and more than six hundred thousand chainmen's stakes scattered across Canada from the Shield to the Pacific. At this point the surveys had cost three and a half million dollars and the lives of thirty-eight men.

Sandford Fleming took charge as engineer-in-chief in April, 1871. His task was not easy. A special kind of man was needed and it was impossible to find enough of them. Many could not endure the toil.

"The leveller in party S is physically unequal to the hard work that I shall unquestionably require from all my staff," Walter Moberly, the pioneer surveyor of British Columbia, scribbled in his journal when he reached the Athabasca country in November, 1872. "He is a capital man, nevertheless I *must* have strong men for my work."

But even if enough good men could have been found, it is doubtful whether Fleming would have been able to employ them. Political considerations entered into the question: various sections of the country had to be considered, different nationalities and creeds had to be consulted, and there was constant pressure to give jobs to friends or protégés of politicians. Often appointments were made over Fleming's head. The chief engineer found he had men of whom he had never heard working for him who could not be fired. Sometimes work had to be invented just to keep the political appointees busy.

One man Fleming was apparently forced to put up with for political reasons was the surly photographer-explorer Charles Horetzky, who was given his job as a result of the intervention of Sir Charles Tupper. Horetzky, after parting from John Macoun at Fort St. James, had pushed on westward towards Port Simpson. When he returned to Ottawa as a fanatical advocate of the Pine Pass–Port Simpson route, Fleming dismissed him. Horetzky always insisted that Fleming, who favoured the Yellow Head Pass, acted out of pure jealousy. Fleming's version differed. "It was sometimes necessary to employ persons who were not adapted to the work or qualified to be chief engineers."

Whatever the reasons, Horetzky ingratiated himself with the new administration and was soon back on the job in British Columbia. There was nothing, apparently, that Fleming could do. In the summer of 1875, Marcus Smith, in charge of surveys in British Columbia, had a raging row with Horetzky near the head of Bute Inlet. "He flew at me like an enraged tiger, defied me in my instructions and said he was going home to Ottawa," Smith reported. Nevertheless, Horetzky kept his job until the administration changed in 1878.

After the first year of surveys, Fleming reported that it was impossible to obtain "the class of men required." That year two crews, working through the unexplored and impenetrable country between Ottawa and Fort Garry, simply gave up the ghost. There was a seller's market in survey labour and, like it or not, Fleming and his staff had to retain incompetents.

"I wish you would find out what Walter Dewdney is doing," Marcus Smith wrote to a subordinate in May of 1875. "I heard last week that [he] was seen on the wagon road blind drunk and making an ass of himself." Since Dewdney's brother Edgar was Member for Yale and a strong political power in the province, the erring Walter could scarcely be dismissed.

The wonder was that anyone worked on the surveys at all. There was little long-term job security, even for experienced engineers. Crews were discharged at the end of the summer and re-engaged the following spring. When the work began to diminish towards the end of the decade, there was real hardship. Early in 1878, Marcus Smith reported that his men had been set adrift on a month's notice "and have not a shilling to maintain their families. If all the surveying staff is now dismissed there will be wholesale distress."

It was a lonely, remote existence the surveyors led in the field, cut off from news of family, friends, or the world at large in a land where the native rites and customs were as foreign as those of an oriental satrapy. In the spring of 1875, Henry Cambie, exploring the east branch of the Homathco, came upon Indians so removed from civilization that many of the women had never seen a beard "and would not believe that mine really grew on my chin." One of Walter Moberly's men unwittingly accepted an invitation to visit an Indian lodge and made the mistake of sitting on a bear rug next to a strapping maiden. Too late he realized that this was tantamount to an offer of marriage. In desperation he traded her back to her father for a handsome finger ring.

Yet out they went, year after year, men who were for the most part tough, intelligent, and uncomplaining. They drank anything they could get, and when they drank, they sang their theme song – sang it from the ravelled coastline of British Columbia to the gloomy granites of northern Ontario – the song of the Canadian Pacific Survey:

Far away from those we love dearest,
    Who long and wish for home,
The thought of whom each lone heart cheereth,
    As 'mid these North-west wilds we roam,
Yet still each one performs his duty
    And gaily sings:
Tra, la, la, la, la, la, la, la, la, la, la, la,
    Hurra! The jolly C.P.S.!
They're at home upon Superior's shore,
    Hurra! we'll drink to them success,
And a safe return once more.

In 1872, it was a nightmare just to reach that "home upon Superior's shore." Charles Aeneas Shaw graphically recalled his initiation in November of that year. A wiry eighteen-year-old, "keen to learn and a hog for work," he was hired as a packer under William Murdoch, seeking to locate a line west from Prince Arthur's Landing. The trick was to try to reach the Landing before winter sealed off the lake.

The group attempted it first in a cockleshell of a steamer; it foundered on a reef in a howling blizzard, drowning three of the party. The survivors bought a small fishing boat and started off in mid-December from Duluth, rowing and sailing to their destination. The temperature sank to 52 below zero – so cold that each crewman had to chip from the blades of his oars a ball of ice the size of a man's head. They crept along the shoreline, sleeping in the snow at night, existing on frozen pork and hardtack and even surviving a full-force gale. When the lake froze on New Year's Day they finally abandoned the boat, built toboggans out of strips handsawn from frozen birch logs, and hiked with their supplies the last fifty miles to Prince Arthur's Landing.

Such hardships in the Lake Superior area were commonplace in the winter of 1871-72: in the Lake Nepigon area, J. H. E. Secretan was reduced to eating rose haws washed down with swamp water. Near Jackfish River, seven men perished as the result of a forest fire so hot that the very soil was burned away. Near Long Lake, William Kirkpatrick had to take his party off surveying to pick blueberries to save their lives. And in central British Columbia that same winter, Roderick McLennan's survey party lost almost all of its pack animals; eighty-six died from cold, hunger, or overwork.

An even worse winter expedition was the exploration launched in 1875 by E. W. Jarvis, who was charged with examining the Smoky River Pass in the Rockies. Fleming had already settled on the Yellow Head as the ideal pass for the railway, but this did not prevent him from carefully examining half a dozen others. Jarvis set off in January from Fort George with his assistant, C. F. Hanington, Alec Macdonald in charge of dog trains, six Indians, and twenty dogs.

Both Jarvis and Hanington left graphic accounts of the ordeal, illuminated by uncanny episodes: the spectral figure of Macdonald knocking on the door of their shack in 49 below zero weather, sheathed in ice from head to toe; the lead dog who made a feeble effort to rise, gave one spasmodic wag of his tail, and rolled over dead, his legs frozen stiff to the shoulders; and the auditory hallucinations experienced one night by the entire party – the ghostly sound of a tree being felled just two hundred yards away but no sign of snowshoes or axemanship the following morning.

The party travelled through unmapped country with only two blankets per man and a single sheet for a tent. Much of the time they had no idea where they were. They camped out in temperatures that dropped to 53 below zero. They fell through thin ice and had to clamber out, soaked to the skin, their snowshoes still fastened to their feet. They stumbled down box canyons and found the way blocked by frozen waterfalls, two hundred feet high. One day they experienced a formidable change of temperature – from 42 below zero to 40 above – and this produced a strange exhaustion, as if they were suddenly plunged into the tropics. One morning, while mushing down a frozen river, they turned a corner and saw an abyss yawning before them: the entire party, dogs and men, were perched on the ice ledge of a frozen waterfall, two hundred and ten feet high; the projection itself was no more than two feet thick.

By March, the dogs were dying and the Indians were "in a mournful state of despair, declaring that they . . . would never see their homes again and weeping bitterly." Hanington himself felt a sense of despair: "I have been thinking of 'the dearest spot on earth to me' – of our Mother and Father and all my brothers and sisters and friends – of the happy days at home – of all the good deeds I have left undone and all the bad ones committed. If ever our bones will be discovered, when and by whom. If our friends will mourn long for us or do as is often done, forget us as soon as possible. In short, I have been looking death in the face. . . ."

Jarvis described "the curious sensation of numbness, which began to take hold of our limbs" as they pushed slowly forward on their snowshoes, giving the impression of men marking time in slow motion. Yet they made it. Hanington had lost 33 pounds; Jarvis was down to a bony 125. The food given them when they finally reached Edmonton produced spasms of dysentery and vomiting. Still they kept on, setting off once more across the blizzard-swept prairie for Fort Garry. All told, they spent 116 days on the trail, travelling 1,887 miles, 932 of those miles on snowshoes and 332 of them with all their goods on their backs, the dogs being dead.

Why did they do it? Why did any of them do it? Not for profit, certainly – there was little enough of that – nor for adventure: there was too much of that. The answer seems clear from their actions and their words: each man did it for glory, spurred on by the slender but ever-present hope that some day his name would be enshrined on a mountain peak or a river or an inlet, or – glory of glories – would go into the history books as the one who had bested all others and located the route for the great railway.

2

One man who thought he had the route and who spent the twilight of his life recalling, with increasing bitterness but not always with great accuracy, the attempt to "humbug" the route away from him, was Walter Moberly.

Moberly was working in Salt Lake City in 1871 when the news came of the pact with British Columbia. He went immediately to

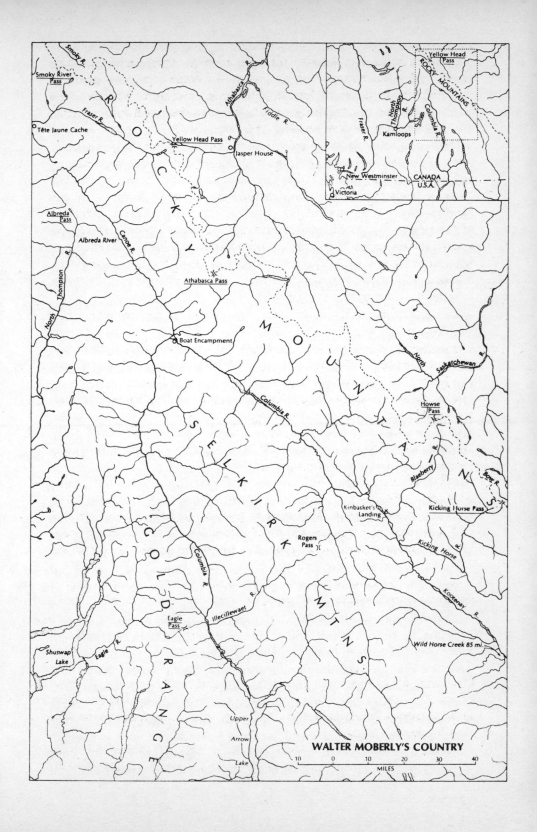

WALTER MOBERLY'S COUNTRY

Ottawa where his enemy, Alfred Waddington, was already trying to promote a railway company. Moberly hated Waddington for the same reason he hated anyone who tried to promote a railway route to the Pacific that did not agree with his own conception. Waddington was a fanatic on the subject of Bute Inlet as a terminus for the railway. It was "his" inlet; he had explored it. Moberly was equally fanatical on the subject of the Eagle Pass, the Fraser River, and Burrard Inlet. That was *his* inlet; he had trudged along its shore before any white man had settled there.

Moberly had gone to school with Lady Macdonald and she introduced him to the Prime Minister. The weathered surveyor insisted, with superb confidence, that he could tell Macdonald exactly where to locate the line from the prairies to the seacoast. Not only that but "you can commence construction of the line six weeks after I get back to British Columbia."

"Of course," Moberly added, "I don't know how many millions you have, but it is going to cost you money to get through those canyons."

Macdonald was impressed. Moberly, who was half Polish, had been lured west by the Fraser gold rush of 1858. He had helped to lay out the city of New Westminster and had located, surveyed, and constructed part of the historic corduroy road from Yale to the Cariboo gold-fields in central British Columbia. After a bout in politics, he had been named assistant surveyor general for British Columbia. In this role he discovered the Eagle Pass in the Gold Range (later called the Monashees) by watching a flight of eagles winging their way through the mountains. Moberly knew that eagles generally follow a stream or make for an opening in the alpine wall. Eventually he followed the route of the birds and discovered the pass he was seeking through the Gold Range. According to his own romantic account, he finally left his companions after a sleepless night and made his way down into the valley of the Eagle River, where he hacked out a blaze on a tree and wrote the prescient announcement: "This is the Pass for the Overland Railway."

Moberly returned to British Columbia, with the Prime Minister's blessing, as district engineer in charge of the region between Shuswap Lake and the eastern foothills of the Rockies. He was in his fortieth year – a man of legendary endurance who could dance, drink, and sing all night and plunge into the wilds the following morning.

He was as lithe as a cat and seemed to have as many lives. Once, in the Athabasca country, he was swept, horse and all, into a river and carried two hundred feet downstream. He seized an overhanging tree, hoisted himself from the saddle, and clambered to safety. On a cold January day he fell through the ice of Shuswap Lake and very nearly drowned, for the rotten surface broke away under his grasping hands. Nearly exhausted, he still managed to pull the snowshoes from his feet, one in each hand, and by spreading out his arms on the ice, climb to safety. Once, on the Columbia River, he gave chase, in a sprucebark canoe, to a bear, cornered it against a river bank, put a military pistol against its ear, and shot it dead, seizing it by the hind legs before it sank – all to the considerable risk and apprehension of his companions in the frail craft.

Moberly, in short, was a character: egotistical, impulsive, stubborn, and independent of spirit. He could not work with anyone he disagreed with; and he disagreed with anyone who believed there was any other railway route to the Pacific than the one that had been developing in his mind for years. Moberly had been thinking about the railway longer than most of his colleagues, ever since his explorations in 1858. Now, thirteen years later, he set out to confirm his findings. He began his explorations on July 20, 1871, the very day the new province entered Confederation.

He took personal charge of his favourite area bounded by the Eagle Pass of the Gold Range and the Howse Pass in the Rockies, just north of the Kicking Horse. Between these two mountain chains lay an island of formidable peaks – the apparently impassable Selkirks. It was in the hairpin-shaped trench around this barrier that the Columbia flowed, first northwest, then southeast again, until it passed within a few miles of its source. It was Moberly's theory that the railway would cut through the notch of the Howse Pass, circumvent the Selkirks by following the Columbia Valley, and then thread through the Gold Range by way of the Eagle Pass, which led to Kamloops and the canyons of the Fraser.

Moberly spent the next eight months in the mountains and trenches of British Columbia. He travelled down the olive-green Columbia with a crazy flotilla of leaky boats and bark canoes, patched with old rags and bacon grease. He trudged up and down the sides of mountains, clinging to the reins of pack horses, accompanied always by a faithful company of Indians.

When winter began, he set off on snowshoes for New Westminster, a distance of more than four hundred miles, as casually as if he were heading off on a pleasant Sunday hike. He went straight over the top of the glacier-capped Selkirks, seeking a practical pass, and was almost buried by an avalanche en route. New Year's Day, 1872, found him all alone in a trapper's abandoned hut, scrawling in his diary that it was "the most wretched New Year's Day I ever spent." He could not find a pass through the Selkirks.

When Moberly emerged from the mountains, he had so convinced himself that his route was the only conceivable one that he determined to take it upon himself to push forward immediately locating the actual line through the Howse Pass. He would get permission later. He set about hiring extra men for the 1872 season, engaging trains of pack animals and buying thousands of dollars worth of supplies, great quantities of which he had cached at Eagle Pass since he reckoned his men would spend two seasons locating the line and would stay out all winter.

Four hours before Moberly and his party were scheduled to leave Victoria for the hinterland, he received a staggering blow. The Lieutenant-Governor had a telegram for him. When he tore open the message, his head must have reeled: it was from Fleming, announcing that the Yellow Head Pass had been officially adopted for the route of the Canadian Pacific railway and that the Howse Pass survey was to be abandoned. He was to move his men north and take charge of a survey through the Yellow Head. All of Moberly's dreams dissolved at that moment. "His" route was not to be *the* route, after all.

Bitterly disappointed, the surveyor rushed to Portland, Oregon, where he tried to buy his way out of his costly contracts. But most of the supplies had already been dispatched to remote mountain areas where they could never be used. Seven thousand dollars' worth were abandoned forever at Eagle Pass.

There was another problem: Moberly needed to hire pack trains to move men and supplies north from the Columbia. If the packers knew of his dilemma they would charge extortionate rates. Moberly would have to outflank the packers, who were moving towards the foot of the Howse Pass, race ahead of them, intercept them, and re-engage the horses for the Yellow Head survey before their owners learned about the official change of plans.

He set off, first through Oregon by stagecoach (which broke down) and by steamboat (which sank), and then up through Washington Territory on horseback into British Columbia where he managed to intercept the packers. Then, with a heavy heart, he began moving his men north towards the despised Yellow Head Pass where Fleming had arranged to meet him on his trip with Grant from ocean to ocean. "Move" is scarcely an adequate verb to describe Moberly's transit: the pack trail had to be carved, foot by foot, out of the tangle of fallen cedars that barred the way up through the cavernous valleys of the Columbia, Thompson, and Albreda rivers.

Moberly himself reached the Yellow Head in early September. In Grant's *Ocean to Ocean* there is no hint of the disagreeable encounter that took place between the engineer-in-chief and his errant British Columbia deputy, but it must have been a painful one. Fleming was taken aback at the slow progress made on the surveys and by

Moberly's reckless spending. Tons of supplies left at Eagle Pass! And four hundred pack horses! The chief engineer could not understand the need for so many. At that point his impulse was to fire Moberly. He could not afford to: somebody had to take charge at the Yellow Head and push the surveys forward.

Moberly's attitude to Fleming's verbal spanking was one of disgust, not with himself but with Fleming for his "unpatriotic action" in abandoning his own pet line. To Moberly, the decision to use the other pass was little short of treason. By his own account, he was on the point of leaving the service.

A decade later, the embittered Moberly came very close to suggesting, publicly, that his chief had tried to starve him to death in the Yellow Head by ordering all purchases stopped. "Had such an order ever reached me I should simply not have gone to the Yellow Head Pass, for I would not have taken a number of men into the mountains to starve to death when winter set in."

As Moberly took his leave of the Fleming party, he was himself plagued by worry over the slow progress of the surveys under his command. Ill fortune seemed to dog his footsteps; the survey parties were taking an unconscionable time to arrive from the Howse Pass. Actually, with Moberly so long gone they had simply settled down to wait out the winter. Moberly got them moving again: it would be touch and go if they could get through the high Athabasca Pass before the blizzards blocked it and cut them off from their work at the Yellow Head.

Another party, under a veteran British Columbia surveyor, Edward Mohun, had lost six precious weeks because its supplies had unaccountably failed to reach him from Victoria. It later turned out that the purveyor and accountant there – another political appointee – was incompetent. Moberly, as the man in charge, took most of the blame.

By this time Fleming had lost all confidence in Moberly. He sent him a message by Indian runner ordering him back to Kamloops. Fleming was convinced that this raw tactic would force Moberly to quit the service, but his stubborn duputy decided simply to ignore the order and press on with the survey of the Yellow Head come hell or blizzard.

Fleming tried again after the new year. In another message he informed Moberly that Marcus Smith had superseded him and would be in charge of all exploratory surveys in British Columbia. To Moberly "this was joyful news . . . for I saw the way clear to get out of the distasteful occupation of making useless surveys." He did some further work for Marcus Smith, who wanted to see if there was a suitable pass up the North Thompson. Moberly reported "an impenetrable wall of rock, snow and ice." Then he quit the service and left for Ottawa where he was "very coldly received by the Engineer-in-Chief." He lingered in the capital waiting for Fleming to sign his expense accounts. Fleming rejected the first audit and passed the accounts on to a second auditor who went over them again. They were passed at last, but not until the frustrated Moberly had been forced to borrow money to pay for his room and board.

Disheartened, Moberly moved to Winnipeg where, presently, he busied himself at the comparatively prosaic job of building the city's first sewers. For all of his life he complained bitterly about the treatment he had received at the hands of Fleming, but he did enjoy one moment of triumph: twenty years after he discovered the Eagle Pass, the last spike of the CPR was driven almost on the very spot where Moberly, in a moment of clairvoyance, had chalked on a blazed tree his prophecy that the overland railway would have to come that way.

3

Marcus Smith, who took over all surveys in British Columbia in the spring of 1873, was without doubt the most controversial figure that the Canadian Pacific Survey produced. No two men in the service seemed to agree about him. Moberly liked him. C. F. Hanington wrote that he was a wonderful man. Harry Armstrong, who worked first in Smith's drafting room in Ottawa and became his friend, described him as "a very crabbed and impatient man, though withal very kind of heart." But some of the men who worked under Smith used harsher terms. Robert Rylatt, a member of Moberly's Howse Pass survey party, wrote in a fury that Smith was "a hard, unjust and arbitrary wretch." In the summer of 1872, a young rodman named Edgar Fawcett, toiling in the Homathco country, called him "an old devil" and wrote in his diary: "I did not come here to be blackguarded by Mr. Smith for $45 a month." And when Smith announced he was leaving the party and moving on, another member wrote in *his* diary that it was "the best news we [had] heard since we left Victoria."

Smith was a pretty good hater himself. He referred to Henry J. Cambie as a sneak and a toady. Fleming was subjected to an entire lexicon of epithets. Fleming's successor, Collingwood Schreiber, was "mean and inferior," Major A. B. Rogers was "a thorough fraud," and Charles Horetzky was "a crazy, conceited fellow." Smith was suspicious of all politicians: Alexander Mackenzie was dishonest, in his view; the Governor General, of all people, he suspected of railway land speculation; and John A. Macdonald would "sacrifice anything or anybody to smooth down difficulties."

Smith reserved his most withering contempt for those who dared to oppose the route to the Pacific in which he had come, by 1877, to believe. This route led from the Pine Pass southwest through Fort George, across the Chilcoten Plains to the headwaters of the Homathco, and thence down that turbulent river to its mouth at Bute Inlet. Smith quarrelled bitterly with anyone who favoured any other line for the railway. He fought with Fleming because Fleming continued a strong advocate of the Yellow Head Pass–Fraser River–Burrard Inlet route. He fought with Cambie because Cambie sent back favourable reports on both the Fraser River route and the northern alternative from the Yellow Head to Port Simpson. He was angered by Horetzky, who also wanted the railway to keep to the north and come out to the mouth of the Kitlope. He became such a monomaniac on the subject of "his" route that when he took Sandford Fleming's place during the latter's leave of absence, Mackenzie, who was both Prime Minister and Minister of Public Works, refused to talk to him.

Smith employed every device he knew to force the government to accept the Pine Pass–Bute Inlet route. He wrote to Members of Parliament, dispatched secret surveys into the north, arranged for letters and articles in the newspapers, and bombarded everybody, including two prime ministers, with his views. He was darkly suspicious of conspiracies, which he believed were being mounted against him, and he accused Fleming of suppressing his reports out of jealousy. Fleming bore it all with remarkable equanimity, at least in public, but he did his best to get rid of Smith. At one point he thought he *had* fired him. Smith stuck around. Fleming acted as if he did not exist. Smith may have been erratic but he was a good engineer and he was a born survivor; long after Fleming himself had been eased out of the service, he was still part of the Canadian Pacific Survey, though his position was less exalted.

In 1872, when Smith first entered the long fiord of Bute Inlet and then made his way up the Homathco – "a scene of gloomy grandeur, probably not met with in any other part of the world" – it was love at first sight, as it had been with Moberly and Horetzky and all the other enthusiasts who championed a line of route, including the chief engineer himself.

In his diaries and official reports, he waxed positively lyrical about the region. His description of the "charming" mile-wide valleys of the Chilcoten and Chilanko rivers had the ring of a hopelessly infatuated suitor composing a paean to his intended. He wrote of the bottom lands, ripe and mellow with bunch growth, with the clear streams meandering through them in graceful curves, of the pale, greyish-green of the grasses "in agreeable harmony with the dark foliage of the spruce," and of the "picturesque irregularity of the evergreens," the whole "forming a scene of pristine beauty rarely to be met with." Compared with the routine prose of some of his colleagues, Smith's, on occasion, seemed almost sensual.

He had just turned fifty-six – a stubby man with a barrel chest, tough as shaganappi and bristly as a wart-hog – when he first clambered up the dripping cliffs of the Homathco. He was a Northumberland man who had been a land surveyor all his life, first in England and Wales, then in South Africa and, since 1850, in Canada. He had worked for Fleming on the Intercolonial, as had so many of the men on the C.P.S.; and like so many of the others – men accustomed to fend for themselves in wild and inhospitable climes – he was totally self-confident and more than a little proud.

He was a hard drinker. On the prairie surveys, where prohibition reigned, his keg of "lime juice" contained straight whiskey. On the Homathco, he and his subordinate, W. O. Tiedeman, broke open a case of brandy and fought and drank an afternoon away. He was not an easy man to work under for he did not suffer incompetence, fatigue, or any kind of human frailty. Young Edgar Fawcett, the rod-man on the Bute-Homathco survey, was toiling up a steep, rock-strewn hill in June, 1872, when a tumbling boulder struck him a blow that knocked him insensible. Smith took personal affront at the mishap: "That boy who could not keep out of the way of stones would have to be sent home."

Anything that interfered with the progress of the survey distressed him, as several entries in the diary of George Hargreaves, the leveller in the Bute survey party, reveal:

June 26, 1872: "Old Smith came to camp about 7:30 and boiled over, accusing us of putting obstacles in his way and saying he would carry through with the survey if he had to send 5,000 miles for men."

July 3: "Had a row with Old Smith for not bringing the levels through before stopping work. . . . Says he, 'what did you mean by saying you was through, you must be an idiot.' "

July 5: "It appears Smith had a big row with two or three of the men and also with Bristow, the Transit. Called him a Gd. dmd. fool and Idiot, who said he would not have such language used to him that he would go home to Canada if he continued to use it, and also told Smith he was stopping the work by carrying on so. Smith told him to go back to his instrument or he would give him the Gd. damdist daming ever he had dam'd. . . ."

"It was most awful the way that old devil swore and went on generally," young Fawcett wrote of Smith in his own diary a week

94

after the incident with the boulder. "He swore at me for the most ordinary things and kept us from dinner till half-past two."

Yet, Fawcett admitted, he was treated no worse than the others, for Smith made no distinctions. He barked at Tiedeman, the head of the party, and at transit men, levellers, axemen, and Indian packers with a fine democracy. The Indians calmly unloaded their canoes and prepared to head off into the wilderness. Smith called in Hargreaves and asked him who had authorized the Indians to leave. Hargreaves replied that the Indians did not require any authorization to do anything, a remark that seemed to astonish Smith, who asked what the Indians wanted. The Indians said that they did not want to work for Smith. Hargreaves prevented a wholesale desertion by apologizing for Smith and agreeing to pay the Indians in cash at the time of every trip.

But if Smith was hard on others, he was equally hard on himself. When he was sixty years of age, he travelled for one thousand miles through the Lake Superior country by canoe, all in a single summer, making two hundred portages that varied from a few yards to four miles.

He must have seemed a superman, albeit a satanic one, to the young chainmen and rodmen who, at the end of each day, found themselves so exhausted they were ready to throw in the sponge. Again, their diary excerpts tell the story:

"So tired I could hardly drag myself along. After one of the hardest, hottest and longest days I had ever experienced in my life, we arrived at 'W' camp. I was so far done in I could not get up and sat down to rest."

"Yesterday I really thought I should have to give in I felt so the loss of having eaten nothing all day but a bit of bread and fat pork in 12 hours. If this is surveying, I have had my bellyfull of it."

"I am heartily sick of the whole business and feel like turning tail."

Yet here was the demonic Smith, a man twice their age, driving late into the evening, scaling the rocks and forging through the glacial waters with enough breath left in his barrel chest to shower curses and imprecations upon the stragglers.

The truth was that he was as exhausted as any. "Felt terribly used up," he wrote in his journal on July 9, 1872. But he would not give up that night until he had worked out the calculations of his travels across the mountains. Four days later, when he boarded the boat to Victoria, he was near collapse: "Fatigue set in after a

95

month of excessive labour and anxiety and I lay and dozed the hours away, totally unfit for anything.''

Sick or not, Smith was back a month later. He was tortured by cramps in his hip and left leg and by August 11 was so ill he could not rise until noon. But rise he did, saddled a horse, and headed off across a swamp. The horse became mired. Smith tried to spur it on. The saddle slipped off and Smith tumbled into the morass. He was too weak to re-saddle the horse but he managed to crawl all the way to the head of a lake where he found two Indians who cared for him.

He was still at it, in the same country, in the summer of 1875. He was then in his sixtieth year and he confided to one of his surveyors that he had ''less heart for this journey'' than any he had undertaken. ''I am far from well and very weak and the mountain torrents are very high.''

When he wrote that letter, Smith was planning to force his way from the Chilcoten Plains through the Cascade Mountains to Bute Inlet. He set off on foot with six Indians, struggling for two and a half days along the perpendicular cliffs of the canyons. Sometimes it took several hours to move a few yards, since they had to climb as high as fifteen hundred feet and descend again to circumnavigate the spurs of rock. At one point, unable to bridge a torrent, they were forced to detour by way of a glacier fifteen miles long, whose sharp ridges they crossed on hands and knees.

It was not the kind of summer excursion a doctor would prescribe for an ailing man in his sixtieth year, especially as the bridges had been swept away by the mountain floods. It took Smith and his men seven hours to construct a fly bridge over the Grand Canyon of the Homathco; it ''looked like a fishing rod and line hanging over the torrent.'' Smith crept gingerly over this precarious filament, dropped heavily to the rocks below, and then spent six hours scrambling over tangled creepers, huge deadfalls, and masses of detached rocks before reaching camp.

Smith's love-hate relationship with this strangely compelling land of grim canyons and smiling meadows had, to borrow his own phrase, used him up. Would all this travail be in vain? Survey parties were crawling over the rumpled face of British Columbia and probing the ragged fiords of the coastline, seeking a feasible method of reaching the Pacific. Sandford Fleming was contemplating no less than eleven different routes leading down from the mountain spine to salt water. Only two led through Smith's country. What if another route should be chosen? What if all those ghastly days in the numbing bogs and among the brooding crags should end in defeat? Marcus Smith was not a man to contemplate defeat; and he had not yet begun to fight.

Chapter
Four

THE
NOBLE
MAN

1

"I will leave the Pacific Railway as a heritage to my adopted country," Alexander Mackenzie is said to have declared in his dry, Gaelic accent, when Donald A. Smith, the Member for Selkirk, tried to argue the merits of using a private company to build the line. Smith, nonetheless, remained in Mackenzie's camp. "He is a noble man," Smith said of him, and the voters, who returned him with a landslide early in 1874, seemed to agree.

They wanted a noble man and they got one: a high-principled Scot with honest eyes of piercing blue. Though not immune to the pressures of nepotism and patronage, he appeared to be a man of probity. The public had reduced Macdonald's following in the House to a corporal's guard, as he ruefully remarked, and placed his antithesis on the pedestal. With his metallic voice, his rigid attitudes, his Baptist teetotalism, and his blunt manner, Mackenzie was the exact opposite of the rounded, soft-spoken, tolerant and indulgent politician whom he replaced.

As Prime Minister he lacked Macdonald's conciliatory gifts and in debate he tended to continue as if he were in opposition, striking down his opponents with the blunt bullets of his words. Mackenzie could never quite let well enough alone and his tendency to want to rub his adversaries' noses in their mistakes, or imagined mistakes, was to affect his railway policy.

Though he never allowed an early adjournment of the Commons if there was business to fill up the time, he sometimes worked unnecessarily hard, for he found it difficult to separate small details from over-all plans – a stonemason's trait, perhaps. In his chosen trade he had created fortifications, canals, and court houses, and when a huge piece of cut stone once fell upon the lower part of his foot he allowed no cry of agony to escape from his thin lips. In his political career, too, he masked his inner tortures. He was not one to cry out in public; but then he was not one to chuckle, either.

It was remarked, wickedly, that while Mackenzie's strong point as a political leader consisted in his having been a stonemason, his weak point consisted in his being one still. This was not quite fair. The Governor General, who still yearned secretly for Macdonald, found him "industrious, conscientious and exact." Dufferin had thought him terribly narrow, but he was not so narrow in his interests.

He had once owned and used a telescope. He was a lover of poetry and English literature. He had not had much formal schooling, but he had managed to read everything to which his better-educated peers had been exposed and seemed to remember far more of it. Though he had, in his younger days, been an incorrigible practical joker, his public image was one of uncompromising sobriety. It is difficult to imagine anything but the bleakest of smiles illuminating those chiselled features. The church, to Mackenzie, was the rock on which civilization rested; scarcely a day went by on which he did not read his Bible and fall on his knees to ask his God for forgiveness and guidance.

As a Liberal, he stood for a retrenchment of government spending. He could not stomach the grandiose schemes of the Conservatives which all too often seemed to him to be designed as much for profit and patronage as for empire building. To Mackenzie and his followers, Macdonald's Pacific railway scheme was precipitate, rash, and spendthrift. The Tories, with their big business connections, were temperamentally attuned to taking chances; but Mackenzie's political base was in the sober farming districts and small towns of Ontario.

During Mackenzie's term of office, only a few miles of the CPR were built, but it is arguable that Macdonald, in those lean years, could not have done much better. Mackenzie was unlucky. For the whole of his term the country was in the grip of a serious continental depression.

Like so much else, the depression was imported from the United States – touched off by the spectacular failure of Jay Cooke's Northern Pacific. On September 17, at the very moment the royal commission was considering the implications of Cooke's secret deal with Allan, the great financial house closed its doors. Five thousand commercial houses followed Cooke and his allied brokers and banks into failure; railroad stocks tumbled; by midwinter, thousands of Americans were starving.

It was an accident of economic history that the crash, which affected all of settled Canada, neatly bracketed the Mackenzie regime; the new prime minister was shackled financially. Yet it is doubtful whether given prosperity he would have accomplished any more than he did. He could gaze upon the universe with his telescope, but he did not see his country as a great transcontinental nation, settled for all of its length from sea to sea. Canada, to Mackenzie, lay east of the Shield; far off were two small islands in the Canadian archipelago: the Red River settlement and British Columbia. These were necessary nuisances. In addition, Mackenzie could not refrain in his speeches from the kind of wild remark that filled British Columbians with dismay and goaded them into retaliation. As late as 1877 he was still using the word "insane" to describe the pact with the Pacific province.

Clearly his predecessor had saddled Mackenzie with an impossible burden. The policy was scarcely insane, but some of the terms were certainly foolhardy. In the prosperous glow of 1871, Macdonald had blithely promised the British Columbians that he would commence construction of the line in two years. *Two years!* In the spring of 1873, with the surveyors bogged down in the bewildering mountain labyrinth, Macdonald realized he must pay lip service to his incautious pledge. A few days before the deadline he recklessly picked Esquimalt, the naval harbour on the outskirts of Victoria, as the terminus of the Canadian Pacific Railway.

In practical terms, this meant that the railway would run to Bute Inlet on the mainland; it would then thread its way down for fifty miles from the head of the inlet through the sheer, granite cliffs of the coastline, leap twenty-nine miles across the Strait of Georgia to Nanaimo on Vancouver Island, and follow the east coast of the island to Esquimalt. It would require eight miles of tunnelling and untold rock cuts to negotiate those sea-torn precipices. Then the track would have to hop from island to island over six deep channels through which the rip tide sometimes tore at nine knots; that would require eight thousand feet of bridging and in two instances the spans would have to be thirteen hundred feet in length. That was greater than any arch then existing anywhere in the world.

This, then, was the *fait accompli* Mackenzie faced: a deadline determined, a terminus established, and a province militant. In this fertile ground were sown the seeds for the uneasy relationship between the Pacific province and central Canada that was to be maintained into the nation's second century. Right from the beginning, the British Columbians viewed "the East" with suspicion. On its part, the East – for Mackenzie unquestionably had the support of the public at large outside British Columbia – saw the new province as greedy, shrill, and bumptious, prepared to wreck the economy of the nation for the sake of petty provincialism and real estate profits.

During the election Mackenzie had been at pains to water down Macdonald's impossible dream. He talked about a land and water route across the nation, with the rail line to be built piecemeal. There was no real hope of attracting private capital during the depression. If the railway was to be commenced, it would have to be built in sections as a public work. The first, a line from Lake Superior to the Red River to replace the Dawson Route, and the second, a branch line in Manitoba from Selkirk to Pembina on the United States border, would, it was hoped, give the Red River its long desired connection with the outside world. After that, as funds were available, other sections would be built – but scarcely within ten years. That was not good enough for British Columbia whose premier, George Walkem, jumped with both boots into the heated Battle of the Routes, which was to last the rest of the decade.

In spite of Macdonald's choice of Esquimalt, the engineers had not made up their minds about the location of the terminus. At the close of 1873, Sandford Fleming was considering seven alternative routes to the coast. No fewer than six passes in the Rockies were being explored. By mid-decade Fleming was able to report on twelve different routes through British Columbia to seven different harbours on the coastline.

But as far as British Columbia was concerned, there were only two routes that really mattered. One was the fur traders' trail through the Yellow Head Pass and down the Fraser Canyon to Burrard Inlet; if chosen it would guarantee the prosperity of Kamloops, Yale, and New Westminster. The mainland of British Columbia fought for this route. The other would lead probably from the Yellow Head through the Cariboo country and the Chilcoten Plains to Bute Inlet, then leap the straits to Nanaimo and thence to Victoria; it would guarantee the prosperity of the dying gold region and of Vancouver Island.

The Premier, a Cariboo man who knew a political issue when he saw one, opted instinctively with the Island interests for the Bute Inlet route and decided to go over the Prime Minister's head to the Crown itself. The Crown, in the person of Lord Carnarvon, the Colonial Secretary, offered to arbitrate the dispute between the province and the federal government.

Mackenzie's immediate instinct was to reject the offer; here was the Colonial Office interfering in the domestic affairs of an independent dominion! But the Governor General persuaded him to give in and accept arbitration. Under the resultant "Carnarvon Terms" of 1874, it was agreed that a railway would be built on Vancouver Island, the surveys would be pushed, and, when the transcontinental line was finally launched, the government would spend at least two millions a year on its construction. In return, the province accepted an extension of the deadline to December 31, 1890.

Now the stoic stonemason, who had forborne to cry out under physical pressure, began to suffer under the millstone of office. He was plagued with intestinal inflammation and insomnia, both the products of political tensions. "I am being driven mad with work – contractors, deputations and so on," he told a colleague early in 1874. "Last night I was in my office until I was so used up I was unable to sleep." Two years later, he complained to a friend about "a burden of care, the terrible weight of which presses me to the earth." The railway – the terrible railway – a dream not of his invention, a nightmare by now, threatened to be his undoing. On one side he felt the pull of the upstart province on the Pacific, holding him to another man's bargain – a bargain which his honour told him he must make an honest stab at fulfilling. On the other, he felt the tug of the implacable Edward Blake, the rallying point for the anti-British Columbia sentiment and a popular alternative as Prime Minister.

The rebellious Blake had left the Cabinet and in October, 1874, delivered himself of the decade's most discussed public speech at Aurora, Ontario. In a section devoted to railway policy he dismissed British Columbia as "a sea of mountains," charged that it would cost thirty-six million dollars to blast a railway through it, and declared the annual maintenance would be so costly that "I doubt much if that section can be kept open after it is built." If the British Columbians wanted to separate from Canada, Blake said, in effect, then let them.

Mackenzie knew Blake must be lured back into the Cabinet. Blake was willing, but he had a price. Mackenzie was forced to add a hedge to the Carnarvon Terms; they would be carried out *only* if that could be done without increasing taxes.

That done, Blake returned in May, 1875, as Minister of Justice. Together, he and the Prime Minister worked out a compromise offer to British Columbia. In lieu of the Island railway, the government was prepared to pay the province $750,000. But the Order in Council was not worded that way. The money was to be advanced, it said, "for any delays which may take place in the construction of the Canadian Pacific Railway." There was that word again – *delays*! British Columbia had had nothing but delays, and now the government was practically promising more and offering hush money to boot.

But opinion in the rest of Canada had by this time swung solidly behind Blake and Mackenzie. In April, 1876, when Parliament passed the taxation declaration that Blake insisted upon, the vote was 149 to 10. Only the Island members opposed it. The Government of Canada had resolved to go its own way in the matter of the railway and to stop trying to conciliate British Columbia. If that meant separation, so be it.

2

Frederick Temple Blackwood, Viscount Clandeboye and Earl of Dufferin, was chafing with inactivity. He longed to get away on a voyage of conciliation for which he felt his undoubted gifts as a diplomat superbly qualified him. Specifically, he wanted to go out to British Columbia as both a spokesman of the federal government and an agent for the Colonial Secretary.

Mackenzie, Blake, and Richard Cartwright, the Minister of Finance, greeted His Excellency's proposal with something akin to terror – at least that was the word the Governor General used. The idea of the Queen's representative, especially *this* Queen's representative, plunging into the most delicate problem in Canadian dominion politics did not make them rest easily. Dufferin loved making speeches; he made them on every possible occasion. He would undoubtedly make speeches all over British Columbia. His speeches were full of Irish blarney and could be calculated to butter up his listeners to the point of embarrassment. Would he unwittingly inflate the expectations of the people to the point where a revival of understanding would be more impossible than ever? The three called on the Governor General on May 26 and "there ensued a long and very disagreeable discussion." Finally it was agreed that Dufferin would make a state visit to British Columbia but must maintain the traditional vice-regal attitude of strict neutrality.

The Governor General and his countess went by rail to San Francisco and there embarked by naval vessel for the "nest of hornets," as Dufferin called Victoria. They debarked from H.M.S. *Amethyst* at Esquimalt harbour on August 16, 1876, and drove through the streets of the capital, cheered on by the entire populace – canoe-loads of Indians, Chinese in pigtails, Cariboo miners, scores of little girls in private-school uniforms, old Hudson's Bay hands and, most of all, hundreds of loyal English men and women – retired army officers, former civil servants, newly arrived immigrants.

The handsome figure in the carriage, acknowledging the cheers that engulfed him, had just turned fifty. There was a certain haughtiness to the tilt of his head for he was not without vanity: he was in the habit, for instance, of sending reports of his speeches to the press with bracketed phrases, such as "Prolonged applause," "Great laughter," "Cries of Hear! Hear!" inserted in the appropriate places. But they were good speeches for all of that, the sentences nicely turned, the local allusions graceful. Dufferin, after all, came from the best literary stock. His mother – hers was the Sheridan side of his family – wrote ballads; his aunt was a poet and singer. He himself had produced an amusing book of travel. A product of the British class system, Eton and Oxford educated, he knew all the titled families of England, but he also hobnobbed with Tennyson, Browning, and Dickens.

As a newcomer, he was able to see Canada whole and not as a loose collection of self-centred and often antagonistic communities. The petty provincialism of the Canadians bothered him, and he tried throughout his term to encourage in them a feeling of common pride. But in Victoria he was dismayed to find no flicker of national feeling. The island town was in every sense a little bit of Old England. Most of the residents had been born in Britain and "like all middle class Englishmen, have a vulgar contempt for everything that is not English." Not only did the capital consider itself separate and distinct from Canada, but it also considered itself apart from the rest of the province.

Dufferin's preconceived notions about the greed of British Columbians for the money the railway would bring in were largely confirmed in the remarkable week that followed. Day after day, beginning at nine in the morning and continuing without interruption until seven at night, he found himself receiving delegation after delegation to discuss the most controversial question in the country. "Lord Dufferin," his private secretary wrote to Mackenzie, "bids me add that he finds great difficulty in keeping his temper with these foolish people." At that point, the Governor General had spent seven days, ten full hours a day, "listening to the same old story, abuse of Mackenzie, of Canada, of Sir John Macdonald and the absolute necessity of bringing the Pacific Railway via Bute Inlet to Esquimalt."

But then, Victoria was literally fighting for its life. The depression had dealt the community a blow more staggering than that which the rest of the country had suffered. The cost of living remained astronomical because of the town's isolation. As Dufferin reported to Carnarvon, "In Victoria the one idea of every human being is to get the railway to Esquimalt. It is upon this chance that the little town must depend for its future . . . most of its inhabitants have wildly speculated in town lots. . . . You can therefore imagine the phrensied [sic] eagerness with which Victoria grasps at every chance of making itself the terminus of the great transcontinental railway."

When he reached the mainland, it was the same story. "The location of the Canadian Pacific Railway, and its terminus along such a line, and on such a spot as may enhance the value of his own individual town lot, or in some other way may put money into his pocket, by passing as near as possible to where he lives, is the common preoccupation of every Columbian citizen."

Yet in spite of the constant pressure upon him, he returned to Ottawa with considerable sympathy for the British Columbians. He suspected that Mackenzie, pushed by Blake and Cartwright, was trying to wriggle out of his commitments. As a result, the "horrid B.C. business," as Lord Dufferin branded it, touched off an extraordinary scene at Rideau Hall. Here, for the first and only time in Canadian history, a governor general and his two chief advisers came perilously close to fisticuffs.

Dufferin was convinced that Lord Carnarvon should re-enter the picture to arbitrate the question of the Island railway, which Victoria continued to claim was part of the main line of the CPR and which

Mackenzie insisted was a local project divorced from the transcontinental route. The Governor General even suggested raising the $750,000 offered in lieu of the line to an even million: any reasonable sacrifice was worth while, if Confederation was at stake.

On Saturday, November 18, he met with Blake and Mackenzie at Rideau Hall. Both men were stubbornly opposed to him and the scene that followed was stormy and disagreeable. They "nearly came to blows . . . Mackenzie's aspect was simply pitiable and Blake was on the point of crying as he very readily does when he is excited."

The day after this extraordinary encounter, everybody cooled off and a face-saving formula was evolved, hoisting the matter for eighteen months until the surveys could be completed and a route fixed; failing that, Mackenzie cautiously agreed to some sort of London meeting under Carnarvon's auspices.

With that, the importunate Dufferin had to be content. He had pushed his ministers as hard as any governor general could or ever would; he undoubtedly felt he had been successful; but the hard fact was that he had battered his noble head against an unyielding wall of granite.

3

By 1877, the Battle of the Routes had reached the stage of a pamphlet war, and still Sandford Fleming had not chosen a pass through the Rockies or a terminus along the coastline. Some of this apparent dallying had to do with the nature of the country itself, but much of it was clearly political procrastination.

Fleming's own opinions in his massive report of 1877 were clouded in ambiguity. By 1875 there was a general understanding that Bute Inlet would probably be the terminus. Then, in November of 1876, it occurred to Fleming, rather tardily, that the Admiralty might be asked its views on the various harbours along the coast. The opinion of the seamen was overwhelmingly in favour of Burrard Inlet.

In spite of that, Fleming still could not make up his mind. Obviously, he felt the final decision was up to the politicians; and in case they could not decide, he had a suggestion: there was another choice at the mouth of the Skeena River, a harbour five hundred miles closer to the Orient than the other two.

Fleming at that time was an absentee engineer-in-chief. He had been a robust man who thought nothing of warding off a bear with an umbrella or unrolling his blankets in two feet of snow, as he had done on his twenty-fourth birthday, but by 1876, in his fiftieth year, he was exhausted. A Fifeshire Calvinist, who prayed aloud on the

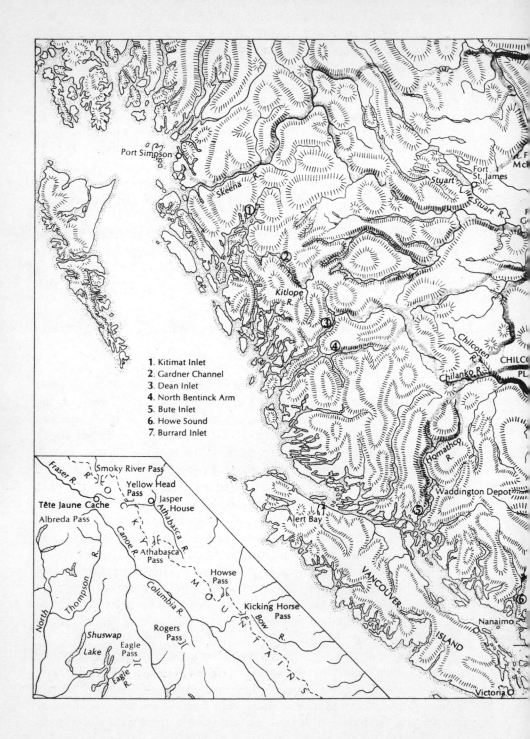

Port Simpson

Skeena R.

Kitlope R.

1. Kitimat Inlet
2. Gardner Channel
3. Dean Inlet
4. North Bentinck Arm
5. Bute Inlet
6. Howe Sound
7. Burrard Inlet

Stuart L.

Fort
St. James

Mc

Stuart R.

Chilcoten R.

CHILC
PL

Chilanko R.

Homathco R.

Waddington Depot

Alert Bay

VANCOUVER

ISLAND

Nanaimo

Victoria

Fraser R.

Smoky River Pass

Yellow Head
Pass

Jasper
House

Tête Jaune Cache

Albreda Pass

Athabasca R.

Canoe R.

Athabasca
Pass

North Thompson R.

Howse
Pass

Columbia R.

Kicking Horse
Pass

Rogers
Pass

Shuswap
Lake

Eagle
Pass

Eagle R.

MOUNTAINS

Bow R.

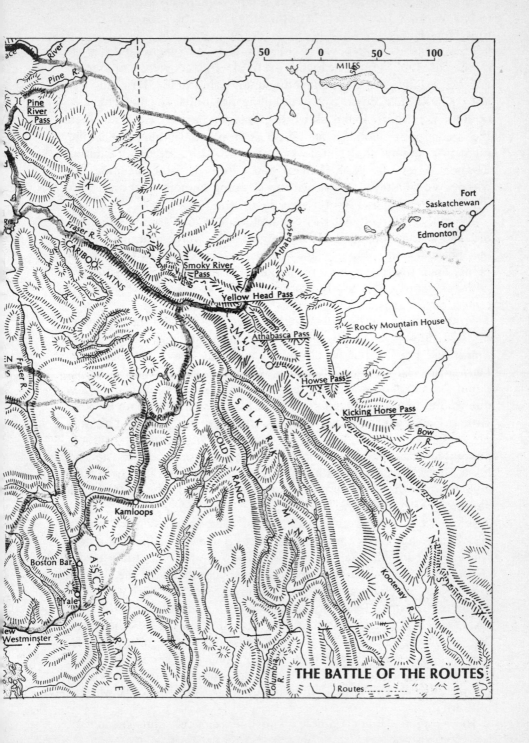

50   0   50   100

MILES

Fort
Saskatchewan

Fort
Edmonton

River

Pine R.

Pine
River
Pass

C
A
R
I
B
O
O

Fraser R.

CARIBOO MTNS

Smoky River
Pass

Athabasca R.

Yellow Head Pass

Rocky Mountain House

Athabasca Pass

Fraser R.

Howse Pass

SELKIRK

Kicking Horse Pass

North Thompson R.

GOLD

RANGE

Bow
R.

Kamloops

K MTNS

Boston Bar

CASCADE RANGE

Kootenay R.

Yale

New
Westminster

Columbia R.

THE BATTLE OF THE ROUTES

Routes ---------

tops of mountain peaks, he had as a boy copied out a maxim from *Poor Richard's Almanack:* "Dost thou love life? Then do not squander time, for that is the stuff life is made of." Fleming loved life; he held gay parties in Ottawa; he was fond of champagne and kept it by the case in his office; he loved rich food – oysters were a favourite; and he certainly did not believe in squandering time. Between 1871 and 1876 he held down two man-killing positions as chief engineer of both the Intercolonial and the Canadian Pacific. He had taken the second job reluctantly and at no extra pay. "I laboured day and night in a manner that will never be known," he reminded Charles Tupper. After all, Poor Richard had said: ". . . the sleeping fox catches no poultry . . . there will be sleeping enough in the grave." The boy Fleming had written that down, too.

When the Intercolonial was completed in 1876, Fleming's doctors ordered a complete rest. He was granted a twelve-month leave of absence and went off to England but was twice recalled by the government, once to write the monumental 1876 report and again to deal with his deputy, the bristly Marcus Smith. The leave stretched out over a two-year period.

For nineteen months, between the spring of 1876 and the beginning of 1878, Fleming was absent and Marcus Smith was in his place. Smith had the job but he did not, apparently, have the authority. During his visits back to Canada, Fleming would countermand his deputy's instructions or disagree with his views. Much of this was due to Smith's furious championing of a single railway route through British Columbia from the Pine Pass to Bute Inlet. But Smith was never an easy man to get along with. Some of Fleming's personal appointees clashed with him. James Rowan, for example (he had been Fleming's chief assistant before Smith took over), ignored for eighteen months the letters that Smith sent out to him on the north shore of Lake Superior.

Smith would not give up on Bute Inlet. The obvious impracticality of a causeway across the strait had not cooled his ardour for "his" route. A steamboat, he insisted, could move an entire train across to the island. He had also become disenchanted with the Yellow Head Pass, which his absent chief favoured. By 1877 there had taken shape in the back of that mysterious mind a preference for the Pine Pass, which Horetzky had first explored. In April of 1877 he asked Mackenzie for permission to probe the pass with three survey parties, adding that he himself would like to go along. Mackenzie, who was trying to slash expenses in the department, turned him down, whereupon the irrepressible Smith determined to go ahead secretly without authority.

He wrote to Henry Cambie, who had replaced him as chief of

surveys in British Columbia, to send Joseph Hunter to the Pine River country with two or three men and some packers. The trip was to be completely confidential. Snoopers were to be told only that Cambie was extending his explorations of the Skeena country.

Meanwhile Smith went out to British Columbia himself on a tour that took on some of the aspects of a political campaign. A friend later told Mackenzie of "the insolence of Marcus Smith, who . . . everywhere and most industriously spoke of your railway policy as shuffling, bumbling, declaring that you had really not the slightest intention of going on with the work in British Columbia and predicting very positively the return to power of the Conservatives . . . ."

Smith now accelerated his behind-the-scenes manoeuvres to get "his" route approved. On December 7, he wrote to Hunter that Mackenzie and Dufferin were "moving Heaven and Earth" to get the Fraser River–Burrard Inlet route adopted. He instructed Hunter that the time had arrived for him to leak some information unofficially to the press about his Pine Pass explorations. Smith actually composed a press release which began: "Notwithstanding that the matter has been kept very quiet, it has leaked out that the explorations of the acting Engineer-in-Chief, Marcus Smith, from the East, and Mr. Hunter, from the West, last summer have been most successful." The release went on to say that the Pine Pass was shorter and lower than the Yellow Head and would connect favourably with Bute Inlet.

An accomplished intriguer himself, Smith was a man who saw dark plots and sinister motives everywhere he went. He lived in a cloak-and-dagger world of the mind in which he imagined himself desperately staving off, at great personal and financial risk, the sombre forces of treason and corruption.

"I see now that the storm is going to burst as regards myself," he wrote to Fleming on December 7, 1877. "At Victoria, I found out about this Burrard Inlet mania, which is a huge land job in which the Minister and his friends are concerned – the latter certainly are from the Lieutenant Governor downwards. It was first started by Lord Dufferin in 1876 . . . ."

In Smith's dark view, the Governor General, cheated of a victory that "would help him much in his diplomatic career," promised the Burrard terminus to the mainland as an act of revenge.

Meanwhile, Henry Cambie in British Columbia had been caught up in the intrigue. Mackenzie, unable to budge Smith, had gone around him and wired direct to Cambie to commence the survey of the Fraser, which the Governor General had so urgently recommended on his return. When Smith returned from the West, he found himself snubbed.

At length, Mackenzie asked Cambie for a written report on the Fraser. This put Cambie in a dilemma. Properly, reports should go to the engineer-in-chief. Cambie was being asked to go over Smith's head. He brought his plight to the crusty Smith, who gave him a fierce reception: after all, Cambie was opposed to the Bute Inlet route and therefore an enemy.

The strange spectacle of a cabinet minister (and Prime Minister to boot) trying to circumvent his own department head in order to obtain information from a subordinate continued all that month. Mackenzie kept on ignoring Smith and meeting secretly with Cambie. For the wretched Cambie, the squeeze was getting tighter. He had been in some tight fixes in his time – just that summer he had taken a leaky boat, caulked only with leaves, for 150 miles down the rivers of the Rocky Mountain Trench, one man bailing furiously all the way – but never had he encountered a situation fraught with such tension. Cambie kept putting off his written report to Mackenzie. Mackenzie kept demanding it. He did not, however, ask for any special report from Marcus Smith. "He shall get one nevertheless whether he likes it or no," Smith remarked grimly. He firmly believed that Cambie was being used as a tool by Fraser Valley speculators to push the Burrard route. As he put it, "I have made up my mind to take the bull by the horns and am prepared to resign my post rather than truckle to the whims or political necessities of the Government against my better judgement."

Cambie, complying with Smith's instructions, ventured no opinion on the relative merits of the various routes proposed through British Columbia. Smith sent the report along to Mackenzie with a laconic note stating that it was "about as full and accurate as it could be in the present unfinished state of the plans." He added that he was in no position yet to make a comparative judgement on the various routes. But Mackenzie had other sources. Quite clearly, the Prime Minister had settled on the Burrard route. There were many reasons for his decision: the Admiralty report; the skilful advocacy of the mainland Members of Parliament; Lord Dufferin's own opinion; the new surveys by Cambie; and, finally, Smith's bull-headed intransigence. The acting chief engineer had got his minister's back up. By March, 1878, Mackenzie had ceased to consult him or even speak to him.

On March 29, Smith sent in his own official report. Predictably, he advocated the Pine Pass–Bute Inlet route, but suggested another year's delay to settle the final location of the line. This presented Mackenzie with a new dilemma. He could scarcely settle on Burrard Inlet in the face of the direct and public opposition of his acting chief engineer. There was only one thing to do: without telling Marcus Smith, he sent for Fleming who for the second time found his sick-leave in England interrupted.

Fleming returned to find his department in an uproar. There were complaints about Smith's language and his treatment of underlings, and there were reports that he had publicly accused some department engineers of working in collusion with railway contractors – a charge designed to infuriate the members of that proud service. In Winnipeg, it was said, Smith had spent more time collecting data to be used against Fleming and Mackenzie than he had on the knotty problems connected with his own department. Mackenzie determined that Smith must go. He told Fleming that he must no longer consider Smith an officer of the department. This resulted in a curious situation: there was the peppery Smith, still fuming away in his office, still, apparently, on the staff, but stripped of his powers.

"He did not receive his dismissal but he was as good as dismissed," Fleming later recounted. No doubt Fleming expected Smith to resign, as he had once expected Moberly to resign, but Smith hung on stubbornly. He even explored, in a letter to a friend, the possibility that Lord Dufferin had an interest in Fraser Valley land – hence his motives in "moving Heaven and Earth" in favour of the Burrard route.

Fleming, meanwhile, set about writing his own report. In this he was finally forced to a conclusion: if engineering decisions alone were to govern the selection of a route, and if that selection could not be postponed further, then the Bute Inlet route should be rejected and the Burrard Inlet route selected. He left the question of a pass open. He thought there should be more extensive surveys in the region of the Peace River Pass in case it proved to be less expensive than the Yellow Head.

Fleming included Smith's report as an appendix to his own. He did not, however, reproduce Smith's map, which purported to show the comparative richness of the country surrounding the Peace and its tributary the Pine. Smith fumed that the map "was cunningly suppressed." Fleming replied that Smith was neither a botanist nor an agronomist, only a surveyor; a map showing soils and fertility had no place in his report.

On July 12, 1878, the government settled officially on the Fraser River–Burrard Inlet route and prepared to call for tenders for the construction of the railway through the dismal canyon of the Fraser. That seemed to be the end of the horrid B.C. business. It was not. Party lines had already been drawn around the opposing routes. The Pine Pass–Bute Inlet route, thanks in part to Marcus Smith's importuning, had become a Tory route. As for Smith, he was still around. Two years later, in a new job and under a new administration he would still be, in his own eyes at least, " the *Bête Noir* of the Govt."

On the morning of October 9, 1877, the citizens of Winnipeg were awakened by the unaccustomed shriek of a locomotive whistle. For the generation to follow, this would become the authentic sound of the prairie, more familiar than the laugh of the loon or the whine of the wind in the wolf willow. But on this crisp October day it was something totally new. There were many there that day who had never heard a train whistle and for some of these, the Indians and Métis, it was as symbolic in its sadness as it was for the white community in its promise.

She was a Baldwin engine – the *Countess of Dufferin* – and she came complete with six flatcars and a van; but she could not arrive under her own steam. She had to be floated down the river because the railway to the boundary was not finished. Even if it had been, there was nothing yet on the other side of the American border with which it could connect.

But a locomotive was still a marvel, and the entire town streamed to the dock to inspect it and to cheer the massive contractor, Joseph Whitehead, who was in charge and who as a boy had worked on horse-drawn railways in England. Whitehead, who was laying track on the line between St. Boniface and Selkirk, had imported her as a work engine. For the white community, at least, she was a promise of things to come, an end to the maddening isolation of half a century and a tangible response to the pleas for a railway which had been issuing from Red River since the beginning of the decade.

This isolation was real and terrible and could be translated into concrete terms. At the beginning of the decade a keg of nails cost at least ten times as much at Red River as in Ontario; small wonder that Red River carts were held together with shaganappi!

The steamboats, which began to arrive on the river in the late sixties, did not appreciably lower prices save during those brief periods when rival lines fought for control. The Hudson's Bay Company held a monopoly of the Red River traffic with its rickety *International* until one spring day in 1871, when a strange vessel loaded with 125 passengers and 115 tons of freight steamed into Fort Garry. This was the *Selkirk,* operated by James Jerome Hill, a one-eyed ex-Canadian with a razor-sharp mind, now operating out of St. Paul. Hill had unearthed an old United States law providing that all goods crossing the border from American territories into Canadian ports must be bonded. He quietly built the *Selkirk,* had her bonded, and persuaded the customs officials at Pembina on the border to hold up all unbonded vessels plying the river. The *International* was legally beached and Hill had a transportation monopoly of the Red River valley. It was said that he paid off the entire cost of constructing his new steamboat with the profits of that first voyage.

Jim Hill had had the audacity to challenge the monopoly rule of the Hudson's Bay Company, which for two centuries had enjoyed the mastery of the North West. Donald A. Smith, the company's chief commissioner, struck back. He had the *International* bonded by assigning the steamer to Norman Kittson, a respected Minnesota fur trader who was the Hudson's Bay agent in St. Paul. Then he leaped into battle with Hill.

They were evenly matched adversaries and, in many respects, remarkably alike – short, fierce-eyed, muscled men with backgrounds crammed with adventure and romance. They knew and respected one another, having met quite by accident in exacting circumstances on the bald, snowswept prairie in February of 1870.

This scene was a memorable one for it marked the beginning of an association which would eventually launch the Canadian Pacific Railway company. Hill, en route to Fort Garry, had made a truly terrible journey from St. Paul at the height of a dreadful blizzard. On his way across the wastes of the southern Manitoba prairie he suddenly beheld, emerging from the curtain of swirling snow, the vague outline of another dog team coming south. Its passenger was Donald A. Smith, en route to eastern Canada by way of St. Paul.

The scene deserves to be preserved on a broad canvas: the two diminutive figures, muffled in furs, blurred by the drifting snow and dwarfed by that chill desert which stretched off for one hundred and forty miles, unmarked by a single human habitation. There they stopped and shared a frozen meal together – Hill, the young dreamer, his lively mind already crammed with visions of a transportation empire of steel, and Smith, the old Labrador hand, who had clawed his way up the slippery ladder of the fur trade. Hill was thirty-two, Smith fifty; within a decade both of them would be multimillionaires as the result of a mutual association. A quarter of a century later, Smith would recall that scene and say: "I liked him then and I have never had reason to change my opinion."

These were the two adversaries who, in 1871, found themselves locked in a cutthroat battle to control the Red River traffic between Minnesota and Fort Garry, where the nearby village of Winnipeg was slowly rising out of the prairie mud. Since it was axiomatic that neither would give way, the two at last agreed to join forces in secret. On the face of it, both retired from the steamboat business, leaving it in the hands of Norman Kittson's Red River Transportation Company. In actual fact, the Kittson Line was a joint venture of Hill, Kittson, and the Hudson's Bay Company. The company's shares were in Smith's name, but he agreed in advance to transfer them

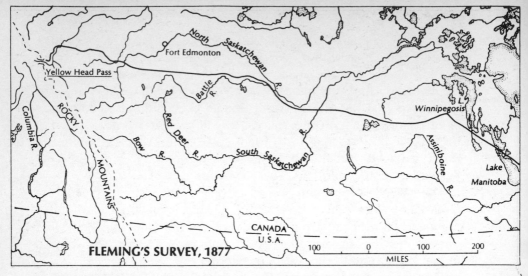

FLEMING'S SURVEY, 1877

to whoever succeeded him as chief commissioner. The Kittson Line gave the Hudson's Bay Company a one-third discount on all river freight and thus a commanding edge on its competitors.

No sooner was this secret arrangement completed than the freight rates shot skyward. In the winter of 1874-75 a group of Winnipeg and Minnesota merchants, incensed at the monopoly, launched a steamboat line of their own. They built two rival boats, the *Minnesota* and the *Manitoba*, and another battle was soon in progress. Norman Kittson launched a rate war, bringing his own prices down below cost. Through friends in the Pembina customs depot, he arranged that the *Manitoba* be held indefinitely at the border. When it was finally released in July, he charged it broadside with his *International,* rammed it, and sank it with its entire cargo. No sooner was it back in service than it was seized for a trifling debt. The same fate awaited its sister ship, south of the border. The merchants sold out to Kittson in September. And the rates soared again. Kittson and his colleagues shared a dividend of eighty per cent and the rising wrath of the Red River community.

There was good reason for this strife. The trickle of newcomers into the Red River valley was rapidly becoming a torrent. Obviously, whoever controlled transportation into the newly incorporated town of Winnipeg would reap rich profits.

Meanwhile, in September, 1874, the first sod had been turned on the long-awaited railway – a branch of the future CPR – that was to run from Selkirk through Winnipeg's neighbour St. Boniface down to Pembina to connect, it was hoped, at the border with a United States line, as yet uncompleted. The construction moved at an unbelievably leaden pace. After the grading was completed, all work stopped: there was no point in building a railroad to nowhere, and construction of the American line had halted ninety miles below the

114

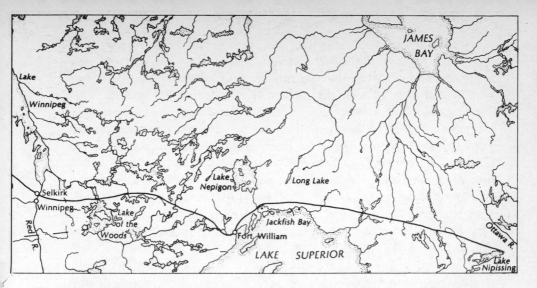

boundary. The contract for laying steel was not let for another three years until it became clear that the moribund St. Paul and Pacific, reorganized and renamed the St. Paul and Manitoba, was actually going to reach the border (as it did late in 1878).

By the time the last spike of the Pembina Branch was driven in November, 1878, the population of Winnipeg had reached six thousand. A gala excursion load of citizens was taken by train to Rousseau for the ceremony. With a single blow, Mary Sullivan, the strapping daughter of an Irish section boss, drove the spike home, to the cheers of the assembly. The cheers, however, did not last long. The rails had been laid, but to describe the Pembina Branch as a railway was to indulge in the wildest kind of hyperbole. Under the terms of the contract, the builders had until November, 1879, to complete the job and turn the finished line over to the government. They determined, in the meantime, to squeeze the maximum possible profit out of it by running it themselves while they continued to build the necessary sidings, station houses, water towers, and all the requisite paraphernalia that is part of a properly run railroad.

In the months that followed, the Pembina Branch became the most cursed length of track on the continent. There was only one water tank on the whole sixty-three miles; there was no shred of telegraph line along the entire right of way; and there were no repair shops or any fences, which meant the train must make frequent stops to allow cattle to cross the tracks. The only fuel was green poplar, which supplied very little energy: the passengers were often compelled to wait at a station while the unmoving locomotive, wheezing and puffing away, finally gathered enough motive power to falter off to the next one.

To travel the Pembina Branch in those days required nerves of steel, a stomach of iron, and a spirit of high adventure. Each time

115

a bridge was crossed, the entire structure swayed and rocked in a dismaying fashion. The road was improperly ballasted so that even at eleven miles an hour, the cars pitched and tumbled about. In many places mud spurted over the tops of the sleepers. A man from *The Times* of London, surely accustomed to the derring-do of Victorian journalism, reported that he and his party were more seasick on the Pembina Branch than they had been crossing the stormy Atlantic. One of the company, so *The Times*'s man said, had not really said his prayers in a long, long time but was so shattered by the experience that he reformed on the spot, took to praying incessantly and, through sheer terror, managed to scare up some extra prayers that had lain forgotten in the dim recesses of his mind since childhood. The Pembina railroad shook them loose.

In Winnipeg, the citizenry could only wait and hold their breath and listen to the faint sounds of activity in the East where, piece by piece, the railway was being built on Canadian soil from the head of Lake Superior.

5

On the afternoon of June 1, 1875, a spirited ceremony took place near Fort William on the left bank of the Kaministiquia River, about four miles from its mouth on Thunder Bay, Lake Superior. Here was turned the first sod of the main line of the Canadian Pacific Railway. The affair was sponsored by the firm of Sifton and Ward, which had secured the contract to grade the first thirty-two miles of roadbed for a line that the government intended to build in sections between Fort William and Selkirk, Manitoba. Like so many contractors in those days, John Wright Sifton and his brother Henry were up to their sideburns in politics, being close friends and supporters of the Prime Minister.

With a crowd of five hundred in attendance, Judge Delevan Van Norman announced the beginning of the actual construction of the Canadian Pacific Railway. Soon, the judge declared, an immigrant with his family might "with celerity, safety and certainty examine the country from Cape Breton in Nova Scotia to Vancouver's Island in British Columbia, in the meantime passing over a space as vast as the great ocean that divides and separates the old world from the new."

Then Judge Van Norman told his listeners what they really wanted to hear: Buffalo had once been no larger than Prince Arthur's Landing, Chicago no bigger than Fort William. "I verily believe," the judge said, "that history is about to repeat itself."

116

Adam Oliver, who had been one of those instrumental in securing the terminus for Fort William, rose as the applause died. He was known as an impassioned player of euchre, whose several variations include "Railroad Euchre" and "Cutthroat Euchre"; Oliver, as events were to prove, certainly knew something about the cutthroat aspects of the railroad game. He and his partners, Joseph Davidson and Peter Johnson Brown (a former reeve of the township), owned forty thousand acres of good timber in the Fort William area together with considerable property and a lumber mill. They already had one government contract – to build the telegraph line accompanying the railroad to the Red River – and were about to sign another for the construction of an engine house. Oliver, like the Siftons, was a prominent Liberal and also a member of the provincial legislature.

Amid loud cheers, Oliver declared: "The place on which you are now standing is destined in no distant day to form one of the most important cities in your great Dominion."

He had reason for his enthusiasm. As a Senate inquiry tardily discovered, the three partners, Oliver, Davidson, and Brown, were planning to make a killing at the taxpayers' expense. The story did not leak out until the summer of 1877, when it was revealed that Oliver and his Liberal friends had been selling their land to the government at fancy mark-ups. Worse than that, they had actually put up part of a building – the Neebing Hotel – on land already appropriated for the railway and had managed to sell it to the Crown at an inflated price.

It was an unblushing piece of jobbery, even for those days. Lots purchased by Oliver, Davidson, and Brown for between sixty and ninety dollars were sold two years later to the government for as much as three hundred. And who was acting as an official government evaluator? Brown! He had one hundred thousand dollars invested in Fort William lands. In one instance the partners had purchased 136 acres for a thousand dollars and laid out a paper town. They sold a mere eight acres of this non-existent community to the government for four thousand dollars. Again, the valuation was Brown's. Actually, there was no real reason for the railway to go through the Oliver townsite at all.

In the case of the Neebing Hotel, Oliver, having been notified of the position of the line of track and having already sold the property to the government for ten thousand dollars, began the hasty construction of a "hotel" on the same piece of ground. For a shell of a building, rudely thrown together out of refuse slabs, the government paid $5,029. Testimony showed that the builder was paid only thirteen hundred dollars for the job and that the books were shamelessly padded.

The case became nationally notorious. During the campaign of 1878,

John A. Macdonald never failed to draw a laugh when he declared solemnly that the only punishment he wished for the Government, if they were defeated, was that they be compelled to board for the next two years at the Neebing Hotel.

Just how much political muscle Adam Oliver had with the Mackenzie administration came to light in 1880 when a royal commission began investigating various contracts awarded along the north shore of Lake Superior. The circumstances under which Oliver, Davidson and Company secured a quarter-million-dollar contract to build the telegraph line from Thunder Bay to Winnipeg were as astonishing as they were suspicious.

Tenders for the line were opened in August, 1874, but the actual contract was not awarded until the following February. The intervening months were spent in what a later century was to brand as "wheeling and dealing." The lowest bid was passed over in a fashion that the royal commission described as "peremptory." The next two lowest bids were both entered, in effect, by one Robert Twiss Sutton of Brantford, who clearly had no intention of fulfilling the contract. He had entered the contest in order to be bought off by his competitors, a fairly common practice in those days. In December, Adam Oliver arrived in Ottawa to do the buying off.

Oliver expected to be able to buy up the lower of the two Sutton bids. But once in the capital he discovered that for mysterious reasons he could actually be awarded the higher one. Oliver promised Sutton a quarter of the profits; Sutton paid off a silent partner (another front man); and Oliver's firm ended up with the coveted contract. It was fifty-three thousand dollars fatter than it would have been had the lowest tender been accepted.

Apart from the cavalier treatment of the lowest bidder, there was never any explanation of how the higher of the two Sutton bids came to be accepted, rather than the lower one. But one thing did develop from the testimony. It was Mackenzie himself who handled the entire business and not one of his underlings, as was the general practice. And all the dealings with the Minister were in the hands, not of Robert Sutton, the official tenderer, but of Adam Oliver. To achieve the kind of financial miracle that Oliver managed required a detailed knowledge of all the tenders for the contract – information that was supposed to be secret.

In Adam Oliver's favourite game, the maker's side must win at least three tricks to avoid being euchred. Oliver had won them all: he had wangled the terminus for Fort William, he had sold property to the government at extortionate prices, and he had gained a telegraph contract at a bonus rate. He was not quite so successful as a builder. The complaints about the state of the line were continual. Poles, badly anchored, kept toppling. Wires stretched over trees in lieu of poles strangled and killed them; the roots decayed and the trees fell over, taking the wires with them. Sometimes it took a message as long as a month to reach Winnipeg on Adam Oliver's expensive telegraph line.

6

The strains of office were beginning to tell on Mackenzie's temper and health; it was the railway that was chiefly to blame. Not only was he Prime Minister, but he had also chosen to assume the burden of the Ministry of Public Works, the most sensitive of cabinet posts in that era of railway contracts. In the spring of 1877, the ex-stonemason revealed a little of his feelings when he exploded in the House that it was "impossible for any man in this country to conduct public affairs without being subjected to the grossest political abuse. Let a political friend get a contract and it is stated at once that [it] is because he is a political friend. Let a political opponent get a contract and we are charged with trying to buy him over to the Government."

Nonetheless, more friends than opponents were awarded contracts on the various sections of the rail and telegraph lines being built along the granites of Superior and the muskegs of Manitoba. The Mackenzie government awarded eleven contracts west of Lake Superior for grading, track laying, and telegraph lines. Eight of the largest contracts – amounting to ninety-five per cent of the total sum paid – went to prominent Liberal wheel-horses, men who in every case were members of a federal or provincial parliament, past, present, or future.

"I feel like the besieged, lying on my arms night and day," Mackenzie told a friend. " . . . A weak minister here would ruin the party in a month and the country very soon." Yet it is debatable how strong the stonemason himself was. Mackenzie took over the Department of Public Works with the memory of the Pacific Scandal haunting him and, before that, distasteful recollections of the Grand Trunk – Conservative marriage and other allied railway schemes. He determined to establish an inflexible method of handling tenders on public contracts: the lowest bidder *must* be given the job. On the face of it this was designed to prevent favouritism. In practice it turned the department into a broker's office.

It did not matter who the low bidder was, or how outrageous his tender. He could be an incompetent, a bankrupt or – as generally developed – a man interested in peddling contracts. The new regulations relieved the government of all responsibility in choosing contrac-

119

tors, so that many bogus ones flourished. Of the seventy-two contracts awarded for the construction of the Canadian Pacific Railway during the seventies, there were ten major ones from which the successful low bidders withdrew. Some of the low bids were entered by men who had no intention of doing the job, others by *bona fide* contractors who saw a chance to make a bigger profit by pretending to drop out while actually joining forces with a higher bidder and splitting the difference between the bids. In addition, many large contracting firms that paid substantial sums to buy up a contract expected to recoup their losses by charging later for "extras" not included in the original specifications.

In 1880, a royal commission began to inquire into government spending on the CPR. It sat for more than a year and took sworn testimony from scores of witnesses. Its exhaustive three-volume report gives a comprehensive picture of the way in which the government sections of the railway were surveyed and constructed, under both Liberal and Conservative regimes. Both were found wanting.

One leading contractor, A. P. MacDonald, himself a former Conservative member, painted an unpleasant picture of corruption in the public works offices. "You do everything in your power to find out where your tender is. You offer inducements to clerks to do things that they would not [normally] do... you offer them bribes to get at things that are dangerous. . . . You take a clerk that gets $1,000 a year salary, and offer him $2,000 to get certain information in his office. . . ." Some people, MacDonald added, thought everyone in the department was corrupt.

Certainly, political friends were able to obtain special favours. For them, in instance after instance, the department found a way to depart from its rigid policy of accepting the lowest bids. One such firm was Sifton, Glass and Company, which managed, in 1874, to acquire a lucrative contract for telegraph construction west from Fort Garry along the proposed right of way. The active partner in this firm was Mackenzie's friend and fellow Liberal, John Wright Sifton. The front man, who did the talking in Ottawa, was David Glass.

Glass was not a contractor at all, but a trial lawyer in London, Ontario. He was also the first Tory to turn against Macdonald in the Pacific Scandal debate of 1873. Now he was a Liberal with a special claim to Mackenzie's gratitude.

That gratitude was not long in appearing. The complicated methods by which Sifton and Glass obtained a contract worth more than one hundred thousand dollars, in spite of the presence of lower tenders, astonished and nettled the royal commission. To put the matter simply, the firm entered a tender that was so ambiguous that Mackenzie and other members of the department appeared to misunderstand it. They not only passed over a better offer, but they also allowed Sifton and Glass to renegotiate the original tender to their considerable advantage.

It took the commissioners some seventy-five hundred words to explain the curious series of steps involved in this political leger-demain. The partners tendered on the basis of the entire line but were awarded the contract for only part of it – the easy part; yet they were allowed to charge for the work as if they were building the difficult parts as well. In short, they were paid an inflated price. Theirs was by no means the lowest bid: two lower bidders mysteriously dropped out and a third firm was passed over on a flimsy excuse. Normally it required an order in council to pass over a low bidder, but Sifton and Glass got the contract without any such authority, even though the department's law clerk pointed out the omission to Mackenzie himself.

The resultant telegraph line was almost totally unsatisfactory. The poles were badly set, so that they often fell into the swamps and muskegs, and, since they were made of the cheapest available wood, quickly rotted and fell away. The contractors, however, pocketed a sizable profit, having received, in the commission's words, "that to which they were not entitled." But a political debt was a political debt and David Glass could not say that his bold support of the party in 1873 had not been recognized in the contract of 1874.

Another political friend was Joseph Whitehead, former mayor of Clinton, Ontario, and a Liberal member of Parliament from 1867 to 1872. He had been a railwayman since the very beginning; as a boy, he had helped drive teams of horses which pulled coaches along wooden rails before the days of steam. At the age of eleven, he had been the fireman on Stephenson's first experimental locomotive. As an old railway hand, Whitehead knew enough to be an old political hand, too. He knew how to buy his way into newspapers or the goodwill of newspapermen, how to peddle influence, how to purchase contracts, and how to deal with politicians. The commission came to the conclusion that "he had a strong belief in the corruptibility of public men." The machinations by which he secured the contract for Section Fifteen of the Thunder Bay–Selkirk line give an insight into the relationship between politics and business in the Mackenzie era.

Section Fifteen was a thirty-seven-mile stretch of right of way that ran through muskeg country between Cross Lake and Rat Portage, near the border between Ontario and Manitoba. Whitehead tendered on the contract for grading and laying track, but when the bids were opened on September 20, 1876, his was certainly not the lowest. The lowest tender withdrew from the contract; accordingly, the next

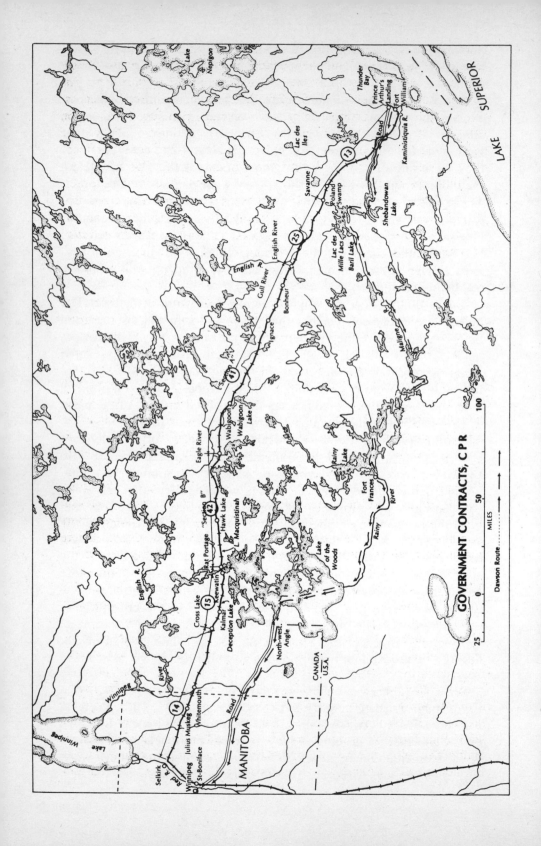

GOVERNMENT CONTRACTS, C P R

MILES

0   50   100

Dawson Route .... ——→

LAKE SUPERIOR

MANITOBA

CANADA
U.S.A.

lowest bidder was awarded the job. Whitehead, of course, knew exactly who had bid and how much had been bid. He also knew whom to pay off. He borrowed twenty thousand dollars from his brother-in-law, Senator Donald McDonald, and paid it to the successful bidder, who withdrew from the contract, pleading "dissension from within and extraordinary pressure from without." Mackenzie awarded the contract to the next highest bidder; Whitehead, in effect, bought their contract for another ten thousand. For his help, Whitehead's brother-in-law was given an equal partnership. Since he was a senator he could not officially be involved in railway construction, and so the industry was treated to the odd spectacle of the senator's son Mitchell, a bankrupt who knew nothing about railways, apparently working in tandem with the veteran Whitehead.

Whitehead, then, had secured a contract worth a million and a half dollars. But this, he figured, would be only the beginning; the area through which Section Fifteen would run had been subjected to the skimpiest of surveys; there would be unavoidable extra charges, not subject to competitive bidding, for which he could bill the government. Before Whitehead was through, these extras, none of them officially authorized by the department, had come to $930,000.

Another firm that obtained extraordinary favours in the fall of 1874 was Cooper, Fairman and Company, a hardware company in Montreal. The Department of Public Works showed an astonishing preference for this concern in its purchases of steel rails, nuts, bolts, and fishplates, bending or breaking the rules in its favour in several instances.

The silent partner in this company was the Prime Minister's brother, Charles Mackenzie, a Sarnia hardware merchant. In 1873 he had put fifteen thousand dollars into the firm – more than the other two partners combined. He was to receive a third of all profits in return. There was little business until the government contracts began to roll in. Mackenzie left the company officially in May, 1875, after the story leaked out, but there is no doubt he was very much a part of the firm for at least a portion of the period when his brother's department was granting it extraordinary public favours.

In the end, it developed that not all the steel rails contracted for were really needed. They had been purchased prematurely apparently because both Fleming and Mackenzie believed they were getting a bargain. The purchase was a disaster for all but Mackenzie's brother's firm. At most, twenty thousand tons were needed for the work in progress. But having purchased that amount, Mackenzie ordered an additional thirty thousand tons, even though the price was higher. Half of this extra order was supplied by Cooper and Fairman at double the going rate. After that, to everyone's discomfiture, the bottom dropped out of the market. The rails rusted for years, unused, while the price of new rails went lower and lower and the interest mounted on the original investment. It was beginning to be apparent to the country at large that the government's venture into the railway business was as disastrous as that of Sir Hugh Allan.

7

From his poplar-shaded mansion of Silver Heights, high above the Assiniboine, Donald A. Smith was contemplating with more than passing interest the future of the Pembina Branch line. He was a member of a syndicate which by 1878 was establishing rail connection from St. Paul to Pembina on the border. If the same group could lease the government road into the Red River Valley they would have a through line to Winnipeg. It was left to Smith to handle the matter politically. As the man who had laid the last straw on the camel's back in the Pacific Scandal debacle of 1873, he had considerable pull with the Mackenzie government.

There was something a little frightening about Donald A. Smith. Perhaps it was the eyebrows – those bristling, tangled tufts that jutted out to mask the cold, uncommunicative grey eyes and provide their owner with a perpetual frown. At fifty-eight, Smith had the stern look of a Biblical patriarch.

He was a stoic – nothing could touch him; the company had seen to that. Years before, in the heart of Labrador, he had suffered an appalling attack of snow-blindness. Accompanied by two half-breed guides, the sufferer set off from his post at Mingan, on the northern coast of the St. Lawrence Gulf, on a fearful snowshoe journey to Montreal, five hundred and fifty-five miles distant by crow's flight. Arriving at his destination, Smith hammered on the door of Sir George Simpson, the company's notorious "Little Emperor." Simpson was not remotely concerned about Smith's plight: "If it's a question between your eyes and your service in the Hudson's Bay Company, you'll take my advice and return this instant." Then, after a perfunctory medical examination, he turned him face-about into the snows. The return journey was so harsh that the guides died before reaching their destination. Smith stumbled the remainder of the way, half dead from exhaustion, fear, and hunger. Years later when asked to describe that ghastly journey he could not bring himself to recall it.

There is no doubt that this incident and others like it had left its mark upon him. All his life he never complained and never explained; that was the company way. Few public men had more vitriol heaped upon them than Smith in his long lifetime; he bore it all without

124

blinking as he had borne the Little Emperor's abuse. In the election of 1874, Macdonald's supporters, incensed beyond reason by his defection from their ranks, had pelted him with raw eggs until he was unrecognizable. He did not flinch. Wintry of temperament, courtly of manner, he wrapped himself in a screen of suavity which masked the inner fires, the bitter furies, and the hard resolution of his soul. It was impossible to panic Smith. He was unshakable in crisis and this, one future day, would stand the CPR in good stead.

In Winnipeg he was admired, hated, feared, respected, but scarcely loved. His political support came from the fur traders, many of whom were shunted across constituency lines at company expense on election day. Thus, for all of his days in Winnipeg, Donald A., as he was called, was a figure of controversy. Seldom quoted in the newspapers, he was constantly attacked in them, especially after he shifted his political loyalties in 1873. But the laird of Silver Heights remained imperturbable. His stays in Winnipeg were solitary enough, for his wife refused to join him in the barbarous North West. She was a child of Labrador and the hub of her existence had always been the fur traders' capital, Montreal. Smith had married her, in the custom of the trade, without benefit of clergy, there being none available in those days. Years later, when he was about to become Lord Strathcona, it was revealed that he had no marriage certificate. This would never do: with his title in the balance, Smith agreed to a hasty wedding in the British Embassy in Paris. He was seventy-seven at the time.

The rail line to the border, which Smith and his partners coveted, was officially a branch of the almost non-existent CPR. Early in 1878 Smith's cousin, George Stephen, arranged with Alexander Mackenzie for a ten-year lease of the government line to the syndicate, which was building the connecting line from St. Paul. That would require an amendment to the Canadian Pacific Railway Act of 1874. On March 18, Mackenzie rose in the House to introduce a bill which would empower Parliament to lease the Pembina Branch to unspecified parties. No mention was made of Donald A. Smith's interest; indeed, the Prime Minister was at considerable pains to conceal it, for Smith's name was an abomination to the Conservative opposition. If, in 1878, the Member for Selkirk had risen in the House to support motherhood, it is conceivable that Macdonald and his followers would have been strongly tempted to opt for matricide.

When the debate began on the Canadian Pacific Railway Act Amendment Bill, at the time of its second reading on April 4, 1878, the Conservatives were ready with sharpened claws. It had scarcely been launched when George Kirkpatrick, a locomotive manufacturer, pointed out that the group seeking the lease were proprietors of the reviled Kittson Line of steamboats, which "had ground down the people of Manitoba." A railway to Winnipeg, Kirkpatrick pointed out, would simply increase their monopoly.

As the debate progressed it grew more personal. One Tory, Mackenzie Bowell, declared that the House was witnessing "the extraordinary spectacle of the champion of this proposed lease using his power and influence as a very humble and obedient supporter of the Government to secure to himself and his partners in this transaction the advantage of a lease."

Macdonald followed that up with a cutting attack. "There was seen the indecent spectacle of an honourable gentleman coming into the House as an advocate and pressing this lease in his own interest ... he advocated more warmly and strongly this Bill, which was in his own interest, and which would put money in his own pocket, than the Minister who introduced it. The hon. gentleman admitted he was a partner in this concern, and the House should know something about it."

"I have admitted no such thing," Smith retorted; but Macdonald pointed out that he had not denied it, "and there is no doubt that, if he could have done so, he would."

In the acrimonious set-to that followed, Smith at no time admitted to his own substantial interest in the company, even when pressed and taunted by the Opposition – though it was clear to all that he was deeply involved. He spoke as one who had inside knowledge about certain "gentlemen of enterprise and means." As for the Kittson Line, "not having been in any way personally interested in that company, even to the extent of sixpence, he had no right to have any knowledge of its internal affairs." This was, strictly speaking, true. Smith's shares, held by Kittson, had belonged to the Hudson's Bay Company and he had turned them over to his successor when he retired from the commissionership in 1874 to take another post. But whether he had the right or not, he was certainly intimately informed about the line's affairs, especially as the firm was about to merge all its assets with the newly purchased St. Paul railway, in which Smith was a major partner.

It was inevitable that the bill should pass; the Government's majority saw to that. But it was a different story in the appointed Senate, where the Tories, who still had a preponderance of votes, had thrown the bill out.

On May 9, the day before the end of the session, Mackenzie took occasion to reprimand the Senate for its actions. This allowed Macdonald to return to the attack. The Senate, he said, put a stop to the Government's bargain with Smith "to make him a rich man, and to pay for his servile support." That sally provoked the most explosive and perhaps the most harrowing scene in the history of the House of Commons.

The House was scheduled to dissolve. The members were in their seats at three p.m. on May 10, awaiting the traditional knock of the Gentleman Usher of the Black Rod, when Smith, brandishing the Ottawa *Free Press* in his hand, rose on a question of privilege. After denying that he had ever admitted being a member of the St. Paul syndicate he began to attack Charles Tupper for some remarks Tupper had made the previous summer.

Tupper, seeing Black Rod at the door (the signal that the session was at an end), realized that he would have no opportunity to answer. The Cumberland War Horse had no intention of allowing that. He rose at once on a point of order, forcing Smith to his seat, and asked the Speaker if it were not an abuse of the rights of Parliament to bring up an old matter, since Smith had had three months to refer to it.

An exchange followed in which Tupper accused Smith of cowardice. He began to bellow across the floor in the face of repeated cries of "Order!" that Smith had telegraphed his support of the Government and then broken his word at the time of the Pacific Scandal debate in 1873. Smith denied it flatly.

Now Macdonald tried to break in and, over more cries, shouted that Smith did not dare listen to an explanation. Smith kept going. He had, he said, expected a different amendment – one in which the Government frankly confessed its faults and took the issue to the country. That he would have voted for.

More bedlam! Tupper managed to call out: "That is not what you telegraphed." He had to repeat himself to be heard, for the Liberal benches were in full cry. "It was a sight to make sluggish blood tingle!" one eyewitness recalled. The vain knocking of Black Rod could be heard faintly at the Commons door behind the uproar; the Speaker tried to answer – then, with resignation, resumed his seat.

Smith continued to speak and with each new declaration the verbal contest grew more heated. The House was in an uproar as Smith threw in a reference to Macdonald's drinking at the time of the scandal. A shouting match ensued.

Smith managed yet another dig: Tupper, he said, had told him that very night that Macdonald was not capable of knowing what he said.

Now Tupper was on his feet, demanding of the Speaker whether it was "competent for a man to detail private conversations while falsifying them." As Smith parried the attack, the Sergeant-at-Arms managed to announce "a message from the Governor General."

The House continued in disorder and the Speaker tried to say that he had "very much pleasure in informing the House it now becomes my duty to receive the Messenger." Then Tupper's powerful voice was heard, over all, bellowing, "Coward! Coward!" at the imperturbable Smith.

Smith held his place.

"Coward! Coward! Coward!" Tupper boomed, ". . . mean, treacherous coward!"

"Who is the coward?" Smith retorted. "The House will decide – it is yourself."

"Coward!" shouted Tupper once again. "Treacherous . . ."

Smith began to speak again, but the harried Speaker interrupted him and asked that Black Rod be admitted.

It was Macdonald who got in the last word, surely the most unparliamentary expression ever to appear in Hansard.

"That fellow Smith," he cried, "is the biggest liar I ever met!"

The Gentleman Usher was admitted to "as excited a mob as ever disgraced the floor of a Parliamentary chamber." Tupper and Macdonald and several other Tories, enraged beyond endurance, rushed at Smith, bent on physical assault. Several tried to strike him. Macdonald had to be pulled away from Smith, crying that he "could lick him quicker than hell could scorch a feather." The disorder was so great that the Speaker could not at once leave the House because of the throng at the door. Finally he was allowed to proceed to the Senate chamber, followed by the dishevelled crowd. Thus did the Mackenzie regime come to an end, not with a whimper but a bang. It could not accommodate Donald A. Smith and his colleagues with an exclusive lease of the Pembina Branch but it could grant running rights for ten years over the line and it did just that in August. That was one of its last official acts.

Chapter
Five

RESURRECTION

1

September 17, 1878, was the day of a political miracle in Canada. Long before the election was called, it was clear that the Conservatives were on the rise; but nobody could be sure of the results. When they began to come in few could give them credence.

The polls closed at five and by seven it was clear that Macdonald had suffered personal defeat in Kingston. But this news was superseded by indications of massive Conservative gains. By nine, it was apparent that the Mackenzie administration had fallen; by eleven, that Macdonald and his party had scored a landslide of unprecedented proportions. In the session just past, the Liberals had held 133 seats to the Conservatives' 73. In the new parliament, the Conservatives would have 137 seats to the Liberals' 69. Both Blake and Cartwright had gone down to defeat. For Macdonald, who would soon win a by-election in Victoria, B.C., revenge was sweet.

He was overwhelmed by the magnitude of his victory. The elections, Lord Dufferin reported to London, had "taken the entire political world by surprise." A week later both parties were still in a state of shock: "Sir John himself was as much astonished by the sweep as anybody." As for Mackenzie, he wrote a friend that "nothing has happened in my time so astonishing."

Mackenzie's railway policy had cost him the West. Worse, he had also lost Ontario. By election day he was an exhausted man, teetering on the edge of a long decline, made irritable by the tensions of office. Macdonald had the ability to bounce back after defeat: unlike Mackenzie, he knew how to delegate authority. Mackenzie attempted personally to handle the smallest details of his department and when his subordinates disappointed him, he broke. He would not lead his party for long for, truth to tell, he was already "a dry shell of what he had been." One day on the steps of Parliament Mackenzie spoke of his depressed spirits to Macdonald, who replied: "Mackenzie, you should not distress yourself over these things. When I fell in 1874, I made up my mind to cease to worry and think no more about [it]." To which Mackenzie made the candid and illuminating reply: "Ah, but I have not that happy frame of mind."

For two years after his defeat, the Tory chieftain had kept his peace while the Liberal press continued to announce his imminent retirement. Then, during the session of 1876, Macdonald revived and the country soon became familiar with the phrase "National Policy."

By then the industrial situation in Canada was critical. United States manufacturers, protected in their own markets by heavy duties, were dumping their surplus products into the Canadian "slaughter market" at cut-rate prices. Industry after industry was forced to the wall and still Mackenzie, the traditional free trader, made no move towards protection.

Macdonald proposed to readjust tariffs so as to support local enterprise, stop the exodus across the border, and protect Canadian interests from unfair competition. But he did not use the word "protection." He talked instead of prosperity and "Canada for the Canadians." In a depression-ridden nation it was an attractive slogan.

Still, in 1878, the National Policy was nothing more than a euphemism for a protective tariff. It was only in later years that it was seen as one leg of a three-cornered foundation on which the superstructure of the transcontinental nation rested. The other two legs were the encouragement of western settlement and the construction of the Pacific railway. The railway was the key: without it western settlement would be difficult; with it there would be more substantial markets for the protected industries. Macdonald himself saw this. "Until this great work is completed, our Dominion is little more than a 'geographical expression,' " he told Sir Stafford Northcote, the Governor of the Hudson's Bay Company. "We have as much interest in British Columbia as in Australia, and no more. The railway once finished, we become one great united country with a large interprovincial trade and a common interest." As it turned out, the National Policy was to become the policy of the country and the future would extend it to include a variety of awkward, expensive, and contentious Canadian devices which, like the railway, would continue the horizontal development of the nation that Macdonald began.

Actually there was not much difference between the Macdonald government's railway policy and that of its predecessor. Mackenzie had clearly wanted to scrap the piecemeal method of construction west of Lake Superior. His excuse for not linking the two main sections in that area was that he wanted the whole undertaking to be in the hands of a single private company. That was Macdonald's hope, too. But in the absence of any offers from private capitalists, his administration was forced to continue Mackenzie's policy of building the line in instalments: the 181-mile gap in the Lake Superior area would be completed; an additional two hundred miles would be contracted for, to run west of the Red River; and it would all be accomplished without raising taxes – or so Charles Tupper insisted.

Tupper announced in May of 1879 several changes of route: the road would be lengthened to pass south of Lake Manitoba, and the selection of Burrard Inlet was considered premature. The government wanted more time to survey the Pine and Peace River passes and Port Simpson on the coast. Marcus Smith's furious efforts had obviously not been in vain. In spite of this, the government felt compelled to let four contracts that year for 125 miles of railway in British Columbia.

One of the bidders on all four sections, though by no means the lowest, was a young American named Andrew Onderdonk, the scion of a prominent Hudson River family. Onderdonk arrived in Ottawa in November, 1879, at the time the tenders were opened, his pockets stuffed with letters of recommendation from Canadian bankers and United States railwaymen.

Tupper was impressed by Onderdonk, who appeared to have almost unlimited means behind him from American financiers. In the muskeg country west of Lake Superior, Canadian contractors were running into difficulties. Some of the low bidders on the four British Columbia sections looked alarmingly shaky. Obviously, a man of experience backed by solid capital could build all the sections more cheaply and efficiently than four under-financed contractors working independently. Onderdonk was allowed to purchase the four contracts. He paid a total of $215,000 for the privilege, arrived at Yale on April 22, 1880, to a salute of thirteen guns, and by May was ready to begin construction. None of Macdonald's followers appeared to grasp the irony of a Conservative government awarding an important section of the railway to a Yankee contractor.

Meanwhile, Marcus Smith, who had been pronounced dead by both Fleming and Mackenzie, refused to lie down on the subject of the Pine Pass–Bute Inlet route. Indeed, he seemed to have gained a new lease on life with the advent of the new administration. There is something madly magnificent about Smith's furious windmill-tilting at this late date. On January 20, 1879, he sent Tupper a confidential memorandum detailing his differences with Fleming. He followed this up with another long memo asking Tupper to give him charge of a two-year survey of the Pine Pass section of the Bute Inlet route. In May he wrote to Macdonald asking him to intercede on his behalf to reinstate him as engineer of the British Columbia division. A week or so later he shot off a private letter to the editor of the Toronto *Mail*, all about the missing map.

In the meantime, Henry Cambie had taken a distinguished party of surveyors and scientists right across the uncivilized hinterland of northern British Columbia. They started at Port Simpson, "one of the finest harbours on the Pacific Coast," worked their way up the Skeena, and then followed a succession of rivers, canyons, and mountain trails on foot and packsaddle and by canoe, raft, and leaky boat until they reached the Peace River country on the far side of the mountains. In all that journey they did not encounter a single human being. Cambie returned on his own with a pack train and reached the top of the Pine Pass in a raging blizzard. He made his way back to civilization down the fast-freezing Fraser, shooting the rapids of the canyon himself, without a pilot. "Sham surveys" Smith called them when Cambie returned; but on the strength of his report the government, in October, 1879, finally gave up on the Bute Inlet route and announced that Burrard Inlet would be the official terminus after all. The Yellow Head, apparently, would be the pass through the Rockies.

Still Marcus Smith would not admit defeat. He wrote immediately to Senator David Macpherson, attacking the whole decision. Then he allied himself with General Butt Hewson, an American engineer resident in Canada who was preparing a pamphlet urging the adoption of the Bute Inlet–Pine Pass route.

All this pressure undoubtedly had some effect on public policy. On February 16, 1880, Tupper told the House that he still wanted more information on the Pine River–Peace River country before finally making up his mind about the choice of a pass through the Rockies. It was now the ninth year of the Canadian Pacific Survey in British Columbia and it seemed by this time that every notch in each of the mountain ranges and all the intervening trenches had been combed as carefully as a Japanese sand garden. Moberly's men had toiled up the slopes of the Howse, Jarvis had almost starved at the Smoky, Cambie and Horetzky had struggled over the Pine and the Peace, Roderick McLennan had lost all his horses probing the Athabasca, Moberly had braved the avalanches in the Selkirks and scoured the Gold Range, while Fleming himself, not to mention a score of others, had come through the Yellow Head.

Every pass had been checked with transit, level, and aneroid, again and again; every pass had been argued over, reported on, discarded or, sometimes, resurveyed – every pass, that is, except the Kicking Horse, which lay to the south, neglected and unsurveyed, waiting to be chosen.

2

Sandford Fleming's days as engineer-in-chief were numbered. The dissensions within his own department, as symbolized by the intractable Marcus Smith, the total identification with Mackenzie's sluggish and sometimes inept railway policies, the bills coming in from Lake Superior, far in excess of estimates, the expensive surveys in British

Columbia – all these were laid at his door. In the spring of 1879 he had been given a hard time as a witness before the Commons Public Accounts Committee and it was clear that more investigations were to follow.

Macdonald intended that Fleming should go, but with as much honour as possible and with the government's blessing; one never knew when he might be needed again. Clearly, Fleming was not the man to prosecute Macdonald's aggressive railway policy. He could be maddening in this caution yet wild in his extravagances. He had, for instance, insisted on a great many instrumental surveys in British Columbia when simple exploratory surveys would have done, for the routes were later abandoned as too expensive, too difficult, or too unwieldy. Even when the explorations revealed little chance of a practical route, the over-cautious Fleming ordered an instrumental survey anyway.

Everybody acknowledged Fleming's genius; yet at times he could be singularly blind. Why, for instance, did he wait five years before consulting the Admiralty about the usefulness of the various harbours on the British Columbia coast? A great deal of money could have been saved if these reports had been in his hands at the outset, for they made it clear that Burrard Inlet was the only really satisfactory terminus on the mainland.

Fleming, of course, had to take the blame for all the manifold political sins of the day. The surveys had to be kept going while the Government tried to arbitrate between warring factions. Untrained and incompetent employees were pressed upon him. Sometimes he had to invent work where no work existed. Often he was late getting his men into the field in the spring because he was forced to wait for the estimates to come down in Parliament before he could know how much money he had to spend.

But Fleming also tried to do too much; and, after 1876, he spent a great deal of time away from the job on doctor's orders. Even in Ottawa a great deal of his time was taken up with preparing for and testifying before parliamentary committees of inquiry.

Overly scrupulous in the Far West, he appeared to have been unduly hasty in his eastern surveys. Here there were terrible delays and extraordinary added charges because his engineers had made only cursory examinations of the ground. In every case between 1875 and 1878, the contractors arrived on the job before their work was fully laid out. Contracts were let on the basis of profile plans only, so that the estimates of the quantities of rock and earth to be removed or filled were mere guesses. On four contracts tendered at a total cost of $3,587,096 the government paid extras amounting to $1,804,830. The surveyors did not know how deep the marshes and muskegs would go; and because they had not studied the nature of muskeg (a deceptively spongy material), its removal and its use as fill was charged for as if it was solid earth. On one contract, the loss from this oversight amounted to $350,000.

Often enough Fleming, the thrifty Scot, was penny wise and pound foolish. The cost of running the railway through the gorges of the Thompson and the Fraser seemed so high that he continued to search for a cheaper route. Eventually even the Pine Pass was abandoned and, in 1880, Fleming's original route of 1871 was selected. On the other hand, the cost of probing the muskegs in advance seemed to Fleming so great that he decided he could not afford it. The price of steel rails seemed so low in 1874 that he ordered far more than he needed, only to see the price go even lower. In all of this expensive penny-pinching Mackenzie was Fleming's partner, but there is no evidence that the engineer-in-chief ever argued with him. For a good deal of the time he simply was not available and his deputy, Marcus Smith, was not on speaking terms with his political master. These displays of temperament were costly and confusing. Sometimes, in fact, because of lack of communication the work proceeded on its own momentum without authority.

Political expediency forced the premature start of construction west of Fort William in 1875. Mackenzie insisted that year that "a most elaborate survey had been made" of Section Fifteen. But the surveyor himself, Henry Carre, later gave the lie to that statement: "We just ran through, using the men that packed the provisions, on days when we were not moving camp, to chop out a line which I ran with my eye and a pocket compass; then as soon as the transit men came along they ran the transit level over it and plotted it; then I put down the location line, and the location men ran that line. If the profile showed a practicable line, then I was satisfied. I never went back over it again, so that I never actually saw the country after the line was located . . . . If I had been asked to estimate the actual cost of the work, I would have refused point blank to pretend to give it. No mortal man could give it."

Yet mortal men did give estimates on those perfunctory surveys and other mortals tendered on the basis of those estimates. Mackenzie had figured the total cost of the Thunder Bay–Red River section at $24,535 a mile; by the time the Government changed, the estimates had risen to $38,092.

The royal commission put most of the blame on Fleming's shoulders. It was not all warranted. Horetzky's testimony, for instance, was venomous: "Mr. Fleming stands convicted of deliberate and malicious falsehood. His malevolence has been directed against me ever since I brought the Pine Pass under his notice. In doing so I unconsciously wounded his vanity, which could not brook the idea of any one but himself proposing a route."

Only a few months before giving this testimony, Horetzky had written to Fleming offering his friendship while attacking Tupper, whose protégé he had been in 1872 ("I have it in for Tupper and will follow him to the last. . . ."). Fleming received "three extraordinary letters in which he volunteered to pledge me his lasting friendship provided I would assist in getting him the money he demanded from the Government, at the same time vowing vengeance if I failed to recommend payment."

Fleming blamed Marcus Smith for much of the extra cost on the work west of Lake Superior, which, he pointed out, was done in his absence. It was, he said, "startling . . . alarming . . . unaccountable . . . incomprehensible." Smith, in his testimony, blamed Fleming. Often enough, he claimed, when he tried to adjust matters during Fleming's absences, the men under him would insist that they were following the chief engineer's instructions.

Fleming was eased out of office in February, 1880, before the royal commission commenced its hearings. The government provided for him handsomely with a bonus of thirty thousand dollars. It also offered him a titular post with the railway, but this Fleming declined; he did not care to be a figurehead.

When the royal commission finally made its report it came down very hard on the former engineer-in-chief, but by then the construction of the railway was proceeding apace. Fleming went off to the International Geographical Congress in Venice to deliver a paper entitled "The Adoption of a Prime Meridian." Greater glories followed. His biography, when it was published, did not mention the petty jealousies, the bursts of temperament, the political jockeying, the caution, the waste, and the near anarchy that were commonplace in the engineering offices of the public works department under his rule. He survived it all and strode into the history books without a scar. The story of his term as engineer-in-chief is tangled and confused, neither black nor white, since it involved neither villains nor saints but a hastily recruited group of very human and often brilliant men, subjected to more than ordinary tensions including the insistent tug of their own ambitions and faced with superhuman problems, not the least of which was the spectre of the Unknown.

3

"We began the work of construction of Canada's great highway at a dead end," wrote Harry William Dudley Armstrong, a resident engineer along the half-completed Fort William–Selkirk line in the mid seventies. It was true. One chunk of railway was begun at the Red River and run hesitantly eastward towards the muskegs on the Ontario-Manitoba border. Another was built westward from Fort William, literally to nowhere. These two pieces were useless because they did not connect. The railway builders were at work in the empty heart of Canada without rail transportation to supply them, in a country scarcely explored. Four years later, when other contractors began to fill in the 181-mile gap between, every pound of supplies and heavy equipment had to be taken in by canoe and portage because the end of steel was still a good hundred miles from the water route. Joseph Whitehead, for one, had a quarter-million dollars' worth of machinery which had to be transported in this manner at prodigious cost. On Contract Forty-two, better known as Section B, eighty thousand dollars was spent moving in supplies before a foot of road was graded or a single rail laid. The distance between Fort William and Selkirk was only 435 railroad miles. But the barrier was so formidable that it took seven years before through rail communication was completed from the lakehead to the Red River.

The land that the railway builders set out to conquer was beautiful in its very bleakness. At the western end of Lake Superior it was almost all rock – the old, cracked rock of the Canadian Shield, grey and russet, striped by strata, blurred by pink lichens, garlanded by the dark vines and red berries of kinnikinnick and sparkling, sometimes, with the yellow pinpoints of cinquefoil. From the edges of the dun-coloured lakes that lay in the grey hollows there protruded the spiky points of the spruce, jet black against the green clouds of birch and poplar. Sometimes there were tiger lilies, blue vetch, briar rose, and oxeye daisies to relieve the sombre panorama; but in the winter the land was an almost unendurable monochrome of grey.

As the line moved west, the land changed and began to sparkle. Between the spiny ridges lay sinuous lakes and lesser ponds of bright blue or olive green from which the yellow flowers of the spatterdock glittered. The lakes became more numerous towards the west, the bright sheets of water winding in chains between the broken, tree-covered vertebrae of granite, with here and there a chartreuse meadow of tall, rank grass. This lake country, smiling in the sunshine, gloomy in the frequent slashing rains, would one day become a tourist mecca; but in the seventies it was a hellhole for the contractors who saw their fortunes sink forever in the seemingly bottomless slime of the great muskegs.

The muskegs came in every size. There were the notorious sinkholes over which a thick crust of vegetable matter had formed. In such a morass near Savanne, north of Fort William, so legend has it, an entire train with a thousand feet of track was swallowed whole.

Worse than the sinkholes were the giant muskegs, like the Poland Swamp or the Julius Muskeg, the most infamous bog of all – a vast bed of peat six miles across, its depth unknown. From these deceptively level, moss-covered stretches the naked trunks of dead tamaracks protruded, their roots weaving a kind of blanket over a concealed jelly of mud and slime. The road was carried over them on log mattresses floated on top of the heaving bog – unwieldy contraptions of long, interlaced timbers, which would sometimes run for eight hundred feet. Later on the muskegs were filled in.

Then there were the apparently placid lakes that seemed so shallow, whose bottoms consisted of unfathomable muskeg which swallowed up tons of earth and gravel fill, month after month. The real lake bottoms were concealed by a false blanket of silt which had never been properly probed during the hasty surveys. Lake Macquistinah, for instance, devoured 250,000 yards of earth fill; and on Section Fifteen the hapless Joseph Whitehead saw his dreamed-of profits slowly pouring into the notorious Cross Lake in the form of 220,000 yards of gravel at a cost of eighty thousand dollars. And still the line continued to sink.

Cross Lake was to prove Whitehead's undoing. The contractor began work on it in 1879 and was still pouring fill into it when the government relieved him of his contract in March, 1880. Ton after ton of sand and gravel vanished into that monstrous gulf without appreciable results. Sometimes the embankment would be built up five or six feet above the water; then suddenly the lake would take a gulp and the entire mass of stone, gravel, and earth would vanish beneath the waves.

At Lake Deception James Ross's huge force of horses and freight cars moved gravel into the water at top speed, using the first steam shovel to operate on the CPR, but the banks slid away faster than the gravel could be poured in. Ross built massive retaining walls with rock blasted out of one of his tunnels. One day in the space of a few minutes the banks settled some twenty-five feet, pushing the protective bulwarks out into the lake for almost a hundred feet so swiftly that the men and horses barely had time to jump clear. Ross tried hammering pilings deep into the lake bottom, building a trestle above them, and filling it in with gravel and rock. One June day, just after a work train had rumbled across the causeway, the pilings sank fifty feet.

There seemed no end to the depth of these incredible swamps. In one muskeg, piles were driven ninety-six feet below the surface before any bedrock was found. Even after the muskegs were conquered, the roadbed tended to creep forward with every passing train. When a heavy engine, hauling thirty-five cars, passed over the track, the rails crept about two feet in the direction the train was moving. As a result track bolts broke almost daily. An actual series of waves, five or six inches deep, rippled along the track and was observable from the caboose.

Temporary trestles were filled by dragging giant ploughs along a line of flatcars loaded with gravel. The ploughs were guided by a single rail in the centre of each car and pulled by a cable powered from the detached locomotive. The most effective of these ploughs was designed on the spot by Michael J. Haney, the colourful Galway Irishman who took over the running of Section Fifteen for the government after Whitehead's downfall.

A lean, hard man with high cheekbones, cowlick, and drooping moustache, Haney was described by Harry Armstrong, the pioneer engineer, as "a rushing devil-may-care chap who did things just as he chose without regard to authority." He seemed accident-prone to an almost unbelievable degree. At one point he was pitched off his horse and badly injured. On another occasion he caught his foot in some wire attached to the rails and a train ran over his toes. On July 18, 1880, he was riding an engine out of Cross Lake when the tender jumped the track and the locomotive with Haney in it rolled over a twenty-foot embankment. Clouds of scalding steam poured out of the wreck, but Haney, who was in the fireman's seat, emerged without a scratch. Two months later he had another close call en route from Lake Deception to Cross Lake. He had just stepped out of the fireman's seat to get a drink of water and was raising it to his lips when the engine rounded a steep curve. Haney was knocked off balance and thrown, head foremost, into a rock cut. The train was travelling at twenty miles an hour and everyone assumed Haney was dead; he escaped with a flesh wound in the forehead.

Haney's particular brand of derring-do was hard on him physically – after two years on Section Fifteen he was a sick man and his doctor ordered a complete rest – but it certainly got results. When Whitehead finally withdrew in February, 1880, matters were in a dreadful snarl. The men had not been paid and another in what had been a series of ugly strikes was in progress. The navvies were in a black mood when Haney arrived, called them together and told them that they would all receive their money as soon as pay sheets could be made up. Some decided to stay on the job, others to strike. Haney warned the strikers that the loyalists would be paid first. Then he set off for Winnipeg to get the needed funds. There he was besieged at his hotel by some of the strikers, demanding their money at once.

Haney was adamant: "I told you what I'd do and I'm going to

do it. I told you the men who stayed would be paid first and you can bet your last dollar that they'll all be paid before any of you get a cent.''

The leader of the group swore that Haney would not be allowed out of Winnipeg with a penny until the strikers got their money. Haney boldly told him that he intended to row across the river to St. Boniface, pick up an engine there at midnight, and steam back to the job. "You can do whatever you please about it," he said bluntly. He was as good as his word. With forty thousand dollars in cash on his person he set off down the track in the dead of night. It was a measure of the man that, in spite of all the threats, none dared stop him.

Back on the job Haney found himself faced with a series of dilemmas. Whitehead's caches were bare of provisions and yet Haney must keep four thousand men working without cessation. He and Collingwood Schreiber, Fleming's replacement as engineer-in-chief, estimated that one thousand tons would be needed – and this amount had to be distributed immediately over some of the roughest country in Canada. It was March 1. In a very short time the trails would be impossibly mired. Hauling could be done only over roads made of hard-packed snow, but there were not enough horses or wagons to do the job quickly. Schreiber figured it was impossible but Haney, moving from farmhouse to farmhouse, brow-beating, cajoling, pleading and promising, managed to hire every team in the country and by March 15 had accomplished a miracle.

Haney's ability to scrounge material became legendary. On one occasion when Section Fifteen ran short of spikes, he simply seized two carloads sitting on the Winnipeg sidings. There followed a wild night ride during which the spikes were unloaded at strategic points and the cars slipped back into the Winnipeg yards without anyone being the wiser. The incident baffled Schreiber more than anything else that occurred that year. The cars had been checked into the yards loaded and, after Haney's secret expedition, were checked out loaded; yet the spikes never reached their destination. Schreiber spent most of the summer tracing the two cars all over the continent. The matter became so nagging that it dominated his conversation.

"What I can't make out is what became of those spikes," he said one day in Haney's hearing.

"Why didn't you ask me about it?" Haney asked.

"What in the devil would you know about it?" Schreiber exploded.

"Well," said Haney, "if you care to walk back a mile or so along the track I think I can show you every one of those spikes."

Schreiber's retort has not been recorded but it was probably tempered with understanding. Haney's methods were unorthodox but they produced results. When he took over Section Fifteen there was a deficit of almost four hundred thousand dollars. Under his management a balance of $83,000 appeared on the black side of the ledger. Haney, of course, was a salaried man. The $83,000 was paid by the government to Joseph Whitehead.

4

In the dismal land west of Lake Superior, nature seemed to have gone to extremes to thwart the railway builders. When they were not laying track across the porridge of the muskegs they were blasting it through some of the hardest rock in the world – rock that rolled endlessly on, ridge after spiky ridge, like waves in a sullen ocean.

Dynamite, patented in the year of Confederation, was as new as the steam shovel; the major explosive was dynamite's parent, nitro-glycerine. This awesomely unstable liquid had been developed almost thirty years before the first sod was turned on the CPR but was only now beginning to replace the weaker blasting powder, being ten times more expensive not to mention more dangerous. It had never before been used as extensively as it was west of the lakehead in the late seventies.

The technique was to pour the explosive into drill holes, each about seven feet deep, and set it off by a fuse. In less than two years some three hundred thousand dollars was spent on nitro-glycerine on Section Fifteen, often with disastrous results. There was among the workmen an almost cavalier attitude to the explosive. Cans of nitro-glycerine with fuses attached were strewn carelessly along the roadbed in contravention of all safety regulations, or carried about with such recklessness that the fluid splashed upon the rocks. Whole gangs were sometimes blown to bits in the resultant explosions, especially in the cold weather, because the chemical was notoriously dangerous when frozen; the slightest jar could touch it off. Under such conditions it was kept under hot water and at as uniform a temperature as possible.

It could not be transported by wagon along those corrugated trails but had to be carried in ten-gallon tins on men's backs. The half-breed packers and the Irish navvies remained contemptuous of it. Armstrong, the engineer, saw one packer casually repairing a leak in a tin by scraping mud over it with his knife, oblivious of the fact that the tiniest bit of grit or the smallest amount of friction would blast him heavenwards. Sometimes the packers would lay their tins down on a smooth rock and a few drops would be left behind from a leak. On one occasion a teamster took his horse to water at just such a spot. The horse's iron shoe touched a pool of nitro-glycerine and the resulting blast tore the shoe from his foot and drove it through his belly, killing him and stunning the teamster.

The number of men killed or maimed by accidental explosions was truly staggering. In one fifty-mile stretch of Section B, Sandford Fleming counted thirty graves, all the result of the careless handling of nitro-glycerine. Mary Fitzgibbon, on her way to homestead in Manitoba, watched in awe as a long train of Irish packers tripped gaily down a hill, each with a can of liquid explosive on his back, making wry, funereal comments all the while:

"It's a warm day."

"That's so but maybe ye'll be warmer before ye camp tonight."

"That's so, d'ye want any work taken to the Divil?"

"Where are ye bound for, Jack?"

"To hell, I guess."

"Take the other train and keep a berth for me, man!"

"Is it yer coffin ye're carrying, Pat?"

"Faith ye're right; and the coroner's inquest to the bargain, Jim."

Mrs. Fitzgibbon wrote that in spite of the banter "the wretched expression of these very men proved that they felt the bitterness of death to be in their chests."

Under such conditions the only real respite was alcohol. Prohibition was in effect all along the line, but this did not stop the whiskey peddlers who had kegs of liquor cached at points along the entire right of way. Since a gallon of alcohol, which was sold in the cities of the East for as low as fifty cents, could, when properly diluted, return forty-five dollars to an enterprising peddler on the line, business continued brisk in spite of the vigilance of the police. The peddlers hid out in the bush or on the islands that dotted the swampy lakes, moving into the work camps in swift canoes of birchbark and darting away again at the approach of the law. If caught, the peddler generally escaped with a fine, since these were the chief source of income for the struggling towns and villages that were springing up at the end of steel.

Harry Armstrong, in his unpublished memoirs, set down a spirited account of one whiskey trial held in the winter of 1877-78 in which he acted as clerk of the court. The trial was held at Inver on Section Fifteen. A man named Shay was arrested with a toboggan-load of whiskey and placed in charge of the local blacksmith. He was duly arraigned before two justices of the peace, one of whom was the government's divisional engineer, Henry Carre, and the other the contractor's engineer. It was their first case on the bench – the bench being literally a bench, since the court was held in the company mess hall.

"Produce the prisoner," called Carre, and the blacksmith entered, holding Shay by the coat sleeve and pulling at his own forelock as he announced: "The prisoner, Your Honour."

The first witness was being questioned when Charles Whitehead, the son of the contractor, acting in his role of prosecutor, "wildly suggested to the bench that it was probably in order to swear the witness." It took some time to find a Bible, but one was eventually located and the case proceeded. A further delay occurred when it was noticed that Armstrong, as clerk, was taking down the evidence in pencil. With difficulty, pen and ink were found, the evidence retranscribed, and the case continued. Without much more ceremony, the prisoner was found guilty. He had formerly been employed as one of Carre's axemen and was well known to him. Obviously he had come up in the world financially, being attired in a fine suit with a fur collar – "the most distinguished looking man in the room."

"Shay," said Carre gravely, "I am very sorry to see you in this position."

"So am I, Mr. Carre," replied the convicted man with disturbing nonchalance.

"The decision of the court is that you pay a fine of twenty-five dollars."

"Well, I won't pay it. I'll appeal."

This was a disconcerting turn of events. There was no jail closer than Winnipeg and no funds to send the prisoner there, and so, after a few days of well-fed comfort in the bunkhouse, the miscreant was allowed to depart, without his whiskey.

Michael Haney's method of handling the alcohol problem was characteristic. He made no attempt to curb the traffic himself but when the men were put on three round-the-clock shifts, whiskey tended to slow down the work. At such times it was Haney's practice to round up the peddlers and secure from them a promise that they would not sell whiskey as long as the 24-hour shift-work prevailed. Generally this agreement worked, but on one occasion the presence of five hundred thirsty men was too much for the entrepreneurs. Haney arrived one morning to find the whole camp roaring drunk. He moved with his usual brusqueness. There were four officials working on the section who were technically known as "whiskey detectives." He called them before him and told them that unless all whiskey peddlers were brought before him by noon, all four would be fired. The peddlers were produced in an hour and haled immediately before a magistrate who was clearly taking his orders from Haney. The law provided increased fines for each recurring offence and the option of jail on a third offence. Haney saw that the maximum fines – a total of thirty-six hundred dollars – were levied. The prison sentences were remitted but all peddlers were packed off to Winnipeg with the warning that if they returned they would be jailed. None of them ever came back.

By the time Haney arrived on the scene, at the decade's end, the solemn, unknown land through which Harry Armstrong had trudged five years earlier had come alive with thousands of navvies – Swedes, Norwegians, Finns and Icelanders, French Canadians and Prince Edward Islanders, Irish, Scots, English, Americans, even Mennonites, all strung out over nearly five hundred miles in clustered, brawling, hard-drinking communities, most of which were as impermanent as the end of track.

Armstrong recalled, not without nostalgia, the days when "life along the railway construction . . . was like one large family. There was hospitality, helpfulness, gentle friendship, good nature and contentedness all about." He described Christmas Eve, 1876, spent in a log cabin on the right of way, with a fiddler playing for dancing couples in a room which also contained a kitchen stove and an immense bed. Everything went fine, he remembered, until someone unwittingly sat on the bed and realized that there was a baby somewhere beneath the sheets.

His account contrasts sharply with that of the postmaster of Whitemouth, a railroad community midway between Winnipeg and Rat River, also describing Christmas Eve, just four years later.

"The demon of strong drink made a bedlam of this place, fighting, stabbing and breaking; some lay out freezing till life was almost extinct. The Post Office was besieged at the hours of crowded business by outrageous, bleeding, drunken, fighting men, mad with Forty-Rod, so that respectable people could not come in for their mail. . . . It is only a few days since in one of these frenzies a man had his jugular nearly severed by a man with a razor."

The one really permanent town along the half-constructed line and by far the largest was Rat Portage on Lake of the Woods. With true chamber of commerce fervour it called itself "the Future Saratoga of America." A less subjective description was provided by a correspondent of the Winnipeg *Times* in the summer of 1880:

"For some time now the railway works in the vicinity of Rat Portage have been besieged by a lot of scoundrels whose only avocation seems to be gambling and trading in illicit whiskey and the state of degradation was, if anything, intensified by the appearance, in the wake of these blacklegs, of a number of the *demi-monde* with whom these numerous desperadoes held high carnival at all hours of the day or night."

The town itself, in the words of one observer, seemed to have been "laid out on designs made by a colony of muskrats." Shanties and tents were built or pitched wherever the owners fancied and without reference to streets or roadways. As a result, the streets were run between the houses as an afterthought so that there was nothing resembling a straight thoroughfare in town.

With a floating population sometimes bordering on three thousand, the community was the headquarters for Section B. The expense of the administration was borne by the contractors, who built the jail and organized the police force. All fines, however, went to the government. Between April and November of 1880, six thousand dollars was collected in fines. The convictions – highway robbery, larceny, burglary, assault, selling illicit whiskey, and prostitution – give a fair picture of Rat Portage as a frontier town.

With both the contractors and the government in the law business, a state of near anarchy prevailed. At one point the company constable, a man named O'Keefe, seized four barrels of illicit liquor but instead of destroying it took it back to his rooms and proceeded to treat his many friends. He was haled before the stipendiary magistrate who fined him for having intoxicating liquor in his possession. O'Keefe paid the fine and then as soon as the magistrate left the bench arrested *him* for having liquor in his possession, an act he was perfectly entitled to perform since he was himself a policeman. When he popped the protesting magistrate into jail, a new magistrate had to be appointed to act in his place. When that was done a hearing was held and the new magistrate fined the old magistrate one hundred dollars. In the end the local government remitted both fines.

In 1880 Rat Portage was easily the roughest town in Canada; eight hundred gallons of illegal liquor poured into town every month, hidden in oatmeal and bean sacks or disguised as barrels of coal oil. So profitable was the business that there was a whiskey peddler for every thirty residents. Here on a smaller and more primitive scale was foreshadowed all the anarchy of a later prohibition period in the United States – the same gun-toting mobsters, corrupt officials, and harassed police. One bloody incident in the summer of 1880, involving two whiskey traders named Dan Harrington and Jim Mitchell, had all the elements of a western gun battle.

Harrington and Mitchell had in 1878 worked on a steam drill for Joseph Whitehead but they soon abandoned that toil for the more lucrative trade. In the winter of 1879-80, a warrant was issued for their arrest at Cross Lake, but when the constable tried to serve it, the two beat him brutally and escaped to Rat Portage where the stipendiary magistrate, F.W. Bent, was in their pay. The two men gave themselves up to Bent who fined them a token fifty dollars and then gave them a written discharge to prevent further interference from officials at Cross Lake. The magistrate also returned to Harrington a revolver that had been confiscated.

It was pay day. The two started east with fifty gallons of whiskey, heading for Hawk Lake. They were spotted, en route, by one of the contracters, John J. McDonald, who realized what was about to happen to his work force. He and the company's constable, Ross, went straight to Rat Portage, got a warrant, and doubled back for Hawk Lake.

They found Harrington and Mitchell in front of Millie Watson's bawdy tent. Mitchell fled into the woods but Harrington boldly announced he would sell whiskey in spite of contractors and police. The two men wrested his gun from him and placed him under arrest. Harrington then asked and was given permission to go inside the tent and wash up. Here a crony handed him a brace of loaded seven-shot revolvers. Harrington cocked the weapons and emerged from the tent with both of them pointed at the constable. Ross was a fast draw; as Harrington's finger curled around the trigger the policeman shot him above the heart. Harrington dropped to the ground, vainly trying to retrieve his guns. A second constable told Ross not to bother to fire again: the first bullet had taken effect.

"You're damned right it has taken effect," Harrington snarled, "but I'd sooner be shot than fined." Those were his final words.

It was such reports, seeping back to Winnipeg, that persuaded Archbishop Taché of St. Boniface that the construction workers needed a permanent chaplain; after all, a third of them were French-Canadian Catholics from Manitoba. He selected for the task the most notable of all the voyageur priests, Father Albert Lacombe, a nomadic Oblate who had spent most of his adult life among the Cree and Blackfoot of the Far West. In November, 1880, Lacombe set out reluctantly for his new parish.

Father Lacombe was a homely man whose long silver locks never seemed to be combed, but benevolence shone from his features. He did not want to be a railway chaplain. He would much rather have stayed among his beloved Indians than have entered the Sodom of Rat Portage, but he went where his church directed. On the very first day of his new assignment he was scandalized by the language of the navvies. His first sermon, preached in a boxcar chapel, was an attack on blasphemy. "It seems to me what I have said is of a nature to bring reflection to these terrible blasphemers, who have a vile language all their own – with a dictionary and grammar which belongs to no one but themselves," he confided to his diary. "This habit of theirs is – diabolical!"

But there was worse to come: two weeks after he arrived in Rat Portage there was "a disorderly and scandalous ball," and all night long the sounds of drunken revelry dinned into the ears of the unworldly priest from the plains. Lacombe even tried to reason with the woman who sponsored the dances. He was rewarded with jeers and insults.

"My God," he wrote in his diary, "have pity on this little village where so many crimes are committed every day." He realized that he was helpless to stop all the evil that met his eyes and so settled at last for prayer "to arrest the divine anger."

As he moved up and down the line, covering thirty different camps, preaching sermons as he went, celebrating mass in the mornings, talking and smoking with the navvies in the evenings and recording on every page of his small, tattered black notebooks a list of sins far worse than he had experienced among the followers of Chief Crowfoot, the wretched priest was overcome by a sense of frustration. The heathen Indians had been so easy to convert! But these navvies listened to him respectfully, talked to him intimately, confessed their sins religiously, and then went on their drunken, brawling, blaspheming, whoring way totally unashamed.

Ill with pleurisy, forced to travel the track on an open handcar in the bitterest weather, his eyes affronted by spectacles he did not believe possible, the tortured priest could only cry to his diary, "My God, I offer you my sufferings."

"Please God, send me back to my missions," he pleaded, but it was not until the final spike was driven that his prayers were answered. He had not changed many lives, perhaps, but he had made more friends than he knew. When it was learned that he was going, the workmen of Section B took up a large collection and presented him with a generous assortment of gifts: a horse, a buggy, a complete harness, a new saddle, a tent, and an entire camping outfit to make his days on the plains more comfortable. Perhaps, as he took his leave, he reasoned that his tortured mission to the godless had not been entirely in vain.

Chapter
Six

TWO
STREAKS
OF
RUST

1

On one of those early trips to the Canadian North West in 1870, when he was planning his steamboat war against the Hudson's Bay Company, James Jerome Hill's single eye fastened upon the rich soil of the Red River country and marked the rank grass that sprang up in the ruts left by the wagon wheels. It was the blackest loam he had ever seen and he filed the memory of it carefully away in the pigeonholes of his active mind. Soil like that meant settlers – tens of thousands of them. Settlers would need a railway. With Donald Smith's help, Jim Hill meant to give them one.

There was a railway of sorts leading out of St. Paul in 1870. It was supposed to reach to the Canadian border but it had not made it that far. One of its branches ended at Breckenridge on the Red River, where it connected with the Kittson line of steamboats. Another headed off northwest to St. Cloud at the end of the Red River trail. An extension faltered north towards Brainerd, where it was supposed to connect with the main line of the Northern Pacific. But neither branch nor extension could properly be called a railroad. They had been built in a piecemeal fashion out of the cheapest materials. Unused piles of bridge timbers, railway ties, and other bric-a-brac littered the right of way, and the farmers along the line were helping themselves to whatever they needed. The rolling stock was incredibly primitive – the engines ancient and creaky, the cars battered and rusty.

The story of the St. Paul and Pacific Railroad is a case history in railway looting. Russell Sage, a railway promoter, had corrupted the Minnesota legislature into handing over vast land grants and bond issues, the proceeds of which he and his cronies coolly pocketed. In just five years the road was bankrupt. The Sage group then reorganized the bankrupt company into two new companies, thereby ridding themselves of all their debts while keeping the valuable land grant. Then they proceeded to lobby for even more land and when they got it floated a bond issue of $13,800,000 in Holland. They diverted some eight million dollars of this sum to their own pockets and plunged the railroad into bankruptcy again.

In the early seventies the railway consisted of some five hundred miles of almost unusable track – "two streaks of rust and a right of way," as it was contemptuously called. One of its lines actually went from nowhere to nowhere, a phantom railroad lying out on

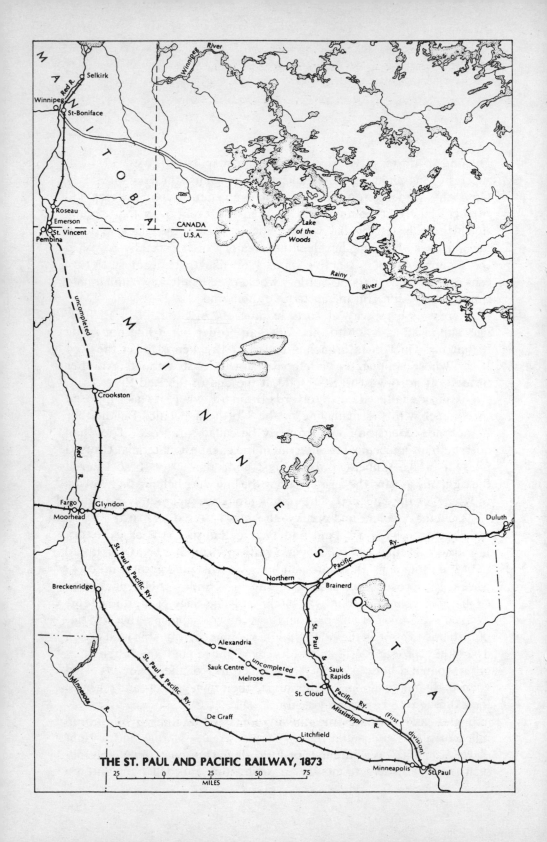

THE ST. PAUL AND PACIFIC RAILWAY, 1873

25   0   25   50   75
MILES

the naked prairie with no town at the terminal end of iron and no facilities created to do business at the other.

Yet this was the line that Jim Hill coveted; and this was the line that would eventually make Jim Hill, Donald Smith, Norman Kittson, and George Stephen rich beyond their wildest dreams and gain them both the experience and the money to build the Canadian Pacific Railway.

In St. Paul, Hill was the town character, a notorious dreamer who would talk your ear off, especially if he got on the subject of railways. Hill was the kind of man who could gaze upon an empty plain and visualize an iron highway. He took a look at St. Paul when it was only a hamlet and realized he was at one of the great crossroads of western trade. Accordingly, he set himself up as a forwarding agent. When the railway first came along Hill began to sell it wood, but he saw that coal would swiftly replace the lesser fuel and so he studied coal. He made a survey of all the available sources of coal and became the first coal merchant in St. Paul. He actually joined geological parties exploring for coal. Years later, when the great coal deposits were discovered in Iowa, it turned out that one-eyed Jim Hill held twenty-three hundred of the best acres under lease. Until his death he was considered one of the leading experts on the continent on the subject of western coal.

But in the early seventies, no one took Jim Hill seriously. Perhaps it was because he talked so much. There he sat in his old chair in front of his coal and wood store, babbling away, his single black eye burning itself into the listener's consciousness.

Napoleon was his hero. He had first read his biography in Canada at the age of thirteen and nothing else that he read (and he seemed to read everything – Byron, Plutarch, More, Gibbon) made such an impression on him. From that moment, he believed that when a man set his mind to something it was already half done. Later in life, when he had built a mansion in St. Paul and stocked it with costly paintings, he began to think of himself as a Bonaparte. But in those early days he simply brought his Napoleonic determination to bear on the matter of the decrepit railroad, which he saw as the nucleus of a transcontinental line. It was, everyone agreed, a crazy dream, but then Jim Hill had always been a "romancer," in the phrase of a boyhood companion. He had wild ambitions: he was going to be a doctor. (While he was playing Indians, an arrow through the eye ended that.) He was going to be a sailor before the mast. He was going to run a steamboat line in India. He was going to conquer the world.

He was Canadian by birth and a Celt by heritage – half Scottish, half Irish. He was born in a log house at Rockwood, Ontario, and was much influenced by his teacher, the great Quaker educator William Wetherald, who taught him the value of books. For all of his life Hill remained a student: he studied scientific treatises, classical art, geology, finance – everything he could get his hands on. Rockwood could not hold him; at eighteen, his heart fired by the idea of adventure, he set off for the Orient. He got only as far as St. Paul.

For eight years, from 1856 to 1864, Hill worked at a variety of jobs in St. Paul, reading and studying all the while. He read voraciously, at all hours and in every setting. One winter he took a job as a watchman on a steamboat wintering at the levee, arriving with an armful of books ranging from Gibbon's *Decline and Fall* to several difficult scientific treatises. When he emerged the following spring he had read and annotated them all.

By the time he decided to try his hand at business, Hill's knowledge was encyclopaedic and his memory prodigious. He had, it seemed, studied everything. One of the things he studied was the Toonerville operation out of St. Paul; and one of the things he learned was that whoever owned the railway could come into possession of two and a half million acres of the richest agricultural land in the American midwest. The time would come, Hill reckoned, when the railway could be bought for a song. It was all a matter of waiting.

2

In Winnipeg, Donald A. Smith had a similar idea. The Red River needed a lifeline to the East. If such a line could be built from Selkirk to the border and if the bankrupt American line out of St. Paul could somehow be revived to meet it, that connection would be effected.

Smith was also a man who liked to look ahead: a month sometimes, a year perhaps, even a decade or more. He saw, for instance, the coming extinction of the buffalo and kept some captive animals in a corral at his home. When he emerged from Labrador on his first visit to Montreal he decided to learn to cook, for he saw future advantages in that art. On his return, he gave all his employees instruction in serving wholesome meals in order to preserve their health and sometimes their lives in the wilds. More, he picked up a knowledge of primitive medicine. It was this kind of preparedness that undoubtedly saved Smith's own life on the snow-blind journey back to Mingan and on other occasions as well. No matter what the weather, Smith always had the foresight to carry extra clothing and additional provisions with him wherever he went. When a blizzard sprang up, Smith was always ready for it; he was generally ready for any eventuality.

Like Hill, he foresaw the death of the steam packet at a time when the river trade seemed to be at its height. Smith also saw the threat to the fur trade even when the fur trade seemed invulnerable. As early as 1860 he predicted that the Hudson's Bay Company could not go on forever sealing off the North West, and he realized that once the company's charter was modified or cancelled there would have to be a railway from Lake Superior to the Red River.

Thirteen years after that forecast was made, Smith contemplated the two streaks of rust out of St. Paul. The twin railway companies (one was known as the St. Paul and Pacific, the other as the First Division of the St. Paul and Pacific) were in a terrible legal and financial snarl. One was in receivership, the other was about to go into trusteeship. There were suits and countersuits by unpaid contractors, chagrined stockholders, and swindled bondholders. It was not easy to fathom the complicated financial situation, since there were several classes of bonds for the two lines and most of these were held out of the country by Dutch investors.

In the fall of 1873, on his way through St. Paul en route to Ottawa, Smith dropped in on "Commodore" Norman Kittson, the Hudson's Bay representative and the president of the steamboat line which, with the company's secret connivance, held a monopoly on the river. Smith asked Kittson to find out everything possible about the financial and legal position of the St. Paul and Pacific Railroad, especially about the Dutch-held bonds. If the price was right, Smith thought, he might consider raising the money to help complete the line.

Kittson mentioned the matter to his other silent partner, Jim Hill, and it was as if a light had flashed on above that lion's head. Of course! For all these months Hill had been grappling with the puzzle of the bankrupt railway, wondering where the money would come from when the time was ripe to buy it. Now he had the answer: Smith was one of the chief officers of the Bank of Montreal as well as of the Hudson's Bay Company. He was wealthy in his own right. Smith was his man. From that moment on, Hill became a monomaniac on the subject of the St. Paul and Pacific.

When Donald Smith passed back through St. Paul, Hill and Kittson were able to tell him that most of the bonds, totalling almost eighteen million dollars face value, were now held by Dutch investors who had formed themselves into a committee of bondholders.

The strategy was clear: buy the bonds as cheaply as possible, form a new company, force a foreclosure, buy the bankrupt railroad, complete it to the border, cash in on the resultant land subsidy, and reap the profits. But there were many obstacles. It was no use buying the railroad without being certain of getting the free land that was supposed to come with it. The Minnesota legislature, however, had passed a law (no doubt with the bitter memory of Russell Sage's plundering) making the land grant non-transferable to any new company after foreclosure. A good deal of lobbying – and perhaps more than lobbying – would be needed to get that law revoked. There was also a variety of lawsuits pending against the railway lines. Then there were the stockholders, in addition to the bondholders, to be considered. Most of the stock was held by a speculator named Edwin Litchfield, a notoriously difficult man to deal with. Litchfield was trying to get control of the railway for himself through court action. The depression was at its height, money was hard to come by, and plagues of grasshoppers were ravaging the land. For the moment nothing could be done. Smith, Hill, and Kittson bided their time for two full years, but Hill was not inactive. He studied the railroad down to the last cross tie. Within two years, it was said, he knew more about it than the men involved in running it. Two things he certainly knew that few others knew: it was worth far more than it appeared to be; and it could be made to show a profit.

Everybody in St. Paul knew that Jim Hill wanted the railroad and hoped to get the money from Donald A. Smith. An old friend, Henry Upham, admitted that Hill "used to talk so much about this that people were, a little tired of it." Hill lived and slept the railway. Indeed, he neglected his work because of it. His partner in the coal business was annoyed because when Hill turned up on the job all he would talk about was acquiring the road.

One of the men he talked to, long and intimately, was Jesse P. Farley, an old railroad man from Dubuque, Iowa, who had been appointed receiver of the bankrupt St. Paul railroad. The twin to the bankrupt company was under trusteeship, and the trustees made Farley general manager of it, so that he was actually in charge of the entire St. Paul and Pacific line and its branches. As such he was supposed to keep the railroad profitable, try to get it out of trouble, and build more track. He was singularly unsuccessful in doing this, spending in three years only about one hundred thousand dollars on construction and repair. During this period he and his assistant were on intimate terms with Hill, whom they saw almost daily, and they were pleased, on occasion, to do Hill's bidding. The question, which was the subject of a prolonged series of legal battles, was whether or not Hill was simply pumping Farley for information or whether Farley was in collusion with him to keep the railway in a rundown condition so that it could be bought cheaply. That mystery has never been conclusively unravelled.

But then, there are several mysteries connected with the complicated finances and eventual disposition of the St. Paul and Pacific. Another has to do with the role played by John S. Kennedy, a New York banker who was the agent for the Dutch committee that held most of the bonds. Kennedy recommended Farley as trustee. Farley, an almost illiterate man, had previously worked for Kennedy and generally did what the banker told him. What was Kennedy's real role? He was supposed to be looking after the bondholders' interests, but he himself was to become a multimillionaire as a result of his connection with Jim Hill and associates – the men who finally bought the Dutch bonds.

The bondholders in Holland appointed one of their number, Johan Carp, to visit St. Paul and look over the railway, which had cost them so many headaches. Farley intimated to him that the headaches would go on for years. Carp, persuaded of this, told Farley the committee was willing to sell the bonds if a reasonable bid could be obtained. The time for waiting was over. While Farley was running down the railway to Carp, Hill realized that solutions to many of the problems were at hand. Chief of these was the new legislation his political friends were arranging, which would make it possible for the reorganized railway company to keep the land grant. Hill had always known that the real value of the line lay in its capacity to claim free land.

The law was changed on March 6, 1876. With this obstacle removed, Hill left for Ottawa on March 17 to meet Smith. It was now or never. Edwin Litchfield, the chief stockholder, was trying to reach a compromise with the Dutch bondholders which would give him effective control and prevent foreclosure. Hill's whole scheme rested on the certainty of foreclosure. Whoever owned the bonds could foreclose if mortgage payments were in default. Then the railroad would go on the block and the new bondholders could buy it for a song. But how much did the Dutch want for their bonds? If the terms were favourable, Smith told Hill, the money could probably be raised.

Hill departed for St. Paul in a state of jubilation. Up to this time Johan Carp had refused to take Hill and Kittson seriously. An aging steamboat man and a garrulous coal merchant! But when he learned who Donald A. Smith was he began to pay attention.

It was now Hill's task to figure out the price at which the Dutch were prepared to sell. In January, 1877, he pretended he was ready to deal. Actually his plan was to write a letter to the Dutch committee that would sound like an offer so that he might get some idea of the actual price. He had two other purposes: he wanted to keep Carp interested, and he wanted to word the letter in such a way as to convince the bondholders that the railway was practically worthless. Faced with an apparently *bona fide* offer, Hill rightly believed, they would grasp at any straw to sell the white elephant. He spent an entire evening working out the delicate wording and then a full morning with his lawyer rephrasing it.

The Dutch rejected the offer, as Hill knew they would; but their reply indicated the kind of deal they would accept. The time had finally come to stop dreaming dreams and playing games. The time had come to put some money on the line. The time had come to broach the subject to George Stephen, the president of the Bank of Montreal, one of the keenest financial minds in Canada and a first cousin of Donald A. Smith.

3

Ever since 1874, Donald Smith had been boring his cousin with talk about the St. Paul railway. George Stephen listened politely but, like most Montreal businessmen, he had a confused and inaccurate picture of the country west of the lakes. "He thought of Minnesota ... that it was at the North Pole somewhere," Smith later recalled. But, though Stephen thought the railway scheme "an impossible thing for us to accomplish," he agreed to meet Hill and Smith early in 1877 to discuss the matter. Hill, armed with facts and figures, papers and documents, gesturing with an insistent finger, never letting up for an instant in his infectious enthusiasm, changed Stephen's attitude from one of "languid attention" to whole-hearted interest; and Stephen's interests were never idle ones.

Stephen is a shadowy figure in Canadian history. Yet, apart from the politicians, he, more than any other single man, was responsible for the shape and direction of the new Canada that sprang up west of Toronto after 1881. He would have been delighted with his own historical anonymity for he was a man who shunned the limelight. He saw to it that his own personal papers were destroyed. He had no use for scribblers. He thought the newspapers printed a lot of damned nonsense. And in his later years he banned the newly invented telephone from his home; it would be used, he said, for no better purpose than to spread gossip.

Outwardly reserved, publicly reticent, and privately unassuming, he was inwardly subjected to the tugs and pressures of a mercurial psyche, reckless in its enthusiasms, magnificent in its audacities, faithful in its loyalties, consuming in its antipathies, and single-minded to the point of intolerance. He was used to the blunt directives of the business world and was maddened by the circumlocutions of the political. Unlike Macdonald, to whom he poured out his inner soul in an astonishing series of personal letters, he indulged himself in the luxury of maintaining his animosities. As far as Stephen was concerned, you were either for him or against him. There was rarely a middle ground.

He could operate with a gambler's daring when the occasion demanded it. His sudden espousal of Hill's scheme to capture the St. Paul railroad is the first major example of it; but there were hints in his background. As a junior partner for a Montreal drapery firm, he came under the influence, during his trips to England, of James Morrison, whose swift rise to fortune had inspired the phrase "Morrison's Millions." With England on the verge of war in the Crimea, Morrison urged Stephen to buy up all the cottons and woollens he could lay his hands on and ship them to Canada before wartime scarcity shot the price up. Stephen took the plunge. The corner he secured on textiles allowed him to bring off a financial coup. He eventually took over the firm, later formed one of his own, and soon found himself a member of the Montreal business establishment.

In Smith and Hill, Stephen found men like himself: shrewd in business, willing to take long risks, and, perhaps above all, wedded to the idea that a man was placed on earth to work, day and night if need be. To them, idleness was anathema. Hill had never known an idle moment. Of Smith, it was said (by an old Hudson's Bay factor) that he "was a wonder to work. He did not seem to take any sleep. . . . No matter how late at night you looked, you would see his lamp burning in his house. . . ." As for Stephen, "it was impressed upon me from my earliest years by one of the best mothers that ever lived that . . . I must concentrate my whole energies on my work, whatever that might be, to the exclusion of every other thing."

It was this hard ethic that explains the dominance of the Scots in pioneer Canada. The Irish outnumbered them, as they did the English, but the Scots ran the country, controlling the fur trade, the great financial houses, the major educational institutions and, to a considerable degree, the government. Almost every member of the original CPR Syndicate was a self-made Scot. In the drama of the railway it is the Scottish names that stand out: Macdonald and Mackenzie, Allan and Macpherson, Fleming and Grant, Stephen, Smith, Kennedy, McIntyre, Angus, and Hill (who was half Scottish) – living embodiments of the popular copybook maxims of the time: *Waste not, want not. . . Early to bed, early to rise. . . Keep your nose to the grindstone. . . See a pin and pick it up. . . .* Stephen, it is said, got a job through following the last maxim. Unsuccessful in Glasgow, he had moved to London and sought work in a draper's establishment. The store was in chaos for it was stock-taking day, and no one had time to speak to him. Turned away by a prospective employer, he stopped to pick up a pin, which he carefully stuck behind his coat lapel. The foreman spotted the action and hired him as an assistant. Alger could not have improved upon the incident.

Stephen's idea of a spare-time activity was to make a study of banking, and this led him eventually to the top of the financial pyramid. His only real form of relaxation was salmon fishing, a passion which he indulged at his summer retreat of Causapscal on the Matapedia River in the Gaspé. That almost certainly went back to his school days in Banffshire, where he came under the influence of a brilliant mathematician, John Macpherson. Top students were rewarded with an invitation to go salmon fishing. Stephen was certainly a top student; Macpherson was to recall that in thirty years of teaching, Stephen was one of the three best mathematicians he had known. The salmon-fishing expeditions must have been frequent.

A mathematician must think logically and tidily and reason creatively. Stephen had that kind of mind. He has been called, with truth, "the greatest genius in the whole history of Canadian finance." His entire career is a testimony to it.

He met his cousin Donald A. Smith for the first time in 1866 – a chilly and awkward encounter. The contrast between the two men was marked. Stephen had climbed swiftly up the social and mercantile ladder while Smith, eleven years older, had been walled up in lonely corners of Labrador for more than a generation. The sophisticated Stephen was faultlessly groomed, as a good draper should be; Smith was shaggy and weatherworn.

Smith knew only that his cousin was in the woollen trade, but he decided to look him up during a shopping expedition. He took his wife and family along, and en route they purchased a gaudy carpet-bag to take back to Labrador. Later, when Smith was asked if Stephen had been glad to see him, his wife burst out: "He wasn't glad at all. Why should Mr. Stephen be glad to see country cousins like us? I wish he had waited until he met Mr. Stephen before buying that red carpet bag. But he wouldn't let me carry it, and the rest of us waited outside."

But Smith was no bumpkin; as Stephen was to realize, he was an astonishing businessman. For many years his fellow officers in the fur trade had entrusted him with their salaries and this gave him control of large sums of money. He guaranteed the fur traders three per cent a year and invested their money in securities. He was, in short, a kind of one-man Labrador bank, and this became the basis of his fortune. One of the stocks he bought was that of the Bank of Montreal; another, the Hudson's Bay Company. But, true to the copybook maxims, he was not above counting and sorting all the nails in the packing cases that were shipped to him.

When Smith met Stephen and Hill in Montreal in the spring of 1877, he was already a director of the bank. Stephen was its president. Smith was moved permanently to Montreal in 1868 and he and his cousin soon found themselves co-directors and leading shareholders in several industries, including one that manufactured railway rolling stock. Bit by bit Stephen found himself getting involved with railways, almost by osmosis. Now, in 1877, he found himself leaning across the table while a one-eyed ex-Canadian jabbed his finger at him and talked about launching a daring financial adventure.

Stephen's mathematician's mind easily grasped Hill's Niagara of statistics and sorted them into a pattern. His gambler's instincts tugged at him insistently. If the coup could be pulled off it would be a master-stroke comparable to the exploits of a Gould, a Fisk, or a Morgan. If it failed, it would beggar them all.

What did Stephen have to gain at this point of his career? He was president of the most important financial institution in Canada, director of innumerable companies, respected by his peers, socially impeccable. The preposterous scheme of buying into an obscure and rundown railroad somewhere off beyond the mists of the horizon could, unless it worked, bring him nothing but discredit. Perhaps if he could have seen the tortured succession of events that this would finally lead to, the terrible moments when he saw his world, everything that he had built and toiled for, crumbling around him, the sleepless nights when he was close to a nervous and physical breakdown, perhaps even to suicide – George Stephen might have hesitated and backed away. A decade later, after it was all over and the years hung heavy upon him, he gave more than a little indication of this when, on the eve of his birthday, he wrote to John A. Macdonald:

"Tomorrow I begin my sixty-first year, and looking back ten years I am far from being the free man I then was.... When I think of the misery I have suffered in these ten years I cannot help thinking what a fool I was not to end my work and enjoy the leisure which I had earned by forty years hard work. I began to earn my own living at the age of ten. 'But what maun be maun be.' It was not so ordained...."

He could not resist the adventure. He sat down and began to figure, with Hill and Smith, the price at which the bonds should be purchased. They worked it out at a little more than four million dollars. If the Dutch bondholders agreed, Stephen said, he thought he could raise the money in London that fall. He still had to see the railway for himself, but from that day on George Stephen was totally captivated, to the exclusion of everything else.

4

The new associates had a great deal of delicate negotiating to do. Before Stephen could leave for Europe, they would have to make a firm deal with the bondholders. Then, to forestall a legal battle, an attempt must also be made to corner Litchfield's stock. After that Stephen would have to raise the money.

Hill left for New York to see Litchfield, and drew a blank. "The old rat," as Stephen called him, would not even name a price. Then, on May 26, Hill fired off a letter to the Dutch committee so ambiguously worded that it looked like an offer; actually it was only an option. When the Dutch tried to bargain, Hill got tough. The value of the bonds was actually decreasing, he suggested: the grasshoppers had hurt land values and the Northern Pacific was threatening to build a competitive line.

On September 1, 1877, Stephen found an opportunity to see the property for himself. He and R. B. Angus, the bank's general manager – another bearded, self-made Scot – joined Smith and Hill for a weekend in St. Paul. On Sunday, together with Farley, the receiver and manager, they all took the pay car out along the completed portion of one of the lines.

Stephen was dismayed at what he saw. This was the worst year of the great depression: drought had driven the settlers from the land, and grasshoppers had ravaged the country. As Stephen began to shake his head ominously, the others watched in growing alarm. Would he back out now? Stephen began to ask some pointed questions: Where would the business come from in this tenantless desert? When, if ever, would there be settlers here on the parched and plundered grasslands? Then suddenly the little station of De Graff was reached. The several trails leading into the community were speckled with carts loaded with people.

"What is all this?" Stephen wanted to know.

Somebody, probably Hill, made a reply which Smith was later to remember:

"Why, this is but an instance of what is to occur along the whole line of the railroad. This is a colony opened by Bishop Ireland one single year ago. Already the settlers brought in by the Bishop are counted by the hundreds, and hundreds of others are coming to join them from different parts of America and Europe. This is Sunday morning and the settlers are going to Mass."

The scene made an enormous impression on Stephen: the vision of a railway tied to colonization – bringing in the very settlers who would then provide it with its future business – was limned in his mind. Stephen's doubts evaporated and, in Smith's words, "from that moment he was won over." Bishop Ireland benefited, too; Jim Hill saw to it that his church got all the land it needed for next to nothing.

By this time Hill had made a detailed inventory of the railroad's assets and liabilities. His supple mind had grasped a point that eluded everyone else: though the net earnings of the First Division Company seemed to have dropped, they had in reality nearly doubled because almost two hundred thousand dollars had been charged to operating expenses instead of to construction and equipment. This meant that the railroad was doing much better than the books showed.

Hill knew something more: although he figured that it would cost some five and a half million dollars to buy the bonds and complete the line, he was able, by close reckoning, to estimate the total value of the railway and its properties at almost twenty millions. In short, if the bondholders accepted the offer, he and his associates would get the railway for about a quarter of its real value.

By mid-September, the Dutch were ready to deal. If Stephen could raise the money, the partners could buy themselves almost eighteen million dollars' worth of bonds for slightly more than four millions. It was a fantastic bargain.

The four partners agreed to share the risks and the profits equally, each taking a one-fifth share in the enterprise. The remaining one-fifth went to Stephen to use at his discretion in raising a loan. At the end of September he set off for England, full of optimism.

But in London, the bankers were gun shy. The panic of 1873 had made American railway securities a bad risk, and among all the bad risks, the St. Paul and Pacific was held to be the worst. Stephen was not able to raise a shilling.

In Montreal, on Stephen's return, four bitterly disappointed men met on Christmas Day, in no mood for Yuletide merriment. Stephen, however, had no intention of giving up. In that precise mind, an unconventional plan was taking shape which, if accepted, would be far better than the original. Stephen decided to take the negotiations into his own hands and deal directly with the Dutch committee's New York agent.

Early in January, Stephen met John S. Kennedy for the first time. Kennedy was yet another self-made Scot and the two swiftly became friends. Stephen's plan was as bold as it was simple. He offered to buy the bonds on credit, depositing a mere one hundred thousand dollars on account and paying the balance *after* foreclosure. The payment could be made either in cash or in the new bonds of the reorganized company. The Dutch were encouraged to accept the paper by the offer of a bonus of $250 in preferred stock for every thousand-dollar bond they took. The partners, in turn, agreed to finish the railway and put it into working order.

They were, in short, proposing to get control of eighteen million dollars' worth of bonds for a cash outlay of only one hundred thousand dollars. By this time the Dutch had worked themselves into a frame of mind to deal at any price. Under Kennedy's prodding they accepted. The purchase was concluded on February 24, 1878, and the partners took control of the railway on March 13.

One of the mysteries surrounding this remarkable transaction is the disposition of the extra one-fifth share. Did Stephen keep it for himself? If not, to whom did he give it? That it was not divided among the four partners seems clear from their subsequent court testimony, in which they appeared remarkably casual, unconcerned, and even evasive about a slice of stock that came to be worth many millions.

One man Stephen did *not* give the one-fifth interest to was Jesse P. Farley, the receiver in bankruptcy of one of the twin St. Paul companies and the general manager of both. Farley later sued Kittson, Hill, and the newly organized company, charging that in 1876, before the meeting with Stephen, both Kittson and Hill had promised him a one-fifth share in the enterprise in exchange for his help, co-operation, and special knowledge. It was clear that that help consisted in deceiving the courts, which had put him in charge of the property on Kennedy's advice. The circuit court judge who heard the case in 1882 tended to believe Farley. "The plaintiff," he said, "conceived a scheme to wreck the vast interests which it was his duty to protect"; but he threw the case out because "courts will not and ought not to be made the agencies whereby frauds are to be in any respect recognized or aided." Farley appealed, and this time the judge did not believe him. He said, with some sarcasm, that in his opinion Farley did not fail in his official duty "and although such conclusion carries an imputation upon his recollection or veracity as a witness, it sustains his integrity as an officer."

Farley persisted in the courts for a total of thirteen years. By the time the final judgement was read against him in the Supreme Court in 1893, he was dead and the matter was closed. From all this testimony several puzzling pieces of information emerge which do not quite fit together. It is reasonably clear that Farley *thought* he had a secret deal with Hill and Kittson. It is equally clear that Hill did not think so. It is also reasonably clear that Hill, Kittson, and Farley did a good deal of talking together about the railway and that at a time when Farley knew that Hill wanted to buy it, he, Farley, did his best to disparage the line to the Dutch representative.

There is also the puzzling question of Kennedy's role. Farley was Kennedy's man. At a time when the bondholders were in their final negotiations with Stephen – on Kennedy's advice – Kennedy was also writing to Farley, urging him to get in on a good thing.

Then who got the extra one-fifth? After the St. Paul line grew into the Great Northern it was revealed that John S. Kennedy held an enormous quantity of its stock. He, Hill, and Stephen all became close friends and when the CPR board was formed Kennedy was a director. When he died he left an estate estimated at between thirty and sixty million dollars, depending on the book value of the immense mass of railway stock he had acquired. Did Kennedy simply buy into the railway that he had urged his Dutch clients to sell so cheaply? Or was it he who was promised George Stephen's extra one-fifth during those delicate negotiations, which allowed the sale of eighteen millions in bonds for almost no cash at all?*

Certainly the Dutch seemed perfectly satisfied: most of them preferred to take bonds rather than cash – a wise decision as it turned out. It was true that they had sold the railway cheaply; it was also true that the line was worth eighteen million dollars only if and when it could be put into working order. If Hill and his associates had not come along, it is doubtful whether the bondholders would have realized anything on their original investment. As it developed, they were so pleased that they made a gift to Stephen of a valuable bowl commemorating a great victory in which a Dutch admiral, in 1666, burned the best of the British fleet. Years later, when Stephen was entertaining George V of England, that old sailor's eye caught sight of the trophy. The monarch was not amused at this symbol of naval humiliation.

"Why don't you destroy the damned thing?" His Majesty asked.

5

The partners had possession of the bonds but they were by no means out of the woods. A whole series of complicated problems now faced them, any one of which could wreck the enterprise.

---

*The Canadian historian O. D. Skelton, in his book *The Railway Builders* (Toronto, 1916), says that Stephen, Hill, Smith, and Kennedy each took one share and that Kittson took half a share, the remaining half share going to Angus after he left the service of the bank and became general manager of the railway. He gives no source for this statement, which does not square with the court testimony of the principals in 1888. Nonetheless it is a plausible suggestion: Kittson's energies were not really involved in the enterprise to the same extent as the others; Angus could probably be lured away from the bank only on the promise of a sizable interest; and Kennedy's subsequent involvement makes it clear that he was a substantial shareholder. It is reasonably certain that Kennedy was brought into the syndicate by Stephen at the time he convinced the Dutch committee to accept the offer.

First, more money had to be raised. The line owed $280,000 which must be paid immediately. Then there was the one-hundred-thousand-dollar deposit to the bondholders. The stock, if it could be purchased from Litchfield, would cost around half a million dollars. Finally, the railroad must be finished swiftly if the land grant was to be earned.

There was only one place to get this kind of financing – the Bank of Montreal. Stephen was president and Smith was a director, and they were now proposing to borrow money personally from an institution under their care. It did not look well; there would certainly be stockholders' questions and newspaper comment, but there was no help for it.

Stephen wrote to Hill that he and Kittson must pledge everything they owned in order to get a line of credit from the bank. He and Smith had already handed over "every transferable security of every kind we have got." It was all or nothing.

"The risks were very great," Hill later recalled, "and in case of failure so great as to entirely ruin the entire party – financially; wipe out every dollar we owned in the world and leave us with an enormous debt if the enterprise failed."

Stephen's next move was to go straight to Ottawa and negotiate with Mackenzie for a ten-year lease of the Pembina Branch so that the St. Paul road would have a connection to Winnipeg at the border. This, too, was fraught with uncertainty. Smith's name was already being mentioned as a major shareholder in the company and it was impossible for him in Parliament to maintain the fiction that he was disinterested.

Almost simultaneously a new problem arose. The Minnesota legislature passed a new law setting a series of deadlines for the construction of the railway. Two sections had to be completed by the end of the year, otherwise everything would be forfeited.

The partners were juggling several problems at once: they must lobby in Ottawa for the Canadian lease; they must raise funds to build the rest of the railway before the deadline; they must haggle with Litchfield for his stock; and finally, they must fight off the Northern Pacific, which was threatening to build its own line to the border. It seemed an impossible task. If either Litchfield or the rival railway knew how badly off they were, the game would be over. This was where Stephen's control of the bank became so valuable: there would be no leaks from that source.

But there was not a million dollars available for the additional railway construction to the border. The only solution was for the receiver, Farley, to get a court order permitting him to issue receiver's debentures. Thirty-five miles of railway had to be built by August, 1878, from Melrose to Sauk Centre, and another thirty-three by December (to Alexandria) in order to hold the land grant. Hill persuaded Farley to go to court, but the hearings were maddeningly slow. When the judge refused to issue the order, Hill himself went to see him. The judge was impressed by Hill but even as he signed the order, he had his doubts: he said candidly that if the associates failed to carry it out, it would destroy them and ruin him.

From this point on the financing of the railway was left to Stephen while Hill moved in to build the line. He had two months in which to lay track from Melrose to Sauk Centre and he had to find rails, ties, rolling stock, and labourers in a hurry. By the time all this was assembled, Hill realized that he would have to lay at least a mile of track a day to make the deadline. He took charge himself, fighting mosquitoes, sunstroke, rattlesnakes, and dysentery, firing bosses on the spot if they could not maintain the mileage. When one crew rebelled at Hill's methods and quit, he wired St. Paul for replacements, paying the fares in advance and hiring the toughest navvies he could find to prevent the new workers from skipping out before they reached the end of track.

Another crisis arose. The rejuvenated Northern Pacific was threatening to build a line to the Canadian border paralleling the St. Paul line. Hill was convinced his rivals were bluffing; it was his tactic to convince them that _he_ was not. Hill threatened to cancel the agreement by which the Northern Pacific used the St. Paul tracks and, in addition, raise the fees for running rights and boost the rent on the St. Paul terminal. More, he would start at once, he declared, to survey a line all the way to the Yellowstone River and would ask Congress for half of the land grant that had been promised the Northern Pacific as far west as the Rockies. In the face of this bluff – it could be nothing else – the rival railway knuckled under. Hill had won his first corporate dogfight.

He met his first construction deadline with just twenty-four hours to spare and secured the vital land grant. He did not slacken his pace, for he had to finish the second stretch before December 1, 1878. The enemy was no longer the dysentery and sunstroke of the summer but the bone-chilling cold of the Minnesota prairies. Hill walked the line himself, stopping here and there to counsel one or other of the navvies on the way to treat frostbite. At one point he leaped from his private car, seized a shovel, and began attacking the snow, spelling the workmen off while they went inside for a dipper of hot coffee. He made his deadline well ahead of time and kept going, for he wanted to get the full railway operating as swiftly as possible. On November 11, he had the satisfaction of seeing his first through locomotive arrive at Emerson, Manitoba, from St. Paul.

Stephen meanwhile was having his own problems. Mackenzie had given the St. Paul line running rights on the Pembina Branch. But the contractors still had legal possession of the line; their rates were so exorbitant that they amounted to an embargo on all through rail traffic from St. Paul. The new government used these difficulties as an excuse to make a new contract with Stephen. The St. Paul group could use the line only until the completion of the Canadian Pacific Railway.

Stephen's second problem was the recalcitrant Litchfield. As long as he held the stock he could hamper the foreclosure proceedings and prevent the reorganization of the railroad company. The partners launched a legal suit against Litchfield to recover money that had been furnished to complete the main line and that he had converted to his own use; but the financier remained stubborn. In mid-January Stephen personally went to New York and managed to secure all the stock for a half-million dollars. There could no longer be conflicts between stockholders and bondholders since they were one and the same.

The partners borrowed their half million from the Bank of Montreal and moved for foreclosure. It was granted in March, 1879. In May, they formed a new company, the St. Paul, Minneapolis and Manitoba Railroad Company. In June, the new firm bought the bankrupt railway for less than seven million dollars – not in cash but in receiver's debentures and bonds. They floated a sixteen-million-dollar bond issue at once, some of which was used to pay back the Dutch. Then they sold the greater part of the land grant for $13,068,887. Already they had realized an incredible profit.

Hill wanted to create fifteen million dollars' worth of stock.

"Aren't you afraid that the capitalization will startle the public?" Smith ventured. "Isn't there some danger that we will be charged with watering the stock?"

"Well," Hill replied, "we have let the whole lake in already."

Three years after the stock was issued, each partner had made on paper a clear capital gain of more than eight millions. At that point – 1882 – they issued another two million dollars' worth of stock to themselves and then, in 1883, they issued to themselves ten million dollars' worth of six per cent bonds for one million dollars – an additional profit of nine millions.

From the beginning, the railroad was fabulously successful. The grasshoppers vanished. The soil began to yield bumper crops. In 1880, the net earnings of the railroad exceeded the interest on the bonded debt by sixty per cent – an increase of one million dollars in a single year. The "Manitoba road," as it came to be called, formed the nucleus of Jim Hill's Great Northern, the only transcontinental line in the United States that never went bankrupt or passed a dividend. Within two years its four promoters went from the brink of disaster to a position of almost unlimited wealth.

They had also become controversial figures in Canada. The deal with the Bank of Montreal was looked at askance by press, public, and shareholders, who asked pointed questions about the propriety of directors appropriating bank funds for a private venture. The criticisms increased when R. B. Angus resigned as the bank's general manager to take a job as general manager of the new railway.

Meanwhile, Stephen and his colleagues were being attacked on another front. The new company, which operated the only trains from St. Paul to the Red River, had also taken over the Kittson Line and thus had a monopoly of all traffic to Winnipeg. That aroused the full ire of the Conservative press, to whom the name of Donald Smith was still a profanity. The Montreal *Gazette* called for the immediate construction of the Canadian Pacific to remove the "pernicious influence" of Smith and his associates. The Winnipeg *Times* was even more caustic. "The wily Jim Hill," it charged, "had to 'grease' other interests, legislative, judicial and private to the tune, it is said, of a million."

Such was the climate in which the CPR Syndicate was eventually formed. All the controversy served to illuminate one fact: there was now available a remarkable group of successful men who had experience in both railway building and high finance. In the summer of 1880, the Macdonald government was looking for just such a group. It was John Henry Pope, the blunt minister of agriculture, who had first drawn his prime minister's attention to the St. Paul associates.

"Catch them," he said, "before they invest their profits."

Chapter
Seven

THE
GREAT
DEBATE

1

From the moment that George Stephen's success became public property, he was transformed, whether he knew it or not, into a leading candidate to build the great railway. Long before Macdonald took power, Mackenzie had been seeking just such a man – a successful Canadian financier, in league with other Canadians of means, with practical experience in financing and constructing a profitable road. After Mackenzie's fall, Macdonald took up the vain search. Then, just when it seemed impossible to find such a man, an entire group of them suddenly popped out of nowhere, loaded with credentials.

In the fall of 1879, Macdonald, Tupper, and Tilley had set out for England to seek an Imperial guarantee to help build the road. It was all premature and over-optimistic. There was no Imperial guarantee; nor were any contractors willing to gamble on such a lunatic undertaking. One English financier laughed aloud when he first heard of Macdonald's plan to raise a loan to build a railway across the half-frozen continent. Years later he related to Donald Smith his impressions at the time: " 'Good Heavens,' I thought, 'somebody will have to hold these Canadians back, or they will go plunging themselves into hopeless bankruptcy before they come of age.' I felt I would as soon invest in a Yankee 'wild-cat' mine."

By 1880, George Walkem, back again in power in British Columbia, was bluntly threatening secession. It was clear that the Canadian government would have to finance the railway on its own and swiftly if it was to keep the nation whole. The contract for the Yale-Kamloops section had to be let hurriedly as a sop to the British Columbians, and by the spring of 1880, to everyone's relief, Andrew Onderdonk was on the spot preparing to blast his way through the canyons of the Fraser. In April, Blake made one of his interminable speeches – this one lasted more than the usual five hours – in which he demanded that all construction cease west of the Rockies. The Government, he declared, was risking the ruin of the country for the sake of twelve thousand people.

Blake's remarks had considerable effect. The Government, while placating British Columbia with the Onderdonk contracts, determined to move slowly on the prairies. Its plan was to build a cheap railway;

only two hundred miles would be placed under contract, and the construction would be as flimsy as possible. The steel would creep across the plains, year by year, a few miles ahead of advancing settlement. After the House rose, Macdonald told his dubious council that such a local railway was necessary to attract immigrants. He proposed a bonus of land to bring settlers and he spoke of going to England that summer to raise money for the project.

This was anticlimax after all the brave talk of a two-thousand-mile transcontinental line built to Union Pacific standards, and it did not sit well with Charles Tupper.

"Sir John," he said, "I think the time has come when we must take an advance step. I want to submit a proposition for building a through line from Nipissing in Ontario to the Pacific Coast."

Macdonald remained sceptical. He told Tupper that he was afraid it was "a very large order." Nevertheless he added, "I shall be pleased to consider anything you have to submit."

Tupper was more sanguine than his leader on the matter of the railway because he had learned of the incredible success of George Stephen and his colleagues, and in his memo of June 15 to the Privy Council he made reference to it. He recommended that "authority be given to negotiate with capitalists of undoubted means and who shall be required to give the most ample guarantee for the construction and operation of the line on such terms as will secure at the same time the rapid settlement of the public lands and the construction of the work."

There was no doubt about who the capitalists of undoubted means were. Tupper plainly had his eyes focused on the St. Paul Syndicate. But even as the Cabinet met to consider the terms it was prepared to offer – a twenty-million-dollar subsidy and thirty million acres of prairie land – it was obvious that the atmosphere was changing and that other capitalists were sending feelers to Ottawa. The depression was at an end; the harvest had been a bumper one; the climate for railway building suddenly seemed better. There was word that the principals behind Andrew Onderdonk were interested. So was Thomas Brassey's firm, in England. And up from New York came a British peer, Lord Dunmore, a front man for Puleston, Brown and Company, a British financial house.

There was another offer before the government that June. It came in the name of Duncan McIntyre, who was engaged in building the Canada Central Railway from Ottawa to Lake Nipissing. It was no secret that his principals were George Stephen and the other members of the St. Paul group. The arrangement was a marriage of convenience: McIntyre's line stopped where the CPR was to begin; the alliance could mean that the through route from Ottawa to the Pacific Ocean would be controlled by a single company.

The Stephen-McIntyre offer was a tempting one, especially as it was the only one that came from Canada, but it asked more than the Cabinet was prepared to grant: a subsidy of twenty-six and a half millions and a land grant of thirty-five million acres. The Syndicate would not bargain. The subject, McIntyre told Macdonald, was closed "for the present"; but the door was obviously being left ajar. On June 29, Macdonald was emboldened to announce that there were a number of capitalists bidding for the construction of the railway and that negotiations had reached the point where a deputation of ministers to England was indicated.

Macdonald, Tupper, and John Henry Pope sailed for England on July 10. The Prime Minister intended to see both Puleston, Brown and Company and Sir Henry Tyler, president of the Grand Trunk. As for McIntyre, he was sailing on the same ship and, as the mail steamer touched at Rimouski, a letter arrived for Macdonald from George Stephen, from his Gaspé fishing camp. It was an odd missive, diffident yet wistful, and it opened the door a little wider.

"I am aware," Stephen wrote, "it is often impossible for a Government to adopt the best course; and it is the knowledge of that fact that makes me rather hesitate to commit myself to the enormous responsibilities involved in this undertaking. You will have no difficulty, I feel sure, in finding men on the other side, more or less substantial and with greater courage – mainly because they know less of the difficulties to be encountered but also because they will adopt measures for their own protection which I could not avail myself of."

It was a clever letter, though Stephen may not have consciously intended it as such since he himself was of two minds regarding the project. Nevertheless, he managed very subtly to damn all other aspirants to the contract while obliquely selling his own group. He pointed out the difficulties of a large bonded indebtedness in which "the real responsibility is transferred from the Company to the people who may be induced to buy the bonds, while the Company or the projectors pocket a big profit at the start . . . ." He suggested that any English financial organization would indulge in this kind of manipulation at great risk to Canada: "It would indeed be a disastrous affair to all concerned, if the English public were induced to invest in a bond issue which the road could not carry . . . ."

His own plan, Stephen remarked, would have been to limit the borrowing to the smallest point. He would expect his profit to come from the growth of the country after the railroad was built. He had no intention of going to England; he would be outbid there. No English or American organization could do the job as well or as cheaply, yet they would want to pocket the profits in advance while Stephen was willing to take the risk and wait.

Then, once more, the soft sell: Stephen was satisfied that he and his group could construct the road without much trouble and if anybody could operate it successfully, they could. The line from Thunder Bay to Red River would be profitable and they would use the experience gained in Minnesota in the management and settling of the lands. The Canada Central to Ottawa and certain Quebec roads would, of course, have to be incorporated because the terminus must be at Montreal or Quebec City, not Lake Nipissing, far off in the wilds of northern Ontario.

It was a letter dictated from a position of strength and confidence, written when Stephen was salmon fishing with Angus. In it, Stephen played Macdonald like an angler. He had thrust the bait towards him: the Minnesota experience, the desire to take risks, the special knowledge of Canadian conditions, the unquestioned ability of his group to do the job. Then, in a final paragraph, he pulled back slightly but left the bait dangling: "Although I am off the notion of the thing now, should anything occur on the other side to induce you to think that taking all things into consideration, our proposal is better upon the whole for the country than any offer you get in England, I might, on hearing from you, renew it and possibly in doing so reduce the land grant to some extent...."

It was a hard letter for Macdonald to resist; moreover, the other candidates were dropping away. In August, the Onderdonk group passed: the Fraser Canyon was occupying all their efforts. In London, Macdonald and Tupper approached Sir Henry Tyler, the president of the Grand Trunk. Tupper reported his reaction: "If you'll cut off the portion of the railway from Thunder Bay to Nipissing I'll take up the project; but unless you do that, my shareholders will simply throw the prospectus into the wastepaper basket." There it was again: the terrible geography of North America conspiring against the efforts of the struggling nation to consolidate. Tupper replied that Canada could not consent to be for six months without any communication with Manitoba, the North West, and British Columbia except by a long detour through a foreign land. But the Grand Trunk's philosophy did not encompass a transcontinental nation; in the eyes of its absentee owners Canada was not much more than a way point on the route that led from the Atlantic to Chicago.

The offer from Puleston, Brown and Company, which was financially more attractive than Stephen's, also dissolved. That left Duncan

McIntyre, who was also in London. Macdonald and McIntyre began a series of discussions; Sir John Rose, who represented one of the smaller British financial houses, was present and George Stephen, in Canada, was at the end of the cable line. By September 4, the provisional agreement was made: twenty-five million dollars and twenty-five million acres it was to be. McIntyre returned to Canada at the end of the month and so did the Prime Minister, to whom Stephen immediately wrote. He had seen "the important document," he said, and he hoped there would be no difficulty in coming to terms on all points.

He and his colleagues had taken on a job that no one else in the United States, Britain, Europe, or Canada had been persuaded to tackle. It was a huge responsibility, and already in Montreal financial circles there were murmurings that this time the reckless Stephen had bitten off more than he could chew.

". . . my *friends* and my *enemies* agree," he wrote, "in affecting to think [that it] will be the ruin of us all."

And it almost was.

2

All during late summer and early fall the newspapers of Canada were alive with rumour and speculation. During August, the *Globe*, with glee, continued to report the failure of Macdonald's mission. On September 7, the Manitoba *Free Press* also reported failure. By mid-September word of actual negotiations began to leak out. The Montreal *Daily Witness* described the prospective deal as "utterly ruinous."

The English press was generally hostile. The all-Canadian route was universally condemned as useless. *The Times* referred to the Lake Superior section as "the pauper the rest of the family will have to support." The American press was scathing. The New York *Herald* referred to the mission as "abortive" and predicted that Macdonald would fail. For fifty years to come, the paper declared, it would be a sheer waste of capital to build the Canadian Pacific.

Yet in spite of the hostility there was enormous excitement when it was learned that Macdonald would be arriving at Hochelaga Station, Montreal, on the afternoon of September 27. The *Mail*'s correspondent wrote that never in a long experience had he "witnessed such intense anxiety to see a public man and hear what he has to say upon a great question of public interest." By late afternoon people of all classes were streaming towards the station. Almost every prominent Montrealer was present, no matter what his politics. A reception committee of some fifty leading Tories was waiting on the platform; packed behind it, pushing, craning, and buzzing with anticipation, was an immense throng.

The train was dead on time. Macdonald's special car was shunted to a siding and a few moments later a smiling prime minister appeared. Almost everybody remarked that he looked ten years younger. More important, success was written on his features.

Every neck strained forward as the Prime Minister prepared to speak. It was a brief, somewhat vague statement but it was what everyone wanted to hear. The Government, Macdonald indicated, had secured financing for the great railway. He could not spell out the details, for these must first be presented to the Governor General. From this short speech in Montreal and interviews with friendly reporters, no one could have divined that the railway was to be built by a predominantly Canadian group. Macdonald made a good deal of the German element in the Syndicate, which was actually very small. It was considered politically important, however, to get token money from Germany, which would, it was hoped, divert the tide of immigration to Canada. The Prime Minister mentioned no names but in an interview talked about "a Syndicate composed of eminent capitalists from Frankfurt, Paris, London, New York and Canada." Since McIntyre had returned home on the same boat, his connection with the new syndicate was generally accepted. The United States element was played down to a point where the Conservative Winnipeg *Times* even denied its existence. But Macdonald was able to reassure the cheering crowd at the station on several points: the new syndicate would finish the line in ten years, it would not build the easy portions first or save the hard ones for the last, and, finally, the road would not cost as much as Sir Hugh Allan had offered to build it for in 1872. Moreover, it would not cost the taxpayers a cent: the sale of western land would pay for it all.

Before he finished Macdonald could not resist a political gibe. The time would come, he said, when Canada would remember that it was the Conservative Party that had given the country its great railway.

"I shall not be present," said the Prime Minister. "I am an old man, but I shall perchance look down from the realms above upon a multitude of younger men – a prosperous, populous and thriving generation – a nation of Canadians who will see the completion of the road."

This sobering reminder of the Prime Minister's mortality produced a curious lull in the jollity. It was not easy to contemplate a Canada without Macdonald. Loved or hated, despised or revered, he had become a kind of permanent fixture with his silver-knobbed cane, his fur-collared coat, and his familiar Red River sash.

Almost as soon as the train puffed out of the station the great debate over the Syndicate, as it was now called, began. By October, the composition of the new group had leaked out even though the actual contract was not signed and the specific details had still to be worked out. The members were George Stephen and Duncan McIntyre of Montreal; John S. Kennedy of New York; James J. Hill and Richard B. Angus of St. Paul; Sir John Rose's old firm of Morton, Rose and Company, London; and the German-French financial syndicate of Kohn, Reinach and Company. There was one name conspicuous by its absence – that of Donald A. Smith. He was, of course, to be a major shareholder, but since his name was an obscenity to the entire Conservative Party there was no way in which he could be publicly connected with the enterprise.

It had been a bad year for Smith. Following his successful re-election to the constituency of Selkirk in 1878, a petition was filed charging that the seat had been secured through bribery. Behind this move was seen the fine hand of the Prime Minister himself, for Macdonald was still smarting from the parliamentary skirmish of the previous spring. The matter did not come to trial until after the House recessed in 1879 at which time Smith was confirmed in his seat. But a local journalist discovered that the judge who gave the decision had borrowed four thousand dollars from Smith and that a mortgage was registered on the jurist's property in Smith's name as security for the loan. The case was appealed to the Supreme Court, which thought a clear case of corruption had been made – not against Smith personally, but enough to void the election. Smith ran in a by-election in September, 1880, spending, as he later admitted, thirty thousand dollars. His connection with the St. Paul and Manitoba railway told against him and he was defeated. That marked his retirement from politics.

The result was scarcely known when Smith suffered a second blow to his ego: the knowledge that he could not be publicly associated with the greatest of all national enterprises. The Syndicate would take his money but it did not want to be saddled with his name. Nonetheless, his presence as a silent partner was assumed by both press and public and a great to-do resulted.

The usually imperturbably Smith dropped his mask briefly and gave Stephen a rare, private glimpse of his ambitions. "You will have heard of the trouble that Smith has given me . . . because I did not put his name into the contract," Stephen wrote to Macdonald. "I had to tell him that I omitted it to avoid discussion in the House but rather than he should be unhappy I would let him out of the business. He is excited almost to a craze and so troublesome that I do not care if he does withdraw though his money and co-operation would be useful, so would his knowledge and influence in the North West.'' Smith did not want to withdraw his money but he did want recognition, and so the fuss continued.

Stephen was equally exasperated with the French-German element which was in the Syndicate for two reasons only: first, to make a quick profit, and second, in the hope that further business from the Canadian government would be forthcoming. The French at the last moment threatened to back out unless they could get assurance either of a speedy profit or of Stephen's pledge to buy up their shares if the operation proved unprofitable. In the end, Stephen told the nervous French that he would build the railroad himself, with or without their help, and ''this confidence . . . did them good.'' After the contract was signed, Stephen himself went to Paris to stiffen the Frenchmen's resolve.

It was Stephen's first venture into the periphery of politics and the inability to deal swiftly and conclusively with matters he considered to be purely business had already begun to torment him. The wretched contract seemed to be taking weeks to complete, and after it was signed Parliament would have to consider it before any company could be formed and the actual work of construction could be begun. He began to fire off letters to Macdonald urging speed. There must be parliamentary sanction ''at the earliest possible day.'' The European signatories must rush to Ottawa and thence to Montreal to iron out all the differences as swiftly as possible. He was almost breathless with impatience, but nothing moved as swiftly as he hoped. He had expected to embark for London at the end of October to meet Tupper. He had to postpone his sailing date.

Among other things, the status of the Pembina Branch had to be ironed out. Stephen wanted a monopoly and in mid-October he made it clear that he was prepared to cancel the entire contract if he did not get it. The Pembina Branch would have to subsidize the lonely line that ran through the Precambrian desertland. Macdonald was reluctant: he saw the political disadvantages, yet he was caught between two unyielding points of view. He must have an all-Canadian railway; to get it he would have to give in to the importunate Stephen who feared ''strangulation in the hands of our Chicago rivals hanging over our heads.''

Stephen had never talked so toughly before and only Macdonald knew, perhaps, how hard a bargain he was driving. For this was the basis of the ''monopoly clause'' in the CPR contract, which would turn the West against the railway and against the East and lay the basis for almost a decade of bitterness before it was voluntarily revoked. The impotence of the Manitobans in the matter of building their own railway lines became, in that province, a *cause célèbre* which was to lead to a long-term disaffection towards Ottawa and towards the railway itself. Macdonald could see that clause returning to haunt him – returning to haunt the nation. But there was nothing he could do.

3

The contract was finally signed on October 21 and the battle lines were drawn for the greatest parliamentary struggle since the Pacific Scandal. The contract was the most important Canadian document since the British North America Act and one of the most important of all time, for it was the instrument by which the nation broke out of the prison of the St. Lawrence lowlands. It represented a continuation of the traditional partnership between the private and the public sectors, which would continue to be a fact of Canadian life whenever transportation and communication were involved. The geography of the nation dictated that the government be in the transportation business – either fully or in a kind of working partnership with private industry. The express and telegraph systems, the future transcontinental railways, the airlines and the pipelines, the broadcasting networks and communications satellites – all the devices by which the nation is stitched together are examples of this loose association between the political and business worlds. Like the original CPR they are not the products of any real social or political philosophy but simply pragmatic solutions to Canadian problems.

Apart from the all-important subsidies of twenty-five million dollars and twenty-five million acres of land, the chief provisions of the CPR contract, drawn up by the same J. J. C. Abbott who had once been Sir Hugh Allan's solicitor, were these:

The government would turn over to the company all the lines built with public money upon completion.

The government would waive duty on the import of all railway materials, from steel rails to telegraph cable.

The free land would be taken in alternate sections of 640 acres each from a strip forty-eight miles wide running along the route between Winnipeg and the Rockies, but the company could reject land "not fairly fit for settlement." It could issue up to twenty-five million dollars' worth of land grant bonds, secured against this acreage. It must deposit one-fifth of the bonds with the government as security, but it could if it wished sell the rest of the bonds, as the land was earned by construction, in the proportion of one dollar per acre.

The land would be exempt from taxation for a twenty-year period or until sold. Stations, grounds, workshops, buildings, yards, and the like would be exempt forever and the land for these would also be provided free.

For twenty years no other line could be constructed south of the CPR to run within fifteen miles of the United States border.

The company, in return, promised to complete the road within ten years and forever after to operate it "efficiently." That adverb was significant since it relieved the CPR of future responsibility for unprofitable aspects of its operations – passenger service, for example.

The Ottawa *Free Press* figured out that the Syndicate was being handed a gift amounting to a cash equivalent of $261,500,000. Stephen's private estimate was considerably lower, but he neglected to count such items as freedom from taxation, duty-free imports, and free land for company property. He figured the value of the 710 miles of completed government line at thirty-two millions and the cost of the work to be completed by the company at forty-five millions. The Syndicate had thirty millions in hand, including the cash subsidy, and could raise fifteen millions from its own resources. But this was a wildly optimistic piece of reckoning, as future events were to prove.

The press attacked on several fronts. Even such loyal western papers as the Winnipeg *Times* found it hard to stomach the monopoly clause, especially in the light of the experience with the Kittson Line's exorbitant rates. The eastern Opposition press hit hard at the monopoly clause and also the proposition regarding duty-free construction materials; after all, Macdonald's victory had been secured by the promise of increased protection. The great debate on the contract was not without its ironies: one was the spectacle of traditionally free-trade newspapers and politicians bitterly attacking the entry of construction material free of tariff. Nor did the press believe the Syndicate would actually commence building the Lake Superior section. But more than anything else, the papers harped upon the American influence in "the St. Paul Syndicate," as its opponents called it.

The editorials hit home to Macdonald. Almost ten years before he had boasted that he had resisted with every atom of his being the attempts by Americans to buy into the Allan railway syndicate. Now he appeared to be welcoming even more Americans (notably Jim Hill) with open arms. Two years ago he had publicly called Smith the greatest liar in the world. Now he had handed the former fur trader's closest friends – and Smith, too, by all accounts – an enormous slice of Canada. Two years before he had gone to the country with a policy of protecting local manufacturers. Now he had given the Syndicate a unique opportunity to buy on the open market.

These misgivings only reflected the doubts and, in some cases, the shock of Macdonald's own followers. Some said the contract would be the ruin of the country; the obligations were so great the credit of Canada would be destroyed. Others saw in the contract the ruin of the party; an alarmed nation would turn against the Tories. There were other murmurings. It was an American syndicate whose members were either Yankees or annexationists. It was a Montreal syndicate without a single name from Toronto or Ontario. The Manitoba members were angry about the monopoly clause. The Victoria members were disturbed because there was no mention of the Island railway. As the session opened the Ottawa *Free Press* predicted: "Sir John Macdonald cannot carry the Pacific Railway Bill. . . ."

Already some papers, seeing a new crisis in the making, were coining slogans like "the Pacific Swindle" and "the Pacific Disgrace." It was an indication that the great Canadian debate, which had been going on since 1871, was about to reach its immediate climax. Was the country prepared to stand behind this first great national undertaking? How much did the nation care whether it was united by these costly bands of steel? Was the price too high? Was the bargain a fair one? Could the country afford it? Was it just another piece of railway jobbery (as the Grits suspected) or a great nation-building device (as the Tories proclaimed)? Could the opponents of the great railway prolong the debate long enough to rally public opinion, as they had in 1873, and force the Government to climb down? Would Macdonald's own supporters stand behind him or would they again fall away like dying leaves? The battle lines were drawn. As the opening session approached, Macdonald, though ill once more, was reasonably confident of victory. But, unlike the impetuous and optimistic Stephen, he knew the fight would be long and consuming.

4

Macdonald had called the session two months in advance in order to dispose of the contract before the construction season began. That may have been why the opening, December 9, 1880, seemed a little short of the usual pomp. Lord Lorne arrived slightly early but Macdonald was not there to greet him; on doctor's orders he remained in the Commons, husbanding his strength for the ordeal to come.

In the Speech from the Throne, His Excellency explained the "extra session," as some were calling it: "No action can be taken by the contractors to prosecute the work, and no permanent arrangement for the organization of a systematic emigration from Europe to the North West Territories, can be satisfactorily made until the policy in Parliament with respect to the Railway has been decided."

The pageantry was ended; it was time for the politics to begin.

Macdonald was ill and so was Mackenzie, the latter an unhappy ghost in the bulky shadow of Edward Blake, who had, in effect, overthrown him as Liberal leader. Blake was outraged by the contract, which he considered a national scandal, and he meant to oust the Government on the strength of it, as he had seven years before. Across from him sat the bulldog figure of Tupper, eager for the contest.

Blake was convinced that he held in his hands a political issue as explosive as the Pacific Scandal. What he lacked in parliamentary power he felt he could make up in rising public wrath over such a massive giveaway to private capitalists. The ghost of the Scandal still hovered over the House. The Opposition press would open the old sores of 1873, whip up anti-American sentiment and link it to the present syndicate, while hinting at bribery, corruption, and shameless political handouts. The Opposition tactic was to talk forever, to speak at every stage of the debate, to propose amendments at all points, to divide the House at every opportunity, and to portray themselves as the saviours of the country. They would paper the nation with tracts, engulf it with oratory, rouse it with mass meetings, and expose Macdonald's attempt to ride rough-shod over Parliament with his steamroller majority. Blake believed that history would repeat itself, that he could force an election and carry the issue of the contract to the country. If that happened he had no doubt that he would win.

The majority belonged to Macdonald; could he keep them all in line? The task of maintaining party discipline would not be easy; and, Macdonald knew, the debate would be exhausting. Stephen, who was already convinced that what was good for the CPR was good for the country, naïvely supposed that the business would be disposed of by Christmas. Macdonald knew better. "Surely," Stephen wrote, "the Opposition will not be foolish enough to take a line to damage us in the country, too." But the Liberals' whole strategy was to save the country from Stephen.

The debate, which began in early December and ran until the end of January, was one of the longest in all the history of the Canadian parliament. During that period, more than one million words were uttered in the House of Commons on the subject of the Canadian Pacific Railway contract – more words by far than there are in both the Old and the New Testaments. Though the proceedings were not immune from personal invective, there was a very real sense of occasion. Tupper called it "the most important question that has ever engaged the attention of this Parliament" and speaker after speaker on both sides echoed these words. They realized, all of them, that once the contract was committed, the small, cramped Canada they knew could never again be the same. Some felt the nation would be beggared and ruined, others that it would blossom forth as a new entity. All understood that a turning point had been reached.

Meanwhile, the misgivings among Macdonald's followers had to be met head-on. This became Tupper's task. The party caucused in the railway committee room on Saturday, December 11. It was the first time the members had been able to examine the actual bill, and according to George Ross, they were all "shocked and overwhelmed at the enormous concessions made by the Government." Tupper let them talk, and they talked all day. Then, with a forceful speech he brought them round. His most telling argument was political: the construction of the railway would give the party such *éclat* throughout the nation that they would be rendered invincible in the next election. They gave him, finally, a unanimous vote of confidence.

Tupper put the resolutions regarding the subsidy and the land grant before the House on Tuesday, December 14, launching into an exhausting speech that lasted for almost six hours. He wound up passionately:

"If I have no other bequest to make to my children after me, the proudest legacy I would desire to leave was the record that I was able to take an active part in the promotion of this great measure by which, I believe, Canada will receive an impetus that will make it a great and powerful country at no distant date."

The following day was Blake's. His speech was almost as long as Tupper's – indeed, in that great debate any speech of less than two hours' duration would have been called short. It seemed much longer. Though the galleries had been full and the House, too, at the outset, there was a dwindling as Blake droned on and on. Macdonald's illness kept him out of the House. Mackenzie, whose own ailments would soon force him to his bed, seemed half asleep. It was an elaborate speech, designed to show that the contract would "prove disastrous to the future of this country" – but it was a little *too* elaborate.

In his speech Blake had hinted darkly at corruption. When Richard Cartwright rose, he brought the hint out into the open, twisting Tupper's closing remarks in such a way as to cause a verbal Donnybrook. Of Tupper he said: "If I understand him aright, the fact of his being a permanent party in conducting this negotiation would enable him to leave a substantial legacy to his children."

Tupper leaped to his feet; he had, he cried, insinuated nothing of the kind. Cartwright retracted his remark: if it was only a legacy of fame and not a substantial legacy, he was sorry for his mistake and also for the children, he said.

Cartwright's speech did not advance his party's cause. The Montreal

Daily Witness, a Grit paper, found it "objectionable in tone as well as in subject matter." The Commons settled down after that and the speeches were more moderate.

By December 21, the Opposition was itching for a Christmas recess. It needed as much time as possible to take the case to the people through public meetings and massive petitions. But Macdonald did not intend to give them any more time than necessary. The House did not adjourn until December 23. It was due to resume on January 5. That left Blake with less than two weeks in which to rouse the nation.

The Conservatives caucused again as the House adjourned. Macdonald's following had grown alarmingly shaky. A new attempt was made to persuade the Prime Minister to modify the contract terms. Resolutions were read from the Manitoba Tories and the Manitoba legislature urging that the monopoly clause be changed. Macdonald knew how impossible that was. Several prominent members rose to press for the abandonment of the promised tax exemption on railway materials while others pooh-poohed the idea of building the railway through the rock of Superior. The Quebec contingent offered to vote for the contract if the Dominion government promised to purchase the province-owned white elephant, the Q.M.O. & O. Railway along the north shore of the St. Lawrence, presumably at an inflated figure. Again it was Tupper who, in a three-hour speech to the dissenters, held them, for the moment, in line.

Meanwhile, the Opposition was in full cry across the country. Blake's speech was printed as a pamphlet and the Liberals were smothering the nation with it. The Conservatives replied with a similar blizzard of tracts reprinting Tupper's speech. Christmas or not, every Liberal member was under orders to call a series of public meetings, to attack the Syndicate and the contract, and to force through a series of resolutions to be forwarded to Ottawa. Petitions were to be circulated on the same theme so that hundreds of thousands of signatures would fall like a storm upon the capital.

The meetings were lengthy, well attended, and often full of surprises. In East York, one meeting was convened at two in the afternoon and continued until nine. The Liberal chairman tried to break it up for supper but the farmers insisted on hearing both sides of the question and agreed to forgo their evening meal to continue the discussion. The Liberal orators retired anyway, whereupon the farmers voted another man into the chair, a move that brought the Grits scurrying back, their suppers untasted.

The speaker most in demand was Edward Blake. Tupper offered to attend Blake's meetings if Blake would grant him half the time for speaking, an offer which Blake declined. Tupper then detailed a man to attend every Blake meeting to announce that he, Tupper, would reply to Blake, point by point, the following night, and the dramatic spectacle occurred of Blake flying from city to city, in one politician's words, "pursued by the Honourable Minister of Railways as though he were an avenging fury."

It made for exciting holiday fare in an era devoid of electronic entertainment and both Blake's and Tupper's meetings were jammed. After the Grit leader's speech, the usual resolution was offered demanding that the matter of the contract be decided at the polls. At one meeting, the chairman was about to put the question when two Tories sprang up and proposed an amendment, which stated that, as Tupper was scheduled to follow Blake in the same hall, the whole question ought to be held over until both sides had been heard. The chairman tried to put the resolution, the crowd called for the amendment, and an "indescribable uproar" followed, with the chairman ruling the resolution carried. Tupper's meeting followed to scenes of similar anarchy. Tupper felt, however, that he had carried the day.

It was becoming apparent that the great wave of public disapproval that Blake had expected was largely non-existent. Though there were many misgivings, the people manifestly wanted the railway question settled. They had been hearing about the railway for almost a decade. In 1871 it had been a new and frightening idea. Ten years later they had come to accept it as a probability.

Nor were they put off by the cries of scandal. If there was scandal, the people wanted proof, and there was no proof. The Syndicate might be controversial but anyone could see that it was possessed of the kind of boldness that, after a decade of vacillation, could only be refreshing. In vain the *Globe* called for the people to rise up and smother Ottawa with their signatures; the *Globe* had cried wolf too often. A total of 266 petitions arrived at Ottawa, of which 256 came from Ontario. They contained 29,913 signatures, scarcely the avalanche that Blake and his followers had envisioned. Moreover, a suspicious number seemed to be in the same handwriting and one signature, at least, in Sir Richard Cartwright's riding, belonged to a corpse. "Generally speaking," the *Bystander* reported, "the attempts of the Opposition leader to fire the heart of the people were not very successful. . . ."

But Blake and Cartwright had no intention of giving up. They had almost a month left to fight and one more major card to play.

5

Early in January, as the session began, there was a kind of insistent buzzing that something big was being planned: the Syndicate, the contract, and the Government were about to be challenged in a dramatic fashion. On Friday, January 7, Macdonald, over Opposition protests, ruled that the contract debate would have precedence over everything except routine proceedings: "I believe that the settlement of the North West will be greatly retarded by delay...." But the delays continued. That day the House sat until after midnight, but such was the duration of the speeches that only five members were accommodated. On Monday the House sat until three-thirty the following morning, yet there were only four speeches that day. George Ross's took four and three-quarters hours. Years later he admitted in his memoirs that he had spoken at "unpardonable length."

Macdonald had a reasonably clear idea of what his adversaries were planning, but he was more concerned with the troubles he faced from his own supporters. From Halifax came word that several leading Tories were expressing doubts about the Government's policy. The Premier of Quebec was in town trying to sell the votes of his federal followers in exchange for a fancy price for the Quebec-owned railway. Macdonald had to put him off with evasions. The Manitoba members intimated that they could not support the bill unless it were modified; Macdonald did not yield. He was sixty-seven years old and very ill; the Opposition papers were slyly insinuating that he was drunk again; some of his friends feared that he had cancer. But ill or not, he intended to stand firm. There would be no compromise. When the vote came he meant to regard it as a vote of confidence. Let his supporters betray him at their peril! If the bill failed to pass, he intended to resign.

On the night of January 11, when the resolution was finally taken out of committee, the Government whips were busy and at 1:30 a.m. Macdonald's supporters trooped in, filling all the ministerial benches. The Opposition, so the *Mail* reported, was startled by this "sudden display of spontaneous force."

The following day the ailing Mackenzie, absent from his seat for all of that session, made his first speech as the bill was read for the first time. He referred to "public reports that eminent men on both sides of politics are, at this moment, preparing offers to the Government of a much more favourable character than those that are now before it." This was the Opposition's final tactic – to mount a rival syndicate, which would offer the Government a much better proposition divested of all the objectionable clauses in the original contract and at a cheaper price. On the face of it the gambit was irresistible.

Even as Mackenzie spoke, the new syndicate was meeting in Toronto to draw up a tender to be sent post-haste to Ottawa. The chairman and president was Sir William Howland, a former lieutenant-governor of Ontario and a prominent Liberal. The new syndicate was prepared to ask for only twenty-two million acres of land and twenty-two million dollars in cash. They rejected the monopoly clause and wanted no exemptions from the tariff on railway material. Nor would they ask for exemptions from taxation on either land or railway property. On the matter of the construction of the line, they were equally obliging. They would be willing to postpone the building of both the Lake Superior and the mountain sections and would cheerfully release the government from the liability of building the difficult Fraser River section. They would also be willing to construct a line to Sault Ste Marie to connect with the U.S. railhead in return for a bonus of twelve thousand dollars a mile.

Such was the Opposition's ploy – to paint the new syndicate as totally non-partisan and totally businesslike, and to convince the country that all the objectionable clauses in the contract were unnecessary.

Macdonald, weak though he was, knew what he must do. The talk about the new syndicate was having its effect. It had raised the morale of the Opposition and it had caused new murmurings among his own followers in both House and Senate. Until now he had taken only a minor part in the debate, leaving the infighting to Tupper. He saw that he must kill the new syndicate – slay it so thoroughly that no man would ever dare to mention it again. He must lay bare its weaknesses, expose the dangers that it posed to the country, and then assassinate it with ridicule.

He rose on Monday, January 17, as soon as Tupper laid the new tender before the House. Blake, he knew, would follow the next day, with one of those earnest, perfectly constructed and brilliantly contrived orations for which he was so well known and for which he was preparing himself with his usual meticulous labour. There was a strange feeling of repertory about it all: the same chamber and the same adversaries of 1873, the same charges of scandal, corruption, and dictatorship, the same feeling of age and infirmity (though not from drink this time), and the same subject – the railway. In a sense he was back where he had started, fighting on his feet for the contract as he had fought eight years before. But it was not quite the same; this time Macdonald had no apologies to make.

He had to be helped to his feet, but his words carried all the force of a pile driver: the road *would* be constructed. "Notwithstanding all the wiles of the Opposition and the flimsy arrangement which it has concocted, the road is going to be built and proceeded with vigorously, continuously, systematically and successfully" – the adverbs fell like hammer blows – "until completion and the fate of Canada will then, as a Dominion, be sealed."

Now the time had come for him to scupper that "flimsy arrangement," the new proposal: "I may say it is too thin. It won't catch the blindest. It won't catch the most unsuspicious. No one of common sense, no man who can say two and two make four, will be caught for one moment. . . . It was concocted here. It was concocted in Ottawa. It was concocted as a political engine. . . ."

Seven of the signatories to the document, Macdonald pointed out, were disappointed or defeated Liberal candidates in former elections. "No man, be he ever so simple, who is fit to be elected, can read else on these papers than that it is a political trick . . . ."

He had to pause for a moment. "I am speaking at some disadvantage," he said, "because I am not well. But I will make myself heard."

He gathered his strength and continued. The joker in the pack was the optional clause in the proposed contract which suggested that the new syndicate had no real intention of building anything but the easiest section of the railroad. The first clause, Macdonald showed, did away with the Superior section, the second provided for a rail line to Sault Ste Marie and the United States, the third provided for the government to abandon the British Columbia section, and the fourth gave up building anything west of the Rockies. The scheme, then, was nothing more than "an impudent offer to build the prairie section and to do it by means of political friends." Connecting with the Yankee railways at the Sault would be "to the utter ruin of the great policy under which the Dominion of Canada has been created, the utter ruin of our hopes of being a great nation . . . .

"They would be relieved from running any portion of the road that would not pay. Canada might whistle for these connections . . . but the people would . . . see that the colonies would gradually be severed from each other; and we should become a bundle of sticks, as we were before, without a binding cord, and then we should fall, helpless, powerless and aimless, into the hands of the neighbouring republic."

He fought next for the monopoly clause; and here all his passionate distrust of the American colossus came to the fore. The Rhine, he said, had a miserable, wretched end, "being lost in the sands of the approaches to the sea; and such would be the fate of the Canadian Pacific Railway if we allowed it to be bled by subsidiary lines, feeding foreign wealth and increasing foreign revenue by carrying off our trade until, before we arrived at the terminal points of Ontario and of Montreal, it would be so depleted that it would almost die of inanition."

What chances, Macdonald asked, would an infant country of four million have against the whole of the United States' capitalists? "The road would become shrunken, shrunken, shrunken, until it fell an easy prey to this ring. We cannot afford to run such a risk."

He was almost finished, but he wanted to nail down in the clearest possible language his vision of the railway and his vision of the nation. He wanted, he said, an arrangement "which will satisfy all the loyal, legitimate aspirations, which will give us a great and united, a rich and improving, developing Canada, instead of making us tributary to American bondage, to American tolls, to American freights, to all the little tricks and big tricks that American railways are addicted to for the purpose of destroying our road."

He had spoken for two hours and a half and he had made his point. The *Canadian Illustrated News,* which was less partisan than the daily press, reported that his criticism of the new syndicate "was so searching that he practically killed it, even in the eyes of the Opposition members themselves."

The following day the Commons got down to business again. Blake had been waiting for this moment. He had not been at ease during the debate. The Government speakers, knowing his uncommon sensitivity, had baited him continually. When thus attacked he found himself unable to stare his opponents down but instead would pick up a book and pretend to read. Macdonald had challenged him the previous day, asking him to get on his feet and say that he could approve, on the basis of his past declarations, some of the essential features of the new tender. He could not rise to that challenge but now, on this afternoon of January 18, he was prepared to deliver another five-hour speech, crammed with facts and figures to prove why the contract was a disaster and why, indeed, the whole concept of the Canadian Pacific Railway was, as in his view it had always been, insane.

The arguments, by this time, were familiar; they had not changed greatly since 1871; nevertheless, they were often telling. Blake, for instance, made a hash of Macdonald's figures, which had been changing from year to year, showing the sums which the Government expected to receive from the sales of raw prairie land. Indeed, on almost every point Blake was convincing. The idea of the railway *was* insane, if you thought in terms of an undivided continent; it *was* perfect madness to try to punch it through that sea of mountains and across those rocky Precambrian wastes. Immigration would not come as swiftly as the Government implied, and events were to prove

Blake right on that point. The land sales would not pay for the railway. It would be easier and cheaper for everybody to go west by way of the United States, at least in the foreseeable future. Logic, then, was on Blake's side.

The key to Macdonald's argument was emotion: the only way Canada could hold onto British Columbia – and, thus, the land in between – was to build the railway; that was the point he continued to hammer home. British Columbia would not wait, or at least that was what the British Columbians were saying. Meanwhile, the reorganized Northern Pacific was creeping west again; with no parallel line on the other side of the border, this great artery would drain off all the commerce of British North America.

Blake's speech was a model of logical argument. On a previous memorable occasion he had used earnestness accompanied by pitiless fact to bring Macdonald down. In this contest between logic and passion, would logic win again? Blake, the nineteenth-century liberal, was properly suspicious of the "big interests," critical of business speculation, and committed, philosophically at least, to the one-world concept of free trade. But the climate of the times was not conducive to this kind of idealism, especially in Canada where free trade could mean economic strangulation. Macdonald, the pragmatic politician and hard-nosed Conservative, was in tune with his era – an era which saw the commercial interests working hand in glove with the politicians to develop, exploit, or consolidate the nation (one could use all those verbs) for personal profit, political power, and (sometimes incidentally) the national interest. Given the political morality of the day and the prevailing public attitude, this traditional Conservative partnership with business was probably the only way in which the nation could be constructed in a hurry. To Blake, with his literal, legal mind, Macdonald was all bombast and humbug. He himself never stooped to the kind of witty sallies, gossipy small talk, or passionate declarations that were among the Prime Minister's trademarks. Macdonald, though a cynic, was also an optimist and a gambler. Blake, though an idealist, was a pessimist by temperament as well as by conviction. He could see the pitfalls in Macdonald's program – and they were real enough. He himself understood the value of a dollar: he had vowed to make one hundred thousand dollars so that he would have personal and moral security before entering the political lists. The wild extravagance of the railway appalled him. But Macdonald had thrown aside all personal security and bankrupted himself in order to enter and remain in politics.

Blake, the man of ideals, had a strong political philosophy and little imagination. Macdonald, the practical politician, whose only real philosophy was expediency, was endowed with a lively imagination. That, really, was where Blake foundered in the matter of the railway. He could not see the new Canada as Macdonald could see it; nor would he ever see it. Canada in the seventies was an imaginative dream more than a nation. Blake lacked both the imagination and the daring (he thought of it as recklessness) to lead in the development of that dream. If Macdonald's political gamble had failed, then Blake might have been hailed as a Cassandra and have gone on to become the leader of his country – the very epitome of a sober, sensible, frugal Canadian prime minister. But that was not to be.

6

The exhausting drama was drawing to its close but it was not quite over. It was not until January 25 that word spread that Parliament was to see the end of the longest debate in history. Macdonald meant to force a vote even if he had to keep the House in session all night.

Finally, in the small hours of the morning, the time came for a division on the first amendment to the resolution, offered by the Opposition leader. The amendment was typical of Blake, being the longest ever offered in Parliament to that moment. It covered three and a half pages of Hansard's small type and raised fifty-three distinct objections to the proposed legislation.

This was the moment of truth. Macdonald had told his wavering supporters in the bluntest terms that if the bill was lost the Government would resign immediately and they would be forced to go to the country with all the opprobrium of a parliamentary defeat hanging over them. The threat was enough: the first amendment was defeated by a vote of 140 to 54. The House adjourned that morning just before six.

It was not yet over. The Opposition had twenty-three more amendments and it proposed to move them all. The galleries were thin the following day; all the old habitués were asleep. The House reconvened at three and sat until eleven that night. Five more amendments were defeated.

The long nights and the gruelling verbal skirmishes were taking their toll. Macdonald, Mackenzie, Tupper, and Pope were all seriously ill. Amor de Cosmos was ill. Keeler of Northumberland East was ill. Bannerman of South Renfrew was ill. Others, the press reported, were breaking down under the strain. And still Macdonald drove them on. Illness of some sort seemed to be a permanent condition of the political leaders of the day; Macdonald's letters and those of his cabinet colleagues are full of earnest inquiries about each other's health, reports of doctors' advice, and descriptions of their own symptoms. On Government leaders, such as Macdonald, the work load was crushing. One could not pick up a telephone to transact a piece of business with dispatch. A rudimentary typewriter had been invented but it was rarely used. Though Macdonald had a secretary, he wrote almost all of his vast personal correspondence himself – thousands and thousands of letters in a lazy, angular hand. The wonder was not that he was ill; the wonder was that he was alive. The secret lay in his ability to relax totally after a harrowing parliamentary session – to push the fevered events of the day out of his mind. One of his methods was to devour cheap yellowbacks, novels of blood-curdling horror that were the popular mass reading of the day.

Now, ill and exhausted, he was nevertheless determined that, though there be a thousand amendments, the first reading of the bill should be voted on before the next day's sitting ended.

He kept his word. The House sat from three until six, recessed for dinner, and then remained in session for twelve hours without a break while amendment after amendment was offered and voted down. A kind of gay lunacy settled over the House of Commons. The bitterness drained away, and as each amendment was offered it was greeted with cheers by both sides. The speeches were mercifully short but even these were interrupted by whistles and desk-pounding. Paper pellets were flung about and caps placed over the heads of slumbering members. As night gave way to morning, a choir was organized and the members began plaintively to sing "Home, Sweet Home." Josiah Burr Plumb, known as the poet laureate of the Tory party, led one group in singing "When John A. Comes Marching Home." Dr. Pierre Fortin, from the Gaspé, led the French members in the traditional voyageur song, *"En Roulant, Ma Boule, Roulant."* The dapper James Domville, from King's, New Brunswick, arrived at six a.m. after an all-night dinner party and commenced what the *Globe* referred to delicately as "most unseemly interruptions."

There were other diversions. While one French Canadian was speaking, a dummy telegram was thrust into his hand; he asked the indulgence of the House to pause and read the contents, which were unprintable. Auguste-Charles-Philippe-Robert Landry, a young gentleman farmer from Montmagny, devised an original jape. He had his hair and moustache powdered iron-grey and then donned an old pair of green goggles, turned up his coat collar, and took his seat. The deputy sergeant-at-arms tried to throw him out; Landry refused to go. When the votes were being recorded on the latest amendment, the strange figure, gesturing ludicrously, stood up to be counted amid cheers and laughter. The clerk did not recognize Landry, hesitated and blushed, then looked again and again until at length he pierced the disguise.

190

Finally, the last amendment was voted down and the main divisions on the two resolutions – the first on the land and the second on the cash subsidy – were carried. In Tupper's absence, Macdonald introduced the bill founded on these resolutions respecting the Canadian Pacific Railway. Not until it was read for the first time did he allow the weary House to adjourn. By then it was eight in the morning.

There were two more readings to go through before the bill could become law. The first of these was a clause by clause consideration of the full text and this was bound to take time. Even the Governor General's fancy-dress ice carnival on January 31 could not lure Macdonald from his duties in the House. At 12:30 that night, while Lord Lorne and his costumed guests were skating under the glare of two locomotive headlights beneath flag-draped arches, festoons of evergreens, and Chinese lanterns – "an overhanging panorama of grotesque and fanciful figures" – the bill passed its second reading.

The following day, February 1, just before midnight, the bill was given its final reading. The formality of Senate assent was still needed, but it was now as good as law and the Canadian Pacific Railway Company was a reality.

Finally, it was over. It had been ten years, almost to the month, since the subject of a railway to the Pacific had first been broached to the House of Commons. For all concerned it had been a desperate, frustrating, and often humiliating decade; yet it had also been exhilarating. Macdonald was ill with fatigue, stomach trouble, and nervous tension, but he was triumphant. The railway, which had hurled him into the abyss of despond, had now hoisted him to the pinnacle of victory. It had consumed many of the men who were closely allied with it. Mackenzie was a political has-been. Blake was in retreat. Sir Hugh Allan had never lived down the events of the Pacific Scandal. Fleming had been driven back to England. Moberly had quit his profession. Marcus Smith hung grimly on but in a minor post. Joseph Whitehead was out of business. In every instance, the railway had changed and twisted their futures.

Far out beyond the Red River, the prairie land lay desolate under its blanket of shifting snow, still bereft of settlers. In just twelve months, as Macdonald knew, all that must change. Before the present parliament was dissolved, cities yet unnamed would have their birth out on those windswept plains, passes yet uncharted would ring to the sound of axe and sledge. Within one year an army of twelve thousand men would be marshalled to invade the North West. Other armies would follow: ten thousand along the Fraser, twelve thousand attacking the mountain crevices, fifteen thousand blackening the face of the Shield. Nothing would ever be the same again. The tight little Canada of Confederation was already obsolete; the new Canada of the railway was about to be born. There was not a single man, woman, or child in the nation who would not in some way be affected, often drastically, by the tortured decision made in Ottawa that night.

The future would not be easy and all the cries of dismay that had echoed down the corridors of the seventies would return to haunt the eighties. The granite shield of Canada had to be cracked open to let the railway through. The mountain barrier must be breasted and broken. There would be grief aplenty in the years to come – frustration, pain, hard decisions and, as always, bitter opposition.

But the great adventure was launched. Tomorrow would take care of itself, as it always did. At last the dream was about to become a reality. The triumph lay just a few short years ahead.

THE
LAST
SPIKE

Chapter
One

THE
SYNDICATE
TAKES
OVER

1

The Canadian Pacific Railway Company was officially launched on a crisp winter afternoon in an office near Dominion Square in Montreal. That date – February 17, 1881 – marked a change in the fortunes and the future of the Canadian frontier. For the next half-century, this single corporation would be the dominant force west of Ottawa. Already its initials, CPR, had entered the national lexicon; soon they would be as familiar to most Canadians as their own. In the decades to follow they would come to symbolize many things to many people – repression, monopoly, daring, exploitation, imagination, government subsidy, high finance, patriotism, paternalism, and even life itself. There were few Canadians who were not in some manner affected by the presence of the Canadian Pacific; indeed, no other private company, with the single exception of the Hudson's Bay, has had such an influence on the destinies of the nation. Nor has any other come so close to ruin and survived.

When the great debate came to an end, Ottawa settled into a kind of doldrums. The glittering social season burned itself out, the session limped to its close, and the capital reverted to the status of a backwoods lumber village. When Lord Lorne arrived to prorogue Parliament on March 21, there was scarcely anybody left in the House.

The rigours of the debate had wrecked the health of John A. Macdonald, Charles Tupper, and John Henry Pope. The Prime Minister seemed to be desperately – perhaps fatally – ill. A few days before the session ended, he broke down completely: his pulse dropped to forty-nine and he was in an agony from bowel cramps. He was dispatched to England in May with the unspoken fear that he was suffering from terminal cancer, and it was generally assumed that he would shortly resign. As for Tupper's condition, it was described by the press in February as "critical," while Pope, in Tupper's words, was "in a sad condition which promises little for the future."

Remarkably, all three recovered. Tupper's doctor told him that he had been "strained but not sprung." His condition was diagnosed in August as "catarrh of the liver" and Macdonald's not as cancer but as "catarrh of the stomach," phrases that doctors used when they could not explain an illness. "Sir John still suffers from languor and a sense of prostration," the Ottawa *Free Press* reported from London that summer. Obviously, the problem was exhaustion from overwork.

In contrast to the lassitude of the capital, Winnipeg, a thousand miles to the northwest, was in a turmoil. Within a fortnight, the CPR had established a headquarters there. Fourteen new locomotives were on their way – all samples from various makers in the United States, sent up on trial for the company's inspection. Contracts had already been let for half a million railroad ties, six thousand telegraph poles, and fifty thousand feet of pilings. Mountains of timber were heaped in the yards waiting to be moved to the end of track. The great triple-decker construction cars were rolling westward and workmen were pouring into town by the hundreds from Montreal and Minneapolis. Five hundred teams of horses had already been hired to move construction supplies. A trickle of new settlers was already seeping westward.

There were other signs of the swiftly changing character of the old North West. The Ogilvie Milling Company had abandoned millstones and introduced steel rollers to cope with the hard northern wheat. The Manitoba Electric and Gas Light Company was planning to light the entire city by gas. There was talk of a street railway to run the whole length of Main. And the Red River cart was all but obsolete; ingenious Winnipeg wheelwrights were working on new wagons with iron axles and iron tires to compete with the railway.

The railway builders estimated that they had close to two thousand miles of trunk-line to construct.* It could be divided into three sections:

In the East, some six hundred and fifty miles between Callander on Lake Nipissing and Fort William at the head of Lake Superior, all heavy construction across the ridges of the Precambrian Shield.

On the prairies, some nine hundred miles from Winnipeg across the rolling grasslands to the Rocky Mountains.

In the West, some four hundred and fifty miles of difficult mountain construction.

In addition, the railway company was to be given, as a gift, some seven hundred miles of line being built as a public work: the sixty-five-mile Pembina Branch from Winnipeg to the Minnesota border, already completed; the line between Fort William and Selkirk – 433 miles long – still under construction; and the 215-mile stretch that led from Savona's Ferry on Kamloops Lake through the Fraser Canyon to Port Moody on Pacific tidewater.

---

*After the line was shortened, the figure was eighteen hundred miles.

Construction would proceed in four stages:

First, the surveyors would locate the actual line, laying out the curves and gradients and driving stakes along the centre line as a guide to navvies who followed.

Next, the road would be graded, ready to lay steel. This was the most important operation of all. A swath sixty-six feet wide would be chopped out of bushland and forest. Tunnels would be drilled through mountain barriers and galleries notched into the sides of cliffs. Bridges of various designs would be flung across coulees and river valleys. Cuts would be blasted out of rock and the broken debris thus obtained would be "borrowed" to fill in the intervening gorges and declines so that the grade might be as level as possible. Swamps and lakes would be diked or drained. On the plains, huge blades drawn by horses would scrape the sod into a ditched embankment four feet high and nine hundred miles long so that the trains could ride high above the winter snowdrifts.

The third operation was to lay the steel. Ties or "sleepers" would be placed at right angles across the grade at exact distances. Parallel rails would be laid on top of them and spiked to the ties. Fishplates would connect one rail to the next.

Finally, the line would be "ballasted" – the space between the ties filled with crushed gravel so that the line would not shift when the trains roared over it.

In addition, all the varied paraphernalia of an operating line – stations, sidings, water towers, turntables – would have to be installed before the railway could be said to be complete. Later on, branch lines to serve neighbouring communities would connect with the main trunk so that the railroad would resemble an intricate tree more than twenty-five hundred miles long, coiling through all of western Canada.

Almost twenty years before, Sandford Fleming had reckoned that such a trunk-line would cost about one hundred million dollars. That rough estimate was probably in the minds of the men who contracted to build the railway. In addition to its twenty-five-million-dollar subsidy, the Syndicate hoped to turn the land grant into an additional twenty-five million by mortgaging it, at the rate of a dollar an acre, through the issuance of "land grant bonds." Unlike other North American railway companies, the CPR shunned the idea of bonded indebtedness and heavy stock promotions. It expected – naïvely, as it developed – to build the railway with the subsidy, the proceeds of the land sales, the operating profits, and a minimum of borrowing. Its first stock issue was only fifty thousand shares at a par value of a hundred dollars a share.

The hustle in Winnipeg, that spring of 1881, was in sharp contrast to the vacillations of the previous year. Though the government had let contracts for two hundred miles beginning in 1879, only about seventy miles had actually been laid, to Portage la Prairie. This section of the line, which the CPR purchased from the government, was virtually useless; the company determined to rebuild it entirely and relocate most of it. A different mood had settled upon railway construction in Canada. For the first time in the long, tangled history of the Canadian Pacific, the rails were being laid under the supervision of the same men who would eventually operate the road; it would not profit them to cut corners.

On May 2, 1881, the company was ready to begin. At the end of track, the little community of Portage la Prairie clattered with activity. Strange men poured off the incoming coaches and elbowed each other in the mire of the streets, picking their way between the invading teams of snorting horses. Great heaps of construction materials transformed the railway yards into labyrinths. An army of ploughs and scrapers stood ready to rip into the unbroken prairie. Like soldiers poised on the start line, the navvies waited until the company's chief engineer, General Thomas Lafayette Rosser, ceremonially turned the first sod. Then the horses, the men, and the machines moved forward and began to fashion the great brown serpent that would creep steadily west, day after day, towards its rendezvous with the mountains.

2

Canada is deceptively vast. The map shows it as the second largest country in the world and probably the greatest in depth. Yet for practical purposes Canada is almost as slender as Chile; traditionally, ninety per cent of its people have lived within two hundred miles of the United States border. It is a country shaped like a river – or a railway – and for the best of reasons: in the eastern half of the nation, the horizontal hiving of the population is due to the presence of the St. Lawrence, in the western half to that "sublime audacity," the Canadian Pacific.

The CPR was the natural extension of the traditional route used by the fur traders on their passage to the West. If that natural extension had been continued as was originally planned through the Fertile Belt, Canada might today have a different dimension. But that was not to be. In the spring of 1881 a handful of men in St. Paul, Minnesota, altered the shape and condition of the North West. Their decision affected the lives of tens of thousands of Canadians and ensured the establishment of cities close to the border that otherwise might not have existed for another generation, if ever. It affected aspects of Canadian life as varied as the tourist trade and the wheat economy.

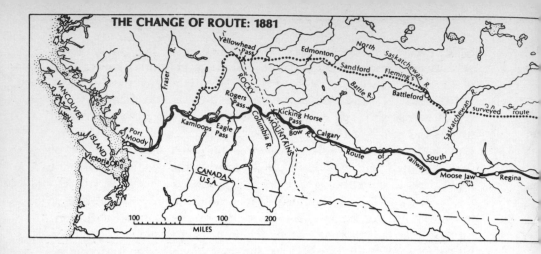

THE CHANGE OF ROUTE: 1881

In addition, it gave the railway company something very close to absolute control over the destinies of scores of embryo communities along the right of way.

The new route was determined by three members of the four-man executive committee of the CPR – George Stephen, Jim Hill, and Richard Angus. Only Duncan McIntyre was absent, that day in St. Paul. The catalyst was John Macoun, the same botanist who had accompanied Fleming and Grant on their trek from ocean to ocean a decade before.

Macoun had come to St. Paul at Hill's behest because he was familiar with the southern prairie. As a result of that original trip he had become enamoured of the North West. In 1879 and again in 1880, the Canadian government sent him on further explorations. As a result he had become convinced that the southern plains were not the desert that almost everybody thought them to be.

In spreading this dogma, Macoun was flying in the face of previous scientific reports by Palliser and Hind. Macoun resorted to the public platform to discredit both explorers, and his enthusiasm drew large crowds. "I was so full of the question," he recalled, "that I could talk for a week without stopping." His estimates of arable prairie soil were far in excess of anyone else's and helped confirm John A. Macdonald's conviction that profits from the sale of prairie land could underwrite the cost of the railway subsidy – a telling point with Parliament as well as the public.

Both Macdonald and his minister of railways, Sir Charles Tupper, were a little wary of Macoun – a man with a fixed idea that had come close to being an obsession. The evidence suggests that he was prejudiced in advance: long before he actually visited the southern prairie he was making pronouncements about its riches. After he did see it, he tried to show that its fertility was even greater than that of the land to the north.

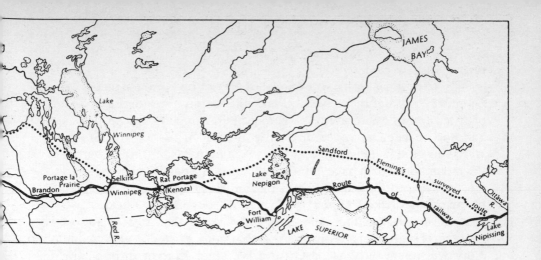

How could one explorer have seen the plains as a lush paradise while another saw them as a desert? How was it that Macoun found thick grasses and sedges where Palliser reported cracked, dry ground? The answer lies in the unpredictability of the weather in what came to be called Palliser's Triangle. Palliser saw the land under normal to dry conditions; Macoun visited it during the wettest decade in more than a century. If the former was too pessimistic, the latter was too enthusiastic.

Macoun was brought to St. Paul to convince the Syndicate that a more southerly route to the Rockies was practicable. Hill and his colleagues were already partially convinced. Early in November, 1880, Angus had made inquiries about this possibility and had received from Winnipeg some optimistic reports through the amiable American consul, James Wickes Taylor, the man who had originally influenced Macoun. Immediately the new company was formed, Jim Hill hired an American railway surveyor, Major A. B. Rogers, and sent him off to the Rocky Mountains, which Rogers had never seen, with orders to examine the four most southerly passes – the Kicking Horse, Vermilion, Kootenay, and Howse – all virtually ignored by the government's survey teams.

All that was needed was Macoun to convince the CPR executives that Palliser and Hind were wrong, and it did not take that voluble naturalist long to effect their conversion. The three old friends together with the CPR's new chief engineer, Thomas Lafayette Rosser, a one-time Confederate general, sat around a table littered with maps of the Canadian North West while a torrent of words poured from Macoun's lips. After he was finished, a brief discussion followed. Then Hill, according to the botanist's own account, slammed his hands on the table.

"Gentlemen," he said, "we will cross the prairie and go by the Bow Pass [Kicking Horse], if we can get that way." With that statement, ten years of work was abandoned and the immediate future of the North West altered.

Why were they all so eager to push their railroad through unknown country? Why did they give up Fleming's careful location in favour of a hazardous route across two mountain ramparts whose passes had not yet been surveyed or even explored? If the Kicking Horse were chosen it would mean that every pound of freight carried across the mountains would have to be hoisted an additional sixteen hundred feet higher into the clouds. Even more disturbing was the appalling barrier of the Selkirk Mountains, which lay beyond the Rockies. No pass of any description had yet been found in that great island of ancient rock; the general opinion was that none existed. Yet the company was apparently prepared to drive steel straight through the Rockies and right to the foot of the Selkirks in the sublime hope that an undiscovered passage would miraculously appear.

The mystery has never been convincingly unravelled though a variety of theories has been advanced, some of them conflicting. The CPR's own records provide no additional clues as to the real reason for the decision.

The chief reason given by Charles Tupper in Parliament a year later was that it would shorten the line by seventy-nine miles and give it a greater advantage over its American rivals. Yet if no pass in the Selkirks could be found, the railway would have to circumvent those mountains by way of the hairpin-shaped Columbia Valley and most of the advantage would be lost.

It is unlikely that the shortening of the line was the chief reason for changing the route. Subsequent accounts have generally attributed the move to fear of competition from American lines, which could send feeders into the soft underbelly of the country if the Canadian Pacific trunk-line ran too far north. Stephen, certainly, was concerned about the Northern Pacific. Its new president, the brilliant if erratic journalist and financier Henry Villard, had already succeeded in buying control of a local Manitoba line, the Southwestern, and was planning to cross the Manitoba border at three points. If he did he would certainly siphon off much of the Canadian through trade and make the CPR line north of Lake Superior practically worthless.

On the other hand, Stephen had the controversial monopoly clause to protect him: no competing federally chartered Canadian line could come within fifteen miles of the border, and Macdonald was prepared to disallow provincial charters for similarly competing lines. No doubt Stephen felt that the more southerly route would provide him with extra insurance when, in twenty years' time, the monopoly clause ran out. Almost certainly, this was one consideration in adopting the new route.

Was this the chief consideration? Perhaps – the hindsight of history has made it appear so. Yet Hill himself was already dreaming dreams of a transcontinental line of his own, springing out of the St. Paul, Minneapolis and Manitoba road. Stephen and the other major CPR stockholders had a substantial interest in that American railway. If the frustration of United States competition was the reason for the decision of 1881, why was Hill the man who made the decision to move the route south?

Hill did give one reason, and Macoun, in his autobiography, quoted it:

"I am engaged in the forwarding business and I find that there is money in it for all those who realize its value. If we build this road across the prairie, we will carry every pound of supplies that the settlers want and we will carry every pound of produce that the settlers wish to sell, so that we will have freight both ways."

This was Hill's basic railroad philosophy: a railroad through virgin territory creates its own business. It was for this reason that Hill was able to convince Stephen that the CPR should not attempt to make a large profit out of land sales but should, instead, try to attract as many settlers as possible to provide business for the railway. The philosophy would have applied to a considerable extent to the original Fleming line; on the other hand, that line ran through country where some settlement already existed and where real estate speculators expected to make profits out of land adjacent to the right of way. It undoubtedly occurred to the CPR that it would be easier to control an area that had never known a settler. Why should the road increase the value of other men's property? Why should the CPR become involved in internecine warfare between rival settlements? The row between Selkirk and Winnipeg was still fresh in the minds of Hill and Stephen. Winnipeg businessmen had forced a change in the original survey to bring the main line through their community. In striking comparison was the CPR's founding of the town of Brandon that spring of 1881. The company arbitrarily determined its location in the interests of real estate profit, and the company totally controlled it.

That was to be the pattern of future settlement along the line. It was the company that dictated both the shape and the location of the cities of the new Canada – and woe to any speculator who tried to push the company around! The company could, and did, change the centre of gravity by the simple act of shifting the location of the railway station. With a scratch of the pen the company could, and did, decide which communities would grow and which would stagnate. As the *Globe* observed, "the Syndicate has a say in the existence of almost every town or prospective town in the North-

West." Since some eight hundred villages, towns, and cities were eventually fostered in the three prairie provinces by the CPR, the advantages of total control were inestimable.

Few single decisions by a private corporation have had such widespread repercussions. As a result, the most spectacular mountain scenery in North America was opened up: Banff, Lake Louise, Glacier, and Yoho parks were all by-products of Jim Hill's tablepounding. So were the mines and farm lands of southern British Columbia. So were the costly locomotives that had to be harnessed to haul the trains over the Great Divide. So were the miles of snowsheds in the Selkirks and the costly diversions of the spiral and Connaught tunnels. From the company's point of view, it remains to this day a toss-up whether or not the change of route was really an economically sensible decision. Who can say how important the mountain scenery was to a once-profitable passenger trade? Who can estimate whether or not the profits on townsites and the advantages of a shorter line cancelled out the increased construction costs and additional carrying charges over the mountain peaks?

From the point of view of the nation, a better guess can be hazarded. It is probable that the switch to the southern route was one factor in delaying the settlement of the North West for twenty years and thus partially frustrating John A. Macdonald's dream of filling up the empty plains. The settlers tended to take up land as close as possible to the railway; often enough they were driven off it by drought conditions.

Significantly, it was the CPR itself that implicitly debunked Macoun's enthusiastic reports by refusing to accept much of the acreage set aside for it in the belt along the railway route. The contract allowed the company to choose the best available acreage; it could reject any land "not fairly fit for settlement." This land was set aside ostensibly in alternate sections along the line of the railway in a belt forty-eight miles thick between the Red River and the Rockies. In 1882, the company's most generous estimate of "fit" land within the belt stood at six million acres; later that estimate was reduced to five million acres. Clearly, the CPR was saying that the land could *not* be settled. To keep its bargain with the railway, the government was forced to give it land elsewhere, and much of this substitute acreage was found in the Fertile Belt, along the original route. If the railway had followed the valley of the North Saskatchewan the pattern of western settlement would undoubtedly have been a different one.

The CPR rejected tens of thousands of acres in the dry country west of Moose Jaw. By 1885, the year the railway was finished, only twenty-three homesteads had been taken up in that four-hundred-mile section of Palliser's Triangle. The settlers, used to eastern Canadian conditions, were not prepared to cope with the special problems of prairie agriculture, especially in dry country.

The wet cycle, which had such an effect on Macoun in 1879 and 1880, continued through 1881 and 1882. Then, in 1883 – the peak year for immigration – the dry cycle returned. By 1886 the land was so dry in many places that cracks a foot wide opened up in the parched soil. Immigration figures in the North West began to decline after a record year in 1883. In 1884 homestead entries were halved. Thousands abandoned the embryo farms they had so eagerly taken up. By 1896, half of all contracts entered into with the railway by the various colonization companies had been cancelled; a total of 1,284,652 acres reverted to the CPR.

With the acceptance of more adaptable farming methods, the prairie country became, after the turn of the century, the granary of the world; Regina, which might not have existed had the northerly route been chosen, was found to be in the very heart of the richest grain-growing soil on the continent. In those portions of Palliser's Triangle where cereals would not grow, a healthy ranching economy developed. But the cycle of drought continued. The undue optimism of the seventies and early eighties was replaced in the decade from 1884 to 1894 by an extreme pessimism. So many farms were abandoned that the Canadian government began to entertain doubts about the future of the West. Once again, John Macoun was dispatched to the southern prairies to report on the seriousness of conditions and once again, just as he arrived on the scene, the rains came and Macoun was able to predict the end of the drought. The vast wave of immigration that filled up the prairies in the following years appeared to vindicate him. When he died in 1922, his friends triumphantly published his autobiography with a flattering foreword by Ernest Thompson Seton. It was not until the desperate years of the 1930's, when the rains ceased once more and the grasshoppers and the cutworms and the hot, dry winds returned, that there took place a rueful reassessment of his strange role in the shaping of the nation.

3

General Rosser's newly surveyed route led out of Portage la Prairie towards Grand Valley on the Assiniboine and then through the Brandon Hills to Flat Creek (later known as Oak Lake). It was here, near the crossing of the Assiniboine, that Brandon, the first of the CPR towns, sprang up. The method of its selection by the General provided an object lesson for the company in the value of establishing its own communities instead of building on existing ones.

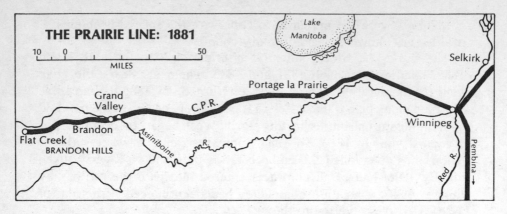

THE PRAIRIE LINE: 1881

MILES

Lake Manitoba

Selkirk

Portage la Prairie

Grand Valley

C.P.R.

Winnipeg

Brandon

Flat Creek

BRANDON HILLS

Assiniboine R.

Red R.

Pembina →

Rosser was a Virginia gentleman of the old school – tall, handsome, swarthy, and popular. A West Point chum of General Custer, he had fought opposite him as a guerilla officer during the Civil War. After the war he had risen to become chief engineer of the Northern Pacific. Later he had helped build part of Jim Hill's Manitoba line. He was a man of precipitate action, as events were shortly to prove. He had refused to surrender with Lee at Appomattox, preferring instead to charge the Federal lines with two divisions of cavalry. His subsequent civilian record was equally dashing. He had begun as an axeman and worked his way up through the ranks to chief surveyor. He was surrounded by an aura of legend – a record of hairbreadth escapes in war and peace. On one occasion when surprised by Yankee cavalry and wounded above the knee by a bone-shattering bullet, he had ridden all night to safety with the broken limb swinging back and forth and the enemy hard on his tail. A decade later near Bismarck, North Dakota, he had shot his way out of a Sioux ambush. In 1881, as the chief engineer of the CPR, he brought the same dash and impulsiveness to the establishment of townsites.

A fortnight before the first sod was turned, rumours of a great new city west of Winnipeg began to fly. Everyone knew that the railway would require a divisional point about one hundred and thirty miles west of Winnipeg. That fitted almost to a mile the location of the little settlement of Grand Valley, clustered on the banks of the Assiniboine at the exact spot where the railway was to cross the river. Tents and shacks began to spring up in the vicinity as the surveyors drove in their stakes. Land speculators poured in. The excitement increased day by day as a general store and a "hotel" of canvas spread over wooden frames sprang up. Dugald McVicar, the pioneer resident, whose wife was the local postmistress, began making improvements to his home. His brother John announced that he would also extend the size of his house. It was on the McVicar property that the new city would presumably be situated.

The McVicar brothers were humble, illiterate men who had come west in 1879 from Quebec to build the first sod dwelling in the region. The community might have borne their name had it not been for their innate modesty; they refused the offer of the chief dominion postal officer in Winnipeg to call it after them. The little town grew around the site of their original homestead, and the McVicars expected to get rich from the Grand Valley boom.

In April, General Rosser paid a visit to John McVicar and made him an offer for his property as a future townsite for the CPR's divisional point. The accounts of exactly what took place are conflicting, but one thing is clear: McVicar, prodded by speculators, held out for double the amount offered. Whereupon Rosser is said to have retorted: "I'll be damned if a town of any kind is ever built here." The railway simply moved the site of its station two miles farther west. This would be the pattern in all future dealings when private individuals tried to hold up the company for speculative profits.

The new site, on the south bank of the river in the Brandon hills, cost the CPR a fraction of the Grand Valley price, and its choice marked the end of Grand Valley as a viable community and the beginning of the town of Brandon. What was not realized at the time was that Rosser and his immediate superior, Alpheus B. Stickney, the general superintendent of the western division of the CPR, were themselves speculating in real estate, using the inside knowledge that their positions provided them.

The main street of Brandon was named after General Rosser, who decreed that the lots should be small, since more money could be made from the land in that way. Once the location of the new town was known, people began to appear and tents to blossom all along the high bank of the Assiniboine. After the realtors, the first businessman on the scene, not unnaturally, was a lumber merchant: Charles Whitehead, the son of Joseph Whitehead, the railway contractor. Whitehead, whose descendants would own the Brandon *Sun,* purchased the first parcel of land sold by the CPR.

On Whitehead's heels, in late May, came a doctor, a grocer, and a hotelman. The grocery store was the one that had been erected the previous month at Grand Valley, but when it became clear that the original settlement was dying, the proprietors moved it in sections by barge to the new townsite. The McVicar brothers were stubbornly trying to sell lots on the old site in the wistful hope that the CPR might locate a station on their land, but their neighbours were less sanguine.

By June, two more stores and a billiard hall had been moved to Brandon. The first post office was nothing more than a soap box with a slit in it placed outside the tent of L. M. Fortier and his new bride. The first restaurant was a plank laid across two barrels on the trail that was to become Pacific Avenue. The first church service was held out of doors in a driving rainstorm in June by the Reverend Thomas Lawson, a Methodist. The local harness-maker held an umbrella over the minister's head while the congregation, composed entirely of young men, sang lustily, oblivious of the downpour. Lawson was able to move his service indoors thanks to the hospitality of a Mrs. Douglas who operated one of the two tent hotels. Double-decker bunks screened by curtains ran along one side of the tent, a lean-to at one end served as a kitchen, and the rest of the tent did duty as dining room and lobby and, on Sundays, as a church. An early Brandon settler, J. A. Smart, who was a regular attendant, remembered noticing with some amusement the ample landlady accompanied by her daughter emerging silently from a corner of the tent, "dressed in her most stately attire, not omitting bonnet, coat and gloves," creeping out the back flap through the kitchen, manoeuvring round to the front, entering through the front flap, and marching up before the congregation "in high reverential style" to a front seat a few feet from the curtained bunks from which they had just emerged.

In that golden summer of 1881, the pattern of the new Canada began to take hesitant shape along the line of the railway. Brandon was the beginning – the first of the scores of raw communities that would erupt from the naked prairie. Its birth pangs would be repeated over and over again as the rails moved west. There was a kind of electric feeling in the atmosphere – a sense of being in on the start of a great adventure – which those who arrived in Brandon that summer would never forget. In future years, when recollections of later events became blurred, they would still retain unclouded the memory of those first months when the sharp spring air was pungent with the incense of fresh lumber and ringing with the clamour of construction; when lasting friendships were forged among the soiled tents on the river bank; when every man was young and strong and in love with life; and when the distant prairie, unmarked by shovel or plough, was still a mysterious realm waiting to be claimed. Some forty years later, J. A. Smart, who had stood out in the rain during that first church service, wrote about those days "when the world, full of opportunity and hope," lay before him. "No small town in Canada or elsewhere," he wrote, "could possibly have contained a happier army of young men than did Brandon in its earliest years."

For the newcomer the opportunities were almost unlimited. Of the first seven lawyers who arrived, four became ministers of the Crown, and one the Leader of the Opposition in the Manitoba legislature. The first organist in Thomas Lawson's new frame church became mayor four times running. Douglas Cameron, from grading the bumps out of Sixth Street, rose to be Lieutenant-Governor of his province. And a jovial young Irish ploughboy from Kirkfield, Ontario, named Pat Burns, who broke sod on J. W. Sifton's farm at six dollars an acre, went on to become the meat-packing king of the Canadian West. Sifton's own sons, Arthur and Clifford, became, respectively, Premier of Alberta and Minister of the Interior in the federal government.

By October 11, when the first official passenger train pulled into the new station, a boom of epic proportions was in full swing. The coming of the railway was already transforming the West and the changes were spectacular enough to set the continent buzzing.

As for Grand Valley, which might have been the new metropolis, it lapsed into decay. In September, the McVicar brothers, still trying to peddle lots, offered a Winnipeg banker a half interest in the site if he could persuade the CPR to build a station on their property; he was unsuccessful. In January, the McVicars tried again, offering eight hundred acres of their land free to two lumber merchants if they could persuade the CPR to put in a station by May, 1882. But the trains went roaring through without stopping and the McVicars eventually sold out their townsite for fifteen hundred dollars. A visitor in 1882 described the community as "a living corpse." Some years later, Charles Aeneas Shaw, one of Rosser's surveyors who had tried to persuade John McVicar to sell, happened upon him ploughing in the vicinity with a team of mules. The farmer ran out onto the road. "Oh, Mr. Shaw, I was a damn fool. If I had only taken your advice, I would have been well off now!"

To future speculators in townsites, the fate of the little community on the Assiniboine was an object lesson in how not deal with the great railway.

4

Sir Henry Whatley Tyler was the kind of man who enjoyed riding conspicuously on the cowcatchers of locomotives. He had been, variously, a captain in the Royal Engineers, a British railway inspector, and a Member of Parliament. Since 1876 he had been president of the Grand Trunk Railway of Canada, an enterprise that was directed from England. He might also have been president of the Canadian Pacific, but he could not concur with the idea of an all-Canadian route over the barren desert of the Canadian Shield. His own road ran south of the Great Lakes on its route from Sarnia to Chicago. That, clearly, was the sensible route to take.

A handsome and debonair man with a military bearing, Tyler was noted for the brilliance of his conversation and his effectiveness at repartee. The easy, sophisticated façade concealed a core of steel. With the help of his shrewd general manager Joseph Hickson he had pushed his railway into Chicago, consolidated several lines in New England, and made the Grand Trunk one of the great railway systems of North America. But was it a Canadian system? Its ownership and its direction were largely British. Its main purpose seemed to be to link the American midwest with the U.S. Atlantic coast, using Canada only as a convenient route between Chicago and Portland. Its directors clearly did not grasp the significance of the Canadian North West.

Tyler had never thought of the CPR as a competitor. Indeed, until the contract was signed, he considered the entire transcontinental railway scheme an elaborate political pipe dream. It did not, apparently, occur to Sir Henry that a railway of that length, built at enormous cost, would have to continue on into the settled East. If the CPR had stopped at Callander Junction on Lake Nipissing it would, of course, have become a valuable feeder for the Grand Trunk. But it is clear from the CPR charter that the Syndicate intended from the outset to establish a complete transcontinental system.

In the midsummer of 1881, Tyler woke up to the fact that the Canadian Pacific was to be a major competitor. The first CPR shareholders' meeting, held in London on May 31, had approved the amalgamation of the new company with the government-subsidized Canada Central whose president, Duncan McIntyre, was also vice-president of the CPR. The Canada Central linked Lake Nipissing with Ottawa. On July 20, the CPR moved to extend its operations further into Grand Trunk territory. Stephen and McIntyre were elected directors of the Ontario and Quebec Railway, a company that held a charter to build from Montreal to Toronto. It shortly became apparent that the CPR intended to swallow this line. The CPR, through Stephen, also had an interest in the Credit Valley Railway, which connected Toronto with Georgian Bay. In addition it had announced a branch line to Sault Ste Marie to connect with another line on the United States side being taken over by Jim Hill. The new company was not yet six months old and already it was posing a serious threat to the older railway.

Thus was the scene set for a battle between the two roads – a battle that was to run unchecked for the whole of the construction period. The Grand Trunk's strategy was to discredit the CPR in public while crippling it financially behind the scenes. In his campaign of attrition, Tyler had some powerful allies. Two great British financial houses, Baring Brothers and Glyn, Mills, were on his side; they had originally financed the Grand Trunk. So were a large number of newspapers, many of which profited from Grand Trunk advertising. Sir Alexander Galt, Canada's new high commissioner to London, was one of the Grand Trunk's friends; he had made a fortune out of GTR contracts. Joseph Hickson, Tyler's general manager in Canada, was on friendly terms with Sir John A. Macdonald, and the Grand Trunk could always be depended upon to deliver the vote of its employees to the Conservatives in federal elections. These links with the Canadian government were not decisive ones, but they might serve as a brake on the ambitious plans of George Stephen.

The Grand Trunk's English shareholders had some cause for discontent. For the best part of thirty years the company had teetered on the edge of financial disaster. Now, when its prospects seemed brighter, a rival line came along to dampen that future. No wonder the overseas investing public looked with jaundice on the CPR: the Canadians, having asked Englishmen to pump millions into one faltering railway, were now asking them to pour more millions into its chief competitor! The Grand Trunk propaganda to discredit the CPR in the British market found fertile ground.

All that summer and fall, the Canadian Pacific Railway and the Canadian North West were subjected to a torrent of abuse in the press of Canada, the United States, and Great Britain. The American attitude was summed up in a brief interview in the New York *Herald* with the taciturn Jay Gould, the American railroad financier, shortly after the CPR was formed:

REPORTER: There is a great project underway up in Canada?

GOULD: The Canadian Pacific Railroad?

REPORTER: Yes; what do you think of it?

GOULD: Visionary.

REPORTER: No dividends?

GOULD: Perhaps in one hundred years. It will be a good excursion line for English tourists and Canadian statesmen when Parliament adjourns.

REPORTER: But they say there are great possibilities. How about the great agricultural resources...?

GOULD: One, the chief one, of the successful agricultural conditions is not there.

REPORTER: Which is?

GOULD: Population.

A large section of the British press, led by *The Times* of London, had convinced would-be immigrants that Australia was a better prospect that the forbidding Canadian plains. The Governor General, Lord Lorne, determined to remedy this impression by a personal tour of the railway's route to the Rockies with four British journalists, including a man from *The Times,* invited along. The coverage was good and the newspaper changed its editorial line and ceased to thunder against Canada; but the gibes from other British journals continued.

The most memorable, entitled "The Canadian Dominion Bubble," was published in *Truth* on September 1, 1881. The author said flatly that the floating of a Canadian government bond issue in England and ten million dollars worth of CPR land grant bonds in New York and Montreal was a fraud. New York investors, he declared, would never be such fools "as to put their money into this mad project. I would as soon credit them with a willingness to subscribe hard cash in support of a scheme for the utilization of icebergs." As for the Canadians, they were "not such idiots as to part with one dollar of their own if they can borrow their neighbours'. The Canadians spend money and we provide it."

"The Canadian Pacific Railway will run, if it is ever finished, through a country frost bound for seven or eight months in the year, and will connect with the eastern part of the Dominion a province which embraces about as forbidding a country as any on the face of the earth."

As for British Columbia, it was "a barren, cold, mountain country that is not worth keeping." It would never have been inhabited at all had it not been for the mining boom: "Ever since that fever died down the place has been going from bad to worse. Fifty railroads would not galvanize it into prosperity." The CPR was "never likely to pay a red cent of interest on the money that may be sunk into it."

This broadside and others that followed had their effect on the British money market. They were accompanied that fall by the first of the anti-CPR pamphlets, said to have been written by the Grand Trunk's "paid ink-slingers," as Stephen called them. In Stephen's view, those who were not passionately devoted to the cause of the railway were enemies, traitors, blackguards, and cowards. Such terms cropped up constantly in his astonishingly garrulous correspondence with Macdonald, almost all of it scrawled in Stephen's own sloping hand.

Stephen saw himself beset on all sides by formidable forces intent on crushing the CPR. One of these was the Northern Pacific, whose dynamic new president, Henry Villard, seemed determined to thrust his rapidly expanding railway into the Canadian North West. In Manitoba two private railways were being built towards the United States border. The Northern Pacific had bought control of one and was ready to buy control of the other, believing, in Stephen's words, that "they can force a connection at the boundary and so strangle the Canadian Pacific; which they are determined to do if they can." With both Macdonald and Tupper absent from Ottawa, Stephen feared the government might yield to pressure from the prairie province and allow the two lines to connect at the border with a spur from the Northern Pacific's through line. Stephen urged Macdonald to instruct Ottawa at once to hold matters over until he returned; he cabled him that a decision in favour of the Manitoba lines "must effectually destroy Pacific as National through line, rendering Eastern section useless . . . ."

All that fall of 1881, Stephen kept up a continual pressure on the Prime Minister to disallow by federal decree any provincially chartered lines that came within fifteen miles of the border. Again and again he made the point that a "Yankee line" into Manitoba would make it impossible to operate or even to build the Lake Superior section of the CPR. With such competition no one could prevent the products of the North West being drawn through the United States to Chicago, whose attraction as a market for wheat was almost irresistible. Stephen used every argument in his power to convince Macdonald to disallow the Manitoba charters: it would, he told him, mean the disgrace not only of the railway but also of the Conservative government itself, since the country would not stand for the enormous expense of the Lake Superior line if it turned out to be worthless. "It would be a miserable affair to find that the benefit of all our efforts to develop the North West had by our own acts, fallen into Yankee hands."

Many of Macdonald's followers, especially those in Manitoba, were eager to subvert the spirit of the contract which protected the railway through its monopoly clause. Because of the British North America Act the clause did not prevent the provinces from chartering lines to the border in competition with the transcontinental railway. This was Stephen's fear.

There is no doubt that Macdonald intended to back Stephen up, but there is also no doubt that the monopoly clause was already causing him grave uneasiness. To ride roughshod over the legitimate desire of Manitoba settlers for more railways to service their communities was to alienate politically an entire province. From the beginning he had seen the railway as a device to unite the nation – to tie the settled East to the new country beyond the Shield. Now in the very first year of its construction the railway had become a divisive force, antagonizing the very people it was supposed to link together. The Prime Minister gave vent to his view in the presence of some of Stephen's colleagues on the subject of the "cussed" Manitoba charters, and Stephen wrote to him in alarm that "they have all come back more or less full of misgivings and fears lest in some way the 15 mile Yankee barrier will not be maintained."

There was another threat on the horizon. The ubiquitous Northern Pacific was about to purchase the railway owned by the Quebec government – or so the Premier, J. A. Chapleau, kept insisting. This was the Quebec, Montreal, Ottawa and Occidental and its eastern section, familiarly termed "the North Shore Line." Quebec had been trying to unload this white elephant ever since the days of Sir George Etienne Cartier, who had promised to make it part of the CPR. The previous winter, Chapleau had tried to make the purchase of the partially completed railway a condition of French-Canadian support for the CPR contract.

Macdonald had managed to evade such an out-and-out promise; now he was again facing the same kind of blackmail. Suppose the aggressive Henry Villard came to the rescue of Quebec by buying up the railway? With one stroke he would occupy a key position between the government-owned Intercolonial on the east and the Canadian Pacific on the west. If he linked the Quebec line with the Northern Pacific at Sault Ste Marie, as he clearly meant to do, the country would be faced with a Yankee transcontinental railway mainly on Canadian soil. But there was more: By taking the faltering railway off the hands of the Quebec government, Villard would be buying considerable political leverage in that province and, consequently, in Ottawa. Macdonald feared that he would use this new political strength to persuade the Quebec members to vote in a bloc against federal disallowance of the Manitoba railways. If Villard's gambit succeeded, he would have a through line from Quebec City to Winnipeg by way of Sault Ste Marie and Duluth, and Macdonald's dream of an all-Canadian route would again be shattered.

The Prime Minister confessed to Stephen that he was very uneasy. A Quebec election was coming up. The president of one of the Manitoba lines was tactlessly predicting that the Northern Pacific would be a factor in that election. If Stephen was to act at all, Macdonald urged, he must act at once. The CPR president decided he must make an offer for the section running west to Ottawa from Montreal in order to head off the American attempt to control Canada's transcontinental transportation system.

Stephen, who had once thought the idea of building the line north of Lake Superior "great folly," was becoming an enthusiastic champion of an all-Canadian route. In August, 1881, he confessed to the Prime Minister that "all misgivings I had last year ... have disappeared with a better knowledge of the position of the whole country. I am now satisfied that the C.P.R. without the control of a line to the *Atlantic* seaboard would be a *mistake*. If for instance, it terminated like the Northern Pacific, at Lake Superior it never could become the property it is certain to be having its own rails running from sea to sea. I am sure you will be glad to hear this from me because I do not think but for your *own* tenacity on that point, would the line North of the Lake *ever* have been built, events have shown you were right and all the rest wrong."

Some of this was flattery and some of it was close to being blackmail. Stephen had been aware, from the outset, of Macdonald's obsession with an all-Canadian railway. He used his knowledge to good advantage – to bargain toughly for the insertion of the monopoly clause in the contract. The Prime Minister was made to understand that he could not have one thing without the other. If the CPR was to pay through the nose for an unprofitable line through an uninhabitable wilderness, it must receive compensation. Stephen might argue that this was merely an extension of the Conservative Party's National Policy of protection, but that protection was paying big dividends for the proprietors of the CPR and of the St. Paul, Minneapolis and Manitoba Railway, whose directorates interlocked. The contract gave them a monopoly of all traffic out of Winnipeg into the United States and they made the most of it.

Stephen had an additional reason for his enthusiasm. He had discovered that the white elephant might not be so very unprofitable: lumber from Ottawa could be laid down in Winnipeg at ten dollars a thousand less than the city was paying elsewhere. He confided to the Governor General that the company would not give up the controversial portion of the line "even if the Government wished us."

Again Stephen and his colleagues had rejected Sandford Fleming's surveys. The Fleming line took the easiest route, well to the north of Lake Nepigon, but Stephen wanted to adopt a new location that would hug the granite-ribbed shores of Superior. "The line north of Nipigon would be easy of construction and operation too, but it *never* can support settlers, there is absolutely no *land*, nothing but bare rocks and pools of water." Moreover, by building close to the lake the contractors could be supplied by water transport. Stephen argued that because of this construction time would be cut, perhaps in half.

Though he thought the new route ought be to acceptable to Ontario, Stephen had no illusions about the *Globe,* which he believed was "conspiring with the Northern Pacific to strangle Canada's national road." The *Globe* could be depended upon to blackball the idea and "perhaps declare that we do not mean to build the Lake Superior section at all."

It was "simply disgusting" to have to swallow the "lying charges" of such newspapers. The best answer was "to take care to avoid anything that even looks like a breach, or even an evasion, of the terms of the contract. It will be the duty as well as the interest of the Company to ask nothing of the Government savoring of a favoritism not provided for in the contract, and you may be sure, that so far as I know, I will be guided by this principle. Acting in this way and pushing our work with the utmost energy and especially that part of the contract which the *Globe still insists we mean to shirk.*"

Few railroad executives in North America had ever talked this way before, but then Stephen was not cast in the traditional mould. Among his own colleagues he was unique. Certainly Jim Hill had no intention of blasting a railroad out of the black scarps that frowned down on the slate waters of the great lake. Like Villard of the Northern Pacific, Hill saw Canadian freight being diverted south of the lake and up through the underside of Manitoba. One of his chief reasons for joining the CPR Syndicate was that his St. Paul road would get all the construction traffic for the line being built west of Winnipeg. The line across the Shield, he was convinced, "would be of no use to anybody and would be the source of heavy loss to whoever operated it."

In the fall of 1881, Hill picked the best railwayman he could find to look over the Precambrian country to the north and west of Lake Superior. According to William Pearce of the Dominion land department – a man privy to a good deal of CPR gossip – Hill's plan was to have the visitor damn the all-Canadian route as impractical. He chose for this task the dynamic young general manager of the Chicago, Milwaukee and St. Paul Railroad; though no one yet realized it, his influence on the future of the young nation was to be enormous. His name was William Cornelius Van Horne.

5

The new man was being considered for something more permanent than a mere report on the Lake Superior route. The CPR badly needed a new general manager. Stickney had managed to build only one hundred and thirty miles of railway that season; moreover, he was under a cloud because of his land speculations.

As usual George Stephen turned to Hill, who had done the major share of the hiring and whose preference for American railroad men and engineers had already caused rumblings in the Canadian press. Hill recommended Van Horne. Of all the men he knew, Van Horne was the best equipped mentally for the job, and in every other way as well. A pioneer was needed, Hill told Stephen, "and the more of a pioneer, the better."

"You need a man of great mental and physical power to carry this line through," Hill said. "Van Horne can do it." He added a word of caution: "But he will take all the authority he gets and more, so define how much you want him to have."

Stephen undoubtedly recognized the type; he had seen the same qualities in Hill. Physically and temperamentally, Hill and Van Horne were very much alike; that similarity may help to explain the unyielding antagonism that developed between them over the rival interests of the Great Northern and the Canadian Pacific. They were both powerful men, their strong faces half hidden by short beards. The eyes differed: Hill's single eye was like a smouldering coal; Van Horne's, impassive and ice-blue, were the product of his Dutch-German ancestry. Like Hill, he was used to controlling armies of men – "the ablest railroad general in the world, all that Grant was to the U.S.A.," in the admiring phrase of a fellow railroader, Jason C. Easton, president of the Chicago, Milwaukee and St. Paul. It was small wonder that Stephen was prepared to pay Van Horne the largest salary ever dangled before a railroad man in the West – a princely fifteen thousand dollars a year.

Van Horne's speech was military in its decisiveness. So was Hill's; the ex-Canadian hated adjectives, preferring short, pungent words. Both men were ruthless and single-minded in any cause they served. Both knew how to seize and hold power. Hill, the Canadian-turned-American, and Van Horne, the American-turned-Canadian, would both push their railroads through to the Pacific. It was inevitable that when their interests clashed they would find themselves locked in battle.

On October 7, Hill brought Van Horne into Winnipeg to look over the CPR's prairie construction and also the government line being built out of Fort William. Winnipeg was a city of contrasts – buildings springing up everywhere; "the streets full of garbage, egg shells, rinds of lemons and other forms of refuse cast out in broad daylight"; stray horses prowling around the suburbs where they "mangle shade trees, stamp around at nights and make a nuisance of themselves generally"; tents blossoming so thickly in St. Boniface along the Assiniboine that the police tried to burn them out; workmen and settlers jamming the broad, muddy avenues.

Nevertheless it was beginning to acquire a patina of culture. The Nathal Opera Troupe performed at the city hall on the very day Hill and Van Horne arrived. "Miss Louise Lester. . .was particularly effective, her performance in the wine drinking scene being most artistic in every respect." The wine drinking was not confined to the stage: "This city," the *Free Press* had complained the previous month, "is suffering from drunken Indians. They are to be met on almost every street at almost every hour. They seem to have no difficulty in procuring whiskey."

The white population was as addicted to drink as the Indians. The opening that August of Winnipeg's pride, the Louisa Railway Bridge, had been accompanied by an "incarnal orgy. . .a great, hilarious, illimitable guzzle," in which small boys quaffed glass after glass of free champagne and beer, provided by the city, "with the easy nonchalance of veterans," and the crowd, on learning that the liquor was cut off, "acted generally more like wild beasts than rational creatures," tearing down the ceremonial tent, appropriating the forbidden stock of spirits, and indulging in a "debauch . . . the largest and most varied the city has seen for many a day."

Hill and Van Horne stayed overnight in Winnipeg and then went west through Brandon to the end of track and then east again along the still unfinished line to Thunder Bay. It must have been a stimulating journey. Both men were insatiably curious. Van Horne was an amateur geologist who constantly chipped away at rock cuts in his search for new fossils, nine of which carry to this day the descriptive suffix *Van Hornei*. Once, in Alton, Illinois, he had been tantalized for several weeks by the spectacle of a fine trilobite embedded in a slab sidewalk until, unable to resist the impulse, he had smashed at the pavement with his hammer and borne the trophy away.

Of the two, Van Horne was the broader in his interests. Hill usually made his curiosity work for him in a business sense; transportation, fuel, forwarding attracted him. But Van Horne indulged his varied fancies for the sheer love of it. He was a first-rate gardener; he was a caricaturist; he was a conjuror; he was a mind reader; he was a violinist; he was a practical joker; he was a gourmet; he was a marathon poker player.

He was also the more sybaritic of the two. Both Hill and Van Horne were furious smokers but the latter's long Havana cigars were to become such a trademark that a brand was named after him, his likeness on every band. All his appetites appeared to be gargantuan. He ate prodigiously and was known as a man who fed his workmen generously. He could sit up all night winning at poker and go to work the following morning without showing a trace of fatigue. He liked his cognac, his whiskey, and his fine French vintages, but he did not tolerate drunkenness in himself or others. Inebriates were fired out of hand. So were slackers, dunces, cravens, cowards, slow-pokes, and labour organizers. Van Horne did not suffer laziness, stupidity, inefficiency, or revolt.

He was probably appalled by what he found between Winnipeg and Thunder Bay. Later Van Horne was to describe a section of the desert east of Fort William as "200 miles of engineering impossibilities." It may be that, at this juncture, he shared Hill's belief that it would be madness to try to push a railroad across the Shield. Did he actually damn the Lake Superior route? William Pearce, the land commissioner, believed that he did. "I have no doubt he carried out what he was asked to do," he wrote in a memoir years later.

But Van Horne at the time was not a committed officer of the company, nor had he yet fallen under the spell of George Stephen.

Events, however, were moving rapidly. The pressure was on him to take over the Canadian railway. It was an enormous risk. His prospects south of the border were as bright as those of any rising young railway executive in the country. He could have had the pick of half a dozen sinecures, yet he chose the CPR. Certainly the salary that Hill was dangling before him was attractive, but it was not really the money that turned William Cornelius Van Horne into a Canadian. The Canadian Pacific Railway Company was launched on a breath-taking gamble. The steel was creeping across the prairie like an arrow pointed at the successive bulwarks of the Rockies and the Selkirks. At that moment, no one knew exactly how the rails were to penetrate those two mountain series or, indeed, if they could get through the Selkirks at all. The railway's future depended on that eccentric little wisp of a surveyor Major Rogers, who all that summer had been clambering over the naked peaks looking for a notch in the rampart. Few Canadian engineers believed he would find what he was seeking, but Van Horne, the poker player, had talked to Rogers. The gamble, the challenge, the adventure, the desire "to make things grow and put new places on the map" were too much for a man of his temperament to resist.

Van Horne's appointment was confirmed on November 1. He began work on January 2, 1882, in the CPR offices in the new Bank of Montreal building. By that time the astonishing real estate boom, which swept across all of western Canada from the Red River to Fort Edmonton and electrified most of the continent, was at its height. The smell of money was in the air. For the past several months, ever since the founding of Brandon, the people of Manitoba had seemed to be going stark, raving mad over real estate. When Van Horne arrived the insanity had reached a kind of crescendo. It would continue unabated until the snows melted and it was snuffed out by the angry floods of spring.

Chapter
Two

THE
GREAT
MANITOBA
LAND
BOOM

1

Van Horne's first official act was to place a small advertisement in the Winnipeg newspapers cautioning the public against buying lots at prospective stations along the line until he had officially announced their locations. All but five sites, he pointed out, were still temporary. Future townsites would be chosen by the company and by the company alone, "without regard to any private interest whatever."

This clear warning went unheeded, and the little ad was lost in an ocean of screaming type, trumpeting unbelievable bargains in non-existent townsites and in "cities" that could scarcely be found by the most diligent explorer. Such ads had fattened Winnipeg's three dailies, the *Free Press, Times* and *Sun,* for all of the latter half of 1881; they would continue to dominate the press for most of the first half of 1882. "MAKE MONEY!" the advertising shrieked. "GET WEALTHY!" "GOLDEN CHANCES! GOLDEN SPECULATIONS!" "MILLIONS IN IT!"

The boom had been launched the previous June with the opening sale of lots in Brandon. By January the value of those lots had tripled, the town had been sold seven or eight times over, and the price was said to be rising at a rate of one hundred dollars per lot per week.

In Winnipeg real estate was more expensive than it was in Chicago; on Main Street the price rose as high as two thousand dollars a front foot for choice locations – exactly what it was worth in 1970. But in 1882 the dollar value was worth at least four or five times its 1970 value.

The town was said to have been surveyed into city lots for ten miles – enough to support a population of half a million. By April it was estimated that fifteen million acres of land had changed hands. To eastern ears this was little short of miraculous. In all of southwestern Ontario, which had a population seventeen times that of Manitoba, there were only eleven million acres of land.

Winnipeg, with a population of some sixteen thousand, supported no fewer than three hundred real estate dealers. Its population had doubled in a year. Accommodation was at such a premium that the smallest building – a storey-and-a-half structure, thirty feet by thirty

– could rent for five thousand dollars a year before it was completed.

The boom caught the imagination of the continent. The New York *Graphic* devoted two full pages to "the wondrous city of northwestern Canada." "Think of $1000 a front foot!" exclaimed the Fargo *Argus*. "If you haven't a lot in Manitoba you had better buy one at once," cried the London, Ont., *Herald*. The eastern press covered the story as if it were a war, sending correspondents into the front lines. Some stayed to speculate themselves. "I have yet to hear of any one who has not made money," the reporter for the St. Catharines *Journal* enthused to his readers at the end of January.

Stories of fortunes made and lost excited the nation. There was, for instance, the tale of one elderly man who owned a parcel of fifty-four acres of land on the outskirts of the city. In 1880 he had tried, unsuccessfully, to sell it for seven hundred dollars. He moved to Toronto and tried to sell it there, again without success. In 1881 he returned to Winnipeg, intending to pack up and leave the country. Soon after his arrival two strangers knocked on his door and asked if he wanted to sell his land. The old man was afraid to ask for seven hundred dollars for fear of driving them away. Seeing him hesitate the visitors jumped in with an offer of forty thousand dollars. The old man, concluding that he was in the presence of lunatics, shooed them off his property and then went to his lawyer with tears in his eyes and told him that a couple of scamps had been poking fun at him. It was some time before he could be convinced that the offer was genuine. By the time he had been persuaded to sell, the price had risen by another five thousand dollars.

A visitor from St. Catharines purchased several lots on Portage Avenue well before the boom. In September, 1881, a friend dropped in and offered him twenty-five hundred dollars for one lot. When the owner hesitated the friend increased the offer to three thousand. The news of the available property travelled swiftly. The following morning, as the St. Catharines man walked down the street he was besieged with offers that seemed to increase block by block. An acquaintance rushed up to him and offered to buy all his lots at three thousand apiece. A few hundred yards farther along, a man popped his head out of the window and raised the price to thirty-five hundred. Another few hundred yards and he was stopped by a stranger who offered four thousand dollars per lot. He had scarcely moved another block before the figure had reached six thousand.

Such tales crowded the world news out of the papers:

"W. J. Ovens used to sell nails for a cent in a hardware store in Yorkville four years ago but he can draw his check for $100,000 to-day."

"A man who worked on the street here last spring, wore a curly dog-skin coat this spring, smokes 25 cent cigars and talks with contempt about thousands."

"Mr. Wm. J. Twigg, of Thompson, Twigg & Co., Real Estate, has retired from business after making one hundred thousand dollars . . . ."

It puts matters in perspective to realize that twelve hundred dollars a year was considered, in 1882, to be a very good income. A hundred-thousand-dollar profit then could keep a man and his family in luxury for life. But many of these fortunes were paper ones. George Ham, one of the great raconteurs of the West, was staying that winter in the Queen's Hotel along with La Touche Tupper, a government employee who was deeply involved in land speculation. "He was a fairly good barometer of the daily land values," Ham recalled. "Some days when he claimed to have made $10,000 or $15,000 everything was lovely. The next day, when he could only credit himself with $3,000 or $4,000 to the good, things were not as well, and when the profits dropped, and some days they did, to a paltry $500 or $600, the country was going to the dogs. We faithfully kept count of La Touche's earnings, and in the spring he had accumulated nearly a million in his mind."

In mid-February, one minister preaching a sermon about Lot's wife had to make it clear to his congregation that it was not his intention to talk about real estate. A performer at a skating carnival that same week costumed himself as a coffin on which was inscribed: "Talked to death by a real estate agent. Lots for sale." In Brandon, the first wedding was provoked by an offer from the municipal council of a free lot to the first bride and groom. A man named Robbins immediately proposed to a woman popularly known as English Nell. One old timer recalled that "no questions were asked whether it was a love match but most folks were satisfied it was principally to get the city lot." The nuptials were celebrated at the city hall and then the entire congregation, singing "One More River to Cross," followed the newly-weds across the Assiniboine, where the city fathers delivered up to them the certificate and title.

Children and teenagers were caught up in the speculative fever. "Little girls gamble in lots for doll-houses," the astonished representative of *The Times* of London reported. In Selkirk, an old resident, Major Bowles, was so bucked up by a local real estate boom touched off by rumours of additional railroad facilities that he was inspired to christen his infant son "Selkirk Boom Bowles" in honour of the event.

Everybody from tradesman to leading citizen was involved in land speculation. The chief commissioner of the Hudson's Bay Company, James A. Grahame, and his land commissioner, Charles Brydges, together with the company solicitor, all of whom had inside knowledge, bought fifty-six of their company's lots at Fort Garry for $280,000 and within eleven days sold eleven of them for $275,000. The company's surveyors speculated in land as did ordinary clerks, all of them privy to information regarding Hudson's Bay property that had not yet been advertised to the public.

So all-pervasive was the talk about real estate that it did not occur to the average citizen that there could be any other topic. In January, a stranger seeking a church service inquired of "a respectable elderly gentleman" where the town hall might be, since it did double service as the Presbyterian meeting place. The Winnipegger jumped to the obvious conclusion that the stranger wanted to buy the property and informed him that it had already been sold at eight hundred dollars a front foot. He "was unable to realize the possibility of any one coming to Winnipeg for any other purpose than to learn how real estate was going."

Early in February, the trustees of Knox Presbyterian Church succumbed to the craze. The church occupied a valuable corner lot on Portage Avenue, and when the trustees announced that it would be auctioned to the highest bidder, the crowd that attended formed the largest congregation the institution had ever known. An eyewitness called it "the wealthiest, as well as the most intelligent, audience that ever gathered in any similar building in Canada," and added that no one removed his hat. "The puffing cigars held in several hundred mouths soon rendered the atmosphere of the sacred edifice disagreeable in the extreme . . . ."

The building and land had cost $23,000. They were knocked down for $126,000. The syndicate that bought it resold the church, realizing a cash profit of fifty thousand dollars. The first tenants included the Bank of Montreal and the Canadian Pacific Railway.

The Anglicans were not far behind the Calvinists. (The Methodists were already renting out their Wesley Hall as a theatre, of all things, on week nights.) On February 26, the congregation of Holy Trinity learned from their rector that a meeting was being planned "for the purpose of considering whether it was advisable to sell the church." That was too much for one aggrieved parishioner. "To what are we tending?" he cried, and then he quoted St. Paul's familiar dictum about the love of money being the root of all evil – an admonition which for all that winter had been ignored by Christian and heathen alike. Few paid him any attention.

2

"If there ever was a fool's paradise," wrote George Ham, "it sure was located in Winnipeg. Men made fortunes – mostly on paper – and life was one continuous joy-ride."

The joy-ride lasted from June, 1881, until mid-April, 1882. For all of that time, the business section of the city resembled a giant carnival. Almost every visitor remarked on the immense crowds jostling each other on the streets, on the general air of wealth, on the feeling of hustle and energy, and on the smell of money. J. C. McLagan in a contemporary essay wrote of "magnificent turnouts with coachmen and footmen fully equipped," ox sleds laden with lumber and produce, dog trains of great length yapping their way through the throngs, and farmers, newly rich, driving spanking teams.

Two-thirds of those on the streets were men. "I doubt if to-day any other city on the continent, according to its population, can boast of so many wealthy, young and middle-aged men," one eyewitness wrote in March. "In physique and general appearance no place can produce their equal. This is the general theme of conversation indulged in by all newcomers, who stand in utter amazement admiring the busy throng as they pass by. Eagerness and determination are depicted on every countenance."

Samuel Benfield Steele, one of the original detachment of North West Mounted Police that went west in 1874, saw Winnipeg in its salad days and recalled it in his memoirs. "People were ready to buy anything," he remembered. "The hotels did a roaring trade and the bars made profits of hundreds of dollars a day . . . . In the forenoon the speculators were at their writing tables going through their correspondence; the city was quiet, though crowded with men. At noon there was the usual hearty luncheon; at 3 p.m. the fun began, and was kept up until a late hour. Those who had made money were ready to re-invest it, and the real estate offices were crowded with men ready to buy or sell lots."

The "king of the land," in the Winnipeg *Sun*'s phrase, was 36-year-old Arthur Wellington Ross, M.P., a real estate agent who had presided at the founding of Brandon. An opportunist, Ross was reputed to be worth half a million dollars at the height of the boom. He was an Ontario-born schoolteacher turned lawyer who became a solicitor for the Mackenzie administration on moving to Winnipeg. Then, after the Tory victory, he switched his allegiance to the party in power and ran successfully as a Conservative, first for the Manitoba legislature and later, in 1882, for the federal seat of Lisgar. He was a man who clearly made it a practice to be in with the right people. He

225

also had a shrewd eye for land. As early as 1878 he was buying lots in St. Boniface for three hundred dollars an acre; within three years their value had increased eightfold. He always seemed to know where opportunity lay; wherever the CPR went, there was Arthur Wellington Ross, quietly moving ahead of it, buying up property, always unobtrusively. He was, the *Sun* declared, known for his tact. He was also known for his Calvinist principles: "While others played, he worked. While others were enjoying themselves in social festivities, he was thinking and working and he has only himself to thank for his present success."

Ross's advertisements overshadowed the slender columns of news on Winnipeg's front pages as did those of the two colourful real estate auctioneers, Jim Coolican and Joseph Wolf. Wolf, "portly and indefatigable," sold half a million dollars' worth of real estate in the first six months of the land fever. When the CPR placed a second Brandon section on the market in February, Wolf was chosen to handle the bidding. The crowds were so huge that the city hall itself had to be transformed into a real estate office. Wolf, working for three nights in a row, sold $133,000 worth of North Brandon lots. His exertions were so great that he suffered a collapse in the late spring and was ordered east by his doctor for a five-week rest.

Coolican, "the Real Estate King," was perhaps the most resourceful real estate man in Winnipeg, a rotund and florid Irishman with a huge black moustache, his plump fingers and silk tie glittering with "real diamonds," in the phrase of the day. Coolican sported the status symbol of the city – a five-thousand-dollar sealskin coat with matching cap – and was building what was described as a "palatial residence" on the Assiniboine to which he was conveyed in an English state coach, the first of its kind ever brought into the North West.

Coolican's advertisements for the paper towns he auctioned off – often a half or a full page in size – were masterpieces of hyperbole. In a single fortnight in February he auctioned off almost a million dollars worth of property. He did his business at the very hub of the city, in the Exchange at the corner of Portage and Main which he was forever enlarging to handle the crowds, "a transformation more wonderful than anything experienced in the Arabian nights."

He was an expansive and popular figure about town. On one night he bought out the stock of a passing apple vendor and scattered the fruit "promiscuously amongst the audience." The next night he gave away seven hundred cigars to his customers. This was in mid-February, when Coolican had placed the entire "city" of Cartwright on the market. Coolican's silver tongue moved Cartwright lots at the rate of twenty thousand dollars a night. The town itself, as the investors discovered, consisted of a single building, a general store that also did duty as a post office. Everything else – the advertised shops, mills, schools, and churches – were, as one investor ruefully put it, "the merest castles in the air."

For every two hundred permanent residents in Winnipeg that winter there was a liquor store or a saloon. Champagne replaced whiskey as the class beverage. One man actually bathed in it. He was Captain Vivian, a monocled English aristocrat who had arrived in the summer of 1881 with a thousand pounds in his pocket which he sank into a quarter section homestead in the Brandon district. By February he was said to be worth four hundred thousand dollars. Unable to drink up all the champagne he had purchased, he filled a bathtub with it and invited his friends to watch him splash about.

The scene is no more unreal than was Winnipeg itself that winter and spring. It seemed as if all belief had been temporarily suspended, all rational conjecture swept aside. One easterner wrote home that "women, who a few years ago were cooking and washing in a dirty little back kitchen, now ride about in carriages and pairs, with eccentric looking individuals for coachmen sitting in the back seat driving, the mistress looking as if the world were barely extensive enough for her to spread herself in." But it was not easy to secure such servants. *The Times* of London reported that "you find that your hackney coachman is a landowner, and cease to feel surprised at this when he declines to drive you five miles for less than $4 or to drive you at all at any but his own pace."

It was a winter of conspicuous extravagance. Diamonds became baubles on scores of fingers and "twenty-dollar gold pieces were just nothing." Next to the advertisements for lots were others for crystal ware, mantle ornaments, music boxes, choice gas fixtures, fine Etrus can jewellery, India and China tea, Weber pianos, cornice poles, and "beautiful dado hand painted shades." The Palace Hotel advertised quail on toast, and no luncheon could be considered complete without the customary dozen oysters on the half-shell. Woltz, "the princely Toronto jeweler," set up shop in March. "Even if you buy nothing," the *Sun* told its readers, "the rich splendor of his wares will feast you with the artistic and educate you in the beautiful."

Woltz pressed a gold watch as a gift upon the reporter who wrote that embroidered prose. He accepted it with alacrity and boasted about his good fortune in print. In Winnipeg that year the accumulation of sudden and unexpected wealth was greeted with applause. Speculators were heroes; profiteers were the new nobility. Businessmen, normally reticent, boasted openly about their killings and gave interviews to newspapers detailing their worth. The *Sun*, revealing some of the largest of the new fortunes, reported that the mayor himself led the list with an accumulation estimated at three hundred thousand dollars. Cabinet ministers, back-benchers in both parties, and the Queen's representative were all speculating in real estate in the most open manner possible. It was publicly reported, with approbation, that the Lieutenant-Governor had cleared a million dollars out of his knowledge of Northwest speculations. M. C. Cameron, one of the powers in the Liberal Party, made a seventy-five-thousand-dollar killing and cheerfully gave the details to the press. The property was quickly resold for one hundred thousand, but Cameron announced that he was perfectly satisfied with the lower figure, "having got the price he asked." The point was implicit: no one had put anything over on M. C. Cameron. Shrewdness was more highly prized than virtue during the boom.

Everybody in Winnipeg, it seemed, was affluent – or believed himself to be. The signs of prosperity were everywhere. By March, one hundred and eighty of Alexander Graham Bell's newly developed telephones were in operation. Gas lighting, hailed the year before, was already becoming obsolete. On June 13, three sample electric lights were installed on the grounds of the CPR station at the head of Main Street, which was "illuminated as if by sunlight.... Books and newspapers could be read with ease."

In eastern Canada, thousands of adventurers were preparing to set out for "the New Eldorado," as the Winnipeg *Times* dubbed the North West. By early April, every train from St. Paul was bringing in hundreds of immigrants from eastern Canada and from every part of the world. One traveller taking an immigrant train from Toronto to Winnipeg described the scene: the men, women, and children crowding aboard at every stop with their kits and baggage and all their household goods, "their faces beaming with satisfaction at being at last on the way to Manitoba." During the journey, "nothing was talked of but Manitoba and the North-West...."

The influx created an unprecedented demand for space. By the spring of 1882 the hotels were so crowded that people were sleeping in the parlours, corridors, and lobbies. Beecham Trotter, who arrived in Winnipeg during the boom, put up at a "miserable hotel" on Main Street, where he paid two dollars to spend a night in a chair. One mathematically inclined newcomer figured out that in his boarding house each occupant had exactly twenty-eight square feet of floor space or about one-tenth of the average in Ontario. Meal times, by all accounts, were savage: ". . . long ere the dining room doors are thrown open, a crowd gathers, eager to charge the tables and anxious to satisfy the cravings of the inner man. Frequently weak men are seriously injured in these jams. The tables have to be cleared and re-set several times ere the guests are all dined." At one of the leading hotels the crush was so great that one diner suffered a broken arm.

In March an Ottawa manufacturer rushed fifteen hundred cotton tents to Winnipeg. On the outskirts of town giant tent boarding houses began to rise in rows. These gargantuan marquees were large enough to accommodate within their folds a cluster of smaller tents, each capable of sleeping eight men. By May, the ever-alert Arthur Wellington Ross was importing portable houses from an eastern manufacturer. Space was at such a premium that he was able to rent them all before they arrived.

That social phenomenon, the Winnipeg boarding house – half tent, half ramshackle frame – had its birth that year:

"You open the door and immediately there is a rush of tobacco smoke and steam mingled with indescribable results which makes you want to get outside and get a gulp of fresh air. You go to the counter and get tickets from the man behind the desk for supper, bed and breakfast. There are no women about and no children. Nor are there any elderly people – they are all young men. You have no time to study them for through the mist of smoke in the great room there breaks the jangling call of a bell and a terrible panic seizes the crowd. It is not an alarm or fire nor is there any danger of the building caving in, neither is it a fight nor a murder – it is only supper."

Supper consisted of a plate of odorous hash, flanked by a mug of tea and a slab of black bread, served up by a number of "ghastly, greasy and bearded waiters with their arms bare to their elbows and their shirt bosoms open displaying considerably hairy breast." The meal was devoured in total silence, the only sound being "a prodigious noise of fast-moving jaws, knives, forks and spoons."

The boarders themselves were a motley lot: "Men who were at one time high up in society, depraved lawyers, and decayed clergymen brought down by misconduct and debauchery, but still bearing about them an air of refinement ... carpenters smelling strongly of shavings, mill hands smelling of sawdust and oil, teamsters smelling of horse, plasterers fragrant with lime, roofers odorous with tar, railway laborers smelling of whiskey, in short all sorts and conditions of men."

At night, when the tables were cleared and the occasional drunk subdued with a club, a man at the end of the building picked up a ladder, planted it against the wall, and told the inmates to clamber into their bunks among the grey horse-blankets that served as bedding.

Yet the immigrants poured in. Often their enthusiasm was dampened when they reached the city. One carpenter, arriving in March, found he could get no work because his employer had no shop. Moreover, the station platform was covered with tool boxes and he realized that his fellow artisans, arriving by the score, would make his services a drug on the market. In St. Paul that same week, an unnamed Canadian uttered one of the few murmurs of gloom voiced about the prospects in Manitoba. "When the tumble comes in Winnipeg it's going to be something awful," he said. But among the swirling crowds in the auction rooms of Main Street, bidding higher and higher for lots in towns and "cities" like Emerson, Shoal Lake, West Lynne, and Minnedosa, there was still no hint of the reckoning to come.

3

The Winnipeg land boom can be divided into two parts. The boom of 1881 was followed by a lull in late January and February before the spring boom of 1882 began. On February 16, the city fell under the lash of one of the worst storms it had yet known. Speculators who had come into town from outlying points found themselves imprisoned by the cold. Even the trains were unable to travel west to Portage la Prairie and Brandon; although the track had been built high and ditched carefully to prevent just such a calamity, the roadbed was effectively blocked by a wall of packed snow.

At first, the storm seemed to act as a depressant; the demand for city property ebbed. Undismayed, the entrepreneurs began to boost other Manitoba metropolises and the boom moved on to a score of unfamiliar communities where, it was whispered, new railroads would soon be built.

As a result, extraordinary efforts had to be made to sell outlying lots in the immediate Winnipeg area. Curiously, the prices of these lots did not go down; rather they rose. The asking prices were so high, in fact, that it was doubtful whether any purchaser would be able to make more than the downpayment. This, apparently, did not matter. Real estate speculation in Winnipeg that spring resembled very much the dime chain-letter crazes and the pyramid clubs of a later era. Everybody reasoned that the real profits would be made by those who moved in early and got out swiftly, but no one was so pessimistic as to believe that he would be caught with worthless property.

The sellers tried to get the largest possible down payment and the shortest terms. The new purchasers, in turn, arranged at once with a broker to have their interest transferred to a syndicate at a handsome advance. The syndicates, in their turn, hired groups of smart young men to extoll the virtues of the property by a variety of dubious methods. Maps were cut and pasted, for example, so that outlying properties seemed to be much closer to town than they really were. But the real action was taking place in the smaller communities of Manitoba.

The safest investments were to be found at Brandon and Portage

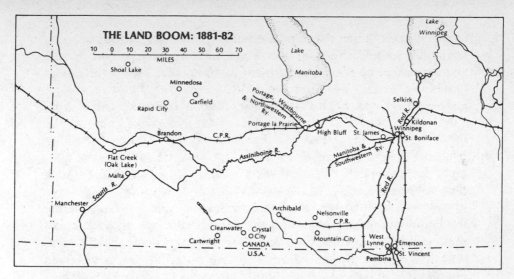

THE LAND BOOM: 1881-82

la Prairie, for these were on the main line of the CPR. The boom in Brandon had not abated since the summer of 1881. "Nobody who saw Brandon in its infancy even forgot the spectacle," Beecham Trotter wrote. Trotter nostalgically recalled a variety of sights and sounds: the hillside littered with tents, the symphony of scraping violins playing "Home, Sweet Home" and "The Girl I Left Behind Me," the cries of the auctioneers: "All wool from Paisley; and who the hell would go naked?" So all-embracing was the real estate fever in Brandon that when the town was laid out no provision was made for a cemetery. The dead had to be brought to Winnipeg for burial.

Portage la Prairie was in a perfect frenzy of speculation. "A craze seemed to have come over the mass of the people," an early chronicler recounted. "Legitimate business in many cases was thrown aside, and buying and selling lots became the one aim and object of life . . . . Carpenters, painters, tailors, and tradesmen of all kinds threw their tools aside to open real estate offices, loaf around the hotels, drink whiskey and smoke cigars. Boys with down on their lips not as long as their teeth would talk glibly of lots fronting here and there, worth from $1,000 to $1,500 per lot." Portage, at that time, had a population well below four thousand. Of its 148 business institutions, 58 were involved in some way with real estate.

The Portage boom was at least understandable. The Rapid City boom was more mysterious. The town was one of the most remarkable paper communities in the province: although its population was well under four hundred, the city was surveyed for eight square miles. The fever persisted in the face of the obvious fact that the CPR had passed Rapid City by. The road between Brandon and Rapid City was lined with wagons loaded with speculators, settlers' merchandise and effects, and with horses, cattle and sheep. Every hotel and every stable in town was overcrowded. Vacant land was being snatched up so swiftly that two or three men would sometimes arrive at the land office within minutes of one another, each intent upon grabbing the same section.

As late as May 30, the Rapid City doctor reported that "Rapid Cityites are not at all despondent over the change of route of the CPR but confidently expect having a railway connection with some place or other before twelve months . . . ." Advertisements in the Winnipeg papers actually boasted that *six* railways would soon run through the community.

In that demented winter people no longer asked, What will the land produce, only, What will it sell for? "People seem to have forgotten," the Edmonton *Bulletin* wrote, "that towns cannot live of themselves." Cities that did not exist, such as Garfield, were given non-existent suburbs such as North Garfield. One series of lots purporting to be in the West Lynn subdivision (on the banks of the Red River just opposite Emerson, near the border) sold for ten thousand dollars. Actually the property was two miles away, far out on the empty prairie.

For the moment at least the railway was king; it seemed to bring the Midas touch to the smallest shack-towns. Like a golden highway, the CPR had brought prosperity to Manitoba beyond the wildest dreams of the most optimistic pioneers. The very whisper of a railway – *any* railway real or imagined – drove people to greater and greater financial excesses. Local councils offered fat bonuses for CPR branch lines to their communities; rumours of newly formed railway ventures were greeted with the greatest enthusiasm and a resultant rise in real estate prices. The day would come when the people of Manitoba, in their grief and disappointment, would turn against the railway; but in the early months of 1882, the CPR could do no wrong.

Emerson, the customs point on the Pembina Branch of the CPR, confidently expected that it would be *the* great railway centre of the North West, easily outdistancing Winnipeg. As one eastern visitor described it, "Nothing is to be heard but 'boom', 'boom,' 'boom,' in every hamlet you pass; 'boom' in every person's mouth. In fact the excitement is fully as great as if a mountain of gold had been discovered near Toronto."

That was in the first week of January, 1882. Three weeks later it was Selkirk's turn. The excitement stemmed from a new by-law guaranteeing a bonus of seventy-five thousand dollars to the CPR to construct a branch line into the community. The news instantly raised real estate prices in Selkirk and reporters on the scene could hardly contain themselves: "In the carrying out of this the owners of lots in Selkirk see a great city rising to rival, and possibly eclipse, Winnipeg."

In the same week, lots in as yet unpopulated "Manitoba City" began to boom with the news that the terminus of the Pembina Mountain branch line of the CPR had been settled upon. Minnedosa, "the railway centre of the North West," had, like some other towns, been by-passed, but that did not seem to matter. "Thank fortune, the 'boom' has also struck Minnedosa!" the *Times*'s resident correspondent burbled. "Happy name! High flown and sweet sounding. A place with such a name and such a vicinage, and, shall I say it? such people, could not but boom. Again, I say, the boom has struck Minnedosa...."

Though Manitoba's population, in 1882, was only sixty-six thousand, a casual newspaper reader in a foreign country, perusing the advertisements, might have believed it to be the crossroads of the continent, teeming with people and jammed with great cities. There was Crystal City, "the featured great city of Manitoba"; Mountain City, "the embryo city"; Dobbyn City, "the future great manufacturing city of the Souris district"; St. Vincent, "one of the leading cities of the Great North West"; Manchester, "the future great manufacturing town of the North West"; Clearwater, "the Brandon of Southwestern Manitoba"; Nelsonville, "the largest town in Southwestern Manitoba"; Kildonan, "the Yorkville of Winnipeg"; Rapid City, "the Minneapolis of the North West"; Malta, "situated in the garden of the North West"; Cartwright, "unquestionable the best situated and rising town in the province"; Pembina Crossing, "the most prosperous town in Southwestern Manitoba"; and High Bluff, "the best chance of the season."

As the frenzy continued the advertisements became larger and shriller, the methods used to peddle property wilder and more unscrupulous, and the paper communities more ephemeral. The land sharks used patently transparent devices to victimize the newcomers. Two men from Barrie, Ontario, were persuaded to buy, sight unseen, for sixty thousand dollars, a piece of swamp five miles from Winnipeg. The sellers played upon their greed: as the easterners were mulling over the deal, a third man came up and, pretending to believe the transaction was closed, offered them eighty thousand dollars for the property. It did not occur to the two that the offer was bogus and that the new buyer was operating as a shill. They handed over the money cheerfully and ended up in possession of a piece of useless prairie.

Such tales, filtering back east, helped to drive a wedge between settled Canada and the new North West. "At this moment Winnipeg is filled with thousands of the vilest villains," the Bobcaygeon *Independent* declared in an editorial in late March, "and it is possible that never before on this continent was there assembled together so large a congregation of scoundrelism.... It is a saddening spectacle to observe the universality of this disgusting degradation.... It is an outbreak of the worst passions of human nature .... The business of men's lives in Winnipeg ... is the gratification of that vile lust of gold which completely overpowers the moral sense, extinguishes reason, annihilates the sense of responsibility, renders crime no longer repulsive, and unfits the miserable and wretched beings for any other companionship than that of themselves and the devil."

To this Victorian invective, the Winnipeg *Times* made a scoffing reply: "Listen to the sage of Bobcaygeon," it sneered, "– and laugh." One of its own editorial writers, C. R. Tuttle, had himself become a leading Winnipeg speculator.

4

Two events, one man-made and the other natural, following hard upon each other in mid-April, killed the great North West boom. The first was the sale of Edmonton lots beginning April 12, which soured the most optimistic speculators. The second was the three-week rampage of the Red River, which began a week later.

Fort Edmonton lay on the very rim of the unknown. Perhaps for that reason it caught the fancy of the Winnipeg land buyers. The word was that the Hudson's Bay Company had surveyed the environs of the old trading post into town lots and was about to throw them onto the market. On April 12, the news was made public in gigantic advertisements by Arthur Wellington Ross, whose office was quickly jammed with purchasers. The previous fall, Edmonton lots had sold for about twenty-five dollars each; now three hundred went in a single night at prices ranging between two and four hundred. But a strange thing happened. On April 13, scores of speculators had poured into Ross's office, waving marked cheques for thousands of dollars, intent on picking up Edmonton lots. The following day, when almost all of them tried to sell the lots at a profit, there were no buyers. The boom was collapsing, though nobody would yet admit it.

Coolican, the auctioneer, tried to resuscitate the good times. On the day of the Edmonton collapse, he engaged a private train for himself and a group of Winnipeg businessmen and steamed off to St. Paul to sell Manitoba lots. It was a gala excursion, a kind of last gasp by Winnipeg's leading speculators. Coolican was promising to turn St. Vincent into a great "International City" straddling the border and including within its limits all of Pembina, Emerson, and West Lynne. He took St. Paul by storm. "There is a smack of enterprise, push and dash in the Winnipeg boomers who are now visiting St. Paul which commands admiration," a local editor wrote. It was strange to see such phrases applied by Yankees to Canadians; for years it had been the other way around. In Sherman's Hall, St. Paul, Coolican sold one hundred thousand dollars worth of Canadian border lots.

There was only one problem: the boomers could not get back to Winnipeg. The Red River was on the rise. Bridges were being ripped away. Entire communities were half submerged. Many of the lots sold in St. Paul had turned to lakes, and the CPR line between Minnesota and Winnipeg was washed out. For the so-called International City, the result was catastrophic. The bridge at Emerson was swept away on April 16. By April 19, West Lynne had almost disappeared beneath the waves. Across the river, Emerson's citizens were forced to live for weeks on their second floors. The steamer *Cheyenne,* pushing a barge-load of lumber, steamed right up the main street and unloaded its cargo at the steps of the Presbyterian church.

The crest hit Winnipeg on April 19. Shortly after one o'clock that afternoon, the Broadway Bridge, nine hundred feet long, began to surge and sway until it plunged down the river on the breast of a six-mile current, its piers toppled by tumbling ice floes. By April 23, train service to and from St. Paul was suspended because of washouts along the line. Thousands were thwarted in their desire to reach Winnipeg and the town was like a morgue. Mail failed to arrive. Freight was at a standstill. Some immigrants managed to reach the city by boat, but since no food was carried, shortages began to drive the prices higher and higher. Building operations came to a stop; there were neither nails nor lumber available. Trade fell off. Artisans found there was no work at any price. The gigantic advertisements vanished from the newspapers as swiftly as the snows. By the time the floods subsided, the boom was finished. The railway blockade lasted for three weeks and did irreparable harm to Winnipeg's business community.

By this time the CPR had moved against the speculators by changing its regulations for the sale of prairie lands. The nominal price was raised from $1.25 to $5.00 an acre, a quarter of which had to be paid at the time of sale and the balance in five years without interest. But the rebate for land placed under cultivation was also raised to three-quarters of the original five dollars. Thus *bona fide* settlers who were prepared to work the land actually got it for $1.25 an acre. Those who bought land in the hope of a quick turnover paid four times as much.

Coolican, who finally managed to get back to Winnipeg by boat on April 28, took one last advertisement on the front pages headed: "COOLICAN'S RETURN! and the Boom Returns Also!" But the boom did not return. When Coolican tried to auction off lots in Prince Albert a month later, there were no takers. Coolican was reduced to auctioning off carpets and tapestries. Arthur Wellington Ross also tried again, vainly offering lots at Port Moody, British Columbia, the terminus of the CPR. Ross, too, was at the end of his financial rope. When real estate values plunged, he lost most of his huge fortune.

Of those who speculated in land in Manitoba in 1881 and 1882, it was estimated that only about five per cent made any money at all. The lucky ones broke even. The less fortunate ended their days in destitution – like Harry Armstrong's Toronto friend, Helliwell, "who cleaned up sixty thousand dollars, put it in his pocket, went broke and walked the streets till he died," or a Brockville man named Sheppard, whose obituary appeared in the dying days of the boom: "The rumour current Sunday evening was that he had lost $30,000 in speculating and hanged himself in consequence."

As a result of the bubble's sudden collapse, Manitoba entered into a period of recession which had far-reaching effects. Confidence in the North West was badly shaken. The international financial world began to look askance at any venture in the new Canada; the CPR would feel the pinch especially. The breach between West and East widened; the depression left by the boom prepared the climate for the farm agitation that followed. People who had once extolled the railway as a bearer of gifts now looked on it darkly as the source of their misfortunes.

The immediate effects were devastating. It was estimated that seventy-five per cent of the business institutions in the province wilted away. Robert Hill, Manitoba's pioneer historian, wrote eight years later that men "once deemed honest and good for any amount, were turned out of house and home, their goods and chattels liened on and sold by the sheriff." The wide-open credit system, which saw properties sold for small down payments, was the real culprit. People had been speculating with money they did not have. Buggies, buckboards, and wagons were shipped to Manitoba in wholesale lots by Ontario manufacturers and sold to anyone who would buy them on time. So extravagant was the spirit of optimism engendered by the coming of the railway that any newcomer who claimed to have taken up a farm or who said he had come to stay was granted almost instant credit; indeed, it was considered well-nigh an insult to turn him down. As a result of this reckless policy, scores of farms and even entire townships fell eventually into the hands of the loan companies. Worse, *bona fide* settlers, hacking away at the tough prairie sod, found they could get no further loans for stock, farm equipment, or seed. The boom collapsed just as the first great wave of immigration reached the prairies. The newcomers ran squarely into a wall of pessimism. The financial hangover that followed was one of the reasons why so many were forced to leave their new-found homes and retreat to the East and why the immigrant tide, which seemed to be unending during that roseate spring, eventually slowed to a halt for another generation.

In the years that followed, the pioneers of Manitoba looked back upon those bizarre months and wondered how they could have been so foolish. There was the case of Roderick McLeod, who owned a river lot of two hundred and forty acres at Portage la Prairie. He sold it for fifty thousand dollars of which fifteen thousand was the down payment. When the boom burst, the purchaser, unable to pay the balance, offered to return the land. Such was McLeod's avarice that he refused and the case went to court. In the soberer climate of a later period, the judge saw that the land had been overvalued. McLeod did not receive a nickel more for his inflated property; worse, the legal expenses gobbled up all of his original fifteen thousand and his homestead as well. Perhaps he contemplated, ruefully, the irony of his stand. Stretching off from that disputed parcel of real estate, in every direction, were millions of acres of prime farmland, available for homestead or pre-emption, all free for the asking.

The boom had a sobering effect on Winnipeg. All during the decade of the seventies it had been a lusty infant of a village. In one incredible winter it had reached its adolescence and sowed its wild oats. By the fall of 1882, it had matured to become a sadder and wiser city. As men recall their lost youth, old timers recalled wistfully those halcyon days before the bubble broke. One of these was George Ham, who wrote in 1921 that "since the boom of 1882, the soul of Winnipeg has never been what it was before."

"The later Winnipeg may be a better city," Ham admitted, but he regretted the good old days. "It was a short life from '71 to '82, but while it lasted, it was a life with a 'tang' to it – a 'tang' born of conditions that cannot be repeated and therefore cannot be reproduced."

Chapter
Three

FIVE
HUNDRED
MILES
OF
STEEL

1

Van Horne arrived in Winnipeg that January with a considerable reputation among railwaymen. The previous year, the *Railway Journal* had called him "a man of wonderful power and shrewdness." He was known, too, as "an idol-smashing heathen" who had no respect for the rigid dogmas of a tradition-ridden business. It was said that he could make eight hundred freight cars do the work of a thousand by his ingenious methods of loading. In Chicago he had astonished his contemporaries by the amount of trackage he had managed to work into a limited area in the yards. He had a reputation for doctoring sick railroads until they were made to pay. He was also known as a fighter: he had fought the grasshoppers, he had fought the labour unions, he had fought the encroachment of other railroads, and always he had won.

He seemed to know a terrifying amount about railroading. He knew all about yards and repair shops, he understood the mysteries of accounting, he could work out a complicated system of scheduling in his head, he could comprehend the chatter of the fastest telegraph key, and he could operate any locomotive built. He had even redesigned, with considerable grace and taste, that ugliest example of nineteenth-century American architecture, the railroad station.

There are a great many adjectives that apply to Van Horne: buoyant, capable, ingenious, temperamental, blunt, forceful, boyish, self-reliant, imaginative, hard-working, ruthless, puckish, courageous. But the word that best sums him up, and the one that his contemporaries used more than once, is "positive." He exuded confidence. J. H. E. Secretan, who worked for him as a surveyor, recorded that "the word 'cannot' did not exist in his dictionary." Was he ever bedevilled by doubts of his own or haunted by fears of private failure? If he was he hid his emotions well behind the grave mask of his face and those unrevealing eyes of penetrating blue.

He believed in coming to the point swiftly, with an economy of words. It was the same with railway lines. One of Van Horne's first tasks was to ensure that the CPR would reach Pacific tidewater by the shortest possible route. He had not yet met George Stephen, but he had encountered Major A. B. Rogers, "the Railway

Pathfinder," a gnarled little whipper-snapper of a man, notorious for the length of his white Dundreary whiskers, the astonishing profanity of his speech, and his apparent ability to exist for days on little more than hard-tack. After a summer in the mountains, Rogers (though he harboured some secret doubts) had decided to announce that the Kicking Horse Pass in the Rockies was feasible. In the second week in January, 1882, he and Van Horne went to Montreal to meet Stephen, McIntyre, and Angus to discuss the matter.

This resulted in two major decisions, the first of which was communicated to the press by Van Horne himself, with characteristic bluntness.

"We have changed the point," he said, "at which the road will enter the Rockies." Although, as the *Globe* pointed out, only the Dominion government could "change the point," it had in fact been changed almost without that authority.

The second decision was that there would be an alteration of route between Lake Nipissing, the official start of the railway, and Fort William, to allow the line to hug the shore of Lake Superior. In addition, a branch line contemplated from Lake Nipissing to Sault Ste Marie would be greatly shortened, placing the Sault virtually on the main line.

This announcement underlined the company's intention of proceeding with the Lake Superior section. Jim Hill and several other directors had not contemplated building the line across the Precambrian Shield. Their plan was to divert it from Callander Junction, on Lake Nipissing, by way of the Sault, to join up with the St. Paul railway in which Stephen, Donald Smith, Angus, and Kennedy were all leading shareholders.

From a business point of view, that plan made great sense. Had it been adopted, it is conceivable that the CPR might have become part of the railway empire that the ambitious Hill was constructing – a Canadian feeder line for the Great Northern, which was to grow out of the original St. Paul railway.

But Van Horne had become that year the most trenchant advocate the Lake Superior line had. His railway sense rebelled against a connection with another railroad. He wanted a through line, independent of local traffic; and there is little doubt that he saw more clearly than the others the consequences to the CPR of linking up with Hill's road. When Hill heard of Van Horne's opposition to his plan he burst out that he would get even with him "if I have to go to hell for it and shovel coal."

No doubt Hill ruefully recalled his advice to Stephen that Van Horne would take all the authority he could. The new general manager was a man of towering ambition whose love of power had its roots in his youth. At the age of eighteen, he had breathlessly watched the arrival of the general superintendent of the Michigan Central coming forward to meet his assistants. When the "mighty man," as Van Horne called him, moved away, the youth walked around the official car and gazed on it with awe. He found himself wondering if he might not some day attain the same rank and travel about in a private car of his own. "The glories of it, the pride of it, the salary pertaining to it, all that moved me deeply," he told his grandson many years later, "and I made up my mind then and there that I would reach it." He did, in just ten years; at the age of twenty-eight he became the youngest railway superintendent in the world. Now, with a new railway in his grasp – the longest in the world and potentially one of the mightiest – he had no intention of sharing his power with any man.

He could get along quite easily with George Stephen, for Stephen was a financier, not a railroad man. The two men hit it off from the beginning, though their backgrounds were dissimilar. Stephen, the Highland Scot, was single-minded in his interests while Van Horne's enthusiasms were multitudinous. The new general manager was a mixture of Dutch, French, and German; in his drive and hustle he was the epitome of the American businessman – Macdonald's "sharp Yankee" – so despised by Canadian merchants and politicians. But there was a quality of enthusiasm about him that Stephen must have admired, for Stephen had it too. When Stephen threw himself into a project he went all the way; so did Van Horne. Once he became general manager of the CPR, he was a Canadian railwayman through and through. The difference was that Van Horne, unlike Stephen, seemed able to switch from one pursuit to another and make himself master of all of them. As a gardener he bred new varieties – a triple trumpet flower, for example, and a perfect hyacinth. As an amateur geologist he discovered and named new trilobites and brachiopods. He carried his rock collection about with him as other men carried a dispatch case.

Like Stephen, Van Horne had been raised in poverty. Like Stephen, he revered his mother, "a noble woman, courageous and resourceful." His father had died when he was eleven; at fourteen he had been forced to forsake his education to support his family. Again like Stephen, he had worked hard all his life to achieve his ambitions. In his ten-year drive to the top he had never known a holiday. When others sought respite, the young Van Horne cheerfully assumed the burden of their tasks; that was how he learned so much about railways, haunting the repair shops, mastering the use of every tool, watching the engineers building bridges, learning line repairs from roadmen and section hands, studying accounting and figures. He was convinced that "an object can usually be attained through persistence and steadiness of aim" and in all his activities – from track-laying to poker – he held fast to that credo.

Van Horne had been in office only one month and was still in Montreal when he fired General Rosser, who was using inside knowledge of future railway locations to speculate in real estate. Van Horne came across a letter in which the General had revealed to a railway contractor the exact location of the terminus of the CPR's Pembina Mountain branch. This was valuable and privileged information. On February 1, Van Horne wired to Rosser that he had seen the letter and on account of his "unwarranted and unauthorized action on this and other matters" he was notifying him that his services were no longer required.

Rosser was not an easy man to dismiss. The wire had come at an extremely awkward time. He was about to leave for the western foothills on a twelve-hundred-mile reconnaissance, which had already received considerable publicity. The party planned to cover forty-five miles a day, using husky dogs "with wolf blood in their veins" hitched Eskimo-fashion eight to a sled, each team pulling eight hundred pounds. This romantic odyssey, which would have provided the chief engineer with priceless information about the future location of western townsites, was quashed by Van Horne's blunt telegram. Rosser was forced to postpone his journey. He rushed to St. Paul where he planned to intercept Van Horne who was returning from Montreal. Meanwhile he denied the inevitable rumours.

But matters could not be adjusted. In Van Horne, Rosser was up against an unyielding obstacle. The two met on February 10; Rosser asked the general manager to reconsider; Van Horne gave him a blunt No. He added that he was not disposed to do anything that would unnecessarily injure the reputation of the old cavalryman. On reaching Winnipeg, Rosser would be allowed to resign. Rosser did so on February 13, asking that his resignation take effect on March 10. Again, Van Horne was blunt: he wanted him out immediately, with his desk cleared, that very day. Indeed, he had already replaced him temporarily with his wife's cousin, Samuel B. Reed of Joliet, Illinois.

Rosser's dismissal was followed shortly afterward by that of his entire engineering staff. On March 13, a fire destroyed the new Bank of Montreal building, in which the CPR had its offices. During the transfer of some of the engineering department's documents it was discovered that several were missing, including plans of the contemplated route of the railway west. Van Horne told Reed to find the leak, and if he could not, to fire the whole staff on the spot. At the same time, Reed laid an information against his predecessor, charging that Rosser had fraudulently obtained the profiles of the line extending all the way to Calgary.

In the end, the CPR dropped the case. That might have been the end of matters had Rosser not accidentally encountered Van Horne on a hot July evening in the Manitoba Club. Van Horne was no man to back away from any encounter – as a child in Joliet he had taken on every boy in school. Winnipeg almost witnessed its only Western-style gunfight. Rosser and Van Horne both drew pistols, and a serious battle was averted only when, in the spirited account of the Winnipeg *Sun*, "the better counsels of cooler heads prevailed, and the belligerents were separated before their passions were cooled in gore."

2

When Van Horne met the CPR directors in Montreal, he was able to convince them that he could lay five hundred miles of track during the 1882 season. Stephen had already told Macdonald that the company was planning to finish the railway in half the ten-year period allowed by the contract. It was, indeed, essential that the through line get into operation as swiftly as possible; the CPR would stand or fall on its transcontinental trade – cargoes such as silk, for example, that demanded speedy dispatch. The Canadian road was far shorter than any United States transcontinental route, but it could not turn a dollar of profit on its through line until the last spike was driven.

Van Horne's announcement was greeted with considerable scepticism, but he gave no hint that he was embarked on anything remarkable. Back in Winnipeg in mid-February, 1882, he told J. H. E. Secretan, the surveyor, that he wanted "the shortest commercial line" between Winnipeg and the Pacific coast. He added that he would not only lay five hundred miles of track that summer but would also have trains running over it by fall. Secretan ventured a modicum of doubt, whereupon Van Horne declared that nothing was impossible; all he wanted his engineers to do was to show him the road; if Secretan could not do that, then he would have his scalp.

The general manager did not care much for engineers. He resented their professional interference; it clashed with his own dictatorship. "If I could only teach a section man to run a transit," he once remarked, "I wouldn't have a single damned engineer on the road." Secretan himself was as snobbish an engineer as ever took a level; but he admired Van Horne, "the most versatile man I have ever encountered."

Secretan noticed that as Van Horne talked he had a habit of making sketches on blotting pads. All his life the artist in Van Horne had struggled to be released; indeed, in another age and another climate – the Renaissance, perhaps – the artist might have won out over the hard-headed man of action. One of the most telling incidents in his biography is the story of how he fell so much in love with Hitchcock's *Elementary Geology* that he determined to use his copyist's skill to make it his own. Night after night by candlelight the determined child copied the book in ink onto sheets of foolscap – copied every page, every note, and every picture right down to the index. It did great things for him, as he later admitted: "It taught me how much could be accomplished by application; it improved my handwriting; it taught me the construction of English sentences; and it helped my drawing materially. And I never had to refer to the book again."

Not surprisingly, his art was meticulously literal. Once, he purloined a copy of *Harper's Weekly* before it reached his mother. With great care, he transformed a series of portraits of American authors into bandits. His mother complained to the mystified editor about his apparent policy of desecrating the images of great Americans. The baffled illustrator, Wyatt Eaton, when shown the same copy some years later was equally indignant. The issue became a collector's item.

This was the puckish side of Van Horne's nature. He was thirty-one at the time and a colleague described him as grave and thoughtful: "His constant manner was that of a person preoccupied with great affairs." But behind that poker face lurked the curiosity, the high spirits, and the ingenuousness of a small boy. Thomas Shaughnessy in his valedictory of Van Horne said truly that "he possessed the splendid simplicity of grown up boyhood to the end."

His reputation as a Yankee go-getter had a reverse side to it. It was generally held, and not without considerable evidence, that he was favouring Americans over Canadians when new employees were hired for the railway. This was especially true in the key jobs, but it was not in Van Horne's nature to take notice of such criticism. In the summer of 1882 he was doing his best to lure another American into the fold, a Milwaukee Irishman named Thomas Shaughnessy who had once been on his staff in the United States. Van Horne needed Shaughnessy to act as quartermaster-general for the vast army he intended to throw into the West once the floods subsided that spring. Shaughnessy required some persuading and did not arrive until late in the year, "a fashionably-dressed, alert young man, sporting a cane and giving general evidence of being what we call a live wire," in the words of Van Horne's private telegrapher, E. A. James.

It is an irony that from the very beginning the CPR – that most nationalistic of all Canadian enterprises – was to a large extent managed and built by Americans. The government section in British Columbia was contracted to an American engineer, Andrew Onderdonk, backed by a syndicate of American financiers. On the prairies another American company, Langdon and Shepard, held the prime contract. The remainder of the railway was given to a third American concern, the North American Railway Contracting Company of New Jersey. This firm was to be paid partly in CPR stock but in November, 1883, after the shares tumbled, the company backed out and the CPR took over construction in the mountains and across the Shield. On both these sections most of the subcontractors were Canadians, several of whom went on to become internationally famous entrepreneurs.

But in the eighties, most of the experienced railway talent was American. No major trunk-line had been built in Canada since the Grand Trunk, almost thirty years before. It was natural that Van Horne should employ men he knew something about and felt he could depend upon. Many of these came from the Milwaukee and St. Paul railroad, such as his old colleague John Egan, the CPR's western superintendent, and his hometown in-law, S. B. Reed. Neither was popular with Canadians. In the summer of 1884 Macdonald reported to Stephen that Egan's policies had, rightly or wrongly, "made the CPR so unpopular that the feeling amounts to hatred." But Van Horne stuck by his friend.

The presence of so many Americans continued to be the subject of bitter complaint; but there was another side to the coin. The brain-drain was being partially reversed by the great project of the railroad. Many of the "sour mash," as Americans were called, became dedicated Canadians. As someone remarked, the building of the CPR would make a Canadian out of the German Kaiser. It certainly made Canadians out of Van Horne, Shaughnessy, and Isaac Gouverneur Ogden, the company's western auditor, who, after he became vice-president, was known as the Finance King of the CPR. These men, and many lesser executives, turned their backs on their native land forever when they joined the railway. Shaughnessy, the policeman's son who became a baron, was so British in outlook that he was offered a cabinet post (which he declined) in the Asquith government. As for Van Horne, he was more Canadian than any Canadian. "I am a Chinese-wall protectionist," he told a reporter shortly before his death. "I don't mean merely in trade. I mean – everything. I'd keep the American idea out of this country."

But in the late spring of 1882, Van Horne was more concerned over floods than he was with "sour mash." The high water had already thrown his schedule off balance. The *Globe* ignored the unseasonable weather and laid the blame at the feet of the general manager. On June 23 it reported that "Van Horne's men have not laid one solitary rail upon the grading done under his regime." The paper dug up "a well known track-layer who has been in the business out west for 20 years" who claimed it was impossible to lay five hundred miles of track that season, and that there was "more construction in Stickney's little finger than in Van Horne's body."

Nonetheless, the general manager was making his presence felt. He was positively indefatigable. Years later, when asked to reveal the secret of his stamina, he summed it all up with characteristic candour. "Oh," said he, "I eat all I can; I drink all I can; I smoke all I can and I don't give a damn for anything."

"Why do you want to go to bed?" he once asked Secretan. "It's a waste of time; besides, you don't know what's going on." He could sit up all night in a poker game and then, when seven o'clock came, rub his eyes, head for the office, and do a full day's work. He loved poker and he played it expertly. It was not a game, he would say, but an education. He enjoyed all card games and he was good at them all. James Mavor, the Toronto professor who knew him well in later years, thought this was his secret – his ability to "turn rapidly from one form of activity to another and to avoid over-anxiety about any one of his enterprises."

Many colleagues were to remark upon this characteristic in Van Horne. When he had done his work he was free to play games, to eat a good supper, to smoke one of his gigantic cigars, to pore over his collection of Japanese porcelains, to work with his rock specimens, or to best a colleague at billiards or chess. He loved to play and he loved to win. He was reluctant to leave any poker table when he was losing. He liked to dare his associates to duplicate his astonishing feats of memory. Armstrong, the engineer, had one experience of it that remained with him all his life. Early in 1882 Van Horne told him to substitute nine-inch discharge pipes for the seven-inch on a water tank in order to save six minutes' time. Armstrong did not receive any nine-inch pipe before he and his fellow workers were dismissed. Two years later, when he was once again working for the CPR, he received a note from Van Horne, naming the date on which the order had gone out. "I told you to have those goosenecks made 9 inches," Van Horne wrote. "Why wasn't it done?"

By June, Van Horne had become the terror of the railway. The *Sun*'s uninhibited columnist, R. K. Kernighan, who signed himself "The Dervish Khan, the Screamer of Qu'Appelle," had been dispatched to Flat Creek – or Flat Krick, as he invariably called it – the transitory community at the end of track. There he watched the descent of Van Horne upon the unsuspecting settlement.

"The trains run in a kind of go-as-you please style that is anything but refreshing to the general manager. But when Manager Van Horne strikes the town there is a shaking up of old bones. He cometh in like a blizzard and he goeth out like a lantern. He is the terror of Flat Krick. He shakes them up like an earthquake, and they are as frightened of him as if he were the old Nick himself. Yet Van Horne is calm and harmless looking. So is a she mule, and so is a buzz saw. You don't know their true inwardness till you go up and feel of them. To see Van Horne get out of the car and go softly up the platform, you would think he was an evangelist on his way west to preach temperance to the Mounted Police. But you are soon undeceived. If you are within hearing distance you will have more fun than you ever had in your life before. He cuffs the first official he comes to just to get his hand in and leads the next one out by the ear, and pointing eastward informs him the walking is good as far as St. Paul. To see the rest hunt their holes and commence scribbling for dear life is a terror. Van Horne wants to know. He is that kind of man. He wants to know why this was not done and why this was done. If the answers are not satisfactory there is a dark and bloody tragedy enacted right there. During each act all the characters are killed off and in the last scene the heavy villain is filled with dynamite, struck with a hammer, and by the time he has knocked a hole plumb through the sky, and the smoke has cleared away, Van Horne has discharged all the officials and hired them over again at lower figures."

Yet the general manager rather enjoyed it when somebody stood up to him. In June he finally managed to secure the services of Michael Haney as superintendent of the Pembina Branch and the Rat Portage division, both of them originally built under government contract. It was inevitable that, sooner or later, Haney and Van Horne would clash.

Haney was in the Winnipeg freight yard one day when his secretary came hustling down the track to warn him that Van Horne was on the warpath. Haney was feeling pretty hot himself at the time. Everything seemed to have gone wrong that day. Instead of getting out of Van Horne's way he stalked resolutely down the yard to meet him.

Van Horne began an exhaustive recitation of the system's defects, punctuating his remarks with a colourful selection of profanity that turned the air blue. The pugnacious Haney waited until the general manager stopped for breath.

"Mr. Van Horne," he said, finally, "everything you say is true and if you claimed it was twice as bad as you have, it would still be true. I'm ready to agree with you there but I'd like to say this: Of all the spavined, one-horse, rottenly equipped, bad managed, badly run, headless and heedless thing for people to call a railroad, this is the worst. You can't get anyone who knows anything about anything. You can't get materials and if you could it wouldn't do you any good because you couldn't get them where you wanted them."

Haney followed up this outburst with a list of counter-complaints far more complete than Van Horne's, since he was in closer touch with the work. His tirade made Van Horne's explosion "sound like a drawing room conversation." The general manager waited patiently as Haney unleashed his torrent of grievances; by the time Haney had finished he was grinning.

"That's all right, Haney, I guess we understand one another," he said. "Let's get to work."

3

The contract to build the prairie section of the Canadian Pacific Railway was probably the largest of its kind ever undertaken. The prize was awarded in February to the partnership of General R. B. Langdon of Minneapolis and D. C. Shepard of St. Paul. The firm undertook to build six hundred and seventy-five miles of railroad from Flat Creek to Fort Calgary. This was a formidable task – just fifteen miles short of the entire length of the Central Pacific.

On the day after the contract was signed, Langdon and Shepard advertised for three thousand men and four thousand horses. They faced a staggering job. Between Flat Creek and Fort Calgary the partners would have to move ten million cubic yards of earth. They would have to haul every stick of timber, every rail, fishplate, and spike, all the pilings used for bridge-work, and all the food and provisions for 7,600 men and 1,700 teams of horses across the naked prairie for hundreds of miles. To feed the horses alone it would be necessary to distribute four thousand bushels of oats every day along one hundred and fifty miles of track. It was no wonder that Van Horne's boast about building five hundred miles in a single season was openly derided.

Winnipeg was transformed that spring of 1882 into a gigantic supply depot. Stone began to pour in from every available quarry, railroad ties from Lake of the Woods, lumber from Minnesota, and rails from England and from the Krupp works in Germany. Since the St. Lawrence would still be frozen well into the construction season, Van Horne had the steel shipped to New York and New Orleans and dispatched to Manitoba by way of St. Paul. Whole trainloads of material destined for the Canadian North West were constantly passing through American cities where hundreds of checkers reported on them daily so that the exact moment of their arrival could be plotted. As fast as the supplies arrived they were hauled away to the end of track. No newly completed line of steel had ever known such activity in the first year of its construction.

The April floods halted this activity, causing formidable log-jams in Winnipeg and St. Paul. By the time the water subsided, scores of would-be homesteaders were disheartened and ready to quit the North West. Trunks were piled along the grade like cordwood, as high as men could throw them, but many of the owners were already trying to sell their outfits and leave. In late May an unexpected blizzard struck, destroying scores of tents and causing great suffering. Fuel was at such a premium that men resorted to stealing lumber, stick by stick. The first passenger train to leave Brandon for Winnipeg after the flood pulled three coaches loaded to the doors with men and women leaving the North West, never to return.

At last, with the waters subsiding and blizzards ended, the sun came out and warmed the frigid plains. The prairie evenings grew mellower and soon the sweet incense of the wolf willow drifted in from the ponds and sloughs to mingle with the more familiar odours of salt pork, tamarack ties, wood smoke, and human sweat. The early spring blossoms – wild pansies, strawberries, and purple pasqueflowers – began to poke their tiny faces between the brittle grasses. Then, as a flush of new green spread over the land, the ox carts started west again until they were strung out by the hundreds ahead of the advancing line of steel.

As soon as the waters ebbed, a mountain of supplies descended upon Winnipeg. With the freight came people. By June, three thousand immigrants were under canvas in Winnipeg, all buoyed up by the expectation of an entirely new life on the Canadian prairies.

Though few people believed it would be possible for the CPR to achieve its season's goal or anything close to it after the delays, Van Horne was immovable. The general manager made it clear that he would cancel the contract if Langdon and Shepard did not live up to their obligations. "We shall show a record at track-laying which has never been surpassed on this continent," Shepard replied.

There followed a whirlwind of construction that was, in the words of the *Quarterly Review,* "absolutely without parallel in railway annals." The grade, winding snakelike across the plains, moved so swiftly that Secretan and his surveyors were hard put to stay ahead. Sometimes, indeed, they were awakened at night by the rumble of giant scrapers being dragged past their tents.

The prairie section of the CPR was built telescopically from a single base. Winnipeg was the anchor point: from there the steel would stretch for a thousand miles into the mountains; there would be no supply line for the railway builders other than the rails themselves. Van

Horne's army worked that summer with a military precision that astonished all who witnessed it. "Clockwork" was the term used over and over again to describe the track-laying technique.

The pulse of the operation was at "End of Track," that unique community that never stayed in one place for more than a few hours at a time. Its nerve centre was the line of boarding cars – eight or nine of them each three storeys high – that housed the track crews. These formed part of a long train of office cars, cooking cars, freight cars, shops on wheels and, on occasion, the private car of the general manager himself. Van Horne was continually to be found at End of Track, spinning yarns with the workmen, sketching buffalo skulls, organizing foot races and target-shooting at night, and bumping over the prairie in a buckboard inspecting the grade. Every day some sixty-five carloads of railroad supplies were dumped at End of Track. Most of these supplies had been carried an average of a thousand miles before reaching their destination.

The organization was meticulous, down to the last railway spike. Each morning two construction trains set out from the supply yards, far in the rear, each loaded with the exact number of rails, ties, spikes, fishplates, and telegraph poles required for half a mile of railway. One train was held in reserve on a siding about six miles to the rear; the other moved directly to the front where the track-laying gang of three hundred men and seventy horses was waiting.

The tracklayers worked like a drill team. The ties were unloaded first, to be picked up by the waiting wagons – thirty ties to a wagon – hauled forward and dropped on both sides of the graded embankment for exactly half a mile. As the ties were thrown out, two men with marked rods laid them across the grade, exactly two feet apart. Behind the teams came a hand-truck loaded with rails, fishplates, and spikes. Six men marched on each side of it, and when they reached the far end of the last pair of newly laid rails, each crew seized a rail among them and threw it into exact position. Two more men gauged these two rails for alignment. Four more followed with spikes, placing one in each of the four ends of the rails. Four others screwed in the fishplates and another four followed with crowbars to raise the ties while the spikes were being hammered in. All worked in a kind of rhythm, each man directly opposite his partner on each separate rail. More men followed with hammers and spikes to make the rails secure, but by this time the hand-truck had already moved forward, passing over the newly laid rails before the job was complete.

As each construction train dumped its half-mile of supplies at End of Track, it moved back to the nearest siding to be replaced by the reserve train. There was no time lost. As the track unfolded the boarding cars were nudged ahead constantly by the construction train locomotive so that no energy would be wasted by the navvies in reaching their moving mess halls and dormitories. Right behind the track-laying gang came the telegraph teams, working so efficiently that one hour after the day's track was laid, End of Track was in telegraphic communication with the outside world.

The operation was strung out for hundreds of miles across the open prairie. Up ahead were the survey camps, followed by the grading gangs and the bridge-makers. Far to the rear were other thousands – saddlers and carpenters, cooks and tailors, shoemakers, blacksmiths, doctors, and provisioners. Supply trains moved out of Winnipeg on schedule, unloading thousands of tons of goods at yards established every hundred miles. Here the material was sorted daily into train lots and dispatched to the front. When the steel moved past the hundred-mile point the yards moved, too. An entire community of office workers, sorters, dispatchers, trainmen, labourers, and often their families as well, could be transported a hundred miles in a single night without the loss of an hour's work, because the houses were all portable and could be fitted easily onto flatcars.

Far out on the barren plains, miles to the west of End of Track, were the bridging teams, grading units, and surveyors, all driven forward by the knowledge that the tracklayers were pressing hard behind them. The head contractor had a flying wing of his own men standing by, prepared to complete immediately any work that seemed unlikely to be ready in time for the "ironing" of the track.

The grading was accomplished by immense scrapers pulled by teams of horses. Their task was to build an embankment for the railway four feet above the prairie and to ditch it for twenty yards on either side. At that height the rails would be protected from the blizzards of winter and costly delays from snow blockage would be avoided.

The bridgers worked in two gangs, one by day and one by night. Every sliver of bridging had to be brought from Rat Portage, one hundred and forty miles east of Winnipeg, or from Minnesota; for this reason the bridge-builders were seldom more than ten miles ahead of the advancing steel. Timbers were unloaded as near End of Track as possible and generally at night so as not to interfere with other work. "Sometimes," one eyewitness reported, "not a stick of timber nor any preparation for work could be seen one day, the next would show two or three spans of a nicely finished bridge. Twenty-four hours afterwards the rails would be laid, and trains working . . . ."

"The history of the world offers no such evidence of push as the work of this year has done," R. B. Conkey, Langdon and Shepard's general manager, declared at Winnipeg in August. "Sherman's march to the sea was nothing to it. When the road is completed there will be nothing in history to compare with it."

The nation was electrified by the speed with which the railroad was being forced across the plains. One man on the scene noted that it seemed to move as fast as the ox carts of the settlers who were following along beside the tracks. Alex Stavely Hill, a visiting British Member of Parliament, went in for lunch on one of the boarding cars around eleven one morning and noted, on emerging at two that afternoon, that a wagon that had been parked beside the car was already two miles to the rear. William White, homesteading near Pile o' Bones Creek, left his camp one morning to bring in wood from a copse six miles away. When he left there was no sign of construction for two miles to the east. When he returned, he and his companions had to cross a newly completed track.

The North West of Canada, once so haunting and so mysterious, was being transformed by the onslaught of the rails. One railway employee wrote that the progress of construction was so swift that antelope and other game that migrated north were cut off on their return that fall by the lines of rails and telegraph posts, "and terrified by the sight . . . gathered in hundreds on the north side, afraid to cross it." It was probably the last summer in which herds of buffalo and antelope freely roamed the prairie.

Father Albert Lacombe, back among his beloved Blackfoot nation, watched the approach of the rails with resignation:

"I would look in silence at the road coming on – like a band of wild geese in the sky – cutting its way through the prairies; opening up the great country we thought would be ours for years. Like a vision I could see it driving my poor Indians before it, and spreading out behind it the farms, the towns and cities . . . . No one who has not lived in the west since the Old-Times can realize what is due to that road – that C.P.R. It was Magic – like the mirage on the prairies, changing the face of the whole country."

Onward the track moved, cutting the plains in two. It moved through a land of geese, snipe, and wild ducks, fragrant in the soft evenings with the scent of willow and balsam. It cut across acres of yellow daisies, tiger lilies, purple sage, and briar rose. It bisected pastures of tall buffalo grass and skirted green hay meadows, which in the spring were shallow ponds. As it travelled westward it pushed through a country of memories and old bones – furrowed trails fashioned decades before by thousands of bison, vast fields of withered herbage, dead lakes rimmed with tell-tale crusts of alkali. Day by day it crept towards the horizon where, against the sunset, flocks of wildfowl, disturbed by the invaders, could be seen in silhouette; or where, sometimes, a single Indian, galloping in the distance, became no more than a speck crawling along the rim of the prairie. This had been the Great Lone Land, unfenced and unbridged, which the early explorers had described as if it were on the dark side of the moon. The line of steel made Butler's phrase obsolete, for the land would never again be lonely. All that summer it reverberated with the clang of sledge and anvil, the snorting of horses and mules, the hoarse puffing of great engines, the bellowing of section bosses, the curses of thousands of sweating men, and the universal song of the railroad navvies: "Drill, ye tarriers, drill."

History was being made, but few had time to note that fact. Beecham Trotter was to write, a little sheepishly, that "few, if any of us were historically minded enough to think of the interest that might attach to a running diary of what was seen, and said, and done, from day to day." Nor did William Oliver (a future mayor of Lethbridge, Alberta) in his ox cart heading west consider the significance of what he saw: "It never came to my mind in watching the building of the railway . . . that in the next fifty years it would play so important a part in the commerce of the country and in fact of the world . . . ."

At the same time the spectacle of the steel-laying gangs was "a sight never to be forgotten . . . ." They were a mixed lot. Charles Alfred Peyton came upon a gang of Italians who "looked like guys who would cut your throat for a dime." A few miles farther on, however, he joined a team of young Englishmen, "a very nice bunch of lads." Stavely Hill, who was a barrister, encountered a man ploughing, "throwing almost as much strength from himself into his work as he was getting out of his horses." It developed that he was a former doctor. That night, the man who cooked his dinner in the boarding car turned out to be the same solicitor's clerk who had once visited his London chambers with briefs.

The general run of railroad navvies was far rougher. One eastern reporter found them "ill-bred and offensive in their manners, applying the most obscene epithets to every passerby, jostling with their heavy teams every traveller they meet upon the trail, and in all respects making themselves as disagreeable as they know how to be. In their personal habits they are much more uncleanly than the poorest and most degraded of Indians, and in all respects they fairly represent the class from which they were drawn, that is, the scum and offscourings of the filthiest slums of Chicago and other western cities."

As autumn approached, the pace of the railway quickened still more. At the end of August one track crew managed to lay four and a half miles of steel in a day. Next day they beat their own record and laid five miles. It was all horribly expensive, as a worried Stephen reported to Macdonald in September: " . . . the road . . . is costing us a great deal more than the subsidy and a great deal more than we expected. We are just about even with the world at the moment, but to reach this position, we have had to find 5 million

253

dollars from our resources. *To enable me to make up my quota I had to sell my Montreal Bank stock.*"

There were those who thought that Van Horne "seemed to spend money like a whole navy of drunken sailors." Actually he counted every dollar. In the interests of both speed and economy he allowed steep grades and tight curves. In places, the road was like a switchback; it remained that way until the end of the century.

The contractors did not reach Van Horne's goal of five hundred miles; the spring floods had frustrated his ambition. By the end of the season, however, they had laid four hundred and seventeen miles of completed railroad, built twenty-eight miles of siding, and graded another eighteen miles for the start of the following season. In addition, Van Horne had pushed the Southwestern branch line of the CPR in Manitoba a hundred miles and so could say that, in one way or another, he had achieved the aggregate he sought.

As far as the general public was concerned, he had wrought a miracle. Only the waspish *Globe* refused to be impressed: "The public has nothing to gain by this breakneck speed . . . . If . . . a southerly pass had been found across the Rocky Mountains, there might be some object in making haste across the plains. But from present appearances, the entire Prairie section will be crossed long before it is positively known whether or not there is a better crossing than the Yellowhead Pass . . . ."

There was a modicum of truth in the *Globe*'s carping. In the heart of the Rocky Mountains that summer, Major A. B. Rogers was still plagued with doubts about the feasibility of the Kicking Horse Pass as a railway route. Equally serious was the whole question of the barrier of the Selkirks. The plain truth was that Van Horne and his men had been driving steel all summer at record speed, straight at that double wall of mountains, without really being sure of how they were going to breach it.

4

The Honourable Edgar Dewdney, Lieutenant-Governor and Indian Commissioner of the North West Territories, was a handsome giant of a man. With his fringed buckskin jacket and his flaring mutton chop whiskers (which won for him the Indian name of "Whitebeard"), he made an imposing figure as he stalked about accompanied by his two gigantic Newfoundland dogs. It was not difficult to spot Dewdney at a distance – he stood "like Saul, head and shoulders above most men." In the late spring of 1882 there were a good many who wanted to keep him in view: the Lieutenant-Governor had been charged with staking out the site for the new capital of the Territories. No more profitable parcel of real estate could be imagined.

Battleford had been the original capital, but Battleford was no longer on the railroad. For all of the winter of 1881-82, Winnipeg speculators, knowing that the seat of government was about to be changed, had been dispatching platoons of men to squat on every promising location. It is fairly clear that General Rosser himself had his eye on land profits in the vicinity of the new capital; that was one reason why the preliminary survey of the line in Saskatchewan was altered. A likely townsite had been at the crossing of the Wascana or Pile o' Bones Creek. When the railway location was moved half a dozen miles to the south, across an absolutely treeless plain, the land sharks were left out in the cold.

Most Canadians familiar with the country felt that the only possible site for a capital city of the plains lay a few miles to the northeast near Fort Qu'Appelle in the wooded valley of the Qu'Appelle River, perhaps the loveliest spot on all that sere steppe. The railway, however, was designed to skirt the valley. The reason given was that the steep banks would make construction difficult and costly. An equally strong motive was undoubtedly the company's policy of by-passing established communities in the interests of greater land profits.

There was also the fact (mere rumour at the time) that Governor Dewdney had an interest in the land surrounding Pile o' Bones crossing. He and several friends, most of them leading politicians and public officials, had secretly formed a land syndicate earlier that year, in which Dewdney had a one-eleventh interest; it owned four hundred and eighty acres at the very spot that Dewdney selected, on June 30, as the site of the future capital.

At Fort Qu'Appelle, when the news of Dewdney's action came, there was anger, frustration, disappointment, and frenzy. Most of the settlers hitched up their teams and moved themselves and all their worldly goods to the bank of Pile o' Bones Creek. Squatters began to pour towards the embryo city. By fall they held most of the available homestead land in the area. Genuine settlers, who were supposed to get homesteads for nothing, found themselves paying up to five hundred dollars for them. The speculators used a variety of devices to swindle the newcomers. One method was to use a bogus lawyer to confuse settlers about their pre-emption rights to quarter sections adjacent to their homesteads. If that failed, Dewdney noted in an interview that fall, "a revolver is produced."

The matter of the capital was settled on August 12. Lord Lorne, consulted about the name, left the matter to his wife, Princess Louise, who chose Regina in honour of her mother. The choice produced an instant adverse reaction. Princess Louise was not the most popular

255

chatelaine that Rideau Hall had known; nor was the Governor General immune from the political mudslinging that enlivened the period. The comment of the Manitoba *Free Press,* which was typical, might easily have been characterized as lese-majesty in a later and more reverent era:

"... the Governor-General ... after harassing his massive intellect for a few days, evolved the word Regina from the chaos of his thoughts, and now the aforesaid capital will go down to posterity under the aegis of that formidable cognomen.... If we have to put up with such outrageous nomenclature, it would have been better to stick by the old stand-by, Pile of Bones."

The choice of the site provoked even greater controversy than that of the name. Some of this resulted from a Canadian Press Association visit to the townsite in August. The eastern reporters, used to the verdant Ontario countryside, were dismayed to find nothing more than a cluster of tattered tents, huddled together on a bald and apparently arid plain. The London *Advertiser* called it a "huge swindle." The Brandon *Sun* said it should have been named Golgotha because of its barren setting. The Toronto *World* declared that "no one has a good word for Regina."

Early visitors were astonished that such a bleak plain should have been preferred over the neighbouring valley. Beecham Trotter, stringing telegraph wire across it early in July, thought of it as a lifeless land: "... there was not a bush on which a bird could take a rest.... Water was invisible for mile after mile." Marie Macaulay Hamilton, who arrived as a child, remembered the embryo capital as "a grim and dismal place"; to Peter McAra, who later became its mayor, Regina was "just about as unlovely a site as one could well imagine." Even George Stephen was dubious. He would have preferred Moose Jaw.

Dewdney stuck to his stated conviction that he had chosen the best possible location. He publicly declared that the site had been selected because "it was surrounded by the best soil, it has the best drainage, and the best and greatest volume of water, of any place between the Assiniboine and Swift Current Creek." He told Macdonald, quite accurately as it turned out, that the new capital was in the very heart of the best wheat district in the country.

In the light of Dewdney's personal interest in Regina real estate these statements were greeted with jeers. Inevitably there was a clash with the CPR. The railway was already hard pressed for funds. Its main asset was the land it owned on the sites of new towns. It did not intend to share these real estate profits with outsiders.

In Regina and in several other important prairie towns, the govern-

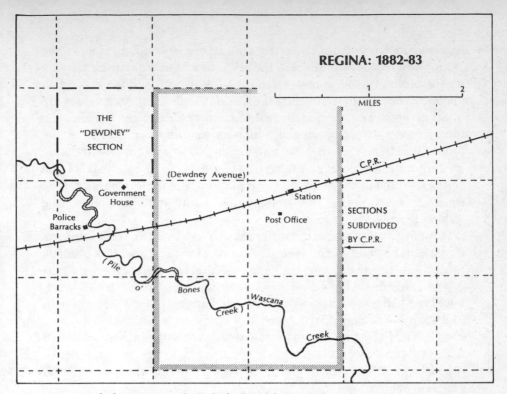

REGINA: 1882-83

THE "DEWDNEY" SECTION

(Dewdney Avenue)

Government House

Police Barracks

Station

Post Office

C.P.R.

SECTIONS SUBDIVIDED BY C.P.R. ←

(Pile O' Bones Creek) Wascana Creek

MILES 1 2

ment and the CPR pooled their land interests and arranged to share the profits equally. That summer the railway, in order to raise funds, agreed to sell five million acres of land to a British-Canadian syndicate, the Canada North-West Land Company. The land company would manage townsite sales in forty-seven major communities, and the railway would receive half the net profits. Thus, in Regina, one quarter of the land profits went to the railway, one quarter to the land company, and a half to the government. Since, in Stephen's phrase, the land company was "practically a branch of the Land Department of the C.P.R.," the railway controlled all of the Regina land save for that held by the Dewdney syndicate.

A struggle now ensued between William Scarth of the land company and John McTavish, the CPR's land commissioner, on one side and the Dewdney syndicate on the other over the exact location of Regina's public buildings. The former wanted the nucleus of the new capital on the railway's land; Dewdney wanted it on his property. The struggle moved to Winnipeg, where the rival properties were touted in huge competing advertisements. The railway won. Scarth sold some half-million dollars' worth of Regina real estate that winter; the rival sales were negligible.

A further struggle developed over the location of government buildings. Dewdney wanted them on the river, where, as he pointed out, the drainage was good (and also where they would be next door to his syndicate's land); Stephen and Scarth wanted them near the station where, they contended, the government as well as the railway would profit. In the compromise that followed Macdonald tried to placate everyone by scattering the various locations. As a result the queer community straggled for two and a half miles across the prairies, the various clusters of official buildings standing like islands in the prairie sea. In all the wheeling and dealing over land profits no public or corporate leader ever bothered to consider the interests of the settlers, who had an awkward town plan imposed upon them by men from eastern Canada, few of whom had any intention of making Regina their home.

It was typical of eastern indifference to local North West interests that when the first train arrived on August 23 with a carload of officials to christen the town, the residents themselves were given no part in the ceremony. They had trekked across the prairie by ox cart, buckboard, horseback, and construction train; but no one thought to ask any of them to participate in the official beginning of the new town. W. H. Duncan, who watched the scene from behind a tent flap, wrote half a century later that "our work clothes were not considered in good enough condition to appear among the well-dressed people from the East."

The ceremony took place in the general manager's private car. Van Horne, Donald Smith, Duncan McIntyre, and John McTavish of the CPR were all present along with the company's solicitor, J. J. C. Abbott. Both the Hudson's Bay Company and the Bank of Montreal were represented on the highest level. Judge Francis Johnson of Quebec, a former territorial official, proposed the toast to Mr. and Mrs. Dewdney and "Success to Regina, the Queen City of the Plains."

It makes, in retrospect, an ironic little scene: there are the eastern dignitaries in their dark coats, wing collars, and striped trousers, lounging on the rear platform of the private car with their well-bustled wives; and there are the first families of Regina in their shapeless clothing, peering curiously out from behind the protection of the canvas flaps. Among the onlookers that day were at least three future mayors and one future chief justice; in the years that followed they and their fellows would help to shape the destinies of Saskatchewan and perhaps to nurture the seeds of dissidence sown in those formative months. But none of this occurred to the gentlemen on the train, sipping their French champagne and squinting across the parched prairie, flat as a deal board, where the little tents stretched off in ragged clusters to the distant river.

5

From his vantage point at Winnipeg, George Stephen must have contemplated the astonishing progress of the railway with mixed feelings. Certainly his strategy, and Van Horne's, was working; but the company itself was in a desperate cash position.

The strategy had been to get the prairie section of the CPR operating as swiftly as possible. In that way a great chunk of the subsidy, which was paid to the company on the completion of each twenty-mile section, could be gained. Equally important, the paying portion of the line could go into operation and begin to show a profit at once.

All that year the climate in the money markets of London and New York had been bad for railway stocks and bonds in general and Canadian Pacific bonds in particular. Stephen made no effort to place CPR securities on the London market, though he hoped to intrigue British investors into ordering land grant bonds from Montreal and New York.

There was a kind of lassitude in England as far as Canada was concerned – an indifference that maddened Stephen who, in February, 1882, noted with disgust that P. T. Barnum's most recent acquisition, the huge elephant Jumbo, was "a matter of ten times more interest to London than twenty colonies." The market was so bad that when the CPR was driven to issue the remainder of its authorized stock in May, 1882, the best price it could get was twenty-five cents on the dollar. Stephen was loath to issue any more stock at all. First, he wanted to prove that the CPR was a paying proposition. But in 1882 he had to find $4,300,000 to buy up the western section of the Quebec government railroad and its branch lines in order to give the CPR access to Montreal. To raise the money he was forced to sell four times as much stock as he originally reckoned on.

He received a second financial blow that month: he had fully expected to lay his hands on an additional million dollars – deposited with the government as security for the construction of the road. Stephen had believed that he could replace the deposit with gilt-edged securities; it did not occur to him that the government would balk, but the government did. He did not get his million until December and only when he put up his personal property in exchange.

One of the unforeseen problems lay in the manner in which the twin subsidies – cash and land – were paid by the government. The money was advanced in equal instalments after each twenty-mile section was completed. This worked very well on the prairie section, where the track was advancing at the rate of twenty miles a week. But Stephen realized that he would shortly be faced with the mountain and Shield country where men would have to struggle for months to complete twenty miles of track. Cash from the subsidy would not be available to the company until long after the actual outlay. The CPR had already spent more than the subsidy on the prairie section. Where would it get the money to pay for labour and materials on the more difficult stretches of the road?

The matter of the land subsidy was even more complicated. On paper it all sounded so simple. Every time the railroad moved twenty miles it was to be given a proportionate number of acres. But even if every alternate section in the forty-eight-mile belt had been fit for settlement, it would have been impossible to locate all of the twenty-five million acres in that strip. Some of it, for instance, had already been sold, some of it belonged to the Hudson's Bay Company, and, in addition, the CPR rejected a great deal of it. Clearly, the government must be persuaded to set aside extra tracts in the North West. The trouble with governments, as Stephen was discovering, is that they do not move very swiftly.

By the end of 1882, Stephen realized, the company would have earned ten million acres of land; but there were only three million available along the completed right of way. Where would the rest come from? The government itself was selling land as fast as it could in the North West. It began to look as if there would not be enough left for the CPR. ". . . we shall need every acre of the grant to enable us to find the money," Stephen wrote. ". . . delay will be fatal to us – we cannot wait . . . ."

But, of course, he had to wait. A hint of panic crept into the letters that arrived, sometimes daily, on the Prime Minister's desk: "I . . . cannot move till I have patents for the lands earned, up to this time." "The demand on us for money is something appalling. *$400,000* went to Winnipeg last week and one million more to be there on the 10th."

Macdonald, however, was not to be pushed. In late October he wrote a soothing letter to Stephen: "Let us go by degrees in what we do . . . . We are endeavouring to discover some plan for the issue of the patents speedily, but I fear that will need legislation."

Stephen was almost beside himself. In his letters he began to under-line words for emphasis with great slashes of his pen: "It is most *essential* it should be settled *where* we are to get these lands." The CPR's account at the Bank of Montreal was badly overdrawn. Without the land the railway had no hope of raising further cash. "Our pinch is *now*," he wrote in frustration at the end of November. Bit by bit the Canadian Pacific Railway got its land, but it was another twenty-two years before the last acre was finally set aside for the company.

Even the acreage the company received at the time did not produce the hoped-for revenue; the land grant bonds were not selling. Again, the only other possible source of ready cash was stock. In December,

1882, the company increased its authorized capital stock from twenty-five million dollars to one hundred million. Stephen, in New York, persuaded a number of leading American financial houses to form a syndicate to take a potential thirty millions in three equal instalments over a nine-month period. To get cash Stephen was forced to sell the stock at slightly better than half price. Moreover, the purchase of the second two instalments was conditional on the successful sale to the public of the first. Stephen set off immediately for London to attempt the impossible: to find buyers for the new issue in a market which, as Macdonald's confidant, the British financier Sir John Rose, wired, was "practically shut against Canada Pacific."

Stephen succeeded. He prevailed on financial houses in London, Amsterdam, and Paris to purchase blocks of the stock from the Americans – a considerable piece of financial legerdemain, given the business climate. As of October 28, 1883, when the final instalment was taken up, 50.3 per cent of all CPR shares were held in the United States.

This did not mean, however, that Americans controlled the Canadian Pacific Railway. The American-held stock was spread among 320 investors. Another thirty per cent was held in Britain and Europe by 157 shareholders. The remainder – just under twenty per cent – was controlled by a tight group of forty-two Canadians. All but a few thousand of these Canadian-held shares were in the hands of four men – Stephen, Angus, McIntyre, and Donald Smith. This Canadian control of the CPR was even more pronounced at stockholders' meetings. At a general meeting in March, 1884, sixteen Canadians voted 96,141 shares while the forty-two Americans voting could muster only 90,212.

It would have taken a major proxy battle to oust the Canadians from control of their own railway. Such a move was unthinkable, for the shareholders had every confidence in Stephen, whose passionate belief in the railway and the Canadian North West had persuaded the businessmen of four capitals to take up his new stock issue. "I have never had misgivings about eventual success in spite of all opposition," Stephen declared, "but sometimes it has taken some courage to keep weak-kneed associates from wilting."

By "opposition," Stephen meant the Grand Trunk, which was continuing to fight the railway on several new fronts. The GTR's forceful general manager, Joseph Hickson, was no minor adversary. He was a Northumberland man who had been involved with railways since boyhood, working his way up from apprentice clerk to the very top, "a straightforward and fair-dealing man," a contemporary biographer called him, punctual as a conductor's watch and tough as a rail-spike. He was known as a shrewd negotiator, patient and tenacious. His brain moved like quicksilver: he had a habit of sizing up a situation almost instantly, recognizing its potentialities, and acting with dispatch. He could, said one admirer, make pounds, shillings, and pence, traffic miles and ton miles, dance in sarabands. In Canada he was a power in both the political and the financial worlds. Married to a member of the Dow brewing family, he was a long-time crony and supporter of Sir John A. Macdonald. During his tenure of office, Hickson had been creating a route for the Grand Trunk through Ontario and into the American midwest, and he did not intend to stand idly by and watch a new railway destroy his creation.

In the election of 1882, Macdonald found himself caught between the Canadian Pacific and the Grand Trunk. He confidently expected that his railway policy would win him the election; but he needed Grand Trunk support, especially in Ontario where he faced a hard fight. The older railway's political muscle in that province was considerable. Among other things it told its employees exactly how they must vote.

The Prime Minister openly solicited Hickson's assistance. "I have, as you know, uniformly backed the GTR since 1854 and won't change my course now," he reassured him in February, 1882, as the campaign started to warm up. In May he was writing to ask him to "put your shoulder to the wheel and help us . . . in the elections." Four days later he was naming specific candidates he wanted the Grand Trunk to back.

Hickson put a private car at Macdonald's disposal for four weeks of the campaign; but he was determined to exact a price for his support. On the very eve of the election he asked the Prime Minister to put a stop to the CPR's invasion of Grand Trunk territory.

Here was a delicate matter for a party leader to face on election eve. Macdonald wired Hickson that he would answer by mail – "meanwhile you may depend on my exertions to conciliate matters." In a later wire he was a little more specific: "Government not committed to any adverse line you may depend upon what I can possibly do personally to meet your views." With that fuzzy promise Hickson had to be content. But the Grand Trunk was moving into the Liberal camp.

Meanwhile, Hickson was attacking on a second front. The Grand Trunk's chief rival in southwestern Ontario was the Great Western, which operated a network of lines between Toronto, London, Hamilton, and Windsor. Hickson, by aggressive competitive tactics, forced an amalgamation in August, 1882. He now controlled every rail approach to the United States. If he linked up with the Northern Pacific at Duluth he would shortly be part of a transcontinental through line that could undercut the Canadian Pacific.

Hickson struck again in Quebec. The CPR now owned half of the

Quebec, Montreal, Ottawa and Occidental Railway – the section between Montreal and Ottawa. Hickson, in a swift coup, bought the other half – the "North Shore Line" – to prevent the CPR from getting into Quebec City.

In London, a propaganda barrage aimed directly at the CPR continued. "The attacks here on the country as a place for settlers to go are abominable," Stephen reported to Macdonald in January, 1883. "The worst feature . . . is that there is hardly a newspaper in the whole country which is in a position to say a word against the G.T.R. no matter what it may say or do against the country without losing Hickson's advertising. . . . I will yet pay off Hickson and his road for the unfair weapons they have used against me." The Grand Trunk pamphlets harped on the foolhardiness of crossing the country north of Lake Superior. A letter in the *Money Market Review,* obviously planted, declared that "no more hopeless project than that line, or a more baseless speculation than its land grant . . . was ever started to enveigle the British public."

Perhaps if the public, which watched the battle of the two giants, had been privy to some of the general manager's private correspondence with his adversary, it might have viewed the contest with more cynicism. For in the matter of passenger and freight rates, business was still business and profits were still profits. Much of Van Horne's invective against Hickson in the years that followed was confined to charges that Grand Trunk personnel were breaking rate-fixing agreements, which the two companies, in spite of their public enmity, had secretly entered into in eastern Canada. Such rate cuts, in Van Horne's words, were "simply idiotic." He gave orders that any CPR agent who dropped rates below those established by the two companies should be subject to instant dismissal – and he wanted the same understanding from his rival.

In areas where direct revenue was not concerned, Van Horne continued to do battle with Hickson. When the Grand Trunk played down the CPR's route on its own folders, Van Horne instructed Alexander Begg, the company's general emigration agent, to strike back with a map of his own. He told Begg to show the GTR's Toronto-Montreal road as a faint line and to drop out their Toronto-Chicago line entirely. In the matter of cartography, the general manager was quite prepared to smite his rivals; but free enterprise in the nineteenth century did not extend to the costly competition of a rate war.

Chapter
Four

HELL'S
BELLS
ROGERS
FINDS
HIS
PASS

1

One of Jim Hill's several executive strengths was an ability to settle upon the right man for the right job at the right moment. His choices, however, were not always obvious. Certainly his decision to employ a former Indian fighter to find a route through the Rockies and Selkirks must have seemed totally outrageous. Major A. B. Rogers had never seen a mountain – he was a prairie surveyor; yet here was Hill, sending him off to explore the most awesome peaks in British Columbia and expecting him to succeed where dozens of more experienced engineers had failed! Rogers was also one of the most heartily disliked men in his profession. He fed his workmen wretchedly, drove them mercilessly, and insulted them continually. Admittedly, he was honest; he would have scorned to engage in the kind of real estate profiteering that had intrigued General Rosser. He pared corporate expenses with a fealty that almost amounted to fanaticism. He was also ambitious, not for money but for fame; and it was this quality that attracted Hill when he called him into his office in February, 1881, and proceeded to dangle before him a chance at immortality.

Hill, who liked to study men thoroughly, undoubtedly knew a good deal about Rogers's background – that he had gone to sea as a youth, that he had studied engineering at Brown University and had then entered Yale. But it is impossible to think of Rogers as a "Yale man." He was short, he was sharp, and he was a master of picturesque profanity. Blasphemy sprang to his lips as easily as prayer to a priest's. Because of this he was saddled with a variety of nicknames, such as "The Bishop" and "Hell's Bells Rogers." The young surveyors who suffered under him generally referred to him as "the old man." He was fifty-two when he set off into the mountains, but he must have seemed more ancient than time – a crotchety old party, seemingly indestructible and more than a little frightening. Small he may have been, but his mien was forbidding: he possessed a pair of piercing eyes, blue as glacial ice, and a set of white side whiskers that were just short of being unbelievable; they sprouted from his sunken cheeks like broadswords, each coming to the sharpest of points almost a foot from his face.

He had won his military title in the Sioux uprising of 1861 and gained his reputation as "the Railway Pathfinder" while acting as a locating engineer for the Chicago, Milwaukee and St. Paul Railroad. Generally he was to be seen in a pair of patched overalls with two pockets behind, in one of which he kept a half-chewed plug of tobacco and in the other a sea biscuit. That, it was said, was his idea of a year's provisions.

The tobacco he chewed constantly. There were many who believed that he was able to exist almost entirely on its nutritive properties. "Give Rogers six plugs and five bacon rinds and he will travel for two weeks," someone once said of him. Everyone who worked for him or with him complained about his attitude towards food; he was firmly convinced that any great variety – or even a large quantity of it – was not conducive to mental or physical activity.

A. E. Tregent, who was with him that first year in the mountains, declared that "his idea of a fully equipped camp was to have a lot of beans. He would take a handkerchief, fill it with beans, put a piece of bacon on top, tie the four corners and then start off." John F. Stevens, who was his assistant, described Rogers as "a monomaniac on the subject of food." The Major once complimented Stevens on the quality of his work but then proceeded to qualify his remarks by complaining that he "made a god of his stomach." Stevens had dared to protest about the steady diet of bacon and beans which, he said, were the camp's *pièce de résistance* three times a day. His demands for more varied fare marked him in Rogers's eyes as an "effeminate gourmet."

Outwardly Rogers was a hard man; only a very few, who grew to know him well, came to realize that much of that hardness was only an armour that concealed a more sensitive spirit. The profane little creature was inwardly tormented by intense emotions, plagued by gnawing doubts, and driven by an almost ungovernable ambition. "Very few men ever learned to understand him," his friend Tom Wilson wrote of him. Wilson, a packer and later a Rocky Mountain guide, was one of those few. Rogers, he said, "had a generous heart and a real affection for many. He cultivated a gruff manner to conceal the emotions that he seemed ashamed to let anyone sense – of that I am certain. His driving ambition was to have his name handed down in history; for that he faced unknown dangers and suffered privations."

James Jerome Hill understood those ambitions when he offered to put Rogers in charge of the mountain division of the CPR. Rogers's main task would be to locate the shortest route between Moose Jaw Bone Creek and Savona's Ferry on Kamloops Lake. That meant finding feasible passes through the southern Rockies and also through the mysterious Selkirks. There were several partially explored passes

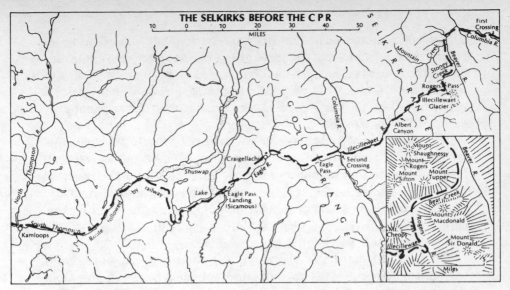

in the former, but no one had been able to find an opening in the Selkirk barrier. Hill made Rogers an offer he knew he could not refuse: if the Major could find that pass and save the railroad a possible hundred and fifty miles, he promised, the CPR would give him a cheque for five thousand dollars and name the pass after him.

Rogers did not care about the cash bonus. But to have one's name on the map! That was the goal of every surveyor. He accepted Hill's offer on the spot, and from that moment on, in Tom Wilson's words, "to have the key-pass of the Selkirks bear his name was the ambition he fought to realize."

Rogers's first move was to read everything that was available about the mountain country. An entry in Walter Moberly's journal of 1866 caught his eye:

"Friday, July 13th – Perry returned from his trip up the east fork of the Ille-cille-waut River. He did not reach the divide, but reported a low, wide valley as far as he went. His exploration has not settled the point whether it would be possible to get through the mountains by this valley but I fear not. He ought to have got on the divide, and his failure is a great disappointment to me. He reports a most difficult country to travel through, owing to fallen timber and under-brush of very thick growth . . . ."

Rogers determined to complete Perry's exploration. With his favourite nephew, Albert, he set off at the beginning of April for Kamloops. It took him twenty-two days to reach the town. When he arrived, he engaged ten "strapping young Indians" through a remarkable contract made with their leader, Chief Louie. Its terms rendered them up to Rogers as his virtual slaves, to work "without grumbling" until they were discharged. If any of them came back without a letter of good report, his wages were to be forfeited and the chief agreed

267

to lay one hundred lashes on his bare back. The Indians were all converted Christians, but the local priest did not complain about this barbarism, possibly because his church was to be the beneficiary of the forfeited wages. It is perhaps unnecessary to add that, in spite of the hardships the party encountered, no murmur of complaint ever escaped the Indians' lips.

The Major spent eight days in Kamloops trying to find out how far an Indian could travel in a day with a hundred-pound pack on his back and no trail to follow, and how little food would be required to keep him alive under such conditions. He concluded, wrongly, that the expedition's slim commissariat could be augmented by game shot along the way and so set off with a minimum of supplies. He was to regret that parsimony.

The twelve members of the party left Kamloops on April 29. It took them fourteen days to cross the rounded peaks of the Gold Range. They proceeded down the Columbia by raft, with the unfortunate Indians swimming alongside, until, about May 21, they reached the mouth of the Illecillewaet. Here Rogers found himself standing on the exact spot from which Moberly's assistant, Perry, had plunged into the unknown, fifteen years before.

It must have been a memorable moment. The little group, clustered on the high bank of the Columbia, was dwarfed by the most spectacular mountain scenery on the continent. Behind them the rustling river cut an olive path through its broad evergreen valley. Above them towered the Selkirks, forming a vast island of forest, rock, ice, and snow three hundred miles long.

Now began a terrible ordeal. Each man balancing a hundred-pound pack on the back of his neck struggled upward, picking his way over mud-falls, scaling perpendicular rock points, wading through beaver swamps dense with underbrush and devil's clubs, whose nettles were almost inescapable. Albert Rogers later wrote that without the fear of his uncle's dreadful penalty, all the Indians would have fled. Rogers himself was to remark later that "many a time I wished myself dead."

In the gloomy box canyon of the Illecillewaet (later named for Albert Rogers) the snow was still several feet deep. Above them they could see the paths of the avalanches – the timber crushed to matchwood in swaths hundreds of feet wide. Sometimes, unable to move farther on one side of the river, they were forced to creep over immense snow bridges high above the frothing watercourse. Occasionally they would catch glimpses of an incredible wedge-shaped glacier, hanging like a jewel from the mountain pinnacles. Before many years passed the Illecillewaet Glacier would become one of the CPR's prime tourist attractions.

The Indians could no longer carry packs weighing a hundred pounds, the game proved to be non-existent, and the party was forced to go on short rations. They were seldom dry. The heavy rains and wet underbrush, the glacial waters and soft snow, the lack of proper bedding (one blanket per man was all that Rogers allowed) – all these privations began to take their toll.

They held cautiously to the lee of an obelisk-shaped peak, which would later be named Mount Sir Donald, after Donald A. Smith. Here, in the cool shadows, there was still a crust on the snow which allowed them to walk without floundering. At four o'clock one afternoon they came upon a level expanse that seemed to be the summit. They camped on the edge of timber, out of range of the snowslides, and when the sun's rays vanished and the crust began to re-form they scurried across the snow-field. At the far end they heard the sound of gurgling water and to their satisfaction saw that it separated, some of it running westward, some to the east. They had reached the divide; was this the route the railway would take?

Mountains towered above them in every direction. A smear of timber extended half-way up one slope and they determined to make their ascent at this point. "Being gaunt as greyhounds, with lungs and muscles of the best, we soon reached the timber-line," Albert Rogers recounted.

Here the going became very difficult. The party crept around ledges of volcanic rock, seeking fingerholds, staying in the shade as much as possible and kicking steps in the crust. The route followed a narrow ledge around a sun-baked promontory. Four of the Indians tied pack-straps to each other's belts and then the leader crept over the mushy snow in an attempt to reach the ledge. He fell back with such force that he lost his footing and all four men plunged thirty feet straight down the dizzy incline, tumbling one over another until they disappeared from sight; miraculously, none was injured.

It was late in the day when the twelve men reached the mountain top, but for Albert Rogers, at least, it was worth the ordeal:

"Such a view! Never to be forgotten. Our eyesight caromed from one bold peak to another for miles in all directions. The wind blew fiercely across the ridge and scuddy clouds were whirled in eddies behind great towering peaks of bare rocks. Everything was covered with a shroud of white, giving the whole landscape the appearance of snow-clad desolation. Far beneath us was the timber line and in the valleys below, the dense timber seemed but a narrow shadow which marked their course."

The Major was less poetic, though he read a great deal of poetry and loved it. On occasions such as this it was his habit to doff his hat, ruffle his long hair, and say, reverently: "Hell's bells, now ain't that thar a pretty sight!"

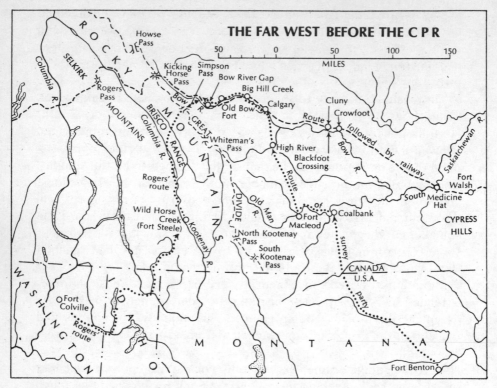

THE FAR WEST BEFORE THE CPR

The party had neither wood for a fire nor boughs for beds. They were all soaked with perspiration and were wolfing great handfuls of snow to quench their thirst. They were perched on a narrow ridge where a single false move could lead to their deaths. They crawled along the razorback until they encountered a little ledge in the shadow of a protective rock. Here they would have to wait until the crust formed again and the morning light allowed them to travel.

It was a long night. Wrapped in blankets, nibbling on dried meat and stamping their feet continually to keep their toes from freezing, they took turns flagellating each other with pack-straps to keep up the circulation. At dawn they crept back to the ridge and worked their way down to the south fork of the river. It seemed to Rogers that this fork paralleled the valley on the opposite side of the dividing range through which, he concluded, the waters of the Beaver River emptied into the Columbia on the eastern flanks of the mountain barrier. If that was true, then a pass of sorts existed.

Unfortunately, he could not be sure. There were eighteen unexplored miles left, but by this time the party was almost out of food. Rogers's notorious frugality had destroyed all chances of finding a pass that season. It would be at least another year before he could say for certain whether it existed at all. By that time the rails would be approaching the valley of the Bow, and he still had not explored the Kicking Horse Pass in the Rockies, which had scarcely been glimpsed since the day when James Hector first saw it in 1858.

Rogers sent all but two of his Indians back to Kamloops. The others guided him to Fort Colville in Washington Territory. There he hired a packtrain and made his way by a circuitous route back into the Kootenay country to the mining camp at Wild Horse Creek. He planned to join his main party of surveyors by crossing the Kootenay River, hiking over the Brisco Range, and then working his way down the Spray to the point where it joined the Bow, where they were waiting for him. It was wild country, unmarked by trails or guideposts, but it was the only route available.

He did not take his nephew with him. It was late June by this time and it was imperative that somebody explore the Kicking Horse Pass from its western approach. Rogers decided that Albert must take the packtrain to the mouth of the Kicking Horse River and from that point make his way to the summit of the continental divide. Only one white man had ever come that way before – James Hector; but he had descended from the summit. Even the Indians shunned the Kicking Horse. Its terrible gorge was considered too difficult for horses. On his first trip into the Rockies, young Albert, aged twenty-one – "that little cuss" as the Major fondly called him – was being asked to attempt a feat that no human being had yet accomplished.

2

Major Rogers and his men were advancing on the Rockies from three directions that spring of 1881. While Albert worked his way towards the Kicking Horse and his uncle guided his packhorses over the Brisco Range, the main body of surveyors was heading westward from St. Paul towards Fort Benton, Montana, the jumping-off point for the eastern slopes of the Canadian Rockies. Waiting impatiently for them at the steamboat landing was a 22-year-old stripling from Ontario. His name was Tom Wilson and he was positively lusting for adventure.

He was a rangy youth with a homely Irish face, easygoing, industrious, good humoured, and incurably romantic. At twenty, he had joined the North West Mounted Police and was stationed at Fort Walsh when he learned that a private company was about to embark on the CPR's construction. Wilson had to be part of the action, and so he wangled a discharge, made his way south with a freight outfit, and reached Fort Benton, Montana, one week before Major Rogers's survey crew – a hundred men in all – disembarked from the steamer. He was the youngest man to be hired by Rogers's deputy, a stickler of a civil engineer named Hyndman, whose rules were so strict that they were promptly dubbed "Hyndman's Commandments." Three aroused the special ire of the men and almost caused a strike: *Not a tap of work was to be done on Sunday. Men caught swearing aloud were to be instantly discharged. Men caught eating, except at the regular camp meal, were to be fired on the spot.*

When the party, still smarting under these harsh strictures, reached its rendezvous at Bow River Gap in the Rockies, it was several days late and there was no sign of Rogers. Then about a week later – the date was July 15 – Tom Wilson was sitting on a narrow Indian trail west of the camp, smoking his pipe, when a mottled roan cayuse appeared around a curve carrying a man wearing an old white helmet and a brown canvas suit. "His condition – dirty doesn't begin to describe it," Wilson remembered. "His voluminous side-burns waved like flags in a breeze; his piercing eyes seemed to look and see through everything at once . . . . Every few moments a stream of tobacco juice erupted from between his side-burns." Wilson realized at once that the tattered creature on the scarecrow horse must be the notorious major.

"This Hyndman's camp?" Rogers asked in his jerky manner.

Wilson nodded and guided Rogers to Hyndman's tent. Hyndman stepped out, but there was no word of greeting from his chief.

"What's your altitude?" he shot at Hyndman. The engineer stammered that he did not know.

"Blue Jesus!* Been here several days and don't know the altitude yet. You —!" There followed what Wilson described as "a wonderful exhibition of scientific cussing [which] busted wide all of Hyndman's 'Holy Commandments' and inspired delighted snickers and chuckles of admiration from the men who had quickly gathered around."

Three days later Rogers announced that he intended to set off on his own to do some exploring, but when he asked for a volunteer to accompany him, the request was greeted by silence. As Wilson put it, "Every man present had learned, in three days, to hate the Major with real hatred." But in spite of himself Wilson thought he might as well take a chance and follow Rogers.

"You were the only man who would go with the old geyser," A. E. Tregent reminded him in a nostalgic letter forty-eight years

---

*Tom Wilson's memoirs, written in the straight-laced thirties, reproduce the Major's favourite bit of profanity as "Blue —!" Since it is doubtful that he would have censored so mild a word as "blazes" (and equally doubtful that the Major himself would have lapsed into such a euphemism), I have filled in the blank with the most obvious expletive.

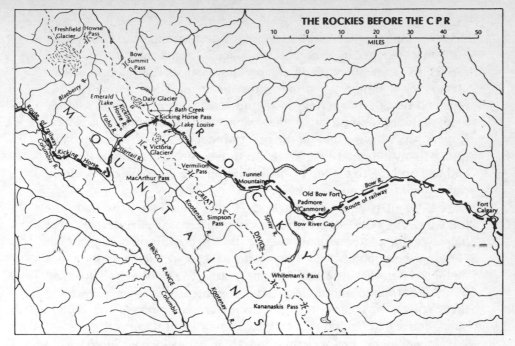

later. "Nobody else had the pluck to run the chance of being starved to death or lost in the woods."

The Major was clearly worried about the fate of his nephew. "Has that damned little cuss Al got here yet?" was his first question on riding into camp one afternoon after an exploration. It was some time before Wilson came to understand that Rogers's manner of speaking about his nephew was part of his armour – a shield to conceal his inner distress.

When Rogers learned that there was no sign of Albert, he began to prance around and shout.

"If anything happens to that damn little cuss I'll never show my face in St. Paul again," he kept saying. The fact that he had given a 21-year-old youth a task that the Indians themselves would not tackle did not seem to have occurred to him.

Two further days of searching failed to locate the missing Albert. When Rogers and Wilson returned to the summit camp, after a long and vain exploration, they were met with silence. The Major tried to rout the men out to search at night, but they sensibly refused. "How the Major put in that night I do not know," Wilson confessed, "but I do know that at daybreak next morning he was on the warpath cursing about late risers." The members of the summit party were dispatched in all directions. Somewhere down below, on the tangled western slope of the Rockies, wrinkled by canyons and criss-crossed by deadfalls, was the missing youth – dead or alive, no one could say.

273

Down that slope Tom Wilson and a companion made their way until they reached the mouth of a glacial stream later to be called the Yoho. There they made camp. They had scarcely finished their meal when a shot cracked out in the distance. They sprang to their feet and began clambering down the stream bed, shouting as they went, until, rounding a curve, they came upon the missing man. Albert Rogers was starving and on the point of mental and physical exhaustion. His rations had long since been used up and for two days he had had nothing to eat but a small porcupine. He had picked it clean, right down to the quills.

The ascent back up the Kicking Horse, which the trio made the following day with Albert Rogers's two Indians, was so terrible that half a century later Wilson insisted that it could not be described. Nearing the summit, they fired a fusillade of revolver shots and a moment later the little major came tearing down the trail to meet them. He stopped, motionless, squinting intently at his nephew; and then Wilson was permitted, for a moment, to glimpse the human being concealed behind that callous armour of profanity.

"He plainly choked with emotion, then, as his face hardened again he took an extra-vicious tobacco-juice-shot at the nearest tree and almost snarled . . . 'Well, you did get here, did you, you damn little cuss?' There followed a second juice eruption and then, as he swung on his heel, the Major shot back over his shoulder: 'You're alright, are you, you damn little cuss?' "

Al Rogers grinned. He understood his uncle. "He also knew that, during the rest of the walk to camp, the furious activity of his uncle's jaws and the double-speed juice shots aimed at the vegetation indicated our leader's almost uncontrollable emotions."

There was an eerie kind of undercurrent drifting about the Rogers camp that evening. As twilight fell, purpling the valleys and making spectres of the glacial summits, the men began to gather around the fire, sucking on their pipes and gazing off across the unknown ocean of mountains. Albert Rogers, still shaky from his ordeal, was present; so was Tom Wilson, together with eighteen others – axemen, chainmen, packers, transit men, and cook. Only the Major, toiling in his tent, was absent.

They were perched on the lip of the Great Divide and they were conscious of both the significance and the loneliness of their situation. In all of that vast alpine domain there was scarcely, so far as they knew, another human soul. The country was virtually unexplored; they themselves had trudged through forests, crossed gorges, and crept up slopes that no man, white or native, had ever seen. What nameless horrors did these peaks and ridges hold? For all they knew (as Wilson was to write), ferocious animals of unknown species or fearful savages of barbaric habit lurked somewhere beneath them in those shrouded hollows. To many it was inconceivable that the mountains would ever be conquered or the chasms bridged.

One declared emphatically that no railroad would ever get through such a God-forsaken land and several grunted agreement. Others argued that the success of the project depended on Rogers's ability to discover a pass in the Selkirks.

"Wonder where we will all be this time next year," someone said.

"Not here! No more of this for me!" another responded. A chorus of approval greeted this remark. For weeks they had all existed on dried salt pork, boiled beans, and tea. They had seen no butter, eggs, vegetables, or fruit; and there was no time to hunt for the game that abounded. The monotonous diet and the need to be one's own bootmaker, tailor, barber, and laundryman were beginning to tell.

Again, they discussed the railroad and again, when one of the party remarked that no line of steel could get through the Kicking Horse – that if a railway ever reached the west coast it would be by way of Fort Edmonton and the Yellow Head Pass – a majority of heads nodded in agreement.

There followed a strange and moving scene. The fire crackled. The peaks above stood out like ghostly shadows against the night sky. The men pulled on their pipes and stared into the flames. Nobody spoke for some time. At length, one man broke the silence:

"Let's make a deal," he said. "Let's promise to keep in touch with each other at least once a year after we get out of here."

The twenty men got to their feet and, without further prompting, took part in a solemn ritual. Each one raised an arm to the sky, and all gravely vowed to keep the Pledge of the Twenty, as it came to be called. In the years that followed, almost all were faithful to it.*

Wilson resumed his job as personal attendant to Major Rogers. A creature of whim, the Major had pinned his hopes on the Kicking Horse, with the Bow Summit as his second choice. Near the end of the season he played one hunch that was to cause him a good

---

*After forty-five years only two of the originals were left alive. The last letter linking the men of the Great Divide was scribbled in pencil by Al Rogers in Waterville, Washington, on two report sheets of the Seattle Grain Company. It reached Tom Wilson in Banff late in February, 1924. "Dear Old Tom," Rogers had written, "you are a loyal soul as ever lived and I love you for it . . . ." Three months later Rogers, too, had gone, leaving Tom Wilson as the sole survivor of the group that sat around the campfire and talked about the great railway on that haunting night in the mountains.

deal of mental anguish during the months that followed: he decided abruptly not to proceed further with the Howse Pass survey. Though he knew nothing about the pass, he had come to the sudden conclusion that it was not a feasible route and was not worth bothering with. As Wilson noted, "Always the Kicking Horse ruled his mind, and although at times he had doubts regarding it being the best route, yet those fears never lasted long." But his sudden decision that morning caused him many misgivings the following summer, long after the Kicking Horse Pass had officially been chosen.

Wilson, also on a hunch, quit Rogers at this juncture. By doing so he saved himself a good deal of hardship. The survey crews lingered too long in the mountains. They did not emerge until late October, and by the time they reached High River they were frozen in. Indians robbed them of their food and some of their clothing. Half starved and freezing, the party managed to trudge to Blackfoot Crossing, where they were given some assistance. Then they began the long, sub-zero trek across the prairies, through the snowstorms and blizzards, to the end of steel near Flat Creek, Manitoba.

J. H. E. Secretan encountered the party, starving and in rags, on the high bank of the South Saskatchewan. The sight of them – and Rogers in particular – offended the sensibilities of the fastidious Englishman who believed, above all else, in cleanliness, good order, and discipline (he even had gunny sacks sewn together to carpet the floors of his tents). Rogers he later described as "the worst looking, long-haired ruffian of them all."

An avid sportsman, Secretan had been living all summer on prairie game birds, which he shot himself. Rogers was as horrified by such Lucullan fare as Secretan was horrified by Rogers's appearance. The two did not get along, but Rogers had his revenge – or thought he had. When he reached Winnipeg he informed General Rosser, who was then in command, that Secretan "was living like the Czar of Russia [with] tents carpeted with Brussels carpet [and] living upon roast turkeys and geese and other expensive luxuries unheard of in the cuisine of a poor, unsophisticated engineer."

"Thus," wrote Secretan, "did the Major bite the hand that fed him."

3

By the time Rogers reached Winnipeg, late in 1881, Van Horne's appointment had been announced. The new general manager took Rogers with him to Montreal in January, 1882, to convince the CPR directors that the Kicking Horse route was practicable with grades of 2.2 per cent and that there appeared to be a feasible pass through the Selkirks.

Rogers had not fully convinced himself, though his pronouncements exuded confidence. In truth, he had discovered half a pass only. To confirm his findings he would have to scale the eastern wall of the Selkirks and make sure that the gap he thought he saw from the Illecillewaet actually pierced the mountain barrier.

That May, he again attacked the Selkirks. No detailed account of that abortive journey remains but it was clearly an ordeal. Once again Rogers had failed to bring along enough supplies. Only the discovery of an old canoe, which brought them swiftly back to camp, prevented the entire party from starving to death. The pass had not been found.

On July 17 Rogers tried once more, setting off from the point where the Beaver flows into the Columbia. Here, before the railway builders helped destroy it, was some of the loveliest scenery to be found in the mountains. The timber was stupendous: the cedars were often ten feet or more in diameter; sometimes they rose two hundred feet above the matted forest floor. Through this unknown country Rogers and his party climbed for hours along a spectacular route that millions would one day traverse in comfort. The brush was so dense they could make little more than two miles a day. Rogers suffered severely from blackflies and mosquitoes. "Not one engineer in a hundred," his friend George Grant later remarked, "would have risked, again and again, health and life as he did."

Above them loomed glaciers fifty feet thick and mountains that would one day bear the names of famous Canadians – Shaughnessy, Sifton, Tupper, Macdonald – and of Rogers himself. The lower mountain slopes were scarred by the paths of snowslides, the trees snapped off dozens of feet from the base. These mountains looked familiar to Rogers, for he had seen them all the previous year from the opposite side. There, before them, was the very peak on which he had stood in the summer of 1881 and there the same broad meadow. He and his party had reached an altitude of forty-five hundred feet and were standing in a valley that seemed completely enclosed by mountains. Ragged black precipices stood guard at the entrance. To the north and west a smudge of timber rose up to blend with sloping meadows, the soft grasses flecked with wild flowers. Beyond these spangled pastures were glacial fields of glistening white, tilting upwards to curved ridges which, in turn, led the eye higher to frosted peaks. To the southwest more mountains stretched off into a haze of misty blue. Somewhere in the distance a brook gurgled above the sound of the rustling spruces. Here the waters flowed in opposite directions, spilling down both sides of the Selkirks. Now the Major knew he had found at last the long-sought passage through the barrier. In the face of considerable hardship – and some foolhardiness – he had done what his detractors had said was impossible. There was a way through the Selkirks after all, and its discovery would make him immortal. Almost from this moment, this smiling, mountain-ringed meadow would bear the name of Rogers Pass. The date was July 24, 1882, and Rogers, after searching vainly for an alternative pass, lost no time in retracing his steps so that he might let the world have the news of his discovery.

Tom Wilson, meanwhile, was engaged in packing supplies from Padmore in the foothills to the summit of the Kicking Horse in the Rockies. One day in August he heard the distant roar of avalanches and inquired about them. An Indian told him that these slides occurred on "snow mountain," which lay high above "the lake of the little fishes." The description intrigued Wilson and he asked the Indian to guide him to the lake. It was well worth the trip. The two men burst out upon a small emerald gem, framed by a backdrop of dark evergreens, a dazzling white glacier, and a curtain of blue mountains.

"As God is my judge, I never in all my explorations saw such a matchless scene," Wilson recalled. He sat down, pulled out his pipe and, as he smoked, gazed for a long time on the mirror of blue-green water, soon to become one of the most famous tourist attractions on the continent. Wilson decided to name it Emerald Lake, and so it appeared on the first geological map. But even as the map was published the name was changed to Lake Louise in honour of the Governor General's lady.

Later that afternoon – the date was August 21 – Wilson arrived at one of the survey camps and ran into Major Rogers, who confided to him that he still had doubts about the Kicking Horse. Perhaps the Howse Pass, after all, was an easier grade. What if, after the road was built, Rogers should be proved wrong? Moberly had been convinced that the pass was the best possible route for the railway to follow. What if Moberly was right? He was not the sort of man who would ever let Rogers forget it.

"Tom," the Major said as the two men sat outside his tent that evening, "I mustn't make any mistakes and I am not quite easy in my mind about the Howse Pass.... I'd like to take a trip over it and I'd like you to go with me."

Wilson agreed, and the two set off with packhorses the following morning, struggling through muskegs and over fallen timber and chopping their way through trails rendered impassable by deadfalls. After the second day they found they had travelled only half the distance they had planned. Rogers began to fret.

"Blue Jesus! We won't get through here to the Columbia in two weeks at this rate. A man carrying a pack on his back could travel twice as fast as we are going. I'll give you a fifty dollar bonus if you'll go through alone on foot.... You ought to do it in ten days easy."

Rogers promised to meet Wilson in ten days' time on the far side of the Rockies where the Blaeberry, flowing down from the Howse Pass, empties into the Columbia. Then he went off with the horses leaving Tom Wilson to face the most terrible ordeal of his career.

There was no trail. He groped his way through a forest of eternal night – the trees packed so tightly that he could get his bearings only by glimpsing the tips of the mountains. Bear Creek, its banks walled in by an impenetrable mass of willows, was in flood and he used it as a guide. It proved to be a fickle ally. At one point he broke out of the labyrinth of the evergreens only to find his way blocked by an immense wall of ice. He had taken the wrong fork and lost a day.

He kept plugging along blindly, following the racing waters, which led him ever upward. There was no sign that any human being, white or native, had passed this way before. Then, when he seemed to have penetrated to the very core of the wilderness, he saw on the trunk of a tree a scar that could only have been made with an axe; it was grey with age and he realized that this must be a surveyor's blaze, left by one of Moberly's men a decade before. He had reached the summit of Howse Pass.

The descent was even more difficult than the descent from the Kicking Horse. Nature, jealous of invasion, appeared to have devised a series of obstacles to frustrate all human passage. Wilson faced mile upon mile of deadfalls – great trees torn up and tossed helter-skelter, as if by an unseen hand, forming an apparently unending series of eight-foot barriers over which he had to scramble. There were other pitfalls. A canyon barred his way at one point; he was obliged to scale a cliff to circumvent it. Later he faced a vast slide – an unstable desert of shattered rock. There was no way around, and so he was forced to strike out directly across it, like a man on shifting ice, knowing that a single slip could send the whole mass roaring into the depths below.

The greatest obstacle of all came to be hunger. After twelve days Wilson was down to a half a bannock. Every mile began to count, but every mile was criss-crossed with uprooted tree trunks. His pace grew slower and for the first time he began to grow alarmed. Would he die in this maze of fallen timber? He decided on a desperate gamble. After a night's sleep he cast aside every scrap of equipment except for his axe and made for the Columbia as swiftly as he could. Late the following day, as fatigue dragged his movements to a crawl, he ran into Major Rogers.

"Blue Jesus! What kept you so long?" was Rogers's only greeting. Then he snorted, turned on his heel, and uttered no further word until Wilson had been fed. The others in the camp later told the packer that the old man had paced up and down for hours like a caged lion, crying over and over again: "If that boy don't show up what in hell will I do? No-one but a fool would send a lad on such a trip alone, and no-one but a fool would try to make it alone." Wilson's journey served to confirm his original hunch that the Kicking Horse provided a better route for the railway than the Howse.

By early fall Rogers was ready to leave the mountains. He wanted to carry the news personally to Montreal. Wilson, who had departed earlier, encountered him on the prairies one Sunday morning in a democrat drawn by four horses, galloping towards the end of steel, "feeling jubilant, for his ambitions were promising realization."

Some time later, George Stephen, faultless in white tie and tails, was entertaining guests in his home in Montreal. His butler was taken aback to discover on the doorstep a wiry little man, roughly dressed and sporting a set of the largest Dundreary whiskers he had ever seen. The butler protested that Stephen could not be disturbed, but the little man was adamant. The CPR president reluctantly came to the door and instantly recognized the Major. He ordered the butler to array him in suitable style and then bring him down to dinner. There he heard at first hand the tale of the discovery of the pass through the Selkirks.

True to Jim Hill's promise, the railway presented Rogers with a cheque for five thousand dollars. To the frustration of the CPR's accounting department, he refused to cash it.

"What! Cash that cheque?" Rogers declared. "I would not take a hundred thousand dollars for it. It is framed and hangs in my brother's house in Waterville, Minnesota, where my nephews and nieces can see it."

"I'm not here for money!" the Major added. It was an unnecessary comment – but one which must have given considerable satisfaction to James J. Hill, the man who originally made that puzzling decision to send a prairie surveyor into the unknown Selkirks.

4

Rogers's discovery of a pass through the Selkirks intensified the Canadian-American rivalry, which was a feature of railway location and construction in the West. How could a Yankee engineer, with no mountain experience, succeed where seasoned Canadians had been forced to admit defeat?

As yet there was not much hard evidence that the pass was practicable. Rogers had measured it with his eye alone. No one had put a surveyor's chain on a foot of the Selkirk Mountains. No human being, white man or Indian, had succeeded in making a continuous passage from west to east along the route that he was recommending.

Stephen was concerned. Could that strange, tobacco-chewing little man really be trusted? The president decided that a disinterested party must be engaged to check up on him. The choice fell on Sandford Fleming, who had been living in England since his dismissal in 1880.

Van Horne also had reservations about both the location survey over the Kicking Horse and the practicability of the Selkirk pass; he was also greatly concerned about Rogers's penchant for economizing on food.

"It is . . . exceedingly important that an ample supply of food be provided and that the quantity be beyond a possibility of a doubt," he told the Major early in 1883; ". . . we must feed the men properly in order to get good service. It will be cheaper for the Company to pay for twice the amount of supplies actually necessary than to lose a day's work for lack of any."

Van Horne, though he defended Rogers to outsiders, decided to send "two competent and disinterested engineers" over the work in the early spring to make sure the pass was suitable. These were Charles Aeneas Shaw, who had spent more than half his thirty years working at his profession, and James Hogg, a cousin of James Ross, the man in charge of mountain construction. Competent they were; disinterested they were not. No surveyor was disinterested in those days. They were ambitious, often blindly stubborn and jealous of their fellows, brave to the point of being foolhardy, and sometimes temperamental; but they were never disinterested. Shaw could not stand Secretan, whom he called "selfish" and "disagreeable." The snobbish Secretan took every opportunity to denigrate Shaw. Shaw despised Hogg, who was to be his companion in the mountains. And all three men had very little use for Rogers.

Shaw first tangled with Rogers, by his own account, in Winnipeg early in March of 1883. James Ross asked him to look over the profile of Rogers's final location line between Calgary and Bow Gap (a distance of some sixty miles): "It's a nightmare to me and I'm afraid it will hold us back a year."

Shaw announced at once that he could get a far better line. A stranger working near by sprang to his feet and cried out: "That's the best line that can be got through the country. Who in hell are you, anyway?'' It was Rogers. Shaw told Ross that he was prepared to relocate the Major's line and ''if I don't save at least half a million dollars over the estimated cost of construction of this line, I won't ask any pay for my season's work.''

A fight threatened to break out between Shaw and Rogers. Ross calmed both men down but, at a later meeting, asked Shaw to go ahead.

Van Horne in the meantime was examining Rogers's profiles and plans out of Fort Calgary and was not happy. He called in Secretan and there took place a memorable encounter, which became part of the Van Horne legend.

''Look at that,'' the general manager exclaimed. ''Some infernal idiot has put a tunnel in there. I want you to go up and take it out.''

''But this is on the Bow River – a rather difficult section. There may be no other way.''

''Make another way.''

Secretan hesitated, whereupon Van Horne hurled a question.

''This is a mud tunnel, isn't it?'' Secretan nodded. Engineers shunned mud tunnels; it was impossible to keep the track in line as the bank tended to move constantly.

''How long would it take us to build it?''

''A year or eighteen months.''

Van Horne swore and banged his fist on the desk.

''What are they thinking about? Are we going to hold up this railway for a year and a half while they build their damned tunnel? Take it out!''

Secretan picked up the profile and studied it as he headed for the door. He turned back for a moment.

''Mr. Van Horne,'' he said in his sardonic way, ''those mountains are in the way, and the rivers don't all run right for us. While we are at it we might as well fix them, too.''

But Van Horne insisted that Secretan personally ''take that damned tunnel out. Don't send anybody else.'' The engineer was spared the trip, however, when Shaw found a route around the offending hill by way of a small creek valley, which actually shortened the main line by a mile and a half.

At the summit of the Rockies, Shaw was met by James Hogg, who had arrived with orders from Van Horne to report on the pass through the Selkirks. The two set off down the difficult incline of the Kicking Horse on the zigzag pathway which the survey crews had already christened ''the Golden Stairs'' because it was the most terrifying single stretch of trail on the entire route of the railway – a narrow ledge, less than two feet wide, cut into the cliffs several hundred feet above the foaming river. It was so frightening that some men used to hang on to the tails of their packhorses and keep their eyes tightly shut until they had passed the most dangerous places. Shaw had one horrible moment when his horse ran into a nest of hornets and another when he met two men with a packhorse coming from the opposite direction. Since it was impossible to turn around, they simply pushed one of the wretched animals over the cliff.

At the base of the Golden Stairs, on the banks of the Columbia, they ran into Rogers. Shaw noticed that the seat of his pants was patched with a piece of buffalo hide that still had the hair on it. Apparently the Major did not recognize his antagonist of the previous spring.

"Who the hell are you, and where the hell do you think you're going?" was Rogers's greeting.

"It's none of your damned business to either question," Shaw retorted. "Who the hell are you, anyway?"

"I am Major Rogers."

"My name is Shaw. I've been sent by Van Horne to examine and report on the pass through the Selkirks."

Shaw recalled that Rogers practically frothed at the mouth when he heard the name.

"You're the — Prairie Gopher that has come into the mountains and ruined my reputation as an Engineer." A stream of profanity followed.

Shaw, a big man with a high intelligent forehead and an all-encompassing black beard, was not inclined to take this sort of abuse. Since the age of fourteen he had been doing a man's work, first as a farmhand and later as a surveyor. He was as hard as nails and would live to his eighty-ninth year. Before Rogers was finished Shaw had leaped from his horse and seized him by the throat; in his own words, he "shook him till his teeth rattled."

"Another word out of you," said the infuriated Shaw, "and I'll throw you in the river and drown you."

Rogers apologized and explained that the engineers in charge of the relocated section had let him down badly. He offered to guide Shaw to the pass in the Selkirks.

"That will be all right," Shaw told him, "as long as you keep a civil tongue in your head."

Shaw's version of the scene at the pass, when they reached it, was told and retold by him in his old age, half a century later. According to his version, Rogers, "in his usual pompous manner," after gazing up at the great Illecillewaet Glacier, turned to him and remarked: "Shaw, I was the first white man ever to set eyes on this pass and this panorama."

Shaw walked over to a small spring to get a drink and there, he related, he found the remains of a fire, some partly rotted poles, and a couple of badly rusted tins. He called Rogers's attention to these.

Rogers's reaction, as quoted by Shaw, was astonishment: "How strange! I never noticed those things before. I wonder who could have camped here."

"These things were left here years ago by Moberly when he found this pass!" Shaw claimed he replied.

It was the repetition of this story that helped convince Canadian engineers and journalists that Major Rogers was a fake and that credit for discovering the pass rightfully belonged to Walter Moberly. Even Moberly began to believe it in his declining years, as his imperfect reminiscences reveal, though he was generous enough at the time. In 1885 he wrote: "I cannot . . . but pay a high tribute to the dauntless energy and untiring zeal that has characterised and, I am glad to say, crowned with success the unwearying struggles of my successor in the mountain surveys, Major A. B. Rogers." Thirty years later he was insisting that Rogers had not seen the pass named after him until the railway had gone through it, and that it should have been named Perry Pass after his assistant who, Moberly came to believe, actually *had* seen the pass. The memoirs of aging surveyors are not very good evidence when set against words actually written on the spot at the time. Moberly's journal of 1866 makes it clear that the campfire Shaw said he found did not belong to his party.

Then who left those relics? Certainly, they could not have been as old as Shaw thought they were. The snow on the top of the Rogers Pass reaches a depth of fifty feet or more in the winter; it is scarcely credible that the remains of a small fire could have survived for seventeen years. It is more likely that (assuming that Shaw was not indulging in a pipe dream) the camp was left by Rogers himself the previous season or by his men, who had hacked a road to the summit and were working on the western slopes of the pass at that very time.

5

On their way back to the summit of the Rockies, Shaw and Hogg briefly encountered the second party dispatched by George Stephen to check up on Rogers: Sandford Fleming, his son Frank, and his old comrade, the Rev. Dr. George Grant. It was almost a dozen years since these two companions had set out, in the prime of life, to breast the continent, and the years were beginning to tell. Fleming, though a superb physical specimen, was fifty-six; for the past three years he had been leading a sedentary life in Europe. Grant, who was forty-seven and inclined to a paunch, had quit his ministry in Halifax for the principal's chair at Queen's. Now these middle-aged explorers were forced to negotiate a trail that terrified the most experienced mountaineers.

Fleming dared not look down. To do so "gives one an uncontrollable dizziness, to make the head swim and the view unsteady, even with men of tried nerve. I do not think that I can ever forget that terrible walk; it was the greatest trial I ever experienced."

At that point the members of the party found themselves teetering on a ledge between ten and fifteen inches wide, eight hundred feet above the river. There was nothing to hold on to – not a branch or even a twig. The one-handed Grant was especially vulnerable: "It seemed as if a false step would have hurled us to the base, to certain death." The sun, emerging from behind a cloud, beat down upon them until they were soaked with a perspiration that was accentuated by their own state of tension. "I, myself, felt as if I had been dragged through a brook, for I was without a dry shred on me," Fleming admitted. It was an exhausted party that finally arrived that evening at Rogers's camp on the Columbia.

Rogers's men were highly amused at the idea of the hard-swearing "Bishop" entertaining a man of the cloth. They warned Grant of the Major's roughness of speech and attitude: "He can blow, he can swar, and he can spit tobacco as well as any man in the United States."

Because Grant was addressed as "Doctor," Rogers at first believed him to be a medical man. When, on the following morning – a Sunday – Fleming proposed that his companion hold a service, Rogers thought the idea was a practical joke. He indulged in a good deal of jubilant profanity and bustled about, drumming up his men for the event, until the truth dawned upon him.

Grant was no mean preacher, and as always when he had a captive and willing audience he preached at great length. Slowly he brought the subject around to profanity and, being careful not to single anyone out, pointed out that it was a useless device and one not generally heard any longer in the conversation of gentlemen. Grant was a shrewd judge of character. He had grasped an essential aspect of Rogers's motivation: above all, the little engineer wanted to be thought of as a gentleman. Then and there Rogers resolved to abstain from swearing. He was not always successful; at one point, when something went wrong with the canoes and Rogers made herculean efforts to suppress his normal vocabulary, Grant took pity upon him. The Major was standing with his mouth open, struggling to force the words back. The minister laid a hand on his arm: "Major, hadn't you better go behind a tree and say it?"

That Sunday evening, Grant and Fleming climbed to the benchland five hundred feet above Rogers's camp to ponder the "noble landscape" and to soliloquize on the future of the virgin country that stretched off below them.

"I asked myself," Fleming wrote, "if this solitude would be unchanged, or whether civilization in some form of its complex requirements would ever penetrate this region? . . . It cannot be that this immense valley will remain the haunt of a few wild animals . . . . How soon will a busy crowd of workmen take possession of these solitudes, and the steam whistle echo and re-echo where now all is silent? In the ages to come how many trains will run to and from sea to sea with millions of passengers?"

The following day he and his son with George Grant, Albert Rogers, and the Major set off up the valley of the Beaver for the pass. The trail was bordered with half a dozen varieties of ripe fruits and berries, which the travellers could pick and eat without dismounting. Refreshed by such luxuriance, they emerged from the forest and into the saucer-shaped meadow where Rogers had planted a yew stake to mark the actual summit.

Fleming had had the foresight to bring along a box of cigars and these were smoked as the group sat down on natural seats of moss-covered rock and listened to the Major tell the story of how he discovered the pass. The whole company was in high spirits. To show that they were still young and unaffected by the journey, Fleming proposed a game of leapfrog, "an act of Olympic worship to the deities in the heart of the Selkirks!"

The following day the Major returned to the Columbia while the others, with Albert Rogers as their guide, set off down the western slope. Twenty-four miles from the summit, the surveyors' freshly cut trail came to an end, and from this point on the party bade farewell to all civilization. After the journey was over, Grant vowed that he would never attempt to pioneer through a wilderness again. "In all my previous journeyings," he later wrote, "other men had been before me and left some memorial of their work, a railway, a Macadamized or gravel road, a lane, a trail, or at least, blazed trees to indicate the direction to be taken . . . . Here, there was nothing even to guide, save an occasional glimpse of the sun, and the slate-coloured, churned-up torrent . . . hemmed in by cañons, from which we turned aside only to get mired in beaver dams or alder swamps, or lost in labyrinths of steep ravines, or to stumble over slides of moss-covered rocks that had fallen from overhanging mountains."

The nettles of the devil's club were so bad that long after reaching civilization again, at Kamloops, the travellers felt the effects of them; their hands had to be wrapped in oatmeal poultices and even then the pain was so severe that one member of the party was unable to sleep.

All this time James Ross had been worrying about the suitability of the Kicking Horse Pass; the terrible descent from the Great Divide bothered him. Finally, he asked Shaw to investigate the Howse Pass; if Shaw found it to be preferable, he was instructed to run an immediate trial line from the summit without waiting for further orders. Ross stood ready to rush a survey crew to the spot. There was not a day to be lost; the rails had moved across the prairies at record speed and were now inching into the mountains.

Rogers was desperately worried when he learned that another attempt was being made on the Howse. Would "his" pass be rejected after all? Was Wilson's report of the previous year accurate? He stoutly defended it, but he was reminded that "Wilson is not an engineer so what does he know about grades?"

By this time it was late October and the snow was already falling thickly. Rogers was forced to leave the mountains without knowing the results of Shaw's explorations. By now Tom Wilson had become his friend and confidant and he revealed to him something of his feelings. He was in a state approaching despondency. All his work, he felt, had been for nothing: the contractors wanted to circumvent his pass in the Selkirks, "and if they did that he would be robbed of his ambition." The Kicking Horse was also in doubt. If it were rejected, too, there would be nothing in the mountains to mark his passing. "Are you sure you're right about the Howse Pass, Tom?" he asked time and time again.

In Calgary, to his great relief, the Major learned that Shaw and Ross had rejected the rival pass. The gradient was easier but the summit was one thousand feet higher than that of the Kicking Horse, and its employment would lengthen the railway by thirty miles. For better or for worse, the route which he had so enthusiastically and so profanely endorsed would become the main line of the CPR, and the name of Rogers would go down in history.

Chapter
Five

ONDERDONK'S
LAMBS

1

Almost every leading figure connected with the building of the great railway – with one notable exception – achieved the immortality of a place name. The map of western Canada is, indeed, a kind of coded history of the construction period. The stations along the way (some of them now abandoned) tell the story of the times: Langevin, Tilley, Chapleau and Cartier, Stephen and Donald, Langdon and Shepard, Secretan, Moberly, Schreiber, Crowfoot, Fleming, and Lacombe. Harry Abbott, the general superintendent, has a street named after him in Vancouver, along with Henry Cambie, the surveyor, and Lauchlan Hamilton, who laid out most of the CPR towns; Thomas Shaughnessy has an entire subdivision. Macoun, Sifton, and even Baron Pascoe du P. Grenfell, one of the more obscure – and reluctant – members of the original syndicate, are recognized in stations along the main line. Rosser and Dewdney are immortalized in the names of the main streets in the towns they founded. Most of the leading figures in the railway's story had mountain peaks named after them; Van Horne, indeed, had an entire range. But the connoisseur of place names will search in vain on mountain, village, park, avenue, subdivision, plaque, or swamp for any reference to the man who built the railway between Eagle Pass and Port Moody through some of the most difficult country in the world. There is not so much as an alleyway named for Andrew Onderdonk.

Perhaps he would have wanted it that way, for he was a remarkably reticent man. No biographer appeared before or after his death to chronicle his accomplishments, which included the San Francisco sea-wall, parts of the Trent Valley Canal, and the first subway tunnels under New York's East River. In the personal memoirs of the day he remains an aloof and shadowy figure, respected but not really known. Rogers, Hill, and Van Horne were each referred to by their underlings as "the old man." Onderdonk was known to everybody by the more austere title of "A.O."

If those initials had a Wall Street ring, it was perhaps because Onderdonk looked more like a broker than a contractor. In muddy Yale he dressed exactly as he would have on the streets of his native New York. His full moustache was neatly trimmed and his beard,

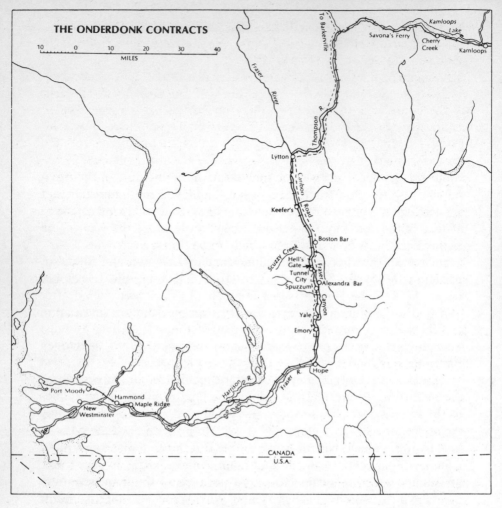

THE ONDERDONK CONTRACTS

when he grew one, was carefully parted in the middle. He was tall, strapping, and handsome, an impeccable man with an impeccable reputation – "a gentleman, always neat, well dressed and courteous," as a contemporary described him. When he passed down the line, the workers along the way – Onderdonk's lambs, they were called – were moved to touch their caps. Henry Cambie, who went to work for him, described him, as many did, as "a very unassuming man . . . possessed of a great deal of tact." In short, Onderdonk had no observable eccentricities unless one counts the monumental reticence that made him a kingdom unto himself and gave him an air of mystery, even among those who were closest to him.

But no one was really close to him. It was not that he shunned company. He was forever entertaining and clearly liked to play the host. "We lived as if we were in New York," Dr. Daniel McNeil Parker wrote of his visit there with Charles Tupper in 1881. Cambie, in his diaries, noted time and again that he dined at the Onderdonks'. But Cambie, who had a good sense of anecdote, never seems to have penetrated that wall of reserve.

If Onderdonk presented a cool face to the world, it was partly because he did not need to prove himself. He differed from most of the contractors of his time and from all the other major figures in the story of the railway, each of whom had been a poor boy who made it to the top on his own. Most were either immigrants or the sons of immigrants; but Onderdonk came from an old New York family that had been in America for more than two centuries. Fourteen members of his immediate family had degrees from Columbia and his ancestral background was studded with bishops, doctors, and diplomats. Onderdonk himself was a man of education with an engineering degree from the Troy Institute of Technology. It was not in his nature to show off; he was secure within himself, a quiet aristocrat, "very popular in local society circles," as the Victoria *British Colonist* put it.

Onderdonk's sense of security was also sustained by the knowledge that he had almost unlimited funds behind him. He was front man for a powerful syndicate whose chief ornament was the legendary San Francisco banker, Darius O. Mills. Charles Tupper, the Minister of Railways, had had his fill of under-financed contractors and so was happy to facilitate Onderdonk's purchase of the four Fraser Canyon contracts. Some time later, when the government let the rest of the British Columbia line from Emory's Bar to Port Moody on the coast, Onderdonk was again awarded the contract, though again he was not the lowest bidder. Certainly in this instance, if not before, the government made use of some fancy sleight-of-hand to ensure that he was successful. Under the terms of tendering, each firm bidding was required to put up substantial security to prove it could undertake the work. The lowest bidder deposited a cheque, which was certified for a specified period. Tupper waited until this period had expired; then he awarded the contract by default to Onderdonk, whose bid was $264,000 higher. This was bare-faced favouritism but Tupper made it stick. There was another suspicious aspect to the case. For the first time the contract was let as a lump sum, without being broken down into component parts. This method, as the *Globe* pointed out, "is essentially a corrupt method, and is so considered by contractors." For one thing, it made it difficult to check up on extras. Normally, the government's practice was to supply its own estimates of quantities to the competing firms, but in this case it declined to do so, thereby putting an enormous financial burden on each company tendering. Clearly, the government wanted Onderdonk to have the job, which was, admittedly, as difficult a one as had ever faced a contracting firm in the Dominion. As Henry Cambie wrote: "No such mountain work had ever been attempted in Canada before."

The CPR under the terms of its contract was to inherit the Onderdonk section of the railway. Onderdonk then, unlike Van Horne, was building a road that he would never have to manage. The distinction was to be the basis of a long and bitter dispute between the CPR and the government.

By the time the CPR turned its first prairie sod in May, 1881, Onderdonk had been at work for a year but had not laid a mile of track. There were four tunnels to be drilled within a mile and a half of his headquarters at Yale; it took eighteen months to blast them out of the rock of the canyon. That left twenty-three more tunnels to be drilled on the Onderdonk line. The blasting was painfully slow; even when big compressed air drills were used, it was not possible to move more than six feet a day. The flanks of the mountains were grooved by deep canyons; as a result, some six hundred trestles and bridges were required above Yale. To build them Onderdonk would need to order forty million board feet of lumber.

At Hell's Gate on the Fraser, a traveller could stand and watch the agony of construction taking place directly across the foaming waters. Splintered trees toppled into the muddy gorge, huge rocks catapulted into the sky, vast chunks of mountainside slid into the river. Men could be seen suspended at dizzy heights against the rock walls, let down the cliffs on ladders secured by ropes to drill blasting holes into the rock face. To escape the resultant explosions they had to clamber back up as nimbly as possible. Engineers made their measurements and took their cross-sections suspended for hours and sometimes days "like Mahomet's coffin between heaven and earth." They worked in bare feet to ensure a better footing, but a break in the rope, a rock toppling from above, or a premature blast meant certain death.

Running along the same cliff face was the old corduroy road to the Cariboo mines, jammed with traffic – twelve-mule teams and ungainly prairie schooners, pulled by sixteen oxen with six spares plodding behind. The road – itself an engineering miracle – was the only link between the coast and the interior of British Columbia. In some spots it was carried around the precipices on trestle-work, like the balcony of a house, so that passengers on the Cariboo stage were travelling directly over the boiling waters three hundred feet below.

Onderdonk was pledged to keep the road open; without it the economy of the Cariboo would be throttled. Besides, he needed it himself to bring supplies to his construction camps. Because the blasting and the building were going on above it, below it, or right beside it, great chunks of road sometimes slid into the Fraser. And when the railway itself required the right of way construction had to be halted until a new section of road was built.

By June of 1882, when Van Horne launched his record-breaking push across the prairies, Onderdonk had driven scarcely twenty miles of steel. An explosives factory was turning out four thousand pounds of nitro-glycerine a day. Ten vessels containing six thousand Chinese coolies were on their way to swell his labour force. Expenses were mounting alarmingly and the freight rates on the old Cariboo corduroy road were strangling him. As a result he decided to attempt a task generally considered impossible: he proposed to build a steamer to negotiate the most treacherous section of the Fraser Canyon, known as Hell's Gate, at a point where the river hurled itself at ten knots over a ledge of black basalt.

The sturdy little craft built on the spot was called *Skuzzy* after a nearby mountain stream and was launched on May 4 by Mrs. Onderdonk. But it was easier to construct such a craft than it was to man it, especially as the river was in spring flow. At the last moment a skipper was found to attempt the feat. He set off on May 17, using every river trick he had learned to pit the *Skuzzy* against the furious waters. Time after time he was beaten back until, at length, he turned the boat about and returned in defeat to Spuzzum.

To the astonishment of all, Onderdonk announced that another attempt would be made to force the boat through the canyon. That summer he went all the way to the upper Columbia to find three expert boatmen foolhardy enough to make the attempt. On September 7, he brought five flatcars loaded with guests from Yale to witness the ordeal. They crowded the high bank of the Fraser, laying wagers on the outcome – the odds running as high as a hundred to one against the boat's getting through.

The crowds could not stay to witness the full struggle. After four days only a few miles of headway had been made. After ten it became apparent that the *Skuzzy* was losing the battle. At this point Andrew Onderdonk took command. He ordered ring-bolts driven into the rock walls of the canyon and he placed one hundred and fifty Chinese labourers at intervals along the banks passing heavy ropes through the bolts. These ropes were attached to the ship's capstan. Finally on September 28, with the aid of the engines, the steam winch, fifteen men on the capstan, and the mass of coolies tugging and straining along the bank, the boat finally got through, and a public holiday was declared in Yale. For the next year the *Skuzzy* worked the river between Lytton and Boston Bar, emerging splintered and battered after every journey.

All this time men were being mangled or killed by falling rock, by slides, by runaway horses, and above all by the incessant blasting. Often, huge rocks came hurtling out of the mouths of tunnels like cannon-balls. One sank a boat, causing a man to drown. Another knocked down a bridge. The larger blasts touched off avalanches and mud slides. Almost every time heavy shots were fired inside a tunnel, great boulders were ripped free from the mountainside. One of these tore through the roof of the engine house at Number One Tunnel, "somewhat injuring a couple of men," in the casual report of the Yale *Inland Sentinel*. One slide came down from such a height that it carried part of an oak forest and an entire Indian burying ground into the river, allowing the oaks to continue to grow "and the dead men's bones to rest without being in the least disturbed – fences, roots, images and all."

A rock slide actually blocked the Thompson River, forming a dam half a mile long and a hundred and fifty feet wide, raising the water two hundred feet and flooding several farms while leaving the channel below almost dry. The Chinese and Indians working in the vicinity dropped their tools and rushed to the river-bed to collect the hundreds of fish wriggling and gasping in the mud and also to recover the gold, which was still plentiful and, with the water low, easy to pan. A slide in November, 1882, blocked the track so badly that it was mid-April before the debris could all be cleared away. A similar heap of debris was struck by a train with such impact that the locomotive became detached. It hurtled over a 250-foot embankment, did a full somersault, and landed upright at the river's edge. The fireman and engineer climbed out, unhurt.

There were other odd mishaps caused by the treacherous terrain. It was not even safe to get drunk. One veteran railroader who did staggered to the top of a bluff not far from the Big Tunnel one January day and toppled to his death. Even as careful and experienced an engineer as Henry Cambie was not immune. His horses bolted on the Cariboo Road – a fairly common occurrence – his carriage struck a new stump, and he, his wife, and his child were thrown out. The child escaped unhurt but both parents were injured, Mrs. Cambie suffering a severe concussion.

The danger was so great that it became difficult to get men who were willing to be suspended by ropes to drill powder holes in the chasm walls. The Indians were the most fearless; fortunately, they turned out to be first-class rock workers. But they also had a habit of quitting on payday.

Six months after Onderdonk began his contract the hospital at Yale had to be enlarged to take care of the accident victims. By August, 1881, the *Inland Sentinel,* which had been reporting deaths almost weekly, had become alarmed at the accident rate: "Life is held too cheap, generally, in this country, and it will evidently require severe punishment to teach parties that they cannot trifle with other people's lives even if they are careless of their own existence." Exactly one week after those words were written, two more men working in Number Seven Tunnel were killed by falling boulders.

2

When Andrew Onderdonk arrived in British Columbia there were only thirty-five thousand white citizens in the province. He would need to employ at least ten thousand men (actually many more, because of the turnover); from the very outset there was a kind of terror that he would solve his labour problem by importing and employing Chinese.

As soon as he arrived in Victoria in April, 1880, Onderdonk was met by a deputation from the Anti-Chinese Association. He assured them that he would always give white labour the preference. When the white labour of the province was exhausted Onderdonk said he would, if necessity compelled him, fall back on the French Canadians of eastern Canada. Should that not be sufficient, he would with reluctance engage Indians and Chinese.

The first Chinese had come to British Columbia from California in 1858, attracted by the Fraser's gold. Anti-Chinese feeling had been rising steadily since that time. By 1878, when their employment in public works was banned, there were some three thousand Chinese in the province. All were prepared to work for lower wages than any white labourer, and that was the chief cause of the discontent. It was considered political suicide for a public figure to take any stand but one that was anti-Oriental.

The feeling elsewhere in Canada, though less intense, was generally against the Chinese. Almost all newspapers were editorially opposed to Oriental immigration. In Winnipeg, where Chinese were all but unknown, the *Times* published a fairly typical series of opinions about "the beardless and immoral children of China," as it called them; they possessed "no sense whatever of any principle of morality"; their brains were "vacant of all thoughts which lift up and ennoble humanity"; and "it is an established fact that dealings with the Chinese are attended with evil results."

The Prime Minister himself agreed that the Chinese were "an alien race in every sense that would not and could not be expected to assimilate with our Arian population," but he was far too pragmatic to exclude Orientals from Canada until the railway was built. He put it bluntly to Parliament in 1882: "It is simply a question of alternatives: either you must have this labour or you can't have the railway."

Onderdonk was operating on a tight budget. He had been forced to accept four contracts at bids that were more than a million and a half dollars lower than his own tendered price. He had paid out an additional two hundred and fifteen thousand dollars to buy up the contracts. He was trying to get men to come all the way to British Columbia for lower wages than the Northern Pacific was offering – as little as $1.50 a day for labourers.

Chinese coolies, on the other hand, could be employed for one dollar a day. In addition, they did not require all the paraphernalia of a first-class camp. The coolie was prepared to move about in the wilderness, set up his own camp, and pack all his belongings, provisions, and camp equipment on his back. Michael Haney, who went to work for Onderdonk in 1883, discovered that it was possible to move two thousand Chinese a distance of twenty-five miles and have them at work all within twenty-four hours. The same task could not be performed with a similar number of white workmen in less than a week. It is small wonder, then, that almost from the outset Andrew Onderdonk began hiring Chinese in spite of a volley of protests. His first consignment came from the Northern Pacific Railroad in Oregon in 1880, the second from the Southern Pacific in California in 1881.

In the winter of 1881-82, Onderdonk, having employed all the west-coast labour he could get at his prices – white, Chinese, and Indian – chartered two sailing ships to bring one thousand coolies each from Hong Kong. They arrived after a long, rough winter passage – "the men below decks slept in closed hatches with bad ventilation," Cambie recalled – but in good physical condition. Altogether in 1882, Onderdonk brought ten shiploads of Chinese, a total of about six thousand.

The coolies came from Kwang Tung province whose capital, Canton, was the only port in China through which foreign trade was permitted. The average wage there was seven cents a day; five years in North America could give any Chinese financial independence if he saved three hundred dollars. No wonder they clamoured to come!

They were not hired individually but in large groups through agents representing the Six Companies of Kwang Tung. Each Chinese promised a fee of 2 1/2 per cent of his wages to the company, together with his passage money – about forty dollars. The company, in its turn, was pledged to look after each man's welfare in North America. From the point of view of the individual coolie, who could speak no English and who was totally uninformed about North American society, the Six Companies represented the only real method of getting to the promised land.

Michael Haney declared that in his entire experience of dealing with the Chinese, he could not recall one case of dishonesty. They lived up to their contracts, and if there was a dispute with a sub-contractor, "it only needed the presence of a representative of the contractor to assure them that their grievances would be considered, to send them cheerfully to work again." But if they thought their rights were being trampled on, they ceased to be docile. George Munro, a construction boss, ruefully recalled his first payday when through an error in the payroll department, the Chinese workers received one cent less per hour than had been agreed upon. " . . . there was a little war declared right there. They stormed the Company's stores like madmen, and it didn't take the men at fault long to discover their mistake. The Chinamen were paid their cent and peace reigned once more."

Such incidents were not uncommon. The coolies were divided by the company that provided them into gangs of thirty labourers plus a cook, an assistant cook, and a bookman, whose task it was to keep count of the payments to be made to each individual. In charge of each work gang was a white boss, who dealt directly with the bookman. Any foreman who did not get along well with his Oriental labourers could expect trouble. Once when a white boss refused to allow his coolies to build a fire along the grade to heat their big teapots, they all quit. On several occasions, white foremen were physically assaulted. One tried to fire two Chinese over the head of the gang's bookkeeper and precipitated a riot near Lytton. He and the white bridge superintendent, the timekeeper, and a teamster were attacked by the entire gang, which seriously mangled one man with a shovel. The following night a party of armed whites attacked the Chinese camp, burned their bunkhouses, and beat several coolies so severely that one died.

In such instances feeling ran high against the coolies. The Chief Justice of the province, Matthew Baillie Begbie, was horrified by "the terrible outrages against Chinamen" in the neighbourhood of Lytton. Begbie was aghast that in all cases "the perpetrators have escaped scot free." In one instance the ringleaders were positively identified by four of the surviving victims but were acquitted by the jury "upon evidence of an *alibi* which the prosecutors might well deem perjured."

Many inflammatory incidents occurred because of accidents along the line, for which the Chinese blamed the white foremen. On one occasion, about ten miles below Hope, a foreman named

Miller failed to give his gang proper warning of a coming explosion; a piece of rock thrown up by the subsequent blast blew one coolie's head right off. His comrades took off after Miller, who plunged into the river to save himself. Several Chinese dived in after him while others on the bank pelted him with stones. Miller was saved by one of the tunnel contractors who rowed a boat through the hail of missiles and hauled him in, but not before one of the Chinese had got off two shots from a pistol. Miller and his rescuer rowed desperately upstream, followed for two miles by an angry mob, before they made good their escape.

Deaths appeared to happen oftener among the Chinese labourers than in the white group. A single month in the late summer of Onderdonk's first season, culled from Henry Cambie's diary, gives an idea of their frequency:

August 13 [*1880*] – A Chinese drilling on the ledge of a bluff near Alexandra Bar is killed when a stone falls from above and knocks him off.

August 19 – A log rolls over an embankment and crushes a Chinese to death at the foot of a slope.

September 4 – A Chinese is killed by a rock slide.

September 7 – A boat upsets in the Fraser and a Chinese is drowned.

September 11 – A Chinese is smothered to death in an earth cave-in.

Yet, in that last week – on September 9 – the *Inland Sentinel* proudly announced that "there have been no deaths since the 15th of June." Clearly, it did not count Chinese.

The coolies were generally fatalistic about death. Haney, calling one day at a tent where a sick Chinese lay, asked the bookman: "Will he die to-day?" The bookman shook his head. "No, to-morrow, thlee o'clock." Haney claimed that at three, to the minute, the man expired.

The Chinese would not work in the presence of death, which they considered bad luck. Haney once came upon two thousand Chinese all sitting idle; one of their number had fallen off the bank and his corpse lay far below, spread-eagled on the rocks. In vain the walking boss argued and swore. He pointed out that it was impossible to reach the body. The bank was a sheer precipice, and no boat could approach it through the boiling waters.

"Well," said Haney, "what do you propose to do? Can't have

these Chinamen standing around until that Chinaboy disintegrates."

The walking boss scratched his head. "There's an Indian who promises to move that body for ten dollars. I've tried to make a deal with him but he won't budge on that price and it's too much."

"Never mind how much it is," Haney retorted. "Pay it and get those men back to work."

He moved off down the line. During the evening a sharp explosion was heard in the canyon. When Haney returned, the Chinese were back at work and the body had vanished. The Indian had stolen some dynamite and caps, lowered them with a smouldering fuse down the canyon wall, and blown the cadaver to bits.

The Chinese subsisted mainly on a diet of rice and stale ground salmon and, as a result, died by the score from scurvy. No real attempt was made to succour them. Two hundred who came over from China died during their first year in Canada. As in other deaths of Chinese there was no coroner's inquest and no medical attention supplied by either the government or the contractor.

The cold winters caused the coolies great hardship. Most found it impossible to work after mid-November. Cambie, one November 22, noted: "Chinamen who are still at work . . . appear to suffer dreadfully from cold. They work in overcoats and wrap their heads up in mufflers." In the winter of 1883-84, when Onderdonk's work force was diminished, the suffering was very great. When the contractors had no more need of them, the Chinese were discharged and left to scrabble for pickings in the worked-out bars of the Fraser or to exist in near destitution in the dying towns along the completed track.

Not all of the Chinese who came to Canada with the hope of securing financial independence achieved their dream. Although a Chinese labourer was paid about twenty-five dollars a month on the railway, it was difficult for him to save very much. He was not paid for the three months of winter when work was at a near standstill, and expenses for clothes, room rent, tools, fares, taxes, doctors, drugs, and other sundries left him with little more than forty dollars after a full year of toil on the railway. That only covered his debt to the steamboat company. The census figures of 1891 indicate that some five thousand coolies were unable to go back to Asia in the years following the completion of the Onderdonk contracts.

Because the Chinese left home expecting to return in a few years, they made no attempt to learn the language or alter their mode of life. Thus they were forever strangers in a foreign land, and their continued presence gave to British Columbia a legacy of racial tension that was to endure for the best part of a century.

The railway workers who remained left few descendants (since they brought no women with them) and few, if any, memories. Some, however, returned to Kwang Tung and then came back to Canada with their families to settle permanently in British Columbia. One of whom there is some slight record was a farmer from Toyshan named Pon Git Cheng. One of his sons became a houseboy for Benjamin Tingley Rogers, the Vancouver sugar magnate. And one of *his* sons, Dr. George Pon of Toronto, was in 1971 a leading scientist in the employ of Atomic Energy of Canada. Dr. Pon was told something of his family background and was able to return to China to visit his grandfather's village in Toyshan. But he never discovered exactly what it was his grandfather did on the railway – how he was hired, where he worked, or what he felt about the strange, raw land which was to become his home. Such details were not set down and so are lost forever – lost and forgotten, like the crumbling bones that lie in unmarked graves beneath the rock and the rubble high above the Fraser's angry torrent.

3

Cheap Oriental labour undoubtedly saved Onderdonk from bankruptcy. Without the Chinese he could scarcely have completed his contracts. Between 1880 and 1884, at their lower rate of pay, the coolies saved him between three and five million dollars.

The Governor General believed that the presence of the Chinese was keeping costs down by at least twenty-five per cent, but even with this advantage Onderdonk's operation was a marginal one. By 1883 he was plainly in financial trouble. Marcus Smith, the government engineer who acted as Ottawa's watchdog on the line, reported that winter that "it was painfully apparent to myself and even to outsiders that the men were not working to advantage nor were they being well directed." Unless some drastic changes were made, he felt, Onderdonk could not pull through without heavy loss.

By March, 1883, Onderdonk was showing a book loss of two and a half million dollars on the work completed. In desperation he hired Michael Haney, who was given the management of the entire line from Port Moody to Kamloops. The crusty Marcus Smith was of two minds about Haney. "He seems to fully realize the gravity of your position and is anxious to improve it," he told Onderdonk, but he added, "I hope Mr. Haney has not caught the disease of the American mind to do something rapid or astounding." Haney, after all, was known as an impulsive Irishman, given to bold escapades; he did, however, know a good deal about saving money. He immediately tightened up discipline and speeded deliveries. He introduced his invention, the wing plough, which unloaded gravel from a line of open cars at bewildering speed. He developed a large nitro-glycerine factory at Yale, and when it blew up, breaking every window in town, he rebuilt it. He travelled the line on horseback, using relays of steeds so that he could inspect as much as a hundred miles of track a day. In this way all of the work in progress came under his personal inspection twice each month.

One of the chief reasons for the delays, Haney discovered, was the huge amount of bridging required. Timbers had to be shaped and cut at each bridging point, always at enormous cost. Haney streamlined the operation by building a mill capable of producing one hundred and fifty thousand board feet of lumber a day – every stick marked and numbered for its exact position on the bridge for which it was destined. By this method, the great trestles, prefabricated in advance, were sent forward for immediate erection.

Haney was a man who did everything with flair, a characteristic that helps explain why he was viewed as a kind of walking accident. When the new governor general, Lord Lansdowne, came out to inspect the line shortly before its completion, Haney insisted on taking him on a wild ride to the coast at seventy miles an hour. Lansdowne scarcely uttered a word until they stopped at a small station to take on water. Then His Excellency spoke up:

"How far is it to Port Moody?"

Haney replied that it was another forty-eight miles.

"Will we be running as fast the balance of the way?"

Haney responded that he thought he could better the pace.

"I have a wife and family in Ottawa and I am rather anxious to see them again," the Governor General replied, "so if you are continuing that rate of travel, I think I will just stay here." A chastened Haney brought the train crawling into Port Moody.

In spite of Haney's cost-cutting, Onderdonk's financial problems continued. In the fall of 1883 he set off for Ottawa to lobby for a further subsidy for the unfinished line. In Victoria he ran into James Hartney, who had been cutting timber for him and who had not yet been paid. It says something for the state of Onderdonk's finances that the railway builder, who had a continent-wide reputation for prompt payment, kept putting Hartney off. He was preparing to leave for San Francisco with his family on a Sunday evening, but just before the ship sailed, Hartney served him with a writ. Thus was the Island community treated to the strange spectacle of the province's biggest employer of labour being pulled from his bunk at two in the morning, haled back to shore, and lodged in jail, where he languished for two hours before his friends bailed him out.

The optimism of frontier communities along the line of the railway in the 1880's knew no bounds. When it became clear that the Pacific railway was finally to be built and the details of the Onderdonk contract were made public, the price of lots rose swiftly in Emory, the steamboat landing at the head of the navigable section of the Fraser. Emory, the real estate ads announced, "cannot fail to become one of the most important and prosperous Cities on the Pacific slope."

But Emory was not destined to be a city. It soon became clear that the real centre of the Onderdonk operations would be at Yale. "Next summer will be a boom for Emory sure," the *Inland Sentinel* wrote wistfully in January, 1881. But in May the *Sentinel* itself moved its offices to Yale – a roaring, wide-open community which for the next three years was to be the railway centre of British Columbia. Then it, too, would fade as merchants, workers, and major institutions – once again including the *Sentinel* – packed up and moved to Kamloops.

The *Sentinel's* editor, a black Irishman named Michael Hagan, belonged to that vanishing breed, the itinerant journeyman newspaper jack-of-all-trades. When he arrived at Emory in the spring of 1880, there was not much about a newspaper office that he had not mastered. Six years before he had launched another *Sentinel* at Thunder Bay when Prince Arthur's Landing was fighting Fort William to secure the CPR terminus. A kind of restlessness had caused him to trek across half a continent and start a new paper in the heart of British Columbia. Hagan's assistant, George Kennedy, always remembered his first sight of Yale. The paper was still being published at Emory when he and Hagan, with the latest edition strapped to their backs, poled and paddled a canoe through the ripples of the canyon the four miles to the neighbouring community.

"The town of Yale was *en fete* that day in a 'wild and woolly' sense, and the one long main 'business' street fronting the river, presented a scene and sounds, at once animated and grotesque – bizarre and risque. The shell like shacks of saloons, whereof every third building, nearly, was one, fairly buzzed and bulged like Brobdignagian [*sic*] wasps' nests, whose inmates, in a continual state of flux, ever and anon hurled in and out, in two's and three's or tangled wrangling masses. Painted and bedizened women lent a garish color to the scene. On the hot and dusty road-side, or around timbers, rails, and other construction debris, men in advanced stages of intoxication rolled and fought or snored in bestial oblivion. One drunken duel assumed a gory and tragic guise, when one of the sweating, swearing gladiators started sawing at his antagonist's neck with a jack knife. A tardy conservor of the peace, at this stage, separated the bloody belligerents, while a handy medicine man did a timely mending job on the lacerated connecting-piece of the chief victim.''

Every shape of face and every kind of costume was observable along Yale's main street. The saloons were packed with gamblers playing faro, poker, chuck-a-luck, and dice. Three-card monte, the confidence man's game, was to be found everywhere. Against the incessant hammering of drills and the periodic crump of blasting powder, there was a cacophony of foreground noises – saw, mallet, and hammer, mouth organ, fiddle, and concertina, blending with the harsher music of rattling wheels. The air reeked with the mingled pungencies of fresh salmon, sawdust, black powder, and tobacco smoke. Yale, in short, was very like any raw frontier town in Wyoming, Montana, or Arizona save for one thing: all the saloons were shut tight on Sunday.

The Toronto *Mail* dispatched a man to examine the phenomenal community. He observed that ''people don't walk in Yale, they rush.... From 'peep o' day' til long into the night the movement of men, horses and wagons along the one business street goes on scarcely with intermission. As we gaze at the hurrying throngs we wonder how on earth they all find beds or even space in which to lie down when they seek repose.''

The *Mail*'s reporter had arrived on a payday and was able to report that ''the 'boys' with the month's wages burning holes in their pockets are making matters lively, keeping the constable's hands full of business....'' Although prices were double and triple those in San Francisco, nobody seemed to grudge spending a dollar. Hagan continually warned his readers – one suspects in vain – of the dire consequences of spending all their wages the day they received them: ''. . . such abuse will undermine health and leave disease and want in train. . . . Let those unfortunately addicted to strong drink take heed . . . .''

For all of the railway period, Yale was a strange and rather artificial community, cut off from the rest of the world. Almost everybody must have known in his heart that its existence was temporary, but no one voiced that feeling. Hagan wrote optimistically about the town's great future from vague mining properties, but in his editorial columns there was a growing peevishness towards the Onderdonk company as the railway neared completion. The feeling of optimism gave way to a kind of carping against established forces. On May 3, 1883, following a rumour that the roundhouse and machine shops were to be moved, Hagan called a meeting to discuss ''this desertion of the town.'' But a year later, he too was forced to desert.

The impermanence of the community was underlined by the shifting population and by the terrible fires that ravaged the business section. Seen from the steamer, the chief characteristic of the community was its newness. The buildings were always new; so were the fences, the sidewalks, and the people. Yale had no opportunity to grow old.

In its brief, three-year joy-ride, the town suffered two disastrous fires, both started by drunks. On July 27, 1880, a third of Yale was burned to the ground, only a month after Hagan had warned the townspeople of the dangers of just such a conflagration. Hagan was a Cassandra whom everyone ignored. It took a second fire in August of 1882, which reduced half the town to ashes in three hours, before there was any serious talk about gathering funds to buy a steam pumper.

After this Yale began to take on a more sober appearance. Concerts, recitals, lectures, and minstrel shows vied with the saloons for patronage. The Chinese opened their own Freemasons' Lodge, with an ornamental flagstaff as well as joss-house. Grand balls were held, in which people danced all night – and even longer – to the music of scraping violins. "A ball out here means business," wrote Dr. Daniel Parker, Charles Tupper's travelling companion. "The last one ... commenced at 12 o'clock on Monday morning and lasted continuously day and night until 12 o'clock the next Saturday."

On the great fête-days the community, bound by a growing feeling of cohesion, turned out *en masse*. The Queen's Birthday on May 24 was an occasion for a half-holiday for whites and Indians. Chinese New Year, celebrated by the coolies early in February, ran for an entire week. The biggest event of all was the Fourth of July, since Yale was very much an American town. Half the population of New Westminster chugged up the river for the occasion. Cannons roared; locomotives pulled flatcars crammed with excursionists from neighbouring Emory; Indians climbed greased poles; "The Star-Spangled Banner" was enthusiastically rendered outside of the Onderdonk home. Couples danced on a special platform erected on the main street. There were horse races, canoe races, caber-tossing, and hurdles. By comparison, July 1, celebrating a Confederation that was less than a generation old, passed almost unnoticed. British Columbia was part British and part American; it would require the completion of the railway to make her part of the new dominion.

Far off beyond the mountains – beyond the rounded bulks of the Gold Range, beyond the pointed peaks of the mysterious Selkirks – the rails were inching west; but as far as Onderdonk's lambs were concerned, that land was almost as distant as China. "... we really knew very little about what they were doing on that side," Henry Cambie recalled. Any letters, if such had been written, would have had to travel down the muddy Fraser by boat, on to Victoria and thence to San Francisco, across the United States to St. Paul, north into Winnipeg, and then west again until they reached End of Track. The distance involved was more than five thousand miles, and yet, in 1883, End of Track, in the foothills, was only about three hundred miles away.

Chapter
Six

THE
PROMISED
LAND

1

By the spring of 1883, Canada was a country with half a transcontinental railroad. Between Port Moody and Ottawa, the track lay in pieces like a child's train set – long stretches of finished road separated by formidable gaps. The easiest part of the CPR was complete: a continuous line of steel ran west for 937 miles from Fort William at the head of Lake Superior to the tent community of Swift Current in the heart of Palliser's Triangle. To the west, between Swift Current and the half-completed Onderdonk section in British Columbia, was a gap of 750 miles on parts of which not even a surveyor had set foot. The section closest to civilization was graded, waiting for the rails to be laid. The remainder was a mélange of tote roads, forest slashings, skeletons of bridges, and engineers' stakes. An equally awesome gap of more than six hundred miles extended east from End of Track near Fort William to the terminus of the newly completed Canada Central Railway on Lake Nipissing. Again, this was little more than a network of mired roads chopped out of the stunted timber and, here and there, some partially blasted tunnels and rock cuts.

By the time the snows melted almost the entire right of way for twenty-five hundred miles, from the rim of the Shield to tidewater, was abuzz with human activity. In the east, the timber cutters and rock men were ripping a right of way out of the Precambrian wilderness. In the far west, more thousands were invading the land of the Blackfoot tribes. Little steel shoots were sprouting south, west, and east of the main trunk-line in Manitoba. And wherever the steel went the settlers followed with their tents and their tools, their cattle and their kittens, their furniture and their fences.

From the famine-ridden bog country of Ireland, the bleak crofts of the Scottish hills, and the smoky hives of industrial England, the immigrants were pouring in. They sat crowded together on the hard seats of the colonist cars – patient people, full of hope, blessed by good cheer. Of the 133,000 who arrived in Canada in 1883, two-thirds sped directly to the North West.

No one, apparently, had expected such an onslaught. The demand for Atlantic passage was unprecedented. In the Toronto immigrant sheds ten thousand meals were served in May alone – as many as

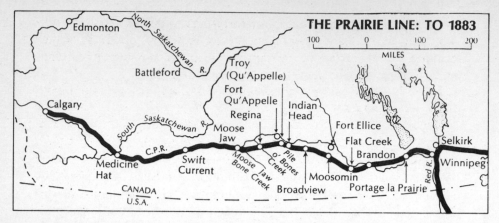

THE PRAIRIE LINE: TO 1883

had been prepared in the entire season of 1882. The postal service was overtaxed with twelve thousand letters destined for the North West. The number had quadrupled in just two years.

As many as twenty-five hundred settlers left Winnipeg every week on trains with every car crammed – some people, indeed, clinging to the steps and all singing the song that became the theme of the pioneers: "One More River to Cross." The CPR by April was able to take them as far as the tent town of Moose Jaw, four hundred miles to the west.

It was not always easy to tell blue blood from peasant. Nicholas Flood Davin, the journalist, on his first day in Regina was struck by the gentlemanly bearing of the waiter in the tent where he breakfasted. He turned out to be a nephew of the Duke of Rutland. And the son of Alfred, Lord Tennyson, the poet laureate, was breaking sod on a homestead that spring.

The immigrants brought everything to the prairies from domestic pets to livestock. One enterprising arrival from Ontario, sensing the loneliness of the settler's life, brought in a crate full of cats. They were snapped up at three dollars apiece. An early pioneer, Esther Goldsmith, always remembered the wild scene at the Brandon station when a birdcage was sucked from a woman's hand in the scramble for the train. Another recalled her first real view of the prairie driving eighty-five miles north from Broadview with a canary in a cage on her lap.

"Freedom?" wrote William Oliver sardonically. "There never was such a thing; every acre was won by hard toil and the sweat of man." The breaking up of the tough prairie sod was gruelling work. A man with a good team of oxen was lucky if he could till three-quarters of an acre in a day.

Government land was free up to a limit of a quarter section; the homesteader who worked it for three years was given title to it and could in addition, pre-empt an adjoining quarter section. Those immigrants who bought CPR land in the forty-eight-mile belt along the railway paid five dollars an acre but were rebated all but $1.25 if they cropped three-quarters of it within four years; if they put up buildings as well, they did not need to crop more than a half.

In the North West, as the rails pushed steadily towards the mountains, new communities began to take shape. "These towns along the line west of Brandon are all the same," the Fort Macleod *Gazette* reported. "See one, see all. There are some board houses, but most of them are board frames (rough) with a canvas roof." Both Moose Jaw, with its "bare, freckled and sunburnt buildings" and Medicine Hat, another canvas town in a coulee of that name, were in this category. The former, in spite of its youth, already had three newspapers by 1883. The latter, by July, boasted six hotels, though most of them were mere tents sheltering half a dozen bunks.

This was Sam Steele's territory. The remarkable Mounted Policeman had been named acting adjutant of the Fort Qu'Appelle district the previous year and placed in command of detachments along the line of CPR construction. As the rails made their way from the coulees of Saskatchewan to the final spike at Craigellachie, Steele would always be on hand to keep the peace. His background was solidly military. At seventeen, he had joined the militia, serving against the Fenians in 1866, and had taken part in General Garnet Wolseley's Red River Expedition against Riel in 1870 (when he managed to hoist three-hundred-pound barrels of flour onto his massive shoulders to negotiate the portages of the Precambrian Shield). When the first permanent force unit was formed in 1871, he rushed to the colours. When the North West Mounted Police were organized in 1873, he joined them immediately, becoming the force's first sergeant-major. He had a habit of being present when history was being made: he took part in the thousand-mile march to the Rockies in 1874; he bargained with Sitting Bull after the Custer affair; now he was presiding at the building of the first transcontinental railway; he would go on to become "the Lion of the Yukon" during the Klondike gold rush.

In his capacity as police magistrate, Steele worked without rest under primitive conditions. In Regina, his courtroom had been a marquee, sixteen by fourteen feet. It was so cold that winter that the water froze in the bathtubs and the clerks had to keep their ink-bottles on the tops of stoves. Between Moose Jaw and Medicine Hat, Steele had no courtroom at all. At Swift Current he tried cases while seated on a Red River cart, with planks stretched across it for a bench and the evidence taken down on the flap of his dispatch bag. As he worked he counted the trains roaring by to End of Track, loaded with ties, rails, and spikes. He could tell by the number how many miles were being laid that day.

By July, the organization had been perfected to the point where ninety-seven miles of track were laid instead of the monthly average of fifty-eight. As Langdon and Shepard approached the end of their contract, the track-laying guides were seized by a kind of frenzy; on July 28, about two weeks out of Calgary, they set a record that has never been surpassed for manual labour on a railroad: 6.38 miles of finished railway were completed in a single day.

The whole country marvelled over the feat of building the railway across the prairies in just fifteen months – everybody, that is, except the people it was displacing. To the Indians, the railway symbolized the end of a golden age – an age in which the native peoples, liberated by the white man's horses and the white man's weapons, had galloped at will across their untrammelled domain, where the game seemed unlimited and the zest of the hunt gave life a tang and a purpose. This truly idyllic existence came to an end just as the railway was thrust through the ancient hunting grounds of the Blackfoot and the Cree. Within six years, the image of the Plains Indian underwent a total transformation. From being a proud and fearless nomad, rich in culture and tradition, he became a pathetic, half-starved creature, confined to the semi-prisons of the new reserves and totally dependent on government relief for his existence.

The buffalo, on which the entire Indian economy and culture depended, were actually gone before the coming of the railway; but the order of their passing is immaterial. They could not have existed in a land bisected by steel and criss-crossed by barbed wire. The passing of the great herds was disastrous, for without the buffalo, which had supplied them with food, shelter, clothing, tools, and ornaments, the Indians were helpless. By 1880, after the three most terrible years they had ever known, the emaciated natives were forced to eat their dogs and their horses, to scrabble for gophers and mice, and even to consume the carcasses of animals found rotting on the prairie.

On top of this the Indians were faced with the sudden onslaught of a totally foreign agrarian culture. Because of the railway, the impact was almost instantaneous. It did not matter that the various treaties guaranteed that the natives would not be forced to adopt white ways. With the buffalo gone and the grasslands tilled and fenced, such promises were hollow.

The government's policy, born of expediency, was a two-stage one. The starving Indians would be fed temporarily at public expense for a period. Over a longer period, the Indian Department would settle them on reserves and try to turn a race of hunters into a community of peasants. The reserves would be situated on land best suited for agriculture, all north of the railway and far from the hunting grounds. Thus the CPR became the visible symbol of the Indians' tragedy.

Only terrible privations could have caused thousands of once-independent people to abandon so meekly an entire way of life. The famine of 1879-80 forced thousands of reluctant Indians onto the new reserves. Others, led by such free spirits as Big Bear and Piapot, briefly defied the authorities but in the end, all the tribes were forced north. To the south lay the line of the railway: a steel fence barring them from their past.

Some of the chiefs accepted the coming of steel with a certain amount of fatalism; Poundmaker, for one, urged his Cree followers to prepare for it. In the spring of 1881, after a fruitless search for game on the prairie, he realized that the buffalo were gone and the old nomadic life was ended. He gathered his followers and told them to work hard, sow grain, and take care of their cattle: "Next summer, or at latest next fall, the railway will be close to us, the whites will fill the country, and they will dictate to us as they please. It is useless to dream that we can frighten them; that time is past; our only resource is our work, our industry, and our farms. Send your children to school . . . if you want them to prosper and be happy."

It was sensible advice, given the inevitability of settlement, but not every chieftain took it, not even Poundmaker himself. His fellow Cree leader, Piapot, ran afoul of Secretan's survey crews in 1882, pulling up forty miles of the surveyors' stakes on the line west of Moose Jaw. Secretan, who had little patience with or understanding of the Indians, threatened to shoot on sight any "wretched ill-conditioned lying sons of aborigines" if they pulled up more stakes – a statement that caused consternation in Ottawa.

In May, Piapot ordered his followers to camp directly upon the railway's right of way. That led to one of those gaudy little incidents that helped to build the growing legend of the North West Mounted Police:

The two young men from the Maple Creek detachment ride up on their jet-black horses. There squats Piapot in front of his tepee, quietly smoking his pipe, directly in the line of the railroad. Around him the young braves wheel their horses, shouting war-cries and firing their rifles into the air, egged on by the usual rabble of shrieking squaws. The prairie, speckled with spring wildflowers, stretches off to the low horizon. From somewhere in the distance comes the ominous sound of hammers striking on steel.

The sergeant tells the chief that he must make way for the railway. The brown old man refuses to budge. The sergeant takes out his watch. "I will give you just fifteen minutes," he says. "If by the end of that time you haven't begun to comply with the order, we shall make you."

The braves jostle the policemen, trying to provoke them into a fight. The two young men in the pillbox hats and scarlet tunics quietly sit their horses. The minutes tick by. Birds wheel in the sky. The chief remains impassive. The young Crees gallop about. Finally, the sergeant speaks again. "Time's up!" he says and, throwing his reins to the constable, he springs from his steed, strides to the tepee, and kicks down the tentpoles. The painted buffalo skin collapses. Other tepees topple under the kicks of his polished boot. "Now git!" says the sergeant and, astonishingly, the Indians obey. Piapot has been stripped of his dignity.

This incident helped to bolster the tradition of the redcoats as fearless upholders of the law. Yet, in the light of the Indians' tragedy, it is inexpressibly sad; and the day was swiftly approaching when no Mounted Policeman would again dare to act in such a fashion. The Indians were growing bolder.

Not far from Calgary, the railway builders encountered the most remarkable Indian leader of all, the sagacious Crowfoot, chief of the Blackfoot nation, renowned for his many feats of bravery. He had fought in nineteen battles, had been wounded six times, and had once rescued a child from the jaws of a grizzly bear, dispatching the animal with a spear while the whole camp watched. Long before his fellows he saw what was coming. He pinned his hopes on the government and signed a treaty.

Thus, when the tents of the construction workers went up on the borders of the Blackfoot reserve, there was anger and bitterness among Crowfoot's followers. The chief sent envoys to warn the foremen that no further construction work would be permitted and that seven hundred armed braves stood ready to attack.

At this point, Albert Lacombe stepped into the picture. For some time he had been concerned about the creeping advance of civilization, which would change his own way of life as surely as that of the natives. "Now that the railway gangs are coming nearer to our poor Indians," he confided to his diary in May, 1883, "we can expect all kinds of moral disorders." When Lacombe learned of the trouble at the Blackfoot reserve, he rode immediately to the construction camp where he tried to alert the foreman to the danger. Rebuffed, he dispatched telegrams to Van Horne, Donald A. Smith, and Edgar Dewdney. The answers were not long in coming: cease all work until the Indians are placated.

The priest had known Crowfoot for years and the two men respected each other. During a smallpox epidemic in 1870 Lacombe so exhausted himself in succouring the victims that hundreds of Indians became Christians in tribute to his selflessness.

At the CPR's behest he set out to soothe his old friend. He arrived at Crowfoot's camp bearing gifts, and at his suggestion the chief called a grand council where the priest, standing before the squatting braves, spoke:

"Now my mouth is open; you people listen to my words. If one of you can say that for the fifteen years I have lived among you, I have given you bad advice, let him rise and speak . . ."

No one budged. It was a dangerous, electric situation. Lacombe kept on:

"Well, my friends, I have some advice to give you today. Let the white people pass through your lands and let them build their roads. They are not here to rob you of your lands. These white men obey their chiefs, and it is with the chiefs that the matter must be settled. I have already told these chiefs that you were not pleased with the way in which the work is being pushed through your lands. The Governor himself will come to meet you. He will listen to your griefs; he will propose a remedy. And if the compromise does not suit you, that will be the time to order the builders out of your reserve."

Lacombe sat down and Crowfoot stood up. "The advice of the Chief of Prayer is good. We shall do what he asks." He had already consulted with Lieut.-Colonel A. G. Irvine, the Commissioner of the North West Mounted Police, and asked him if he thought he, Crowfoot, could stop the railway. Irvine replied by asking Crowfoot if all the men in the world could stop the Bow River running. The perceptive chief resigned himself to the inevitable. He did not believe in fool-hardy gestures. Not long afterwards, Dewdney arrived and agreed to give the Indians extra land in return for the railway's right of way.

2

In a curiously roundabout way, the presence of the Indians in the North West had aided the railway in its swift progress across the plains. Without them it is doubtful whether prohibition would have existed; without prohibition it would have been impossible to drive steel so efficiently. The entire North West Territories were dry by law. Long before the railway was commenced, the liquor traffic west of Manitoba had been driven underground.

A. C. Forster Boulton, a CPR land examiner, gave in his memoirs a remarkable picture of a bone-dry Medicine Hat, as he first came upon it in 1883.

"It was a rough place then. . . . Miners, cowboys, trappers, prospectors gathered in the saloons to drink soft drinks and play cards. I remember I thought at the time what a fine thing it was that no spirits could be bought for love or money. If whiskey had been allowed, then life, with the men gathered in these saloons, would have been cheap." It makes an incongruous and somehow typically Canadian spectacle – the rough frontier town full of men in outlandish dress crowding into the saloons to purchase mugs of sarsaparilla.

Lively they certainly were, and never entirely dry, but the prairie railway camps, in contrast to those south of the border, were relatively tame. "When a man breaks the law here," one American boss told George Grant, "justice is dealt to him a heap quicker and in larger chunks than he has been accustomed to in the States." What he was praising was the Canadian passion for order imposed from above – a British colonial heritage – as against the American concept of localized grass-roots democracy. The symbol of the American West was the gun-toting town marshal, elected by the community; the symbol of the Canadian West was the red-coated, federally appointed, quasi-military Mountie.

For all of the railway construction period, the Mounted Police were locked in a battle of wits with the whiskey peddlers. Every device that human guile could invent was used to smuggle liquor into the North West and to keep it hidden from official eyes. Egg-shells were blown of their contents and alcohol substituted. Imitation Bibles, made of tin, were filled with intoxicants and peddled aboard CPR passenger cars; metal kegs of alcohol were concealed in the centre of barrels of kerosene; mincemeat soaked in brandy and peaches marinated in Scotch were also common. At Silver City, not far from Calgary, the police seized nineteen tins of corn, peas, and tomatoes which, on inspection, were revealed to contain alcohol, not vegetables – all shipped by an Ontario distiller. Eleven barrels supposedly filled with pork, imported into Calgary, were found to contain 1,584 bottles of liquor, which, at five dollars a bottle – the regulation price in those days – would have realized almost eight thousand dollars, a tidy profit at a time when whiskey sold for something like fifty cents a gallon in eastern Canada.

On the treeless prairie where concealment was difficult, the ingenuity of the bootleggers met its greatest test. One favourite hiding place was the boiler of a disabled or wrecked locomotive laid up on a siding. Another was one of the many carcasses of pack horses that lay strewn along the route of the line. It was said that hundreds of these dead animals were used to conceal bottles of liquor. One good-looking man in a plug hat, white tie, and black coat shipped an organ to End of Track, ostensibly for the use of the navvies during divine service. It was actually a hollow shell lined with tin, loaded with spirits. Another walked the line carrying the familiar knapsack which apparently contained nitro-glycerine canisters; he bore a red flag in his hand, which kept the Mounties away – as well as everybody else. Known variously as Chain Lightning, Tangle Foot, Death on Wires, and Injin Killer, prairie booze was generally a fearsome concoction made by mixing a gallon of good liquor and nine gallons of water into which was sunk a quantity of blue-stone and oil of smoke and later, for colouring, a little black tea. The price, in the bootleggers' dives, was twenty-five cents a glass.

Perhaps the most ingenious of the whiskey peddlers on the prairies was a Mrs. Hobourg of Regina, who used to arrive back in town from a trip to the wet cities of Winnipeg and Brandon looking more than pregnant from a circular rubber bag she wore around her waist. Another of her devices was to dress up a keg of liquor to resemble one of her offspring asleep on the seat beside her or to disguise it as a pillow on which she might rest her head while the police rummaged vainly through her old-fashioned bag.

One customer's gloomy description of Regina's sporting life explains the fervour with which the occasional furtive bottle, no matter how villainous, was welcomed:

"The solemnity which perennially reigns in a North-West hotel is beyond words. Long-faced men sit silent around the stove, only varying the grim monotony by an occasional expectoration of tobacco juice. Sometimes they may break out, and engage in the congenial pastime of 'swapping lies.' The bar dedicated to teetotalism (cider is sold and hop beer) makes a ghastly attempt at conviviality and jocoseness, by having an array of bottles of colored water and cold tea marshalled upon a series of shelves and labelled 'Old Tom,' 'Fine Old Rye,' Hennessy's 'Silver Star,' or 'Best Jamaica.' With what hideous humour do these tantalizing legends taunt the thirsty tenderfoot from 'down East.'"

Brandon, on the edge of Manitoba, was the farthest western point at which liquor could be sold. That, no doubt, explained why a visitor from Fort Macleod remarked on the number of men "staggering about the streets considerably under the influence of the juice of Bacchus." The first station west of Brandon was Moosomin, and here the train was supposed to be searched for whiskey but, according to John Donkin, "a constable or corporal merely promenades with clanking spurs down the aisles of the cars."

Prohibition or no, a good deal of liquor was consumed along the CPR right of way during the construction period. Sam Steele, who resented the strict laws and the nuisance of enforcing them, went so far as to claim that "the prohibitory law made more drunkards than if there had been an open bar and free drinks at every street corner." That is scarcely credible. When Edwin Brooks, migrating from Quebec, reached Regina in August, 1883, he was able to write to his wife Nellie: "I can tell you they (the police) look after these whiskey dealers awfully sharp. One never sees a drunken man in this N.W.T. or if ever very seldom. . . ." The truth was that because of prohibition the CPR was able to keep its men on the job and, in spite of occasional sprees, stabilize a work force whose training and precision made it possible to drive almost nine hundred miles of steel in fifteen months. When it was all over and the trains were running from Winnipeg to the base of the Rockies, the Moose Jaw *News* summed it up:

"The order and quiet which have prevailed during the construction of the Canadian Pacific, where thousands of men, proverbially not of the tractable kind, have been employed far in advance of civilization and settlement, have been unexampled in the history of any similar enterprise."

3

Langdon and Shepard completed their contract in mid-August, 1883, when the rails reached Calgary. Until that moment, the old Hudson's Bay fort and its cluster of adjacent log buildings had been more closely linked with the United States than with Canada. To a newcomer from the East, such as William Murdoch, the harnessmaker, who put up the first commercial sign on the site in May, the embryo town seemed like a distant planet. "I was dreaming about home almost all last night," Murdoch wrote in his diary on a bitter, windy June day. "How I long to see my wife, mother and little ones. My heart craves for them all today more than usual." Murdoch, who would become Calgary's first mayor, could not get so much as a sliver of dressed lumber, for there were no sawmills in the foothills. All that was available were rough planks, whip-sawed vertically by hand. Fresh fruit was so rare that when half a box of apples arrived they were sold at fifty cents each (the equivalent of more than two dollars in modern terms); they were the first that had been seen in that part of the North West.

The railway was to change all that. It was even to change the location of the town, as it had in the cases of Brandon and Regina.

Until the railway arrived, Fort Calgary was situated on the east bank of the Elbow River near its confluence with the Bow. As usual, there were squatters living in rough shanties, hired by Winnipeg land speculators to occupy the most likely ground until the townsite was subdivided.

Calgary watched the railroad approach with a mixture of apprehension and anticipation. Where would the station be located? Under the terms of its contract, the CPR had title to the odd-numbered sections along the right of way. The fort and surrounding structures, together with all the squatters' shacks, were situated on an even-numbered section – Number Fourteen. But the adjacent section, Fifteen, on the opposite bank of the Elbow, had been reserved by Order in Council as pasturage for the police horses. Surely then, everyone reasoned, the town would have to be put on the east bank, where the fort was located.

The tension began to mount. The bridge across the Bow was completed on August 10. Two days later a construction train puffed in. On August 15, a train carrying a temporary station arrived, and the community held its breath. Where would it stop? To everyone's dismay it shunted directly through the settlement, across the new bridge and was established on Section Fifteen on the far side of the Elbow.

Nobody quite knew what to do. The ownership of Section Fifteen was in dispute. The town was growing rapidly on the east bank, but because everyone wanted to wait for the decision about the townsite, no one wanted to go to the expense of erecting anything permanent; and so for all of 1883 Calgary was a tent city.

On August 27, the leading directors of the CPR arrived aboard Van Horne's private car and invited Father Lacombe to be their guest at luncheon. On a motion by Angus, Lacombe was made president of the CPR for one hour. Taking the chair, the priest immediately voted himself two passes on the railroad for life and, in addition, free transportation of all freight and baggage necessary to the Oblate missions together with free use for himself for life of the CPR's telegraph system.

All the promises made that day were honoured by the railway. Moreover, Lacombe's rather cavalier use of the passes, which he lent out indiscriminately (as he did most of his belongings), was regularly tolerated. On one occasion the two passes, which became familiar along the line, were presented by two nuns, newly arrived in the West. "May I ask," the conductor politely inquired, "which one of you is Father Lacombe?" He let the blushing sisters go on their way.

After honouring the priest, the distinguished visitors departed Calgary without leaving the settlers any wiser about a future over which they themselves had no control. The state of indecision continued all that fall, with half the community swearing that it would not budge an inch to accommodate the railway. "There are some people here who have a mind of their own and do not propose to follow the meanderings of the CPR," the Fort Macleod *Gazette* declared. Calgary's new paper, the *Herald,* reported in December that "we have much pleasure in announcing that our friends east of the Elbow have definitely decided upon the permanent location of the city in that quarter. Already the surveyors are hard at work upon the sub-division of the Denny Estate, and our next issue will contain the date of the sale of this beautiful spot so well adapted for the future capital of Alberta."

But the CPR itself and nobody else – editor, banker, merchant, or real estate man – would make the decision as to where Calgary was to be; and in January, when the Order in Council regarding the NWMP pasturage was finally rescinded, the CPR spoke. The city would be on the west side of the Elbow River and not on its original location on the east side. To underline that point, the government, which stood to profit equally with the railway, moved the post office across the river to the west.

In vain the Denny subdivision on the east side advertised that it was "the centre of Calgary City." As soon as the post office crossed the river, James Bannerman followed with his flour and feed store. All the solemn pledges about staying put and refusing to follow the meanderings of the railway were forgotten and a kind of wild scramble ensued as butcher shop, jeweller, churches, billiard parlour, and hotels packed up like gypsies and located on the favoured site. The *Herald* reported that buildings were suddenly springing up "as though some magical influence were being exerted" and that what had been barren prairie just three weeks before "is now rapidly growing into the shape of a respectable town."

Once again the railway, in truth a "magical influence," had dictated the lineaments of the new North West.

4

When George Stephen returned from the North West on October 1, 1883, the company's financial situation was even darker than before. Van Horne had spent the thirty million dollars raised the previous year. Hill had left the company and was selling out most of his stock – the decision to build an all-Canadian line north of Lake Superior was too much for him. Both Donald A. Smith and George Stephen resigned simultaneously from the board of the St. Paul, Minneapolis and Manitoba Railway, though they retained their interests. Smith replaced Hill as a director of the CPR. J. S. Kennedy's subsequent resignation from the CPR board – it was inevitable that the New York banker would follow Hill – made a bad impression in financial circles, since Kennedy's firm had made its reputation in railroad securities. Moreover, the country was entering a depression. CPR stock began to drop. By October 31, it had dived to 49 3/8.

That same fall, the North West, still reeling from the collapse of the real estate bubble, was struck a second blow. An early frost wiped out the wheat crop. In the United States, the Northern Pacific was teetering on the edge of insolvency. By December, its president, Henry Villard, would be deposed – his health wrecked, his worldly goods abandoned to his creditors. On October 26, the *Globe* used the word "depression" to describe the economic crisis. A "demoralization in railway stocks occurred" (to quote Charles Tupper); if the CPR were to throw any more of its outstanding common stock on the market it would be sacrificed.

Stephen decided upon a bold gamble. The CPR had forty-five million dollars' worth of authorized stock as yet unissued. No one would buy it, except at a fire-sale price. Stephen wanted to force the price up and make a market for the stock. To do that, he was prepared, with the government's help, to guarantee a five-per-cent dividend for the next ten years on *all* stock.

Stephen wanted the government to guarantee three per cent; the remainder, he felt, could be paid out of the company's resources. He was ready to pay in advance for the privilege; in effect, he was buying a government annuity. The price tag came to twenty-five millions. He was prepared to pay fifteen million dollars down, an additional five millions the following February, and the rest in securities and assets, including postal subsidies. All this would be deposited with the government, which would be acting merely as trustee for the fund.

This was exactly the kind of daring gambit that had won for Stephen a reputation for financial wizardry. He would, he hoped, make CPR stock gilt edged. If it succeeded, Stephen could sell the rest of the company's stock at something close to par and get enought money – he needed about thirty millions – to finish the railway. But if he lost, he would be tying up a huge block of cash at a time when the railway was desperately short of money. The situation was already serious. At Brandon, for instance, the staff of the freight office had not been paid for three months. The town's storekeepers had no other choice but to carry them. As one put it: "We've got to carry them. If the CPR goes bust, we will all have to pack up and go back to Bruce County, Ontario."

Macdonald liked the idea and the Cabinet passed it. The Prime Minister felt that the guarantee would boom the CPR's stock to seventy or more, but that rosy prediction did not come true. The stock shot up briefly to a little over sixty-three dollars, hovered there for a few days, and then began to drop back again. By the end of 1883 it was down to fifty-two.

Long before that point was reached, Stephen was forced to revise his plan. He would guarantee a dividend on only sixty-five millions. Fifty-five millions were already issued. That meant he had only ten million dollars in stock available. He dared not put that up for sale at the reduced price but was able to use it as security to get a loan of five million dollars in New York.

The gamble had been disastrous. To raise five million dollars, Stephen had put up nine millions in cash and pledged another seven millions in securities. The railway was worse off than it had been before he took the plunge. And in December it was hit by another crisis: the Canada North-West Land Company was in difficulties. The CPR was obliged to take back about half of the land grant bonds that it had sold to the company on time and an equivalent amount of land, to bail it out. The railway had scarcely a friend left in the international financial capitals. Stephen was close to despondency, for his reputation had suffered a bad blow.

With great reluctance, Macdonald decided that the Government would have to find some way of forcing a new CPR loan down the throat of Parliament. It had taken considerable persuasion to budge the Prime Minister. One evening late in November a powerful CPR delegation visited Macdonald at his private residence, Earnscliffe. Stephen, Angus, McIntyre, Van Horne, and Abbott, the lawyer, were all present to make the case, but Macdonald could not be moved. "You might as well ask for the planet Jupiter," he told them.

The five men went dolefully back to the old Bank of Montreal cottage to wait for the four o'clock morning train to Montreal. There they encountered John Henry Pope, the acting Minister of Railways, to whom Stephen told the bad news.

Pope rose slowly and called for a carriage.

"Wait till I get back," was all that he would say. It was already past one o'clock, but Pope was prepared to get the Prime Minister out of bed. He used the one argument that could convince his chieftain that the CPR must get its loan. "The day the Canadian Pacific busts the Conservative party busts the day after," he told him.

The following day Stephen and his colleagues appeared before the Council to find the Prime Minister out of sorts, Alexander Campbell totally opposed to further help, and Leonard Tilley, the finance minister, openly advocating that the government take over the railway. Macdonald desperately needed Tupper at his side. Sir Charles, though still a Member of Parliament, had been dispatched to London to replace

Alexander Galt as High Commissioner. On December 1 Macdonald sent him a curt cable: "Pacific in trouble. You should be here." Tupper arrived post-haste and "found everybody in despair."

Stephen was frantic. "Something must be done at *once*," he told the Prime Minister, otherwise he must give up and let the government take over the railway. He needed $3,850,000 cash by January 1, 1884, to pay immediate debts. By January 8, he needed an additional $3,812,240 to pay off a short-term loan in New York. Another payment of $2,853,750 was due the government by February 1. The company's total debt was fifteen millions.

A bank crisis was not inconceivable. Stephen himself feared that if the heavy advances to the railroad, made without adequate security, became known to the public, there would be a run on the Bank of Montreal. The bank's chief executive officers were in a state of terror. Tupper privately told them that they must advance the railway the money it needed; the government would guarantee payment. In a close vote they agreed to extend the loan.

This short-term aid did not solve the railway's long-term problems. There could, in fact, be only one solution – a government loan. Stephen needed thirty million dollars to pay the CPR debts and complete the main line. In mid-January, he asked formally for a loan of $22,500,000, repayable in 1891, and a five-year postponement on the second instalment of more than seven millions that he had so recklessly promised in order to guarantee the dividend. This was an enormous sum; it represented almost a whole year's revenue of the federal government. To get it Stephen was forced to mortgage all the CPR's assets and promise to finish the line in five years instead of ten.

That was the medicine that Macdonald and Tupper must force their reluctant followers to swallow. It would not be easy. A platoon of powerful forces was arrayed against the railway: the Opposition under Edward Blake, the most eloquent man in the House; half the newspapers in the country; the great international press associations – Reuters and AP – which seemed to be spokesmen for the Grand Trunk; the large financial houses; and a good many of Macdonald's own followers, including several Maritimers (who had no interest in a western railroad), most of the Quebec *bleus* (who wanted an equal share in any largesse the government intended to dispense), and the Manitobans, who represented a growing popular antagonism to the CPR.

The building of the railway had laid a bundle of annoying problems at the Prime Minister's door that Christmas season of 1883-84. Disgruntled Manitoba farmers had organized themselves into a pressure group, the Manitoba and North-West Farmers' Union. Its formation marked the beginning of a perennial Canadian problem: the estrangement of the agrarian West from the industrial East. The symbol of that disaffection was the CPR.

The railway was seen mainly as an arm of the eastern industrialists – a tool to crush the farmer. The CPR would haul away the prairie grain to eastern Canada and, in turn, deliver the protected manufactured goods of Ontario and Quebec to the western consumers. As the farmers saw it, they were paying through the nose in two ways: first, by artificially high prices on manufactured goods and, second, through exorbitant freight rates. After all, the CPR Syndicate was the lineal descendant of the hated and monopolistic Kittson Line, whose successor was the Pembina Branch of the CPR and its corporate cousin, Hill's "Manitoba Line," which also enjoyed a monopoly. In 1883, Macdonald, at Stephen's prompting, had disallowed the provincial charters of three Manitoba railways because they came too close to the international border. That did not sit well with the farmers, to whom the building of a railway – *any* railway – meant prosperity.

Stephen, meanwhile, was struggling to keep the company afloat. On January 22, 1884, he scrawled a note to Macdonald that he was going back to Montreal to try to "keep things moving . . . until relief arrives." There was a note of despair and resignation in this letter: ". . . you must not blame me if I fail. I do not, at the moment, see how we are going to get the money to keep the work going. . . . If I find we cannot go on I suppose the only thing to do will be to put in a Receiver. If that *has* to be done the quicker it is done the better."

It was the first time that the possibility of bankruptcy had been mentioned, and Stephen sounded almost comforted at the prospect: "I am getting so wearied and worn out with this business that almost any change will be a relief to me."

When the CPR president reached Montreal, he picked up a copy of the *Star* in which, to his fury, he read an editorial which insinuated that he, Smith, McIntyre, Angus, and the others had been robbing the company for their own personal benefit. Since all of them had pledged their own stock in the St. Paul railway against the CPR's bank loan, the words cut deep. But he had to put up with the "scribblers," as he called them, as he had to put up with the politicians. Macdonald warned him in mid-January that it would take another six weeks to get the loan through Parliament. Stephen was aghast. Six weeks, when every day counted! "Had I supposed it would take to 1st March before help could reach us I would not have made the attempt to carry on."

In Montreal, he learned the magnitude of the railroad's financial dilemma. Every cent coming in from the government subsidy had to go directly to the Bank of Montreal to cover its loan. Nothing could be diverted to pay wages or meet the bills for supplies that were piling up in Thomas Shaughnessy's office. He must have an advance of at least three and a half millions by February 8 to pay off the bank. "If this cannot be obtained," he told Tupper, "it is not a bit of use of my trying to carry on any longer."

But he had to carry on as he had been carrying on all the last year, putting off creditors, trimming costs, postponing expenses. In spite of further threats to Ottawa, cries of despair, and attacks of fatigue and nerves, he would continue to carry on. It was not in his nature to give up.

5

There was trouble north of Lake Superior, where John Egan had been forced to cut off the cost-of-living bonuses. Some thirty-five hundred men struck and the work on the line was suspended. In the end, most were forced to give in because at that season jobs were so hard to get.

In his brusque interviews with the press, the general manager exuded confidence. In Chicago the previous August, he had announced that the CPR was employing twenty-five thousand men and spending one hundred thousand dollars a day.

"How much will it cost per mile through the Rockies?" a reporter asked him.

"We don't know," Van Horne replied.

"Have you not estimated the amount beforehand?"

"The Canadian Pacific Railway," declared Van Horne, "has never estimated the cost of any work; it hasn't time for that; it's got a big job on hand, and it's going to put it through."

"Well, but if you haven't estimated the cost of the construction through the mountains how do you know that you have sufficient funds to push the road as you are currently reported to have?"

"Well," replied Van Horne, airily, "if we haven't got enough we will get more, that's all about it."

The reporter retired, "forcibly impressed with the resolute frankness of character displayed by the man who is the administrative head of this great Canadian enterprise."

But Van Horne, too, was pinching every possible penny. There scarcely seemed to be an expenditure in 1883 that did not come under his personal scrutiny, from the cost of the paymaster's revolvers to the hiring of a cab at Portage la Prairie. He could berate a man for sending a telegram "containing 35 words and costing this Coy about

$2.00 and which could have just as well have been sent by mail," and he could also give orders for mammoth savings north of Superior, where construction had just got underway. When John Ross, his general superintendent there (no relation to the James Ross in charge of mountain work), asked for sixteen steamshovels, Van Horne turned him down. The company could not afford them.

Van Horne's idea was to get a workable line through – one that would stand up for at least six years – make it pay, and then begin improving it. Masonry could wait; all rock quarrying would have to cease. Wooden trestles could replace earthworks; the cuts could always be filled in later.

The general manager was in the House of Commons on February 1 with Stephen and Donald A. Smith when Tupper rose to propose the new Canadian Pacific Railway resolutions. The *Globe* was quick to note sardonically that Smith could lean down "and hear the man who in 1878 denounced him in the most infamous manner in the same chamber labouring hard to show the company of which Mr. Smith is a leading member is composed of men of great wealth, enterprise, unblemished honour and undoubted integrity. Time certainly brings its revenge."

It was time, Stephen realized, for a reconciliation. Stephen felt he owed it to his cousin. When extra money was needed, Smith raised it. When he was asked to put up his personal fortune to back a loan, he signed it away without so much as raising one of his tangled eyebrows. And yet, beneath that hard shell there was a childlike sensitivity. The disaffection of the Prime Minister clearly irked him; he wanted to make up. Now his grateful cousin handed him that prize. Macdonald's reception was kind and cordial and Stephen thanked him for it; the two, it was said, settled their differences over a bottle of good Scotch whiskey. Smith did not mention the particulars to Stephen; that was not his way, but "I know he *felt* a good deal and I know – without his saying it – that he is today a much happier man."

That was the only gleam of light in an otherwise gloomy month. The debate on the railway resolutions turned into a bitter and lengthy parliamentary wrangle, sparked by a daily diet of rumour, speculation, and minor sensation fed to the country through the Opposition press.

One thing was clear to the public: the CPR was in deep trouble. On February 17, a mass meeting was held in Quebec City to protest the Government's railway policy. On February 20, there were rumours of Cabinet resignations; the Quebeckers were locked in a heated caucus. Forty-two of them, it was whispered, had bolted the party. To keep them in line Macdonald was forced to promise a retroactive subsidy to Quebec on the somewhat dubious premise that the line between Montreal and Ottawa, now owned by the CPR, was a work of national importance. To a casual newspaper reader, it must have seemed that the debate was tearing the country apart.

The following week the *Globe,* which never let up, summed up the state of the nation in an editorial that was only too accurate:

"To what a sad condition Sir John Macdonald and his colleagues have reduced the country! Quebec, separating herself from the other Provinces, compels the Government to yield to her demands. Manitoba talks secession, and is certainly discontented. The other Provinces, including Ontario, are dissatisfied, and the Indians – ill-treated, cheated and half-starved by the partisans whom Sir John tries to satisfy at their expense – threaten hostilities. Perhaps it is sufficient offset to all this that the Grand Old Schemer maintains his serenity, that Lieut. Governor Dewdney has received an increase of salary, that Sir C. Tupper is content, and that the CPR Syndicate are satisfied." Only British Columbia, once "the spoilt child of Confederation," appeared to be at peace.

It was the first time, really, that Canadians had become aware of the new kind of nation they were tying together through the construction of the railway – an unwieldy pastiche of disparate communities, authored under varying circumstances, tugged this way and that by a variety of conflicting environmental and historical strains, and all now stirred into a ferment by the changes wrought through the coming of steel. Macdonald had been used to governing a tight, familiar community from the federal capital. Until the coming of the railway he had known most of it intimately – the people, the places, the problems. Suddenly he was faced with an entirely different political situation. Far out along the half-completed line of track, new political leaders whom he had never heard of in communities he had never visited were demanding a say in matters which he only partially understood. It is significant – and tragic – that, though the Prime Minister was also Superintendent General of Indian Affairs, he himself had never been to the North West or entered a Cree or Blackfoot tepee.

Macdonald was forced to offer a familiar threat to keep his irresolute followers tractable: if they did not support him, Parliament would be dissolved and they would face the prospect of going to the country on the heels of a Government defeat in the House. Meanwhile, he told Stephen, "the CPR *must* become political and secure as much Parliamentary support as possible." All railway appointments in Ontario and Quebec henceforth must be made on a political basis: "There are plenty of good men to be found in the ranks."

This was something that both Stephen and Van Horne had fought against; now they had to bow to the inevitable. Before the debate was over Macdonald was able to write to a political friend that Stephen had informed him that Van Horne "is fully aware now of the necessity of not appointing anybody along the line who has not been 'fully circumcized' – to use his own phrase." In future elections the CPR not only persuaded its men to vote for Conservative candidates (and made sure that the Liberal-minded employees did not get to the polls) but it also pumped large sums of money into Conservative election funds. By 1890, Stephen had spent over one million dollars aiding the Tories.

The political arguments in the House were wearing Stephen down. He wanted another extension on his Bank of Montreal loan but, in spite of Tupper's intercession, the bank refused. On February 27, 1884, the CPR president wrote another desperate note to the Prime Minister:

"McIntyre goes down to N.Y. tonight to raise by way of a loan for a few days $300,000 which we think will keep us out of the sheriff's hands till Tuesday or Wednesday. I hope he will manage this, though he may not be able. In that case I do not know what we shall do. . . ."

The following day, the CPR relief bill passed the House. How soon could Macdonald get it through the Senate? Again Stephen implored the Prime Minister to move swiftly. It would have to be made law by Wednesday, when McIntyre's short-term loan (negotiated successfully in New York) fell due; on Wednesday, dramatically, it was done. At the very last moment the company had been saved from ruin. That final denouement was reminiscent of one of the cheap yellow-backed thrillers that Macdonald liked to read to clear his mind from the cares of the day.

Those cares were very real ones. The Prime Minister was in his seventieth year and was complaining more and more of being tired every night. When he had driven the original CPR contract through Parliament in 1881 he had believed his main worries to be at an end, at least as far as the railroad was concerned. Stephen, he thought, would take the responsibility off his back. But the railroad, which was wearing Stephen down too, was pressing upon Macdonald's stooped shoulders like a great weight, as it had a dozen years before in the days of Sir Hugh Allan. Once again the papers were hinting that he would retire – he was suffering once again from an old nervous disease, inflammation of the stomach; but he could not retire while the railway remained unfinished. "It is only because I want to be *in* at the completion of the CPR that I remain where I am," he had told Stephen the previous November. "I may say I groan for rest."

By the summer of 1884, Macdonald was worried that Stephen himself might give in. "I would leave the Govt. tomorrow," he admitted to Tupper in July, "if it were not that I really think George Stephen would throw up the sponge if I did. He was so worried & sleepless that his wife became alarmed.'' The Prime Minister insisted that Stephen go off to the seaside for a vacation. A few days later, he himself came down to visit him, and for three days the two men on whom so much depended basked in the sun and talked about the railroad and the future of the country. Macdonald thought Stephen had "chirped up a good deal" as a result of his rest. He would need to, to survive the trials that lay ahead.

Chapter Seven

NOT A DOLLAR TO SPARE

1

The price of building the line north of Lake Superior was appalling. By the summer of 1884, John Ross had close to fifteen thousand men working between Lake Nipissing and Thunder Bay, which meant that every month the company had to send a pay car out along the line with $1,100,000 in wages. One single, memorable mile of track was laid through solid rock at a cost of seven hundred thousand dollars. To save money and time, Van Horne had three dynamite factories built in the Caldwell-Jackfish area, each capable of turning out a ton a day. The bill for explosives came to seven and a half million dollars. The awesome quantities of food consumed by the workmen flabbergasted old-time traders. In winter it required three hundred dog teams, working incessantly, to keep the railroad supplied.

The line hugged the armoured shores of Lake Superior, where construction was heavy but supply relatively easy. Van Horne had imported two big lake boats built in Scotland to do duty between Algoma Mills and Thunder Bay. In this way freight could be shipped by water from Montreal to Port Arthur and by rail from Port Arthur to Winnipeg – a distance of 1,320 miles – in sixty-six hours. This was the start of the Canadian Pacific Steamship service under Henry Beatty, whose son was to become president of the CPR at a time when it was able to advertise itself as "The World's Greatest Travel System."

To Stephen, watching every penny in Montreal, the whole operation must have been disturbing. This was the section that almost everybody, Stephen included, had once said should not be built. This was the section that had caused Hill's defection – and Kennedy's. Now it was devouring the millions that the company had managed to pry loose from Ottawa.

There was no thought of stopping for winter. Track must be laid in all seasons, in snow five feet deep and in temperatures that dropped to fifty degrees below zero. Sometimes the drifts were so high that in the absence of an embankment it was impossible to locate the centre line of the roadbed, and the rails had to be laid directly on the snow. In some places, when spring came it was found they were not on the grade at all.

All sorts of short cuts were attempted. There was one rock cutting east of White River on which the contractors were well behind. A delay of a month seemed inevitable until it was decided to lay the track directly on top of the escarpment, to one side of the half-finished cut. The first locomotive that attempted to reach the top slipped back. The rails were sanded and the track smoothed out until finally a single car was pulled over safely. When the engine crews grew used to the hazard they were able to cross it easily with two cars. By the time the cut was finished, track had moved on thirty miles.

In the interests of greater speed, Van Horne imported a track-laying machine. This was really a train loaded with rails, ties, and track fastenings. Shallow, open-top chutes, with rollers spaced along the bottom, were hung on either side, and the ties and rails were rolled along by manpower to the front of the device, where they were man-handled onto the grade.

The usual method of cut and fill was abandoned. Van Horne had decided at the outset to carry the line high, building timber trestles over the intervening gullies and filling them in later with materials brought in by rail. The cost of these trestles was about one-tenth the cost of the filling operation.

To Alan Brown, a pioneer in Ontario railway development, "the rock cuttings were wonderful." Brown, who travelled the line shortly after it was completed, said he felt weak in his powers of description: "It is impossible to imagine any grander construction. . . . Everything is synonymous with strength. . . . The bridges, the tunnels, the rock cuttings almost make you aghast. . . ."

The blasting of the Shield was done, as always, at a considerable cost in men's lives. Dynamite had largely replaced the more dangerous nitro-glycerine, but even dynamite, carelessly handled, can bring tragedy. One man tried to pack a dynamite cartridge tighter by tamping it down with an iron crowbar; he was blown to pieces. A hotel proprietor from Port Arthur on a fishing expedition reached into the water and encountered a live discarded dynamite cap among the rocks; it blew his hand off. In another instance a man asleep in a cabin near McKay's Harbour was killed when a rock from a blast tore through the roof and crushed him.

John Macoun, who visited the line in 1884, wrote that it was "indescribable, as we were tormented by flies, and our path was not strewn with roses." Yet there was a kind of perverse grandeur about the country through which the steel was being driven. Superintendent John Egan found himself waxing poetical about it to the press: "The scenery is sublime in its very wildness; it is magnificently grand; God's own handiwork stands out boldly every furlong you proceed. The ravines and streams are numerous and all is picturesqueness itself.

As to the character of the work, it will remain an everlasting monument to the builders."

To the men on the job – throats choked with the dust of shattered rocks, ears ringing with dynamite blasts, arms aching from swinging sledges or toting rails, skin smarting and itching from a hundred insect bites, nostrils assailed by a dozen stenches from horse manure to human sweat – the scenery was only a nuisance to be moved when it got in the way. The summers were bad enough but the winters were especially hard; in the flat light of December, the whole world took on a dun colour and the chill wind blowing off the great frozen inland sea sliced through the thickest garments.

Because of the isolation, conditions in the camps north of Lake Superior were undoubtedly the worst of any along the line of the railway. The navvies lived like men on another planet in gloomy and airless bunkhouses, which were little better than log dungeons. Into these hastily constructed, temporary structures, often badly situated and inadequately drained, between sixty and eighty men were crammed. They slept in verminous blankets on beds of hay in double-decker bunks that extended around three sides of the building. The atmosphere was oppressive and the ventilation meagre. The faint light that entered from two small windows at either gable was rarely sufficient for reading or writing. The nights were fetid with steam from the wet clothes that habitually hung over the central stove. In the summer, the air was rancid with smoke from burning straw and rags set afire to drive off the maddening hordes of mosquitoes and blackflies. The board floor was generally filthy and the roof often leaked. Baths and plumbing were unknown, men washed and laundered or not as they wished; medical attention was minimal.

The conditions north of Superior, especially in the winter, made for a monotonous and unhealthy menu. The only real delicacy was freshly baked bread; otherwise the staples were salt park, corned beef, molasses, beans, potatoes, oatmeal, and tea, varied by the occasional carcass of frozen beef. There was little if any fresh or green food to lighten this excessively coarse and heavy diet which, when it did not lead to actual scurvy, produced in most men a feeling of sluggishness and lassitude.

In spite of these circumstances it was usually not difficult to get cheap labour. Economic conditions were such that, in the summer of 1883, ordinary shovel men were being paid $1.50 for a ten-hour day along Lake Superior and in some instances as little as $1.00 a day, which was the going rate in the eastern cities. In the rare instances when strikes did occur, they were quickly broken.

As the winter of 1883-84 approached, wages rose to $1.75 a day for shovel men, but the board was increased to four dollars a week.

That was only one of several factors that made the pay seem better than it was. If the weather, sickness, or construction delays kept the men in the bunkhouses, they received no wages. Eight wet days a month could reduce a navvy's net pay to four dollars a week. In addition he had the cost of his clothing and gear, much of it purchased at company stores at inflated prices, and sometimes his meals and transporation en route to the site.

The company held him in thrall. If he complained, he could be fired. If he wanted to quit, he had to continue to pay board until the company was ready to give him transport; then he had to pay his fare out as well. Under such a system it was difficult for a man to accumulate much money.

Yet the conditions of the wage earners were far superior to those of the men who worked for themselves on small subcontracts, grading short strips of right of way with shovel and wheelbarrow, or clearing the line of brush and stumps for fixed prices, arrived at by hard bargaining. These subcontracts had one apparent advantage: the men were their own bosses. The advantage, however, was generally illusory; most of the self-employed men worked much longer hours under worse conditions than the wage earners, yet made no more money.

Living arrangements for those employed on small subcontracts were especially squalid. Harry Armstrong came upon one such camp of French Canadians that he thought the worst he had ever seen. It was a windowless cabin with nothing in the way of a floor except black mud, kept thawed by the heat of the stove. To bridge the mud there were several scattered poles across which the men were supposed to pick their way. Armstrong recalled that "all the refuse from table had been scraped off after each meal, which didn't improve the mud."

The camps of the Italian immigrants were even worse. One group, which took a contract clearing the line, lived during the winter in a kind of root cellar, dome-shaped and without windows. To enter, they crawled through an opening in the bottom, and there they lay most of the time, playing cards, but going out into the snow when the sun shone to do a little work. Once a week they bought a sack of flour and a little tea on credit. By spring they had managed to clear half an acre.

Under such conditions the navvies turned inevitably to alcohol. By special act, the government had banned the sale of liquor along the line of the railway as far as the Manitoba border. Here as everywhere else in Canada, government agents fought a running battle with whiskey peddlers. In May, 1881, the Thunder Bay *Sentinel* estimated that no fewer than eight hundred gallons of spirits were sold every month to the twenty-five hundred people living between Whitemouth River and Lake Wabigoon. The price was fifteen dollars a gallon.

A regular count made by the CPR revealed that there were five thousand revolvers and three hundred shotguns and rifles, together with the same number of dirks and bowie knives, in the possession of railroad workers on the Lake Superior line. The North West Mounted Police did not patrol the Ontario section of the road; that job was left to the local constabulary, some of whom were plainly corrupt.

Both Peninsula Harbour and Michipicoten were for several months under the control of gangs of desperadoes euphemistically called "vigilantes," who terrorized the citizens and held a tight rein on the whiskey trade, keeping out all competition and running the community for their own personal profit.

In Michipicoten, the gang that ran the town was actually headed by the former police chief, Charles E. Wallace. In October, 1884, the gang attempted to shoot the local magistrate, whose life had been frequently threatened. A force of Toronto police was called to the scene to restore order and by nightfall had seven prisoners in custody. As a result, their boarding house headquarters became the target of hidden riflemen who pumped a fusillade of bullets into it, grazing the arm of the cook and narrowly missing one of the boarders. The police maintained an all-night vigil to stave off attack.

The force destroyed one hundred and twenty gallons of rye whiskey and laid plans to capture the four ringleaders of the terrorist gang, including Wallace, the ex-police chief. After some careful undercover work they descended upon a nearby Indian village where the culprits were supposed to be hiding. The police flushed out the wanted men, but Wallace and his friends were too fast for them; in the ensuing chase the hoodlums, apparently aided by both the Indians and the townspeople, easily evaded their pursuers.

No sooner had the big city constabulary departed the following day with their prisoners than Wallace and his three henchmen emerged from the woods and instituted a new reign of terror. Wallace, "in true bandit style," was carrying four heavy revolvers and a bowie knife in his belt and a Winchester repeating rifle on his shoulder. The four finally boarded the steamer *Steinhoff* and proceeded to pump bullets into the crowd on the dock before departing for Sault Ste Marie. Their target was actually the CPR ticket office and, more specifically, the railway's agent, Alec Macdonald, who had taken refuge within it. Before the steamer departed, Wallace and his friends had managed to riddle the building with a hundred bullets without, fortunately, scratching their quarry. Wallace and his partners were

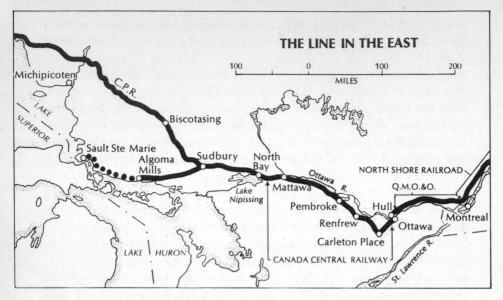

THE LINE IN THE EAST

MILES

Michipicoten

LAKE SUPERIOR

C.P.R.

Biscotasing

Sault Ste Marie
Algoma
Mills

Sudbury

North
Bay

Lake
Nipissing

Mattawa

Ottawa R.

NORTH SHORE RAILROAD

Q.M.O.&O.

Pembroke

Hull

Renfrew

Ottawa

Montreal

Carleton Place

LAKE HURON

CANADA CENTRAL RAILWAY

St. Lawrence R.

not captured until the following February, after a gunfight in the snow in which one of the arresting constables was severely wounded.

Communities like Michipicoten were isolated in winter because there was no continuous line of track between Thunder Bay and Lake Nipissing. The contractors, supplied by boat, were strung out in sections of varying length, depending on the terrain; indeed, some contracts covered country so difficult that only a mile was let at a time. For administrative purposes, the Lake Superior line had to be divided into two sections: the difficult section led east from Fort William to meet the easier section, which ran west from Lake Nipissing, the point at which the Canada Central, out of Ottawa, joined the CPR proper.

In the summer of 1882, a young Scot of eighteen named John McIntyre Ferguson arrived on Nipissing's shore. Ferguson was the nephew of Duncan McIntyre, an uncle who knew exactly where the future railway was going to be located. The prescient nephew purchased 288 acres of land at a dollar an acre and laid out a townsite in the unbroken forest. He also built the first house in the region and, in ordering nails, asked the supplier to ship them to "the north bay of Lake Nipissing." Thus did the settlement unwittingly acquire a name. By 1884, when the CPR established its "company row," North Bay had become a thriving community. Ferguson went on to become the wealthiest man in town and, after North Bay was incorporated, its mayor for four successive terms.

The land between North Bay and Lake Superior was generally considered to be worthless wilderness. The rails cut through a barren realm, denuded by forest fires and devoid of all colour save the occasional sombre russet and ochre, which stained the rocks and glinted up through the roots of the dried grasses on the hillsides. These were the oxides of nickel and copper and the sulfides of copper and iron, but it needed a trained eye to detect the signs of mineral treasure that lay concealed beneath the charred forest floor.

By the end of 1882 the Canada Central had reached Lake Nipissing. By the end of 1883 the first hundred miles of the connecting CPR were completed. Early that year the crudest of tote roads, all stumps and mud, had reached the spot where Sudbury stands today. Here, as much by accident as by design, a temporary construction camp was established. It was entirely a company town: every boarding house, home, and store was built, owned, and operated by the CPR in order to keep the whiskey peddlers at bay.

The first men to examine the yellow-bronze rocks in the hills around the community made little or nothing from their discoveries. The earliest was probably Tom Flanagan, a CPR blacksmith, who picked up a piece of ore along the right of way and thought that he had found gold. He did not realize that he was standing not only on a copper mine but also on the largest nickel deposit in the world. Flanagan did not pursue his interest, but John Loughrin, who had a contract for cutting railroad ties, was intrigued by the formations. In February, 1884, he and three friends staked the land on what became the future Murray Mine of the International Nickel Company. It subsequently produced ore worth millions, but not for the original discoverers.

Other company employees became millionaires. One was a gaunt Hertfordshire man named Charles Francis Crean, who arrived on the first work train into Sudbury in November, 1883. On entering the company store, Crean noticed a huge yellow nugget being used as a paperweight. The clerk said the ore was probably fool's gold, but he let Crean have a piece of it. Crean sent it to a chemist friend in Toronto who told him it was an excellent sample of copper. In May, 1884, Crean applied for a mining claim and staked what was to become famous as the Elsie Mine.

A month later, Crean spotted some copper ore in the ballast along the tracks of the Sault Ste Marie branch of the railroad. He checked back carefully to find where the material had come from and was able to stake the property on which another rich mine – the Worthington – was established. Later he discovered three other valuable properties. Another prospective millionaire that year was a railway construction timekeeper named Thomas Frood, who acted on a trapper's hunch and discovered the property that became the Frood Mine, perhaps the most famous of all.

But for every fortune made in Sudbury there were a dozen lost:

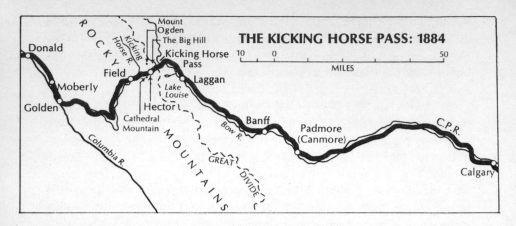

THE KICKING HORSE PASS: 1884

the story of northern Ontario mining is the story of happenstance, accident, and sheer blind luck. Sudbury itself was an accident, located by error on the wrong side of a lake and named by the contractor, James Worthington, after his wife's birthplace in England. Worthington had not intended to use such an unimportant spot on the map to honour his spouse, but the station up the line that was expected to be the real centre of the area had already been named, and he had to settle for the lesser community. He was not the only man to underestimate the resources of the Canadian Shield. Right up until the moment of Sudbury's founding, some members of Macdonald's cabinet, not to mention a couple of the CPR's own directors, were opposed to running a line of steel across those ebony scarps. It was only when the land began to yield up its treasure that the fuss about the all-Canadian line was stilled.

2

In the Rockies, that summer of 1884, the weather was miserable. The numbing rain turned the Kicking Horse into a torrent that spread itself across the Columbia flats, cutting the tote road so badly that it was almost impossible for the teams to struggle through. The speed of track-laying had slowed down once the pass was entered. The rails crept to within a few miles of the summit in the fall of 1883 and came to a halt for the winter. For all of the summer of 1884, the construction headquarters of the Mountain Division of the CPR remained near the summit at Holt City, later known as Laggan (the site of Lake Louise station today).

James Ross had announced that he would need twelve thousand men in the mountains that summer. By June they were pouring in. Every train brought several carloads of navvies who had come across the plains from Winnipeg. They tumbled off the cars and trudged up the right of way to the construction camps, in a land hitherto seen by only a handful of men, singing the song of the construction men in the mountains:

For some of us are bums, for whom work has no charms,
And some of us are farmers, a-working for our farms,
But all are jolly fellows, who come from near and far,
To work up in the Rockies on the C.P.R.

One of them, a young labourer named George Van Buskirk, had arrived in Calgary absolutely penniless, "in a foreign land, 4,000 miles away from home and no money and not a chance to get any." By pawning his baggage he finally managed to reach Holt City one morning with four dollars in his pocket. It was not hard to find work. He hiked ten miles and, about one o'clock that same afternoon, "pretty well fagged out," he found himself erecting tents and chopping down foot-thick trees for shanties. In spite of the scenery, young Van Buskirk was pretty discouraged by evening: "Taking it all and all the North West is not what it is cracked up to be," he informed his mother. "Some of these chaps who write in the papers ought to be shot, for the country although a fine one is terribly overrated & the reports one sees mislead entirely." A fortnight later he had cheered up considerably: "I am very well with the exception that my blood is very coarse from eating strong food. Too much beans."

The British novelist Morley Roberts, who arrived that summer, watched the tenderfeet from the cities heading off up the line to the various camps — a miscellaneous throng of about a hundred, loaded down with blankets and valises – and noted that many had never worked in the open air at all. Some indeed had not done a hard day's work in their lives:

"It was quite pitiful to see some little fellow, hardly more than a boy, who had hitherto had his lines cast in pleasant places, bearing the burden of two valises or portmanteaus, doubtless filled with good store of clothes made by his mother and sisters, while the sweat rolled off him as he tramped along bent nearly double. Perhaps next to him there would be some huge, raw-boned labourer whose belongings were tied up in a red handkerchief and suspended from a stick."

Behind the labourers came the first tourists, some of them travelling all the way from Winnipeg to gaze upon the wonders of the mountain scenery. Some of it was fast disappearing under the human onslaught. "Round me," wrote Morley Roberts, "I saw the primaeval forest torn down, cut and hewed and hacked, pine and cedar and hemlock. Here and there lay piles of ties, and near them, closely stacked, thousands of rails. The brute power of man's organized civilisation had fought with Nature and had for the time vanquished her. Here lay the trophies of the battle." The mountainsides that year were ablaze with forest fires started by the construction workers. At times the entire pass, from the summit to the Columbia, and westward seemed to be aflame.

Avalanches were also frequent in the Rockies that season, many of them set in motion by the continual blasting that went on along the line. Everyone who witnessed one was awestruck. "They resembled exactly a large mow taken down with a scythe in the fields," Alexander Mackenzie wrote to his daughter. (The former Liberal prime minister was on a tour of the North West as a guest of the railway and, as a result, was to change his mind about the barrenness of prairie land.) Sam Steele described glaciers that broke away and tore pathways half a mile wide through the forest. He saw one avalanche descend five thousand feet from a summit with such velocity that it tore directly across a valley and up the opposite side for another eight hundred feet.

Under such conditions, the work went on at a killing pace from dawn to dusk. On one contract the workmen averaged more than ten hours of labour a day every day for a month. Some of them had thirteen or fourteen hours a day to their credit. If rain made work impossible, they caught up in sunny weather. Some even worked by moonlight.

The railway workers lived in every kind of accommodation along the line – in tents of all shapes and sizes, in boxcars rolled onto sidings, in log huts and in mud huts, in shanties fashioned out of rough planks, and in vast marquees with hand-hewn log floors, log walls, and a box stove in the centre. Over the whole hung the familiar pungency of the bunkhouse, an incense almost indescribable but compounded of unwashed bodies, strong tobacco, steaming wood, cedar logs, and mattress straw.

The work was often as dangerous as it was back-breaking. Near one of several tunnels along the Kicking Horse the cut in the hill was so deep that the men worked in three tiers. At the very top, the route was being cut through gravel; in the centre the gravel gave way to blue clay; below the clay was hard rock. The men on the lowest tier, working just above the layer of rock (which would have to be dynamited), attacked the clay from beneath. Twenty to thirty feet above them a second gang worked, chopping out the gravel and wheeling it away in barrows. The high gang removed the top layer of sand and stumps. Those at the very top worked in comparative safety; the middle gang was in some peril because they had to watch out for rocks that might topple down on them; but the lowest gang was in constant danger – from both benches above them came a continual shower of rocks. Morley Roberts, who worked on the lowest tier, reported that he never felt safe for a single moment. Every sixty seconds or so, all day long, a warning cry would be heard and a heavy stone or boulder would come thundering down the slope, scattering the men on both sides. On his third day on the job the impact from an eighty-pound rock put him out of action for five days. The literate vagabond whiled away his convalescence with a copy of Thomas Carlyle's *Sartor Resartus*.

Since it was impossible to take heavy drills down the dizzy inclines of the Kicking Horse, all blasting holes had to be punched out by hand. The men hammered the broken rocks into smaller pieces and shovelled them into carts and barrows. In spite of such primitive techniques, James Ross's work force managed to move a million and a half cubic yards of earth and rock and, in addition, drill half a mile of tunnels during the 1884 season.

Van Horne had decreed that all bridges be made of timber in order to save money. Even without the cost factor, the necessity of pushing the line through on time would have dictated this swifter method of construction. There was no way in which iron girders or quarried stone could be transported down the gorge of the Kicking Horse until the rails were laid.

It was a considerable feat to cross an unfinished bridge, as hundreds of men were forced to do. Along the cross-pieces lay stringers, placed on edge and at varying distances, some close together and some so far apart that a man could scarcely leap from one to the next. These were lying loose, unbolted and trembling with every movement. Some fifty feet below, the water could be seen swirling around the sharp rocks. If a man fell, nothing could save him, especially if he was carrying a load, for there was nothing below to seize hold of save the great timbers of the understructure.

In order to get around the face of some of the bluffs without drilling tunnels or making expensive cuts, the railway resorted to "grasshopper trestles," so called because the outer posts extended far down into the gorges, standing in steps cut in the rock, while the inner posts, like a grasshopper's forelegs, were very short and sometimes non-existent. Later on these trestles were replaced by walls of masonry, built by Scottish stonemasons.

On its queasy descent from the Great Divide, the road switched back and forth across the Kicking Horse by truss and trestle eight times. Before the right of way could be cleared, a tote road had to be constructed to replace the dangerous surveyors' trail cut into the cliffside. This road ran a few feet above the bed of the railway and in one place was notched right into the cliff. It was almost as perilous as the Golden Stairs. On their first journey down the hazardous thoroughfare, men involuntarily hugged the upper side and uttered a sigh of relief when the journey was over.

The choice of the Kicking Horse Pass had presented the CPR with a considerable dilemma. The river drops eleven hundred feet in the first three and a half miles of its headlong race down the western slopes of the Rockies. Under the terms of its contract with the government, the CPR was pledged to a maximum gradient of 2.2 per cent, or about 116 feet to a mile, but to build the road as Rogers had located it, the line would have been forced to cross several unstable boulder slides and to pass under an immense glacier. In addition, it would have been necessary to drill a fourteen-hundred-foot tunnel – and that would have delayed the railway for almost another year. Sandford Fleming suggested to Van Horne that the company build a temporary line dropping quickly down from the summit into the comparative level of the valley of the Kicking Horse by means of a grade of 232 feet per mile – twice as steep as that allowed by the contract and four times as steep as the ideal maximum. Fleming's suggestion was accepted, and thus was born the "Big Hill" between the stations of Hector and Field. It was an eight-mile horror. The grades would be the steepest ever regularly operated for any considerable period of time by a standard-gauge railroad and the so-called temporary line – an eight-mile diversion from the original location – would last for a quarter of a century.

Even a 2.2 gradient can cause runaways. The first train that tried to descend the Big Hill ran away and plunged to the river below, killing three men. Safety switches were installed every two miles and manned twenty-four hours a day, but these did not always work. A second train lost control after passing over a safety switch and headed straight into a tunnel where sixty men were working. The engineer slammed the engine into reverse, set the whistle, and jumped. When the tender derailed, the train came to a stop.

At the top of the Big Hill, every passenger train was required to stop to have its air brakes tested. Brakemen jumped off at intervals and trotted beside the cars to make sure the wheels were not sliding or heating unduly. Boxcars and flatcars were restricted to a speed of six miles an hour. All trains were required to stop at the safety switches and start up again after the switchman re-aligned the track onto the main line. The bigger engines were limited to seventeen loaded cars in daylight and twelve at night; smaller engines could not even pull these loads. Powerful water brakes were brought into service when the steeper inclines were reached and the trains began to slide downhill like toboggans. In spite of these precautions runaways continued to occur. One train lost a forty-ton wing plough, which plunged three hundred feet into the river. And there were several cases of locomotives roaring down the slope so fast that the men tending the safety switches could not operate them in time to save train or crew.

The upward journey was a slow and difficult operation. At least four big engines were required to pull a train of 710 tons to the summit. Under such conditions it took an hour to move eight miles. Such a train could not be long – fourteen to twenty freight cars or eleven passenger coaches. When the Prince of Wales visited Canada, it took five engines to pull his entourage back over the summit of the Rockies.

All of this was expensive and time consuming; the use of four locomotives meant that there were four times as many chances for delay through engine failure. And in the winter, when the winds shrieked off the Yoho ice-fields in forty-below weather, smothering the mountain slopes in immense drifts of cement-hard snow, the difficulties were compounded. But it was not until 1909 that the CPR decided to drill the remarkable spiral tunnels, which make a figure eight deep within the bowels of Cathedral Mountain and Mount Ogden. It took ten thousand men two years to do the job, but there was not an employee in the operating division of the CPR who did not believe that it was worth it.

Nonetheless, the steeper line allowed Van Horne to push the railroad down the Kicking Horse to its junction with the Columbia by September. By January it had moved on down the Columbia for seventeen miles to the point where the line would cross over to the mouth of the Beaver at the foot of the Selkirks.

Here, at a spot known simply as First Crossing (it would later be named Donald, after Donald A. Smith), the work came to an end for the season and another garish little community sprang into being on the frozen river bank. On November 15, Jack Little, the telegraph operator, set down on paper the events of one single moonlit night:

". . . the Italian saloon . . . [is] a little hut, 12 x 16, and it dispenses beer, cigars, and something more fiery, in unlimited quantities. The barkeeper is a woman . . . there is an accordion squeaking in the corner, and it and the loud coarse laugh of the barmaid make an angelic harmony. . . . On all sides we hear the music of the dice box and the chips . . . the merry music of the frequent and iniquitous drunks; the music of the dance and the *staccato* accompaniment of pistol shots; and the eternal music, from the myriad saloons and bars along the street, of the scraping fiddle. In the French Quarter a dance is going on. The women present are Kootenai Squaw, 'the first white lady that ever struck Cypress' and two or three of the usual type of fallen angels. A gang of men and boys line the walls and a couple of lads dance with the damsels in the centre. There is a lamentable want of a sense of shame at Columbia Crossing. . . .

"During our walk we met plenty of 'drunks.' The contractor is as drunk as his employees, and the deadbeats are as drunk as usual. There is a good deal of card-playing . . . all through the night. . . .

"Below the high bank, on the dry land left by the receding river, several teamsters have camped for the night preparatory to crossing in the morning. The ferry boat with its one light is making its last trip for the night across the narrow space of water, becoming narrower day by day as the ice encroaches from the banks. On the opposite side of the river lights shine out from rafts and shacks, while above them the dark pine forest stretches its gloomy line. The scene behind is growing livelier as the hours grow shorter. There is a row at one of the card tables. A pistol shot follows. A man is seen standing back a rough crowd with drawn revolver while another man is lying in a pool of his own blood. Well, it is all very interesting, no doubt, and has the great charm of being 'western' which makes up for a multitude of sins. . . ."

3

All during the spring of 1884, Van Horne, who had moved his headquarters to Montreal, was trying his best to get out to British Columbia to settle on the Pacific terminus of the railroad. A variety of problems kept forcing him to postpone the journey. He was faced daily with a mixed bag of executive decisions, many of them niggling, but all, apparently, requiring his personal intervention. No detail was too small for Van Horne to handle. To a Brockville man who wrote to him personally asking for a job he sent a swift rejection accompanied by a piece of personal advice: "Perhaps you will permit me to say, that in seeking employment in the shape of office work, I think you will find that your hand writing will militate against you." The bill of fare on the newly acquired lake boats offended his trencherman's palate: ". . . altogether too many dishes offered," he told Henry Beatty. "Fewer varieties, but plenty of each, I have always found to be better appreciated than a host of small, made-up dishes . . . . Plenty of fresh fish . . . is what people expect to find on the lakes and it is, as a rule, the scarcest article in the steamers' larders . . . ." From that moment, Lake Superior trout and whitefish became standard Canadian Pacific fare.

Many of his actions in 1884 were designed to further the interests of the railway in the years to come. He worried about grain buyers swindling prairie farmers and told Egan that if the buyers would not pay a fair price the market must be stimulated by dropping in outside buyers with private assistance to shake it up. He was distressed by the erection of flat warehouses. His experience in Minnesota had convinced him that much more modern elevators would be needed. Van Horne also did his best to persuade the farmers to forget soft wheat and concentrate on harder varieties. The best of these was Red Fife and, as an inducement, Van Horne offered to carry the seed free to any farmer who ordered it.

The general manager was equally solicitous of the immigrants pouring into Winnipeg. They were the railway's future customers. In order that they could get immediate access to supplies on the prairies, he had sidings built at intervals along the line on which he placed railroad cars fitted up as stores. As soon as anyone came along who seemed to be a good storekeeper, the business was transferred to him and the store car moved elsewhere.

In spite of the need to cut costs he had no intention of pinching pennies where the railway's public image was concerned. To the president of the Michigan Central, who asked that he use a certain type of economical sleeping car exclusively, he replied that he would not: "If the business is to be successfully worked up, the very best cars will be needed." He was determined that the woodwork of the passenger cars be hand carved. As he told the board of directors: "Every foot of imitation carving will affect the opinion and attitude towards us of the Company's employees. We want them to have confidence in us – we want every clerk, conductor and brakeman to regard this Company as above all mean pretence. So everything must be of the best material, and be exactly what it pretends to be. Otherwise, their attitude and their service to us will not be what it ought to be."

Van Horne took special delight in personally designing sleeping cars and parlour cars. To this end he engaged noted artists to handle the interior decoration. As for comfort, he once, as an object lesson to his own people, made a comic illustration showing a tall, fat man attempting to squeeze into one of the short berths provided by United States railroads. He made sure that CPR cars were constructed of larger dimensions with longer and wider berths. Van Horne himself thought in terms of bigness. He liked big houses, "fat and bulgy like myself," with big doors, big roofs, big windows, big desks, and vast spaces.

His whole philosophy was based on permanence. The railway, as he saw it, was to become a kind of religion among the men who worked on it and also among the people who travelled on it. "You are not to consider your own personal feelings," he told a trainman who had engaged in a dispute with an irritable passenger. "You are the road's while you are on duty; your reply is the road's; and the road's first law is courtesy."

Van Horne was one of the first railroad executives to realize the value of retaining such auxiliary utilities as the telegraph, express, and sleeping car departments. These, he used to say, were not the big tent but the sideshows, and "I expect the sideshows to pay the dividend." It was the custom of other railways to franchise these departments to independent firms which took the cream, as Van Horne put it, off the business and left the skim milk to the railway.

In mid-June, Van Horne decided that he must inspect the line between Lake Superior and Nipissing before making his journey to the Pacific coast. The inspection covered everything, right down to the quality of the lake steamer's coffee, which, he complained, contained "a considerable percentage of burnt peas."

Accompanied by the government's engineer-in-chief Collingwood Schreiber, he took off on an eighty-two-mile walking trip to look over the stretch between Nepigon and Jackfish Bay. He was a corpulent man by this time, spending most of his days at a desk in Montreal, but he amazed Schreiber by his energy and endurance. After walking for miles through fire-blackened rock country, the two men finally reached an engineer's camp at dusk, limp and sore. Van Horne promptly challenged the chief engineer to a foot race.

In the camps along Superior's shore and later in the mountains, Van Horne fitted in easily with the workmen, sitting up all night in poker sessions, swapping stories, and drawing caricatures. He probably preferred them to some of the stuffier members of Canadian society with whom he was forced to put up from time to time. (He often used to test acquaintances for their sincerity. He liked, for example, to sign one of his own paintings with the name Théo Rousseau, a fashionable French artist who was then in vogue, and listen sardonically to the ooh's and ah's of pretentious guests who praised his judgement.)

His power, by 1884, was enormous. Lord Dunmore said that "no other man commands the same army of servants or guides the destiny of a railway over such an extent of country." Van Horne "the ablest railroad general in the world," as Jason Easton, his American contemporary called him, was in charge of the equivalent of several army divisions. Yet at the same time he continued to indulge his various exotic tastes. His collection of Japanese porcelain was rapidly becoming the finest in the world. He collected French Impressionists long before they were popular or valuable. When he discovered, to his chagrin, that his architects had designed the Banff Springs Hotel so that it faced away from the mountains, he personally sketched in

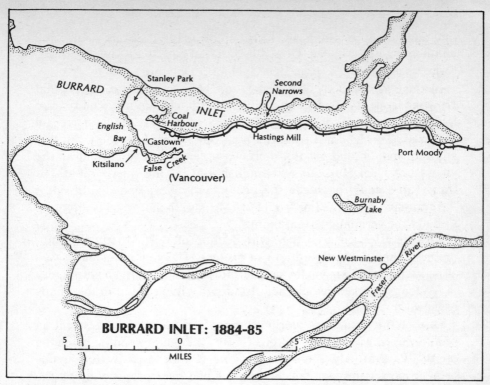

BURRARD INLET: 1884-85

a rotunda that could redress the oversight. The log station houses and chalets in the Rockies and Selkirks were also his idea. He scribbled a sketch on a piece of brown paper and turned it over to a designer with a brief order: "Lots of good logs there. Cut them, peel them, and build your station." In various ways, the general manager was helping transform the face of his adopted land.

He finally saw the Pacific Coast in the late summer. The expedition to British Columbia was arranged in July, and on August 4 a distinguished party arrived at Victoria and moved swiftly across to Port Moody, then designated as the terminus of the transcontinental line. The settlement, perched on a narrow bank at the head of Burrard Inlet, was basking in the belief that it was to become the greatest metropolis on the coast.

"Port Moody . . . has no rival," exclaimed the *Gazette,* the locality's pioneer newspaper. "There is no place upon the whole coast of British Columbia that can enter into competition with it . . . these declarations are sweeping but incontrovertible."

The paper could hardly wait for Van Horne to arrive in order that the new metropolis could be laid out. Its editor wrote lyrically of gigantic markets, theatres, churches, paved streets, hotels, shops, and warehouses rising "like magic." But it was all tragically premature. Van Horne was disturbingly non-committal. He wanted first to examine the mouth of Burrard Inlet and its two settlements – the

345

tiny community of Hastings, surrounding the mill of that name, and another properly called Granville but dubbed "Gastown" after a former saloonkeeper, John "Gassy Jack" Deighton.

In fact, Port Moody would not do. There was no room on that crowded ledge for a substantial city. The railway alone would require four hundred acres of level ground, and even that much space did not exist. To reclaim it from the tidal flats would cost between two and four million dollars. But there *was* plenty of level ground in the vicinity of Coal Harbour and English Bay at the inlet's mouth. If Van Horne could persuade the provincial government to subsidize the continuation of the line from Port Moody, then it was his intention to build the terminus at that point.

This decision ensured the swift decline of Port Moody. In vain, the merchants sent off petitions of protest. The general manager was already planning to name the new terminus Vancouver. The proximity of Vancouver Island would help to identify its position in the minds of world travellers.

One of the influences working upon Van Horne in the selection of a terminus was that of Marcus Smith, the government's watchdog on the Port Moody–Emory's Bar line. Smith was at some pains to keep secret the fact that he himself had held property along the future right of way since the previous July. He made it clear to his banker that he did not want the CPR to know he owned the land.

The spectacle of Marcus Smith secretly dabbling in real estate and urging Van Horne to place the terminus where it was best designed to enrich him is an intriguing one, for Smith was a man who proclaimed his own honesty repeatedly in the face of what he believed to be almost universal corruption. His own dalliance in land speculation did not weaken his personal suspicions. He told his banker that sale of the land would give him a chance "of making a few thousand dollars which will be very acceptable as the Govt. service is becoming very irksome through corruption connected with the Onderdonk contracts so that I fear I cannot stand it much longer." Smith was forever predicting his imminent resignation or dismissal; actually, he survived in the government service longer than most of his colleagues.

Marcus Smith clearly believed that corners were being cut on the Onderdonk section of the line and that many of his colleagues and superiors were purposely ignoring inferior work in accepting the contractor's estimates. Certainly the government engineers had not held Andrew Onderdonk to the letter of his contract. Van Horne was appalled at what he saw that August: the timber trusses were "the worst I ever saw in a railway. In the attempt to strengthen them they have been patched and spliced in a most wonderful manner – boulders and debris are continually coming down on the track."

The situation led to a series of disagreeable battles between Van Horne and John Henry Pope, who was Charles Tupper's successor as Minister of Railways. Pope was in a difficult position. He felt duty bound to stand behind his own people, who had told him that the work was properly done. "It seems to be a very sore question with him," Van Horne told Stephen, "and he usually gets into a rage within ten minutes after we touch upon it." The dispute led to an open breach between Pope and Van Horne. Their feud was so bitter that they did not speak for many years and shook hands only on Pope's deathbed.

Marcus Smith made such a fuss that he was transferred to the section east of Kamloops, which Onderdonk had contracted to build not for the government but for the CPR – or at least that was Smith's suspicion. Certainly he was impolitic in charging Onderdonk, and by inference Collingwood Schreiber himself, with corruption. "It is . . . generally believed," he wrote, "that Onderdonk by corrupt means had the power to get any engineer removed from his contract and that I was removed at his instance."

But there is no doubt that along the Fraser Canyon, the government shaved costs to the bone to the detriment of the line. Henry Cambie was ordered to "locate the cheapest possible line with workable curves and grades." He and his assistant, T. H. White, began adopting eight-degree curves, thereby avoiding tunnels and expensive cuts. According to White, when the curves reached ten degrees, Andrew Onderdonk, "throwing up his arms to high heaven declared that he refused to accept the order to run construction trains on so impossible a curvature." Between Kamloops and Lytton there were 430 curves and virtually no straight track. Not only would the maintenance be costly on such a section but the operating speed would also be slower.

The result of all this parsimony was a long and acrimonious debate between the CPR and the government which finally resulted, in 1888, in a board of arbitration. The company claimed twelve million dollars from the government; the final settlement, in 1891, was $579,255. The dispute embittered Stephen. As a reward for building the line swiftly, he felt he was "forced and cheated into accepting a temporary road, utterly unfit to be operated as a through trunk line. . . ." As for Van Horne, he told a United States Senate inquiry in 1889 that if the CPR had had control of the British Columbia section, "we would not have built it where it is. . . ." He would have found a way to circumvent the Fraser Canyon which he described, not inaccurately, as "one of the worst places in the world."

4

The general manager had his first view of the Fraser Canyon on August 9. He was accompanied by Collingwood Schreiber, Joseph W. Trutch, Major A. B. Rogers, Marcus Smith, Henry Cambie, Michael Haney, and S. B. Reed – as quarrelsome, temperamental, and jealous a company of engineers as it was possible to assemble. Smith had quarrelled with Rogers, bullied Cambie, questioned Schreiber's integrity, and called Trutch an incompetent. The Canadians were all jealous of Rogers, whose crusty personality did not endear him to either casual acquaintances or colleagues. Haney and Smith had fought eyeball to eyeball on several occasions. Reed was known as the man who did the hatchet job in Winnipeg in 1882. In addition, several of the company had apparently been engaged to spy on one another. When the CPR decided to give Onderdonk the subcontract to build east from Savona's Ferry towards the Eagle Pass, it sent Rogers out as supervising engineer. Van Horne, in April, decided to send Cambie out to check up on Rogers. Later he sent Reed to check on Cambie and then, to cap it all, dispatched Marcus Smith to look over Reed's work.

In spite of all this it was a reasonably harmonious group that arrived in Kamloops on August 10, having inspected the steel cantilever bridge across the Fraser near Lytton, "one of the great wonders of the C.P. railway," as the *Sentinel* rightly described it and the first of its kind in North America. Until the bridge was finished a cable was stretched across the boiling Fraser, and freight and passengers were carried over in a basket suspended from pulleys. Cambie actually made the crossing before the basket was used, sitting in the body of a wheelbarrow slung by ropes. As he came hurtling down the cable Cambie saw a man roll two bales of hay into his path and, fighting back the inclination to scream, threw his legs into the air to prevent them from being snapped off. The barrow struck one bale and sent it flying; the second brought it to a stop.

Yale was all but finished as a community. Kamloops was the new mecca. The town, which had suffered a decline after the gold rush, perked up with Van Horne's announcement that it would be a divisional point. Here were repeated all the spectacles attendant on the construction period – the hotels jammed with men, some sleeping in the bar room and some on billiard tables, some gambling their savings away and some drinking them up. The courts were crowded with liquor cases, presided over by the former premier, George Walkem, himself no mean toper. "Judge Walkem carried away dead drunk at 7 a.m. when everybody was looking on," Cambie scribbled in his diary one day, noting, however, that Walkem recovered sufficiently to open court at 10.30 a.m. and, presumably, to levy the usual fines for intoxication.

It was Onderdonk's job to continue the railroad for the CPR from the end of the government section at Savona's Ferry to meet the railway builders coming from the east. On August 11, Van Horne, together with Major Rogers and S. B. Reed, set off along the route of the line that would take them directly through Eagle Pass and then on across the mountains to the Columbia.

It was a truly fearful trip. The members of the party were forced to leave most of their spare clothing at End of Track and push on by freight team, scow, and, finally, pony train. An early fall of snow had deposited three feet of slush on the mountain trails, already littered with the cast-offs of other travellers. While crossing Summit Lake, Van Horne tumbled into water that was only a degree or so above freezing. John Stevens the engineer, who was present, wrote: "I have never forgotten, after 48 years, the vigorous and breezy comments about the country and everybody connected with it which he made when we had pulled him back onto the raft. . . ." The entire trip was one that few people had ever made. In another fifteen months it would no longer be necessary to make the journey on foot.

The party was without food for two days, probably as a result of Rogers's eccentric provisioning. When they finally arrived at the most forward of the camps on Rogers Pass, the general manager's sensitive nostrils detected the aroma of ham cooking. "It was then," he later recalled, "that I learned that a man can smell ham ten miles away."

On this journey several new Van Horne legends were forged. When the general manager reached the Mountain Creek trestle he was told that a few days before several men had crashed to their deaths in the ravine below. The floor of the trestle, one hundred and sixty feet above the torrent, consisted of two loose planks and nothing more. One of the general manager's companions was barely able to negotiate the bridge by crawling inch by inch on his hands and knees, but Van Horne stepped confidently out on the shaky planks, strode across the trestle, and returned just as imperturbably.

He liked to take curves on the newly constructed road at the highest possible speed. Once, with a dangerous trestle looming up ahead, the engineer balked.

"Here," Van Horne said, "get down and I'll take her over myself."

"Well," said the engineer, "if you ain't afraid, guess I ain't neither."

When the general manager left the mountains and rolled across the prairies in the comfort of his private car, he was able to witness the by-products of his handiwork: Calgary, Medicine Hat, Moose

Jaw, and Regina slowly changing from tent and shack towns to permanent communities; crops being harvested; sod houses going up; and a veneer of civilization spreading out over the raw prairie. As he sped towards Winnipeg Van Horne could note at every siding the bleak symbols of a vanished past – great stacks of buffalo bones being loaded into boxcars. The general manager had made his gardening expertise pay off: the bones were shipped to Minneapolis and sold as fertilizer for seven dollars a ton.

Back in Montreal, he plunged once again into the executive routine. Had Alexander Mackenzie been impressed by his trip to the North West? Then a letter giving his impressions would be "of very great use in killing the villanous [sic] slanders that are being published about 'alkali deserts,' 'sandy stretches,' etc." Jim Hill, Van Horne learned, had spies within the company and was boasting that he was in possession of full reports on all the business the railway did at Port Arthur. The general manager moved swiftly to stop the leakage. In British Columbia, Arthur Wellington Ross, the railway's real estate representative, had overstepped the bounds of propriety and had taken a piece of property on the Hastings Mill Tract in trust for Van Horne, with some secret agreement involved. The general manager declined to accept the property. "I do not like transactions of this kind and do not intend to take any chances whatever of having my name smirched by my connection with them," he told Ross.

As always, no matter was too small to occupy his attention. He personally dictated changes in some drawings of the mountains: he wanted to see steam and not black smoke issuing from the locomotives pictured in the foreground of Mount Stephen; that would give more emphasis to the presence of the railway. And, when necessity dictated it, he could be sarcastic. To Harry Abbott he shot off a withering note:

"You have on your Engineering Staff an inspired idiot by the name of Gribble, who is writing letters here complaining of the desecration of the Sabbath Day by barbarians in your employ. These letters are very long and must have taken a considerable time to write; if they were written during the work the time must have been stolen from the company's time, if they were written on the Sabbath he too must have desecrated the Sabbath."

More and more, however, he was concerned about costs. Over and over, in his wide ranging correspondence, he used the phrase "we have not a dollar to spare." Staffs were reduced to the bone, and repairs to locomotives were cut back to the minimum. To John Ross, on the Lake Superior line, he wrote: "By cutting every corner and cheapening the work in every practicable way, we may be able to build the line for the money available. . . . If we cannot do that, we must stop the work."

As the months went by Van Horne's communications with his deputies in the field became more and more insistent. ". . . we are again very near our *danger line,*" he informed John Ross in October. All pretence at building a first-class line had been abandoned. Even the ballasting of the rails had to be discontinued except where it was necessary to preserve them from damage. After November 1 not even a fence could be built or a nail driven without Van Horne's permission. That was how tight money had become.

Outwardly, the general manager maintained his air of bluff confidence. When a Scottish friend of W. B. Scarth's asked if the CPR was a good investment, Van Horne replied: "I have no hesitation in expressing my opinion in the strongest possible terms that it will pay handsomely" – and he went on to say why: its entire debt was only one third that of the Northern Pacific on a mileage basis, and even less in comparison with other United States transcontinental railways. The CPR's advantage as a through line was greater, and the road itself was far better built.

But Van Horne's real expression of confidence in the railroad went much further than words. He himself had sunk almost every dollar he had in Canadian Pacific stock. If the road failed, he was prepared to go down with it.

5

Once again, the railway was in a critical financial position. "I *feel* like a man walking on the edge of a precipice with less 'nerve' than is comfortable or even *safe* in such a case," George Stephen wrote to the Prime Minister at the end of 1884. ". . . the ordeal I am going through is not easy to stand."

The ordeal had begun that summer – only a few months after Parliament reluctantly passed the loan of $22,500,000. By September the credit of the company at home and abroad was gone. Stephen and Donald A. Smith had been dipping lavishly into their private fortunes in an attempt to sustain it. They were close to the bottom of the barrel.

Almost all of the spring loan had been gobbled up by the railway builders on the Shield and in the mountains; what was left was being paid out only as the work was done; often these payments were very late. The grain elevator at the lakehead had cost three hundred thousand dollars. Then there were the terminals, shops, and equipment, spread over more than two thousand miles. In the first ten months of 1884 the company found it had spent eight million dollars on essential work that had not been contracted for.

The railway was working on a margin that was terrifyingly narrow. A few days' delay in the subsidy could mean that thousands of men would not be paid. Yet for a variety of reasons the payments were often slow or slender.

Part of this was the result of pure governmental vacillation or because of a general suspicion that the CPR was not entitled to the amount claimed. The Pacific Scandal still haunted Macdonald and his colleagues. They were fearful of seeming to show any sign of favouritism to the Canadian Pacific. That exasperated Stephen. Such delays, he pointed out, were damaging the company's credit. The Council's apparent lack of faith "weakens me more than I can tell you, denuding me of the power and moral strength which the confidence and hearty co-operation of the government alone can give."

There were other problems. Expensive tote roads had to be constructed out of Lake Nipissing and Michipicoten and across the Selkirk Mountains. Vast quantities of construction equipment and supplies had to be brought in, especially before the onset of winter. For all of this the company was forced to lay out funds months in advance; but in Schreiber's strict interpretation of the contract terms, the subsidy did not apply to these preliminary steps of construction.

The real fear was that the government would stop payment altogether. This it was empowered to do if its engineers estimated that there were not enough funds left to complete the line. By October, 1884, it was becoming increasingly clear that if the company had to find funds to repay its loan of the previous November, together with interest and dividends, the coffers would be empty and construction must cease.

Wages were suspiciously slow. Thousands of men on the Lake Superior section were facing long delays in pay. The company was using every possible excuse to stave off creditors and employees. At the end of October the CPR announced that the men in the eastern division would henceforth be paid by cheques drawn on the Bank of Montreal; the reason given was that it was too dangerous to carry around more than a million dollars in cash. The real reason was that Van Horne had decided on a daring though barbarous gambit. He intended to keep nine thousand men at work all winter in the remotest areas with plenty of good food. They would be paid by cheque, which they would be unable to cash. If any man wanted to get away he would find it almost impossible to do so; the isolated conditions would make it difficult to leave before spring, at which time the general manager believed funds must be forthcoming.

In those desperate months, Van Horne and Stephen leaned heavily on Thomas Shaughnessy, a man apparently able to make one dollar do the work of a hundred. Shaughnessy was rising rapidly in the ranks; one day he would be president. He sprang from humble beginnings; both his parents were immigrants; his father, a Limerick Irishman, was a policeman on a beat in Minneapolis. This modest start undoubtedly contributed to Shaughnessy's later love of ostentation. He was a dapper man, immaculately turned out, a pearl in his tie, a gold-handled cane in his gloved hand – an autocrat who remained aloof from all but his closest intimates. He was, in a contemporary journalist's assessment, "a man almost bloodless in the intensity of his devotion to material ends." In his view, what was good for the CPR was good for Canada; he held no personal or political views save those of the institution he served. That he served it well in the financial crisis of 1884-85 is beyond doubt. He never showed the slightest tremor of panic as he kited cheques, kept creditors at bay, denied funds, made partial payments, and generally held the company together. In Toronto, the heads of the big wholesale houses, under Van Horne's and Shaughnessy's persuasion, extended millions of dollars in credit so that supplies could go forward.

While Shaughnessy was using extraordinary measures to keep the company solvent, Stephen was slowly committing his entire personal fortune and those of his closest colleagues to its further support. The previous winter, he, Donald Smith, Angus, and McIntyre had put up a total of $2.3 million in their own bonds and securities as collateral against CPR bank loans. But in May, McIntyre dropped right out of the Canadian Pacific, refusing to stay even as a director or to have anything to do with the management of a company he clearly believed would go to the wall. Baron Reinach went with him, and Stephen was forced to use more of his fortune to buy out both men's stock. In the president's phrase, these men had "deserted"; they were little better than traitors. McIntyre, he told Macdonald, had been "coarsely selfish & cowardly all through these 5 years. Ruthless in disregarding the interests of others when he could advance his own. . . ." The unkindest cut came a few months after the defection when, in the CPR's darkest days, McIntyre was the first to refuse it credit and threatened to sue immediately unless his firm's accounts for dry goods was paid at once.

In the face of these desertions, the steadfastness of Donald A. Smith was refreshing. Smith was prepared, like Stephen, to invest all of his own money in the Canadian Pacific. Stephen, who went to London in July, was able that month to "*melt*," as he put it, a number of land grant bonds into cash by giving the personal guarantee of Smith, Angus, and himself to a British bank for a four-month loan.

"Smith," he told Macdonald, "has behaved splendidly, promptly doing what I asked him to do. . . ."

It was the second of three trips Stephen made across the Atlantic in that desperate year of 1884. The first, in April, had been a total failure. Stephen had hoped to raise funds to build the Manitoba South-Western, an important branch of the railway, and also to try to boost public confidence in Canada and in the CPR. He failed on both counts and returned to Montreal exhausted.

The continued attacks on the Canadian Pacific affected Canada's own credit position on the other side of the Atlantic. Leonard Tilley, the finance minister, arriving in London in June and hoping to float a loan of five million pounds, was alarmed at the propaganda campaign that had been organized. A "vile article" in the *Mining & Financial Register* referred to the loan as "another crutch for the CPR." A man actually paraded in front of the great financial house of Baring, where the bonds were being offered, advertising the article by means of huge handbills. Tilley, who blamed the Grand Trunk for planting the story, got his money only with difficulty and not at the rate he expected. A week later CPR stock dropped to a record low of 39 on the New York board. The railway's enemies, determined to drive it into bankruptcy, were also apparently prepared to bruise the country as well.

Stephen responded with fury to the "malicious venom" in the *Globe* that summer. There was no doubt in his mind as to who was the grey eminence behind the *Globe*'s continuing attacks: "Hickson is at the bottom of it all. . . ." Finally, Stephen was stung to the point of reply. The *Globe* published it and then turned it against him:

"If Mr. George Stephen's statements that the last loan of $30,000,000 will build and equip the road [are true], why is he so sensitive about the attacks of the Globe? To be frank with Mr. Stephen he has humbugged the public as much as he can. He has a corrupt government and the corrupt Parliament at his mercy; but a few years hence he will have to appeal to the electors of Canada who make and unmake governments and parliaments. He had better made good use of the power he has at present over the creatures who have so shamefully betrayed the taxpayers of this country. Mr. Stephen has lost caste; Mr. Stephen is looked upon now as a pocket edition of Jay Gould. It is his own fault. He has betrayed the public for a fortune for himself and his friends. He has sullied the reputation he once had as a high-toned businessman. He has no one to blame but himself. He sees his downfall near at hand, and hopes that by blaming the Globe newspaper he may fall upon a bed of doom; but we sincerely hope it won't be, as it deserves to be upon something harder."

To the sensitive Stephen, who valued his personal integrity and reputation above all else, these insinuations were almost too much. He seemed to swing from depression to elation and back to depression again. In October, the Prime Minister found him in high spirits. The company's balance sheet showed the railway making money in all its divisions. But he was soon a mass of nerves again. The company could certainly make money, but the shortage of ready cash was killing it. In mortgaging the railroad, Stephen had made it impossible to raise any further funds except through the sale of outstanding stock. But the government lien, together with the bitter campaign being waged against the CPR in New York and London, had frightened off potential buyers. Unless he could make an arrangement to get rid of that lien he faced an impossible situation. It was a maddening dilemma: as soon as the CPR became a through line the profits would roll in, for it held a mileage advantage over other transcontinental railroads. But could the CPR be completed? By October, Stephen realized that there simply was not enough money to do the job.

He set off for England for the third time that year, to raise more funds. The loan he had negotiated in July would shortly be due. Worse, the five-million-dollar loan he had raised in New York the previous year by pledging ten million dollars' worth of CPR stock was also due in November – and the stock was too low to be of any use. There were other worries. Looking beyond the financial watershed of November, Stephen could see the dark month of February looming up. Then the railway would be forced to pay its guaranteed dividend of five per cent. The government was responsible for three per cent, but the CPR would somehow have to find the cash for the remainder – an amount in excess of one million dollars.

Nevertheless, Stephen began to see some tiny pinpoints of light at the end of the tunnel down which he had set his course. The New York loan he solved by the now familiar device of using his own funds and those of some of his friends. He simply bought up the stock held as collateral and paid off the debt. Then in London, Charles Tupper came to his aid and drafted a plan for relief of the railway which he shot off to Tilley in Ottawa. It was all very tentative; nobody knew, certainly not Macdonald, whether any further plan to aid the CPR could be forced down the throats of the Cabinet and the public in time to do any good. Still, it was a straw at which Stephen could grasp. And, finally, by pledging $385,000 worth of Toronto, Grey and Bruce bonds, which he, Donald Smith, and R. B. Angus held among them, he was able to raise a loan of a quarter of a million from a Scottish financial institution. It was this small bit of Highland good cheer that prompted the president to send off to Donald Smith one of the most memorable cablegrams in Canadian history – and certainly the shortest.

Both Stephen and Smith had come from small Scottish towns in the countryside drained by the River Spey, in a land once dominated by the Clan Grant. Stephen remembered, and knew that Smith would remember also, a great rock which dominated the valley no more than three miles from Dufftown, in Banffshire, where he had been born. Everyone knew the meaning of that rock: it was a symbol of defiance. In the brave old days, when clan battled clan, a sentinel had kept watch on its stark promontory, and when the enemy was sighted and a fiery cross borne through Speyside, this rock had become a rallying place for the Clan Grant. The rock was known as Craigellachie, and it was this defiant slogan that Stephen dispatched to his cousin. Into one brief, cryptic sentence, the CPR president managed to convey all the fierce passions, bold defiance, dark hatreds, and bright loyalties inherited from his Scottish forbears. "Stand fast, Craigellachie!" the cable advised, and Donald Smith, when he read it in Montreal, must himself have heard, as in the distance, the clash of warring claymores and the wild skirl of battle.

Chapter Eight

MARCHING AS TO WAR

1

Eighteen eighty-five was perhaps the most significant year of the first Canadian century. After that year nothing could ever be the same again, because for the first time Canadians would be able to travel the length of their nation without setting foot in a foreign land. A series of devices came into being that year that would also help to bind the country together. The single-pole-electric trolley had just been invented and was demonstrated for the first time at the Toronto Agricultural Fair of 1885. That same year Gottlieb Daimler took out his historic patent for an internal combustion engine and Karl Benz built the first automobile – a three-wheeled one. The presence of radio waves was confirmed and the long-distance telephone put into use. Like the railway, these new aids to communication would help stitch the awkward archipelago of population islands into a workable transcontinental reality.

The concept of a transcontinental railway was also responsible for changing the casual attitude towards time. Heretofore every city and village had operated on its own time system. When it was noon in Toronto, it was 11:58 in Hamilton, 12:08 in Belleville, 12:12 1/2 in Kingston, 12:16 1/2 in Brockville, and 12:25 in Montreal. As the railways lengthened across the continent, the constant changing of watches became more and more inconvenient. Schedules were in a state of total confusion. Every railroad had its own version of the correct time, based on the standard of its home city. There were, in the United States, one hundred different time standards used by the various railroads.

On New Year's Day, 1885, the Universal Time System was adopted at Greenwich. About a year earlier the major American railways and the Canadian Pacific had brought order out of chaos as far as their own schedules were concerned by adopting "railway time." The change was a fundamental one, for it affected in a subtle fashion people's attitudes and behaviour. Such concepts as promptness and tardiness took on a new meaning. The country began to live by the clock in a way it had not previously been able to do.

Much of the credit for this went to Sandford Fleming, who had realized very early that a transcontinental railway would immediately raise difficulties in the computation of time. In 1876 he prepared a memorandum on the subject, which was widely circulated, and in 1885 the Canadian Institute recognized him as "unquestionably the initiator and principal agent in the movement for the reform in Time-Reckoning and in the establishment of the Universal Day."

Because of the railway, the settled and stable community of Canada was entering a new period of instability. After 1885, the Canadian Shield ceased to be a barrier to westward development. The railway would be a catalyst in new movements of population (such as the Klondike gold rush) and in a variety of social phenomena that would destroy the established social order.

Eighteen eighty-five was as dramatic a year as it was significant. As the nation became vertebrate, events seemed to accelerate on a collision course. In Montreal, George Stephen was trying to stave off personal and corporate ruin. In Ottawa, John A. Macdonald faced a cabinet revolt over the railway's newest financial proposals. In Toronto, Thomas Shaughnessy was juggling bills like an accomplished sideshow artist in order to give Van Horne the cash he needed to complete the line. On Lake Superior, Van Horne was trying to link up the gaps between the isolated stretches of steel – they totalled 254 miles – so that the CPR might begin its operation. In Manitoba, the political agitation against both government and railway was increasing. In St. Laurent on the Saskatchewan, Louis Riel was back from his long exile and rousing the Métis again. On the far plains the Cree chieftains, Big Bear and Poundmaker, were agitating for new concessions. And in the mountains, the railway builders faced their last great barrier – the snow-shrouded Selkirks.

Van Horne had thought long and hard about using the Rogers Pass in preference to the longer but easier Columbia Valley. On the one hand there would be steep gradients for some forty miles. That would mean heavy assisting engines and costly wear on the track. Against that there was the saving of nearly seventy-seven miles, which meant a reduction of two hours in passenger time and four hours for freight trains. This latter consideration was of great importance when competing for through traffic. Van Horne, who disdained circumlocution, opted for the Rogers Pass.

There were problems in the Selkirks, however, on which no one had reckoned. By 1885 the right of way had been cleared directly across the mountains. More than a thousand men were toiling away in the teeth of shrieking winds that drove snow particles like needles into their faces. Seen from the summit, the location line resembled a wriggling serpent, coiling around the hanging valleys, squeezing through the narrow ravines, and sometimes vanishing into the dark maw of a half-completed tunnel. High above, millions of tons of ice

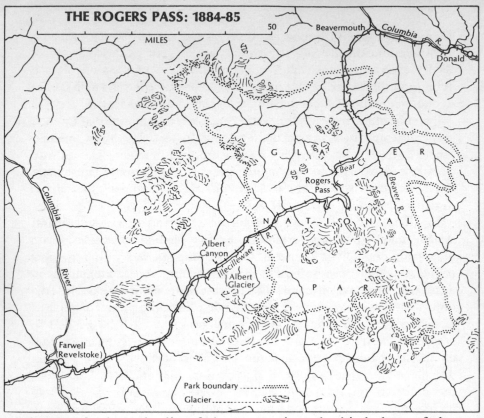

50

MILES

Beavermouth   Columbia

Donald

G L   A   C   I   E   R

Bear Cr.

Rogers
Pass

Beaver R.

N   A   T   I   O   N   A   L

Albert
Canyon

Illecillewaet R.

Albert
Glacier

P   A   R   K

Columbia

River

Farwell
(Revelstoke)

Park boundary ....
Glacier ....

hung poised on the lip of the mountains, the birthplace of the
avalanches and snowslides that constantly swept the area.

The snowslides occurred largely on the western slopes of the mountains. Like the lush vegetation, they were the result of an extraordinary
precipitation. An average of fifty feet of snow fell each winter on
the Rogers Pass.

This natural phenomenon posed a threat to the entire operation of
the railway. In midwinter, the pass was almost impossible to breach.
The snowslides – solid packs of ice – were sometimes fifty feet thick.
Through this frozen jungle the railroad builders intended to force
the line. On February 8, a slide six miles west of the summit buried
an entire camp, killing the cook. On the same day a second slide
buried three men alive. A third destroyed a company store. Workmen
became panic stricken. Herbert Holt lost sixty-five thousand dollars'
worth of supplies, all swept away by a vast slide at the end of February.
By that time all communication between the summit and Second
Crossing was cut off.

A Selkirk snowslide was a terrifying spectacle. A quarter of a million
cubic yards of snow could be detached from a mountain peak and
come tearing down the slopes for thousands of feet, ripping out cedars,
seizing boulders in its grip, and causing an accompanying cyclone

more fearful than the avalanche itself. A few seconds before the body of the avalanche struck, the pressure of this gale force wind, known as the flurry, snapped off huge trees several feet in diameter fifty feet above the base. One such flurry was known to have picked up a man and whirled and twisted him so rapidly that when he dropped he was a limp mass without a bruise or a break in skin or clothing yet with every bone in his body either broken or dislocated. Another knocked eight loaded freight cars off the rails.

Apart from the slides, there were the prodigious falls of snow. In one six-day period, eight and a half feet of snow fell. Sometimes three weeks could pass without the blizzard ceasing. In the winter, the scene from the Rogers Pass was eerie. The traveller, gazing westward, looked down into a two-thousand-foot gorge, muffled in a white blanket twenty feet deep. Above and around him the glaciers dangled, shimmering in the sunlight. At one spot, forty-two glaciers were visible, the largest being the vast Illecillewaet, which would for more than half a century be one of the great Canadian tourist attractions until the changing climate caused it to recede.

This scenery, an uncalculated asset in the summer, was an uncalculated liability in the winter. The problems of the Selkirks delayed the opening of through passenger service to the Pacific by at least six months. In the winter of 1885-86 entire sections of completed track were swept away by snowslides and the line had to be closed. In the end, the company was forced to construct almost six miles of snow sheds at a cost of forty dollars a foot.

For the next quarter-century, this westward descent, like that of the Big Hill in the Rockies, was an operating nightmare. In March, 1910, a snowslide which caused the loss of fifty-eight lives finally convinced the CPR that it must abandon the Rogers Pass. This resulted in a second engineering feat, equal to the drilling of the spiral tunnels – the boring of the longest double-track tunnel on the continent, the five-mile-long Connaught. (Today, the Trans-Canada highway runs through the Rogers Pass, but it is passable only in summer.)

Snow or no snow, the line had to be driven to completion somehow by the end of 1885. As winter gave way to spring, every mile of the right of way was throbbing with activity – teamsters jogging in with wagonloads of supplies, other teams ploughing up the rough, root-ridden earth, small armies of men swinging picks and shovels, others blasting out handcuts and tunnels – trees toppling, stumps flying sky-high, boulders splintering, and always the stench of smoke and horse manure blotting out the subtler scent of the cedar forest.

The mountain streams tumbling down from the glaciers above had cut deep gouges in the naked rock, and it was over these gulches that the longest and the highest bridges were required. Built entirely of timber, they had few counterparts in the world. The Mountain Creek bridge, which rose more than 175 feet above the torrent, was one of the largest wooden structures ever built, being twelve hundred feet long. The bridge over Stoney Creek was the highest in North America, supported on wooden towers two hundred feet high, set in concrete.

It was no easy task to work with the diamond-hard rocks of the Selkirks. The strata often ran at right angles to the course of the stream. Sometimes extraordinarily hard layers of rock would stand out from the cliff face like a kind of fence left behind by the erosion of the centuries. Such irregularities made the work more than usually difficult.

On the wet western slopes of the mountains, the railroad builders encountered another unexpected difficulty, a viscous gumbo which oozed from the sides of the cuts and covered the track with a mucilage that was almost impossible to remove. It was finally conquered by driving a double row of piles on either side of the track and filling the intervening space with coarse gravel or broken rock.

On the far side of the pass, where the Prussian blue waters of the Illecillewaet raced downhill between thick jungle walls, the line made a double loop, curving first to the left, then swinging back across the valley to the very tip of the great glacier and then, a mile farther on, twisting back again in the shape of an inverted S. This was three more miles of railway than Van Horne had counted on; it took nine and a half miles to reach the level of the stream four miles from the summit. But it was necessary to avoid the snowslides, and for future tourists, swaying down this dramatic slope from the vantage point of an observation car, the experience would be electrifying. This was the same trail, bestrewn with devil's club and skunk cabbage, that Major Rogers and his nephew Albert had toiled up on their voyage of discovery in 1881, that Fleming and Grant, badly lacerated from thorns, had managed to negotiate in 1883, and that a hungry Van Horne had struggled over in 1884. Nobody except an enthusiastic mountaineer would ever have to make that journey again; and only a few, gazing up at the shattered rock of the clefts and tunnels and the pilings of the matchstick bridges, would let their thoughts rest upon the thousands of sweating workmen who made it possible.

2

To those who had known the North West before the time of the steel, the railway was a symbol of the passing of the Good Old Days.

To the Indians it was a new kind of boundary, as solid in its own way as a wall. To the white settlers of northern Saskatchewan, its change of route had meant disappointment. To the farmers of Manitoba it spelled monopoly and grinding freight rates. To the half-breeds, it stood for revolutionary social change.

From Winnipeg to Edmonton, the North West was in a ferment. Whites, Indians, and half-breeds were all organizing. At the end of July, 1884, the Crees of the North Saskatchewan, who had come to the point of rebellion earlier in the year, were welded into an Indian council by Big Bear, the most independent of the chiefs. The Indians felt that the government had deceived them, and the Indians were right. Ottawa had promised to save them from starvation, yet already their meagre rations had been cut back as part of an official policy of retrenchment. It was plain that the eastern politicians had little understanding of the North West; the new minister of the interior, Senator David Macpherson, had not ventured even as far as Winnipeg.

The white settlers were equally disaffected. In addition to the burgeoning Manitoba Farmers' Union, other organized groups were petitioning Ottawa for redress. Their demands were similar: local autonomy, land reform, control of their own railways, reduction of protective tariffs, and an end to the CPR monopoly.

The English and Scots half-breeds and the French-speaking Roman Catholic Métis had another grievance. They wanted what the government had granted in Manitoba after the first collision with Louis Riel – a share in the aboriginal title to the land. Time after time they had been put off.

By the spring of 1884, protest meetings were becoming common at St. Laurent near Duck Lake on the South Saskatchewan – the strongest and best established of the Métis communities. ". . . the N.W. Ter. is like a volcanoe ready to erupt," one Métis wrote to the exiled Louis Riel in May, 1884. "On all sides people complain of injustice; they invoke equity, they desire to obtain our rights."

By that time, the united half-breed community in the forks of the Saskatchewan had decided that Riel was the only man who could lead them to force the government's hand. No one else had his charisma, his sense of tactics, his eloquence and, above all, his reputation. Riel was a long distance away and many years out of touch, living in poverty and teaching school at a Jesuit mission at Sun River, Montana. Distance held no terrors for the Métis. Four of them saddled up their horses that May and set out on a seven-hundred-mile ride to meet their Messiah.

The most interesting member of the delegation was Gabriel Dumont, the most popular and respected man along the Saskatchewan – a natural leader, though totally unlettered and almost apolitical. Dumont had been for years chief of the buffalo hunt – a legendary rider, sharp-shooter, drinker, gambler, and even swimmer. He was forty-seven and had been a chief of his people since the age of twenty-five, much beloved by all who knew him, including Sam Steele, the Mounted Policeman, who thought him one of the kindest and best of men, flawed only by an obsession for gambling. He knew the prairies, Steele said, "as well as a housewife knows her kitchen," and was universally respected: "One might travel the plains from one end to the other and talk to the Métis hunters and never hear an unkind word said of Dumont. . . . When in trouble the cry of all was for Gabriel."

In 1884 there was trouble and the cry was for Gabriel again. But Dumont knew that he could not lead his people in a battle with the government of Canada: he had no English and no gift for oratory. He was a man of action, a prairie general who would shortly become the tactician of the last stand of the Métis empire against the onrush of civilization. Riel would be that empire's king.

The four delegates arrived at Riel's home on June 4, 1884. Riel was under doctor's orders to avoid excitement, a counsel he only occasionally remembered to follow. Exiled in 1875 for five years as a result of his role in the Red River troubles, forced to flit back and forth across the border, his already mercurial psyche had been subjected to such stresses that he had gone insane at times, bellowing aloud that he was a prophet, suffering hallucinations, and sometimes running naked down the corridors of the institutions in which he was confined. Twenty months in Quebec asylums (hidden from his pursuers) had calmed him down, but his sense of personal mission was never quenched. He was clearly aroused by the message the delegation brought to him. The sense of power, which he had enjoyed in his brief time as master of Fort Garry, was still within him; so was the mystic conviction that he had a divine mission to perform. Undoubtedly he felt keenly the plight of his people, as he had fifteen years before. Added to that was his own sense of injury at the hands of the Canadian government. Canada, he believed, owed him both land and money. After some consideration he told the delegation that he would return to Canada temporarily to fight not only for his personal rights and those of his people but also for the white settlers and the Indians.

On the surface Riel did not appear to sanction trouble. His meetings were enthusiastic but outwardly peaceful. The Métis demands were codified and sent to Ottawa; they included requests for land scrip, better treatment for the Indians, responsible government with vote by ballot, parliamentary representation, reduction of the tariff, and

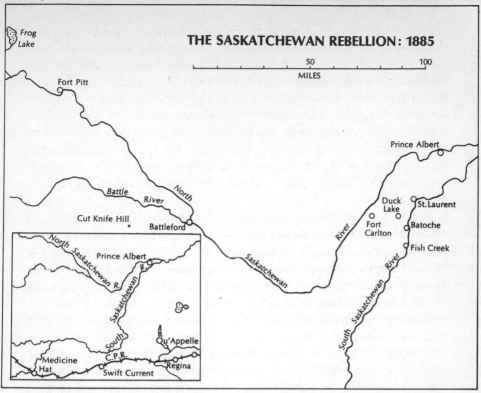

Frog Lake

Fort Pitt

Battle River

North

Cut Knife Hill

Battleford

Prince Albert

Duck Lake

St. Laurent

Fort Carlton

Batoche

Fish Creek

Saskatchewan River

South Saskatchewan River

MILES

50   100

North Saskatchewan R.

Prince Albert

Saskatchewan

South

Qu'Appelle

C.P.R.

Medicine Hat

Swift Current

Regina

the building of another railway to Hudson Bay. In spite of the clamour, the government remained curiously inattentive.

The resident priest at St. Laurent, Father André, wrote three letters to Dewdney in January and February, 1885, stating clearly that unless the government took some action to redress grievances there would be an uprising under Riel in which the Indians would join. By this time Riel was acting very strangely indeed. There is no doubt that he believed himself to be God's envoy. He prayed daily, told of revelations he had experienced in the night, recounted the visitations of saints, and repeated conversations he said he had had with the Holy Ghost.

Father André's repeated warnings were supplemented by others from Joseph Howe, the Mounted Police inspector at Prince Albert, from Major L. N. F. Crozier, his superior at Battleford, and from D. H. McDowell, the representative of the district on the Territorial Council. All urged that Ottawa take some action; but the government's only response was a vague set of promises for the future and the establishment in January of that favourite Canadian device for procrastination, a commission, to examine the question of land scrip for the Métis. This served only to infuriate Riel and his followers.

The fascinating truth seems to be that Riel could have been bought off quite easily for a few thousand dollars. The evidence suggests that he was prepared to desert the cause and return to Montana for hard cash and that he did his best to negotiate that return with the government's representatives.

Riel had made his intentions clear to Father André, who urged Councillor McDowell to meet with him immediately. At the meeting, Riel did most of the talking. McDowell reported that "his claims amount to the modest sum of $100,000.00 but . . . I believe myself that $3,000.00 or $5,000.00 would cart the whole Riel family across the boundary." But to John A. Macdonald, this was simple blackmail, and he refused to countenance it.

In the face of these vacillations Major Crozier's misgivings increased. He wired Dewdney in February urging that some accommodation be made with the Métis; delay would be dangerous. But the Prime Minister's mood that spring seemed to be delay, as George Stephen was finding to his own frustration. Macdonald appeared to exhibit strange blindness towards the North West. There was a curious ambivalence about his attitude towards the new Canada. At the time of Confederation he had ignored it totally; then, when the Americans seemed on the point of appropriating it, he had pushed the bold plan for a transcontinental railway. Suddenly once again he seemed to have lost interest. The railway was floundering in a financial swamp; the West was about to burst into flame. Macdonald vacillated.

Riel's memory went back to those intoxicating moments in December, 1869, when he had been able to deal with Canada on equal diplomatic terms and secure concessions for his people as the result of a bold *fait accompli*. Something along the same lines was in his mind in the early months of 1885. He would not need to resort to bloodshed; the threat of it would bring the Canadian government to its senses. But conditions had changed since 1869 and Riel ignored one vital factor – the presence of the railway.

By March 13, Crozier was expecting a rebellion. The NWMP commissioner, A. G. Irvine, dispatched a hundred reinforcements to Prince Albert. Events began to accelerate. On March 18, Riel took prisoners, seized arms in the St. Laurent–Batoche area, and cut the telegraph line between Batoche and Prince Albert. The following day, he set up a provisional Métis government, as he had done in 1869. He did not want bloodshed, and when Gabriel Dumont urged him to send messengers to enlist Indian support, Riel overruled him, believing Ottawa would now yield to the threat of insurrection.

He was, however, becoming more inflammatory. In the week that followed he and his followers, in Crozier's words, "robbed, plundered, pillaged and terrorized the settlers and the country." Dewdney wired Macdonald on March 22 that it was imperative that an able military man be in the North West in case the militia had to be called out. The next day Macdonald dispatched Major-General Frederick Dobson Middleton to the Red River with orders that the militia should move.

It was Riel's intention to seize Fort Carlton and establish it as the capital of his new government. He demanded unconditional surrender from Crozier:

"We want blood! blood! If Carlton is not surrendered it will be a war of extermination; I must have an answer by 12 o'clock or we will attack and take the fort."

Crozier decided to hold Fort Carlton with his policemen and a detachment of volunteers from Prince Albert. But on March 25, he sent a sergeant and seventeen constables to get provisions and ammunition from the trader's store at Duck Lake. The detachment was halted by a large number of Métis and Indians led by Dumont, who actually went so far as to prod the ribs of the NWMP interpreter with a cocked and loaded rifle while the Indians jeered at the police: "If you are men, now come in." The party retreated.

This was too much for the impatient Crozier. The Force had been slighted. No one who wore the scarlet coat could countenance such a breach of law. Without waiting for Irvine and his reinforcements, the superintendent set out with his fifty-five Mounted Policemen, forty-three Prince Albert volunteers, and a seven-pound cannon in tow.

Dumont, on horseback, watched them come. His Métis dismounted and began to creep forward through a curtain of falling snow, partially encircling the police. Crozier drew his twenty sleighs up in line across the road and ordered his men to take cover behind them. A parley took place under a rebel white flag with Dumont's brother Isidore and an Indian on one side and Crozier and a half breed interpreter, John McKay, on the other. When Crozier extended his hand to the Indian, the unarmed native made a grab for McKay's rifle. Crozier, seeing the struggle, gave the order to fire. Isidore Dumont toppled from his horse, dead. The rebels were already on the move, circling around the police left flank. Crozier put spurs to his horse and galloped back to the police lines through a hail of bullets. The Indian was already dead.

At this moment, with the Métis pouring a fierce fire on the police from two houses concealed on the right of the trail and outflanking them on the left, Louis Riel appeared on horseback through the swirling snow at the head of one hundred and fifty armed Métis. He was grasping an enormous crucifix in his free hand and, when the police fired at him, he roared out in a voice that all could hear: "In the name of God the Father who created us, reply to that!"

Within thirty minutes Crozier had lost a quarter of his force killed and wounded. The Métis had suffered only five casualties. The North

West Mounted Police were in retreat. The Saskatchewan Rebellion had begun.

3

Sunday, January 11, 1885, was the Prime Minister's seventieth birthday, and on Monday all of Montreal celebrated this anniversary, which also marked his fortieth year in politics. It was almost fifteen years since he had promised British Columbia a railway to the Pacific, and in that period he had moved from the prime of life to old age. The rangy figure was flabbier; the homely face had lost some of its tautness; the hair was almost white; deep pouches had formed beneath those knowing eyes; the lines around the edges of the sapient lips had deepened; and on the great nose and full cheeks were the tiny purple veins of over-indulgence.

He was a Canadian institution. There were many at that birthday celebration in Montreal who were grandparents, yet could not remember a time when Macdonald had not been in politics. The reports of his impending retirement through illness, fatigue, incompetence, scandal, or political manoeuvre had appeared regularly in the press for all of the railway days, but Macdonald had outlasted one generation of critics and spawned a second. As he drove through two miles of flaming torches on that "dark soft night," under a sky spangled by exploding rockets, to a banquet in his honour, he was in the mellowest of moods. In his speech he could not help adding to the eulogies that he heard on all sides about the great national project, which was nearing completion. "In the whole annals of railway construction there has been nothing to equal it," he said. Only a few of those in attendance – George Stephen was one – could appreciate the irony of that statement. The Prime Minister might just as easily have been referring to the immensity of the financial crisis that the railway faced.

Just the previous Friday, Stephen had dispatched one of his frantic wires to the Prime Minister: "Imminent danger of sudden crisis unless we can find means to meet pressing demands." That week, rumours of the company's financial straits began to leak out. Within a fortnight the stock was down below 38; not long after it hit a new low of 33 1/3.

Stephen had worked out with Tupper and Macdonald a scheme whereby the unissued stock of the CPR would be cancelled by government legislation, the lien on the railway removed, and a more or less equivalent amount of cash raised by mortgage bonds applied to the entire main line of the railway, with principal and interest on them guaranteed by the government. About half the cash from these bonds would be used to help pay off the loan of 1884. The rest would go to the company as a loan to pay for expenditures not included in the original contract. The remainder of the 1884 loan would be paid off in land grant bonds.

Financially, it was an ingenious scheme. Politically it was disastrous. The previous year, Blake had taunted the Government about the CPR loan: "Don't call it a loan. You know we shall never see a penny of this money again." Macdonald could foresee the hazards of allowing Blake to cry: "We told you so!" He was also an older and wearier man. The picture of Macdonald in 1885 is that of a leader who has lost his way, stumbling from one crisis to another, propped up by bolder spirits within his cabinet and by the entreaties of men like Stephen and Van Horne. His policy of delay, which from time to time had worked in his favour, was disastrous in 1885; it brought bloodshed to the North West and came within an hour of wrecking the CPR.

Stephen's letters to the Prime Minister had taken on a waspish, old womanish quality. "It is as clear as noonday, Sir John," he wrote in January, "that unless you yourself say what should be done, nothing but disaster will result. . . ." But Old Tomorrow would not say. Stephen was almost at the end of his tether – or thought he was: "I feel *my* ability to save [the railway] has gone. I am sorry to confess this even to myself."

The horrifying prospect of the April dividend hung like a spectre over the CPR executive committee. The company's books were about to close. If it did not advertise the dividend, the world would assume that the Canadian Pacific was bankrupt. Again, the only hope was the government. Surely it would come to the assistance of the company on a temporary basis, making an advance on supplies before the end of January: those funds could be paid back out of the monthly estimates. Stephen wired Macdonald on January 20: "The dividend must be cabled to night. . . . Can I trust to this? Please answer. I cannot delay advertizing dividend any longer."

Now the Prime Minister was forced into a corner. He must break the news to Stephen that there was no hope of further assistance. He faced a revolt in his cabinet; three ministers were opposed to further relief and one of these, Archibald McLelan, the Nova Scotian who was Minister of Fisheries, was pledged to resign if any further public monies were advanced to the CPR. The Prime Minister wired Stephen that there was little chance of legislation that session. He would, however, be able to carry an advance of enough money to pay the dividend if it would enable Stephen to postpone matters until 1886.

This was worse than no answer at all. As Macdonald himself knew, the railway could not stay afloat until 1886. Stephen realized what he must do.

In one of his directors' meetings, Stephen, in a speech that Van Horne later characterized as the finest he had ever heard, turned to Smith and said, simply: "If we fail, you and I, Donald, must not be left with a dollar of personal fortune." Smith had silently agreed. Now the two Scotsmen pledged the remainder of their joint fortunes and all their personal assets – everything they possessed – to raise the six hundred and fifty thousand dollars necessary to pay the dividend and an additional one million dollars on a five-month note to provide the short-term funds the company would need to carry it over the coming weeks.

When the treasury officers arrived at his new home on Drummond Street to take an inventory of his personal belongings, Stephen stood quietly by. He carefully examined the long list of his material possessions acquired over a period of thirty-five years in Canada – everything from his marble statuary to his household linen – and then, in the words of an eyewitness, "without a flicker of an eyelid signed it all away."

It was a remarkable act, given the business morality of that day, or indeed of any day, as Stephen himself well knew. What he and Smith had done was "simply absurd on any kind of business grounds." Among the various United States transcontinental lines, bankruptcies had been the rule, but the directors and promoters had rarely lost a penny. But Stephen had not embarked on the Canadian Pacific project so much for profit as for the sheer financial adventure, which he loved, and probably also for kudos. The thing he prized most was his reputation; the idea that he might be the means whereby his friends and business associates would lose money bothered him far more than the possible financial ruin he now courted. It was not enough that he be a man of honour in the business world; he must be *seen* to be a man of honour. If the CPR crashed, Stephen must crash with it.

Donald Smith remained, as always, imperturbable, but Stephen was becoming more emotional as the days wore on. At one point he began to cry while sitting in Collingwood Schreiber's office. His tears of despair were the outward sign of an inner sense of impending personal doom. ". . . I am not *sure* of *myself* being able to stand the strain for an indefinite time," he confessed to Macdonald. "I have had warnings of which no body knows but myself which I will fight against to conceal to the last."

No such melodramatic disclosures issued from Smith's compressed lips. If he had physical warnings, he never betrayed them; if he had emotions, he never revealed them. Storm after storm had broken around that frosty, weathered head, but Smith had never cracked or indicated that he cared. He was a lonely man, subject to considerable gossip about his "strange and complicated" family relationships. But he was always present in the background when needed, as solid and unmoving as the great rock of Craigellachie; and Stephen undoubtedly drew strength from that presence.

The two Scotsmen could not, unaided, save the railway with a million dollars. The demands of the contractors would consume that sum in a few weeks. Already the three-month notes given to satisfy clamorous creditors were coming due and Macdonald was still vacillating. "How it will end God knows," the Prime Minister said, "but I wish I were well out of it." Even the normally ebullient Van Horne was in a private state of gloom. Outwardly he remained supremely confident. "Go sell your boots, and buy C P R stock," he told one worried creditor. Inwardly he must have had his doubts. The absence of the pay car was threatening to close down the railway. At Beavermouth on the Columbia, there was strike talk. On Lake Superior, men were threatening to lynch a contractor whom they blamed for holding back their wages.

Van Horne's own future was secure enough. As a friend told him at the time, he could always return to the United States, where several good posts were available for him. To this suggestion he made a characteristic answer: "I'm not going to the States. I'm not going to leave the work I've begun, and I am going to see it through. I'm here to stay and I can't afford to leave until this work is done no matter what position is open to me."

On March 18, Stephen made an official application to the Privy Council for a loan of five million dollars. It was rejected, and Stephen vowed he would leave Ottawa, never to return. The railway was finished. Its directors were ruined men.

Van Horne this time made no attempt to hide his feelings. Collingwood Schreiber recalled a scene in his office – "the only time I believe his iron nerve was ever shaken" – when the general manager very slowly and very softly revealed the depth of his despair: "Say, if the Government doesn't give it [the loan] we are finished." Van Horne, who had never cast a vote in his life, felt that he had been beaten at the one game he did not understand – the game of politics. He had come within an ace of commanding the greatest single transportation system in the world, and now his ambition had been thwarted by a combination of subtle forces which he could not control. No one had seen him show his feelings to such an extent since that dark day, so many years before, when his small son William had died, and his friend John Egan, driving him in absolute silence to the funeral, noticed a tear fall onto his hand.

And then, as if the railroad itself had given the cue, succour came from the North West in the most perverse and unexpected form. The Métis under Louis Riel had raised the flag of insurrection.

Earlier that year, Van Horne had held a significant conversation with John Henry Pope, who had talked about a possible prairie revolt.

"I wish your CPR was through," Pope said.

Van Horne immediately declared he could get troops from Kingston or Quebec, where the two permanent force units were stationed, to Qu'Appelle in ten days.

In late March, Van Horne was reflecting on that promise: *How could the government refuse to aid a railway that sped troops out to the prairies, took the Métis unawares, and crushed a rebellion?* He immediately offered to the Privy Council the services of the railway to move troops, if needed, from Ottawa to Qu'Appelle. He made only one stipulation: he and not the army was to be in complete control of food and transport. His experience in moving troops during the American Civil War had taught him to avoid divided authority and red-tape interference.

It sounded like a foolhardy pledge. There were four gaps, totalling eighty-six miles, in the unfinished line north of Lake Superior. Between the unconnected strips of hastily laid track was a frozen waste. Could men, horses, guns, and supplies be shuttled over the primitive tote roads which crossed that meeting place of blizzards? The members of the Council refused to believe it.

"Has anyone got a better plan?" Macdonald asked. There was no answer. Van Horne was told to prepare for a massive movement of men, animals, arms, and equipment.

The first intimations of the impending Saskatchewan rebellion appeared in fragmentary reports in Ontario newspapers on March 23. By the following day, Van Horne's plan was in operation, although Joseph-Philippe-René-Adolphe Caron, the Minister of Militia and Defence, was still unsure it would work. The engagement at Duck Lake took place on March 26; when the news burst upon the capital, the country was immediately mobilized.

In Ottawa on the very morning of the Duck Lake tragedy, George Stephen had just finished scribbling a note to Macdonald confessing failure and asking that the Privy Council decision rejecting his proposal be put into writing. There was nothing more that the CPR president could do. The fate of the CPR now lay with the railway itself. If Van Horne's gamble worked, then the politicians and the public would have the best possible proof that the presence of a transcontinental line could hold the nation together in time of trouble.

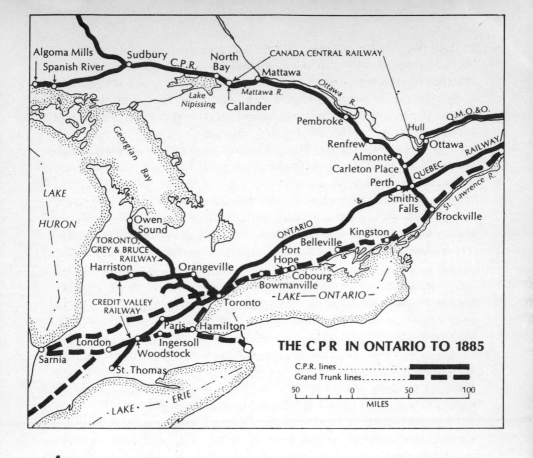

THE C P R IN ONTARIO TO 1885

C.P.R. lines ....
Grand Trunk lines ....

50   0   50   100

MILES

4

On March 27, all of settled Canada learned from its newpapers that a bloody rebellion had broken out in the North West. Ten members of Crozier's mixed force of police and volunteers lay dead at Duck Lake. Thirteen more were wounded, two mortally. Dumont's victory was beyond dispute. The Indians were about to rise. Prince Albert, Fort Carlton, Batoche, Fort Pitt, and perhaps Fort Qu'Appelle, Calgary, Edmonton, Moose Jaw, and Regina, were all threatened. A wave of apprehension, anger, patriotism, and excitement washed over eastern Canada.

The government had already called out the permanent force – A and B batteries from Quebec and Kingston. On March 27, several militia regiments were ordered to be ready to move immediately to the North West. This aroused a flurry of speculation: How on earth were they to get there? There would be 3,324 men in all.

When the news was confirmed that the entire force was to be shipped west on the new railroad, a kind of frenzy seized the country. To a considerable extent the social life of the towns revolved around the militia. Now these men were parading through the streets for the first time in earnest. Never before had Canadians witnessed the kind of spectacular scenes that took place during late March and early April – the cheers for Queen and Country, the blare of martial music, the oceans of flapping banners, the young men in scarlet and green marching behind the colours, the main streets jammed with waving thousands, the roll of drums, the troop trains puffing through the small towns and off into the Unknown – the singing, the cheering, the weeping and the kissing and the bitter-sweet good-byes. All this sound and spectacle, pumped up by a fanfaronade of military oratory – together with the terrible news on April 2 of a massacre of priests and civilians by Big Bear's Indians at Frog Lake – kept the country on an emotional binge for the better part of a fortnight.

The first units called out were the Queen's Own Rifles, the Royal Grenadiers, and the Infantry School, all of Toronto. The scenes on Monday morning, March 30, were chaotic and extravagant. It seemed as if every single citizen who could walk or crawl had come from miles around to line the route of march from the drill shed to Union Station. King Street was a living mass of humanity. Thousands jammed the rooftops. Hundreds offered vainly to pay for positions in the flag-decked windows. Women and children fainted continually and had to be removed by the police. Many were weeping.

About 11:30, the cheering of the troops was heard from the drill shed, and the entire mob of more than ten thousand broke into an answering cry. The cheering moved like a wave along King Street; the crush made it impossible to move. Then somebody spotted the first uniform – that of a member of the Governor-General's Body Guard on horseback, followed by Colonel William Dillon Otter, marching on foot at the head of his men.

Down the streets the young men came, as the crowd around them and above them, before them and behind them, shouted themselves hoarse. Bouquets of flowers drifted down from the windows above. Handkerchiefs fluttered. A thousand flags flapped in the breeze. Those who could not move along beside the troops began to cry "Good-bye, Good-bye!" as the musicians struck up the song that became a kind of theme all over Canada that month, "The Girl I Left Behind Me."

To the foot of York Street, by the station, the people had been pouring in an unending stream. The immense crowd filled the Esplanade from one end of the station to the other, swarming over the roofs of freight cars and perching in every window. The morning had started warm and pleasant; then, as if to mirror the crowd's changing mood, a heavy sleet began to fall; but the people did not move to shelter.

Jammed into the cars, the men leaned out of the windows and

waved. The train began to crawl forward. Above the continual roaring, individual good-byes could be heard. Then the band of the Queen's Own struck up "Auld Lang Syne" and, as the engine bell began to ring, the men joined in. Slowly the train drew away through the yards, where the top of every freight and passenger car was black with waving well-wishers, and then through the driving sleet and the whirling snow towards the dark forests and the unballasted track of the new Canada.

These scenes were repeated over and over again during the days that followed. In Kingston, hundreds crammed the town square to greet the incoming troops. In Montreal, the crush of onlookers was so great that a vast double window burst out from a three-storey building, injuring twelve persons. In Ottawa, the station platform was "a dense mass of enthusiastic, patriotic, jostling, laughing, shouting and war-fever-stricken individuals of all ages, sizes, sexes and complexions." In Quebec, "the scene presented beggars description."

Only the Governor-General's Body Guard, the oldest cavalry regiment in Canada, departed in comparative quiet and secrecy, the authorities fearing for the safety of the horses. The Guard was kept on the *qui vive* for several days while final arrangements were made to get the horses over the gaps in the line. When the regiment left, their colonel, George T. Denison, and his officers had not slept for three nights, having remained booted and spurred and ready to move for all of that time.

The men from the farms and cities were young enough to laugh at the kind of ordeal they would shortly face. They were also woefully under-trained. The York Rangers of Toronto looked more like sheep than soldiers. In Kingston it was noticed that the members of the composite Midland regiment were badly drilled. Among the 65th, in Montreal, there were men who had never fired so much as a blank cartridge.

Few battalions were properly equipped. The belts and knapsacks of the Queen's Own had done duty in the Crimean War. Their rifles were ancient Snider Enfields, most of them totally unreliable. The clothing of the York Rangers was old and rotten, the knapsacks so badly packed that a day's marching would break men down. Several of the Midland companies had no knapsacks at all and were forced to wrap their belongings in paper. Others had no helmets. One battalion set off without uniforms. Many of the 65th lacked trousers, tunics, and rifles; indeed, there was not a company in that battalion properly equipped for service – ammunition was so scarce that each man could be alloted only three rounds. Nobody, it appeared, had ever considered the possibility that one day his unit would march off to war.

The trains sped off at staggered intervals towards Dog Lake, where

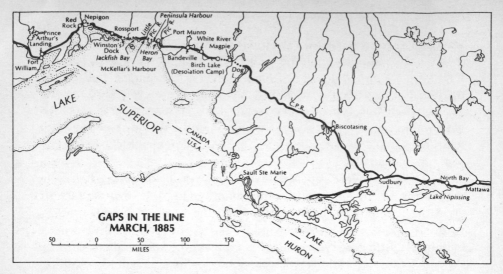

GAPS IN THE LINE
MARCH, 1885

the real ordeal would begin. The officers, at Van Horne's insistence, were given first-class accommodation even though he doubted he could collect for it. But for the sake of the railway's long-term image it was "important that the report of the officers as to the treatment of the troops on our line should be most favourable." As for the men themselves, Van Horne ensured that there would, whenever possible, be mountains of food and gallons of hot coffee. Better than anybody else, he knew what the troops were about to face. He could not protect them from the chill rides in open flatcars and sleighs, or from the numbing treks across the glare ice, but he could make sure that his army marched on a full stomach.

At Dog Lake, the men left the comfort of the cars and were packed into sleighs which set off behind teams of horses down the uncompleted right of way or along tote roads that circumvented the unbridged ravines and unfilled cuts. In some places the sleighs encountered boulders seven or eight feet high; in others they pitched into holes as deep as graves – the occupants flung over the dashboards and into the steaming haunches of the terrified horses. "No description," wrote one man, "could give an idea of the terrible roads through the woods." One sleigh overturned no fewer than thirteen times. Men were submerged in six feet of powdery snow, often with all their equipment. One member of the London Fusiliers was completely buried under an avalanche of baggage; a comrade was almost smothered when a horse toppled onto him.

The men crouched in the bottoms of the sleighs, wrapped in their greatcoats, but nothing could keep out the cold. For some units, it was so intense that any man who left any part exposed even for a few minutes suffered frostbite. "What they passed through that night all hope will never require to be repeated," a reporter travelling with the Grenadiers wrote back.

376

The entire gap between Dog Lake and Birch Lake took some nine hours to negotiate, and at the end stood a lonely huddle of shacks, which was swiftly and accurately named "Desolation Camp." It deserved its title. A fire had swept through the scrub timber leaving the trees a spectral white, and a cutting wind, rattling through the skeletal branches, added to the general feeling of despair. The only real shelter was a tattered tent, not large enough to accommodate the scores who sought refuge in it. Yet some men had to remain there for hours, their drenched clothing freezing to their skins in temperatures that dropped as low as thirty-five below. The 10th Royal Grenadiers arrived at five one morning and waited seventeen hours for a train without even the warmth of a fire to greet them.

Some members of the Queen's Own were rendered hysterical by the cold; when the trains finally arrived they had to be led on board, uncomprehending and uncaring. Although most troops had had very little sleep since leaving civilization, they were denied it at Desolation Camp because sleep could mean certain death when the thermometer dropped. The Halifax Battalion, the last to arrive, had to endure a freezing rain, which soaked their garments and turned their great-coats into boards. When men in this condition dropped in their tracks, the guards were ordered to rouse them by any means, pull them to their feet, and bring them over to the fires to dry. There they stood, shivering and half-conscious, until the flatcars arrived.

In these cars, sleep again was all but impossible. There was no roof, and the wind and snow blew in through the crevices between the planks. Rough benches ran lengthwise and here the men sat, each with his two issue blankets, packed tightly together or huddled lengthwise on the floor.

For the Governor-General's Body Guard, the journey was complicated by the presence of the animals. The men were obliged to gather railway ties and construct flimsy ramps up which the horses could be led to the cars. The boards were sheathed in ice and had to be covered with blankets so that the animals would not lose their footing. All had to be watered and fed before the men could rest. Nor could they be moved by sleigh; the cavalrymen rode or led their animals the entire distance. When the cavalry moved by train, the horses were placed in exactly the same kind of flatcars as the men. Unloading them occupied hours, for it was necessary to remove all the hind shoes to prevent injuries to men and steeds.

The track that led from Desolation Camp to the next gap at Port Munro was of the most perfunctory construction. The ties had been laid directly onto the snow and in some sections where a thaw had set in, four or five ties in succession, spiked to the rails, would be held clear off the ground for several inches. Trains were thrown off this section of track daily and the rails were slowly being bent by the heavy passage. It was rarely possible to exceed five miles an hour. "It was," a member of the Queen's Own Rifles wrote home, "about the longest night any of us ever put in."

At Bandeville, the half-way point, the men were fed sandwiches and hot tea. Some were so stiff with cold they had to be lifted out of the cars. Others were so bone weary that when they reached the warmth of the eating house they dropped off into a sleep so deep it was almost impossible to awaken them to eat. After Bandeville, the troops faced another chilling seven hours before End of Track at Port Munro was reached. Here, in a deep, natural harbour, lay the schooner *Breck,* "open at both ends and leaky into the bargain." It was capable of accommodating some two hundred men who slumbered in comparative comfort, huddled together in the hold on mattresses composed of equal parts of hay and dirt, and later of water.

There followed a forced march across the glare ice of Lake Superior to the next piece of track at McKellar's Harbour, a journey of some eight hours. Here, for many, the sun proved to be the enemy. For those who had been issued with snow glasses the glare on the ice was searing enough; they arrived at their destination with their faces scorched and blistered sometimes almost beyond recognition. Others managed to make eye-coverings, Indian-fashion, out of strips of birchbark with thin slits cut into them. But there were some who were rendered painfully blind; Colonel Otter himself was one of these.

The troops, buffeted by piercing winds on one side and blistered by the sun's glare on the other, were eventually strung out for seven miles across the lake. Marching was almost impossible on the glassy surface. Then, after ten miles, the texture changed and deep cuts, broken blocks of ice, and rocks frozen into the surface began to lacerate the feet of the men and officers, especially those who had left home in light shoes. Some threw their kits away, bit by bit; some collapsed in their tracks; others became temporarily deranged; one man was ruptured. The baggage sleighs picked up the casualties.

"I can tell you I'll never forget that march," a member of the Queen's Own Rifles wrote home. "We dared not stop an instant as we were in great danger of being frozen, although the sun was taking the skin off our faces. One man of our company went mad and one of the regulars went blind from snow glare."

Those units that travelled the same gap by night endured equally fearful conditions. Any man who drifted away from the column knew that he faced almost certain death. To prevent this, guards were assigned to ride around the column to head off drifters and stragglers. At that, the night was so dark and the way so difficult that the guide appointed to lead the troops across lost his way and the ordeal was lengthened by several hours.

The travail of the cavalry was again far more strenuous. The infantry was marched across the ice as far as McKellar's Harbour, where a short piece of line had been laid to Jackfish Bay. But because of the nuisance of loading and unloading horses, the Governor-General's Body Guard decided to ride or walk their steeds the full distance. For the last twenty miles they faced "a vast prairie or desert of ice," with no track of any kind. The surface was obscured by a crust under which two or three inches of water lay concealed. Above the crust there was a blanket of light snow. This treacherous surface was broken by patches of glare ice. Through this chill morass the horses, all of them lacking hind shoes, slipped, floundered, and struggled for mile after mile.

An equally uncomfortable set of circumstances presented themselves to the York Rangers, who after crossing the same gap in a driving sleet storm and trudging up to their knees in a gruel of snow and water, were faced with a six-hour wait for the flatcars. These long waits without shelter were among the cruelest privations suffered by the soldiers *en route* to the North West. The Queen's Own endured three: a two-hour wait in a blinding sleet storm when a train broke down at Carleton Place, a nine-hour wait in the freezing cold at McKellar's Harbour, and a four-hour wait in driving sleet at Winston's Dock. Most of these waiting periods were spent standing up; it was too cold and too wet to sit down.

Out of Jackfish Bay, where the next gap began, the dog-tired troops, gazing from the rims of the cutters, began to gain some understanding of Van Horne's feat of railway construction. There they could see the gaping mouth of one of the longest tunnels on the road, piercing a solid wall of rock, one hundred and fifty feet high, for five hundred feet. For miles on end the roadbed had been blasted from the billion-year-old schists and granites – chipped into the sheer surface of the dark cliffs or hacked right through the spiny ridges by means of deep cuts. In some places it seemed as if the whole side of a mountain had been ripped asunder by dynamite and flung into the deep, still waters of the lake.

The voyage between Winston's Dock and Nepigon was again made on rails laid directly over the snow. The scenery grew grander as the cars crawled along and the soldiers began to stand up in their seats to see "sights which we will never forget" – the road torn out of the solid rock for mile after mile, skirting the very lip of the lake, from whose shores the mountains rose up directly for hundreds of feet above the track.

There was one final gap yet to come, and for many it would be the most terrible of all. This was the short march over the ice of the lake between Nepigon and Red Rock. It was no more than ten miles but it took some troops six hours.

The 10th Grenadiers started out in the evening along a trail so narrow that any attempt to move in column of fours had to be abandoned. It was almost impossible to stay on the track, and yet a single misstep caused a man to be buried to his neck in deep snow. When the troops emerged from the woods and onto the lake they were met by a pitiless rain that seemed to drive through the thickest clothing. Every step a man took brought him into six inches of icy porridge. To move through this slush the men were forced to raise their knees almost to their waists, as if marking time; in effect, they waded the entire distance. Now and then a man would tumble exhausted into the slush and lie immovable and unnoticed until somebody stumbled over him. Captain A. Hamlyn Todd, of the Governor-General's Foot Guards, counted some forty men lying in the snow, many of them face down, completely played out. Some of these could not even speak. A member of the York Rangers described one such case: "On the way across one of the boys of the 35th was so fagged out that he laid down on the sleigh and could not move an inch. Captain Thomson asked him to move to one side but not one inch would he stir, so he caught hold of him like a bag and baggage, and tossed him to one side to let him pass."

When Red Rock was finally reached, the men were like zombies. They stood, uncomprehending, in ice-water ankle-deep, waiting for the trains; and when these arrived they tumbled into the cars and dropped in their tracks, lying on the floor, twisted on the seats all of a heap, sleeping where they fell. There was tea ready for them all but, cold and wet as they were, many did not have the strength to drink it. The ordeal was at an end; the track, as they well knew, lay unbroken all the way to their destination at Qu'Appelle. There would be no more marching until the coulees of Saskatchewan were reached – time enough then to reckon with Dumont's sharpshooters. For the moment, at least, they had no worries; and so, like men already dead, they slept.

Chapter
Nine

THE
LAST
SPIKE

1

William Van Horne was not a man given to rash or boastful promises. When he said that he could move troops from eastern Canada to Qu'Appelle in ten days, he was actually giving himself a cushion of twenty-four hours. The first troops to leave Ottawa on March 28 arrived in Winnipeg exactly one week later. Within two days they were on the drill ground at Qu'Appelle. Two hundred and thirty miles to the north at Batoche, Riel was in control. Battleford was under siege by Poundmaker's Indians. Big Bear's Crees, following the massacre at Frog Lake, were roaming the country around Fort Pitt, killing, looting, and taking prisoners. But by mid-April, not much more than a fortnight after Duck Lake, the entire Field Force, save for the Halifax Battalion, was in Saskatchewan and ready to march.

The rebellion wrenched the gaze of settled Canada out to the prairie country and focused it on the railway. Every major newspaper sent a war correspondent with the troops. For week after week in the columns of the daily press, as the journalists digressed on the grandeur of the scenery, the impressive size of the newly created cities, and the wonders of the plains, Canadians were treated to a continuing geography lesson about a land that some had scarcely considered part of the nation. Until 1885, it had been as a foreign country; now their boys were fighting in it and for it, and soon anyone who wanted to see it could do so for the price of a railway ticket.

The Halifax Battalion was especially delighted to discover so many fellow Nova Scotians working along the line and living in the western towns. "I was surprised at the size of the city of Winnipeg," a Nova Scotian wrote home, "and the magnificent character of the buildings and the splendid wide streets, three times as wide as in Halifax. The stone and brick stores on every hand indicate a surprising degree of enterprise in this city. . . . There are a great many Nova Scotians in both the police and fire departments." No longer would these Maritimers think of the North West as the exclusive property of Ontario.

Until the coming of the railway, all of the North West had been like a great desert with scattered oases of population, each sufficient unto itself. Now, the cross-fertilization process had begun. A new kind of Canadian, the "Westerner," was making his first impact on the men from the sober East. He belonged to a more open-handed and less rigid society; over the century that followed he would help to change the country.

One war correspondent's description of a prairie town mirrored the astonishment of an Ontario city man on first coming up against western life:

"Here is where the man who has a turn that way can study the human face divine, and the human dress astonishing. Men well dressed, fully dressed, commonly dressed; awfully dressed, shabbily dressed, partly dressed; men sober, nearly sober, half drunk, nearly drunk, quite drunk, frightfully drunk, howling drunk, dead drunk; men from Canada, the States, the United Kingdom and from almost every state in Europe; men enormously rich and frightfully poor, but all having a free and easy manner which is highly refreshing to a man fresh from the east who is accustomed to the anxious expressions of men in our silent streets at home."

If Riel's rebellion helped change eastern attitudes to the prairies, it also helped change them towards the CPR. Van Horne was later to remark that the railway should have erected a statue to the Métis leader. As early as April 6, he was able to tell a friend in Scotland that "there is no more talk about the construction of the Lake Superior line having been a useless expenditure of money, nor about the road having been built too quickly. Most people are inclined to think it would have been better had it been built three or four weeks quicker."

Yet and Van Horne must have felt the irony of the situation – the CPR was in worse financial shape than ever. It had cost almost a million dollars to ship the troops west, and that bill was not immediately collectable. It was a strange situation: at the moment of its greatest triumph, while the troops were speeding west on the new steel to the applause of the nation, the CPR's financial scaffolding was collapsing, and scarcely anybody in Ottawa appeared to be concerned.

The president himself wanted out; Ottawa had become painful to him. George Stephen was determined to shake the slush of the capital from his boots, never to return.

On March 26, the day of the bloody engagement at Duck Lake, he went to his room in the Russell House and packed his bags. He had already written to the Prime Minister explaining that, as a result of a conversation that morning, he was satisfied the government could not aid the railway. There was in that letter none of the desperation that characterized so much of his correspondence with Macdonald. Stephen was drained of emotion; all that remained was a sense of resignation: "I need not repeat how sorry I am that this should be the result of all our efforts to give Canada a railway to the Pacific ocean. But I am supported by the conviction that I have done all that could be done to obtain it." That was it. The great adventure was over. Stephen prepared to return to Montreal to personal ruin and public disgrace.

Among the crowd in the lobby that evening were a CPR official, George H. Campbell, and two cabinet ministers – Mackenzie Bowell, Minister of Customs (who had originally opposed the railway loan), and Senator Frank Smith, Minister without Portfolio. Campbell was one of several CPR men lobbying Government members. Bowell had already been converted; Smith did not need to be. A Toronto wholesale grocer and supplier to the CPR, he was personally involved in railways as well as in allied forms of transportation.

Smith spotted Stephen walking towards the office to pay his bill, and, dismayed at his downcast appearance, hurried towards him, urging him not to leave. "No," said Stephen, "I am leaving at once; there is no use – I have just come from Earnscliffe and Sir John has given a final refusal – nothing more can be done. What will happen tomorrow I do not know – the proposition is hopeless."

But Smith, whose powers of persuasion were considerable, managed to win Stephen over, promising that he would make a final effort that evening to change the Prime Minister's mind. He and Bowell drove to Earnscliffe for a midnight interview, leaving Campbell with orders to remain with Stephen and not to allow any other person access to him.

Though Smith held no cabinet portfolio, he was one of the most powerful politicians at Ottawa, a handsome, large-hearted Irishman with a vast following among the Roman Catholics of Ontario. Macdonald believed that he could personally deliver the Catholic vote in Ontario, or withhold it. If any man could swing the Prime Minister and the Cabinet, it was Smith.

It was the second time within a year that a midnight attempt had been made to reprieve the CPR but Smith was less successful than Pope had been in 1884. Macdonald may have been shaken, but he would not move. Nevertheless, when Smith returned at 2 a.m. he was able to convince Stephen that he should not give up the ghost. Guarded by the vigilant Campbell, whose instructions were to keep him incommunicado, the CPR president agreed to revise his proposal for relief while Smith worked on the Cabinet. It was said that for Campbell the three days that followed were the most anxious of his life. He was the constant companion of "a man torn with anguish and remorse whose heart seemed to be breaking with compassion for friends whose downfall he felt himself responsible for."

Stephen had his revised proposition ready for the Privy Council

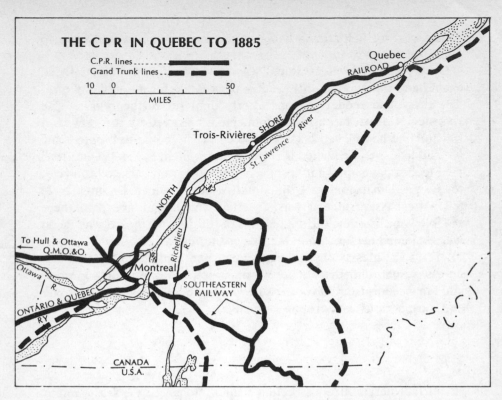

THE C P R IN QUEBEC TO 1885

C.P.R. lines..........
Grand Trunk lines...

10   0   50
                 MILES

Quebec
RAILROAD

Trois-Rivières SHORE

St. Lawrence River

NORTH

To Hull & Ottawa
Q.M.O.&O.

Ottawa R.

ONTARIO & QUEBEC RY

Montreal

Richelieu R.

SOUTHEASTERN
RAILWAY

CANADA
U.S.A.

the following day. That it was not rejected out of hand must be seen as a victory for Frank Smith. McLelan might resign if the loan went through, but Smith made it clear that he would resign if it did not; and Smith controlled more votes.

Over the next fortnight, as the troops from eastern Canada were shuttled off to the plains, a series of protracted negotiations took place regarding the exact terms of the proposed loan. With every passing day, Stephen grew more distraught. The government had him in a corner and was exacting harsher terms than he had expected. It was insisting, for instance, that the CPR take over the North Shore line between Montreal and Quebec City. Under pressure from Ottawa, the Grand Trunk could be persuaded to give up the line to the Quebec government which, in turn, would lease it back to the CPR at an annual cost of $778,000. It was doubtful, Stephen thought, if it could earn one hundred thousand dollars annually, it was so run down. (Later that year the CPR bought the line outright.)

But there was no help for it. Reports were coming in of a serious strike at Beavermouth, where an angry mob of navvies was on the march. Stephen warned Tilley of the "utter impossibility of averting an immediate & disastrous collapse" unless some way could be found to give the company temporary aid to tide it over while the matter was being discussed at painful length in the Cabinet and in Parliament.

Tilley was not helpful; he believed the government would have to take over the railway.

Once again the CPR president was at the end of his tether. Once again he told Macdonald: ". . . it is impossible for me to carry on." The delay had rendered him "utterly unfit for further work." He was sick at heart, fed up with politicians, betrayed by the very man in whom he had placed his confidence. Yet he could not quite bring himself to leave. He waited four more days. Silence. Finally, on April 15, Stephen gave up. That evening he took the train back to Montreal, to the great mansion on Drummond Street in which he must have felt a trespasser since it was, in effect, no longer his. And there the following morning the dimensions of the disaster the railway faced were summed up for him in a curt wire from Van Horne:

"Have no means paying wages, pay car can't be sent out, and unless we get immediate relief we must stop. Please inform Premier and Finance Minister. Do not be surprised, or blame me if an immediate and most serious catastrophe happens."

2

Of all the mercurial construction camps along the CPR's mountain line, the one at the mouth of the Beaver River was the most volatile. It was dominated by saloons – forty of them – all selling illegal whiskey at fifty cents a glass, and it was awake most of the night to the sound of dancing, singing, and revelry.

By late March, the complaints over lack of pay began to gather into a discontented rumble. The men had been content to go without wages in the winter, but by early spring funds were needed for homesteads in Manitoba, Minnesota, and Dakota. Inspector Sam Steele counselled patience. He feared that a strike, if it came, would swiftly develop into a riot, sparked by a large number of "ruffians, gamblers and murderers from the Northern Pacific who had left it on the completion of that road." He wired the Prime Minister that a strike was imminent but got no action. Macdonald had more serious troubles in Saskatchewan on his mind. At this critical point Steele was felled by a massive attack of Rocky Mountain fever; he was so ill he could scarcely lift his head from the pillow. With the strongest force for law and order thus incapacitated, the men struck and began marching by the thousands up the line towards Beavermouth.

The news of the work stoppage had barely reached the Mountie when a frantic wire arrived from the Mayor of Calgary: the entire North West seemed to be up in arms; Riel had struck; the Crees were on the verge of joining the rebellion; Crowfoot and his braves were camped on the very edge of Calgary. "For God's sake, come; there is danger of an attack by the Blackfeet!" Everything seemed to be crowding in on Steele at once. He could only reply that the situation at Beavermouth was so dangerous that he could not spare a man. He had only eight as it was.

Track-laying, which had come to a halt with winter's onset, was about to recommence. Carpenters were strung out on top of the great Mountain Creek trestle, trying to complete it before the track reached that point. The strikers massed on the edge of the ravine below and called to the men to stop work and come down off the bridge. The carpenters, intent on finishing the job, refused. One of the strikers seized an axe and slashed the rope that held the block and tackle used to hoist bridge materials to the top of the trestle. That meant the carpenters could do no further work.

The strikers moved resolutely on to Beavermouth, gathering strength as they went. The ailing Steele received a deputation and warned them that "if they committed any act of violence, and were not orderly, in the strictest sense of the word, I would inflict upon the offenders the severest punishment the law would allow me."

Three hundred armed strikers began to police the line, bringing all work to a halt. A trainload of men sent to End of Track was driven back. James Ross himself mounted the engine, told the engineer to put on all steam, and ran it through the armed mob as bullets whistled past his cab. The train entered the narrow canyon of the Beaver, an easy place to defend with a few men. Here the tracklaying began again.

On came the strikers, firing as they advanced, while the tracklayers worked in the canyon. Steele's second in command, a thickset sergeant with the appropriate name of Fury, drew his party across the mouth of the canyon to meet the advance. When they arrived, Fury announced that he would shoot the first man to cross the line. An uproar followed, but the strikers were cowed and returned to Beavermouth, allowing the tracklayers to finish their day's labour.

Sergeant Fury returned to his bedridden superior to find that one of the constables, attempting to arrest a contractor named Behan for being drunk and disorderly, had been driven off by the mob. "We must take the man at any cost," Steele told him. "It will never do to let the remainder of the gang know they can play with us." Fury accordingly set off with two constables to arrest the offending contractor, whom they found in a saloon "in the midst of a gang of drunken companions." The constables seized their quarry and dragged him out, but an angry mob of two hundred armed men retrieved Behan and the police were forced to retreat.

Fury, badly mauled, returned to ask Steele for orders. "Take your

387

revolvers," Steele said, "and shoot anyone who interferes with the arrest!"

Events were now building to a climax. Steele was too weak to watch what happened, but the local stipendiary magistrate, George Hope Johnston, gave him a running account from the barracks window. He watched Fury and three policemen start off for the bridge across the Beaver, enter the log town, and disappear between the cabins. A few moments later the sharp crack of gun-fire echoed through the valley.

"There is one gone to hell, Steele," Johnston said.

Sick or not, Steele had to see for himself. He crawled to the window in time to see two of his men dragging a prisoner across the bridge. The prisoner was "fighting like a fiend, while a woman in scarlet followed. . . with wild shrieks and curses."

It was time for Steele to take over. He called on Johnston to get the Riot Act and, seizing a Winchester from the constable on guard at the jail, ran to the bridge, levelled his rifle at the crowd, and told the strikers to halt.

"Look at the _____ ," someone cried; "his own death bed makes no difference to him!" Nonetheless, everybody stopped. One of the constables knocked the struggling prisoner insensible and pulled him by the collar the rest of the way. The woman in red started to scream: "You red-coated _____ !" Steele turned to his men: "Take her in, too!" Then he started forward onto the bridge to face the sullen mob.

Johnston had been forced to kick the orderly-room door in, the constable with the key having been too busy with the riot. He arrived at last with the Riot Act. Said Steele: "Listen to this and keep your hands off your guns, or I will shoot the first man of you who makes a hostile movement." There was silence. Sergeant Fury had already put a bullet into the shoulder of a man who tried to keep him from taking his prisoner.

After the Riot Act was read, Steele spoke again:

"You have taken advantage of the fact that a rebellion has broken out in the North West and that I have only a handful of men, but, as desperate diseases require desperate remedies, and both disease and remedy are here, I warn you that if I find more than twelve of you standing together or any large crowd assembled, I will open fire upon you and mow you down! Now disperse at once and behave yourselves!"

Steele's full force of eight Mounted Police now stood in line behind them, rifles cocked. Steele stood his ground with Johnston and watched the grumbling mob slowly break up. The following morning the town and all the line were "as quiet as a country village on Sunday."

Steele arrested all the ringleaders in the riot, brought them to court, and fined them each one hundred dollars or six months in jail.

There was no further violence. Steele, still convalescent, donned his uniform and headed for Calgary where he was given a unique command. His task was to organize a cavalry detachment and strike off in pursuit of the rebel Cree chieftain, Big Bear. It was, perhaps, the most remarkable case on record of instant recovery from Rocky Mountain fever.

3

When Stephen learned from Van Horne on April 16 that the CPR pay car would not be sent out, he immediately wired the news in cipher to John Henry Pope in Ottawa. Van Horne had hinted at the imminence of a "serious catastrophe." Another riot was likely if wages were again held up. The Minister of Railways was Stephen's last hope.

Pope went straight to the Prime Minister and again pointed out the obvious: if the CPR went bankrupt, the Government could not survive. At last the vacillating party leader was forced into a decision. Until this moment he had believed that any further relief to the company would be politically disastrous. The debate of 1884 had been bad enough but it would be nothing compared to the national uproar occasioned by further public handouts to a faltering railroad. Whichever course Macdonald took, he knew he was going to face a storm. If the CPR collapsed, it would undoubtedly touch off a wave of bankruptcies and personal tragedies – bank failures, entire communities facing depression, the country demoralized by the failure of its great national endeavour. He had two unpalatable choices, but one was slightly less distasteful than the other. With very little heart he decided that, once again, he must help to bail out the CPR.

Fortunately, the mood of the country was beginning to change. Because of the railway, the government had a good chance of localizing the Saskatchewan Rebellion. First, however, there was a nasty wrangle in the caucus. McLelan resigned and Macdonald had to use all his political muscle to bring the party into line; he bluntly promised to resign himself if his followers failed to back his proposal for another loan.

In one crowded week, events took on momentum of their own. The railway still had no money to pay its men. The relief bill could not be passed before a long debate in Parliament. Macdonald privately asked the Bank of Montreal to advance five million dollars to the CPR, explaining that he intended to bring some resolutions before

Parliament regarding financial aid "at an early date." That was not good enough for the bank; it refused to advance a nickel to the faltering company. The same day – April 24 – at Fish Creek, a coulee not far from Batoche, a handful of Métis under Gabriel Dumont fought General Middleton's superior force to a standstill, immobilizing him for a fortnight. There was better news from Battleford, where the siege was finally lifted by Colonel Otter's division. In London three days later, Sir Henry Tyler told a Grand Trunk meeting that the CPR was finished.

On May 1, the reluctant Prime Minister acted. He gave notice to the House of the resolutions he proposed to submit. The following day, there was more bad news from Saskatchewan: Colonel Otter had suffered a defeat at the hands of Poundmaker and his Crees. And still there was to be a delay. Macdonald was determined to postpone the debate on the railway resolutions until he had forced his pet franchise bill through the House. This was a measure that would remove control of the terms of the federal franchise from provincial legislatures. To Stephen, it seemed as if the Prime Minister was putting a petty squabble with the provinces ahead of what he was prone to call "this great national undertaking."

He was beside himself at this politicking. J. J. C. Abbott had "fairly scared" him with the news that it might be five or six weeks before the CPR resolutions became law. The railway could not hold out for anything like that time. It was essential that the government guarantee a loan at the bank. Even a million dollars would help. That sum in Thomas Shaughnessy's hands could give the company perhaps three weeks' breathing space. On May 5, at the government's request, the Bank of Montreal advanced three-quarters of a million dollars. It was not much, but it was something.

The real problem was pay. Both the March and the April wages were due and all along the line the grumblings began to be heard, mingled with reports of real privation. Single men had not been able to pay their board for two months. Merchants began to deny further credit to married employees. In Toronto a number of men were forced to cut themselves down to one meal a day. Everybody from office clerk to dispatcher felt the pinch. For the ordinary labourer, who received only a dollar a day and was therefore unable to save any money, the lack of wages was especially severe.

The listlessness seemed to have seized the employees of the railway in Ontario. They continued to work because they had no recourse. When a group of mechanics at Perth told Van Horne that they would quit work unless the pay car came along, the general manager simply informed them he would close down the works. That message travelling up and down the line killed all talk of a general strike.

In Parliament, the debate on the franchise bill dragged on and on. It was clear that the CPR would have to have a government advance or another bank guarantee if it was to stay alive. Somehow the railway had to find money, not just for wages, but also for the interest payments on the bonds of the Ontario and Quebec Railway, due on the first of June. "If we default," Stephen reminded the Prime Minister on May 12, ". . . then goodbye to the C.P.R. . . ."

The resolution of the CPR's various financial crises was always theatrical, fraught with the same kind of tension that audiences had come to expect from the stage melodramas of the era, in which the heroine was saved at the last instant from the Fate Worse than Death. Such a moment came less than a week before the interest on the O and Q bonds was due. The directors of the company waited breathlessly outside the Privy Council door while the Cabinet argued about guaranteeing another bank loan. In later years, Van Horne liked to describe that scene to his friends:

"It was an awful time. Each one of us felt as if the railway was our own child. . . . We men ourselves had given up twenty per cent of our salaries and had willingly worked, not overtime but double-time, and as we waited in that room, we thought about these things and wondered whether all our toil was going to be wasted or not. . . . At last Joe Pope came with a yellow paper in his hand. He said that the Government was prepared to back the Bank of Montreal to the extent then required. I think we waited until he left the room. I believe we had that much sanity left us! And then we began. We tossed up chairs to the ceiling; we trampled on desks; I believe we danced on tables. I do not fancy that any of us knows now what occurred, and no one who was there can ever remember anything except loud yells of joy and the sound of things breaking!"

Van Horne raced immediately to the company's office to telegraph the news to Shaughnessy. The operator seemed too slow and so the general manager pushed him aside and began ticking off the message himself. It had been a near thing. "The advance we are now making is quite illegal and we are incurring the gravest responsibility in doing so," Macdonald wrote to Stephen.

John Henry Pope was not able to present the railway resolutions until June 16. By that time the rebellion in Saskatchewan had been crushed. Riel and Poundmaker were both prisoners. Dumont had vanished over the border. Sam Steele was in hot pursuit of Big Bear. Schreiber had already written to Tupper that "the House and country are both in favour of the CPR and that should now be doubly the case when the fact is patent to the world [that] but for the rapid construction . . . Canada would have been involved in a frightful waste of blood and treasure quelling the rising in the North West."

Edward Blake had no intention of giving in without a fight. He was prepared to oppose the relief bill as he had opposed the whole concept of a privately owned transcontinental railway from the very beginning. His speeches were now lasting for six hours and causing even his own supporters to snore, a situation that might have amused Macdonald had it not been for his own problems. Tupper was out of the picture in London. Pope was ill. Campbell, the Minister of Justice, was incapacitated by splitting headaches. Tilley, also ill, was off to Europe. Macdonald had remarked earlier that year that he could not be away for an hour without "some blunder taking place." He had just come through a savage debate; now he must gird himself up for another struggle. This time, however, he was in a stronger position, for the railway had proved itself; no matter what Blake and his colleagues said, it had saved the country. He made that point when he rose to speak:

"Late events have shown us that we are made one people by that road, that that iron link has bound us together in such a way that we stand superior to most of the shafts of ill-fortune, that we can now assemble together, at every point which may be assailed, or may be in danger, the whole physical force of Canada by means of that great artery, against any foreign foe or any internal insurrection or outbreak."

The debate that followed, as Joseph Pope recalled it, was "acrimonious and unpleasant." It was a foregone conclusion that the measure would pass; what was less certain was the company's ability to survive during the time it would take to turn the bill into law. If the Opposition kept on talking the CPR could collapse.

The loan from the bank ran out; the chances of another were slim. Stephen was so hard pressed that he was forced to delay his continuing visits to Ottawa. "I feel like a ruined man," he said. Yet in spite of all his dark predictions about imminent collapse, in spite of his sinister warnings about his own physical condition, in spite of his pledge never again to visit the capital, even in spite of his declarations that he would turn negotiations over to Van Horne, he somehow hung on and the company somehow hung on.

The melodrama continued until the very last hour. By July, the CPR's credit had reached the snapping point. One creditor would wait no longer. The company owed him four hundred thousand dollars and could not meet its obligations. On July 10, it is said, the debt was due. If it was not paid, the CPR was faced with total collapse.

The debate had occupied the best part of a month. The morning of July 10 came and the bill still had not passed the House, which did not sit until 1:30 that afternoon. According to O. D. Skelton, Van Horne's sometime confidant, the four-hundred-thousand-dollar debt was due at three o'clock. There were the usual maddening parliamentary formalities before a division could be taken, but at two that afternoon a majority of the Commons voted in favour of railway relief. The affirmation of confidence was good enough for any creditor; the measure would become law in a matter of days. With the Lake Superior line complete and only a few dozen miles remaining in the gap between the Selkirks and the Gold Range, the railway was saved. It is doubtful whether history records another instance of a national enterprise coming so close to ruin and surviving.

In England, Tupper was working on the great financial house of Baring Brothers to market the new CPR bonds when they were issued. By the time Stephen reached London, he found they had taken the entire issue. In Canada, the CPR got the money it needed to finish the line; and it never had to ask for a government loan again.

4

The frontier was melting away. The old, free days of whiskey peddlers and gamblers, of log towns and unfenced prairie were vanishing. On the heels of the railway came Timothy Eaton's new catalogue: for as little as two dollars the ladies of Moose Jaw or Swift Current could order one of several models of the new Grand Rapids Carpet Sweeper or for twenty-five cents a patented Hartshorn window shade with spring rollers. The violent days were over – gone with the buffalo and the antelope, gone with the whooping crane and the passenger pigeon, gone with the Red River carts and the nomads who used to roam so freely across that tawny sea of grass.

The native peoples had made their final, futile gesture in the deep coulees of the North Saskatchewan country in May and June. Gabriel Dumont met the militia at Fish Creek on April 23, luring them into a kind of buffalo pound and vowing to treat them exactly as he had the thundering herds in the brave days before the railway. Here his force of one hundred and thirty Métis, armed with obsolete weapons, held back some eight hundred men under General Middleton, the bumbling and over-cautious British Army regular. On May 2, at Cut Knife Hill, Chief Poundmaker and 325 Cree followers emerged victorious against cannon, Gatling gun, and some 540 troops under Colonel Otter.

These were the last contortions of a dying culture. The Canadian government had eight thousand men in the field, transported and supplied by rail. The natives had fewer than one thousand, and these were neither organized nor in all cases enthusiastic. Riel planned his campaign according to the spiritual visitations he believed he was receiving almost daily. The more practical Dumont used his knowledge of the ground, his skill at swift manoeuvre, and his experience in the organization of the great hunts to fend off superior forces. Had Riel given him his head, he might have cut the main CPR line and harried the troops for months in a running guerilla warfare; but the outcome in the end would have been the same.

In mid-May Dumont fought his last battle at Batoche. It lasted for four days until the Métis ammunition ran out. Riel surrendered and Dumont fled to the United States, where he subsequently re-enacted the incidents of 1885 in Buffalo Bill's Wild West Show.

In the weeks that followed, the Indian leaders surrendered too, or fled over the border – Poundmaker, Little Poplar, Lucky Man, Red Eagle, Poor Crow, Left Hand, Wandering Spirit, and finally Big Bear. There was no place any longer for a wandering spirit, as Crowfoot, the wisest of them all, had thoroughly understood. Two days before the Duck Lake engagement, Father Lacombe, at Macdonald's request, had ensured the neutrality of the Blackfoot chief. Crowfoot's steadfastness was rewarded with the present of a railway pass from Van Horne. Thus was seen the ironic spectacle of the withered Indian riding back and forth across the prairies on the same iron monster that had changed his people's ways.

In the great trench between the Selkirk Mountains and the Gold Range through which the Columbia flowed, the old frontier life still existed. The last rail was laid on the Lake Superior section on May 16, but in British Columbia construction continued for most of 1885. On the Onderdonk side, the rails were ascending the western slope of the Gold Range from Eagle Pass Landing on Shuswap Lake. On James Ross's side, the rails were moving up the eastern slopes of the same mountains from Farwell, on the Columbia, soon to be renamed Revelstoke.

Again in Farwell the CPR brooked no opposition from local merchants or speculators in the matter of real estate profits. A. S. Farwell, the surveyor, had secured one hundred and seventy-five acres for himself on the banks of the Columbia; as he had anticipated, the railway location went right through his property. However, he refused the terms offered by the CPR, and a long and expensive lawsuit followed, which he eventually won. For practical purposes, he lost. The company followed its practice of moving the location of the station and laid out another townsite which became the heart of the business section.

What the CPR wanted in British Columbia was a gift of land in return for establishing a town or divisional point. The general manager had no intention of locating the smallest station where "it will benefit anybody who has imposed upon us in the matter of the right of way."

In his dealings with William Smithe, the Premier of British Columbia, he struck a hard bargain. He knew that the provincial government was anxious to see the CPR extend its line to a new terminus at Granville on Burrard Inlet because it would help the sale of public land in the area. In return, Van Horne asked for almost half the peninsula on which the present metropolitan area of Vancouver is situated. He settled for an outright gift of six thousand acres from the government. In addition, the Hastings Mill had to give up immediately four thousand acres of land and an additional one thousand acres annually in return for an extension of its lease to 1890.

Van Horne let the private speculators know that if they did not deal liberally with the company, the CPR shops and works would be moved away from their property. In the end the landholders had to yield a third of the lots in each block they held. The railway, in short, would dominate the new city. No street could be continued to tidewater without its permission.

"Keep your eyes open," Van Horne is said to have told a colleague after an all-night poker session in which he himself had been badly taken. "These damned Vancouver fellows will steal the pants off you." But Van Horne was engaged in a larger game for higher stakes. Besides the huge land grant he had managed to secure almost all of the foreshore of the future city, which he had insisted upon because, he said, the depth of the water made piers impossible; the railway would need all that land for dock facilities. Future events were to prove that this was not necessary, and, as later generations slowly realized, the railway would have had to come to the mouth of the inlet anyway, whether or not it was given as much as an acre of free real estate. Van Horne may have been skinned at poker in the last of the frontier railway towns, but he was the real winner in a much more important game of skill and bluff.

5

Edward Mallandaine, aged seventeen, wanted to fight the Indians. When the news of the rebellion reached Victoria, where he lived and went to school, there was no holding him, and his father, a pioneer architect and engineer, did not try to hold him. He booked passage to New Westminster, took the CPR as far as Eagle Pass Landing, and then trudged along the partly finished railway until he reached the foot of the Kicking Horse, where he learned that the rebellion was over.

Disappointed and disgusted, he headed west again, through the

Rogers Pass and into Farwell, with its single street lined with log and frame shacks. There was a feeling of excitement in Farwell that summer of 1885. The town was the half-way point between the two ends of track: freight outfits bustled in from the Rogers and the Eagle passes; boats puffed into the new docks from the mines at the Big Bend of the Columbia; a new post office was opening. Young Mallandaine decided to stay for a while and go into business for himself. He opened a freighting service between the town and Eagle Pass Landing, taking a pony through the Gold Range twice each week along the tote road carved out by the railway contractors and soliciting orders for newspapers and supplies from the navvies along the way. It was hard going but it made a profit.

For a teenage boy it was an exciting time in which to live and an exciting place in which to be. Mallandaine was bright enough to realize that history was being made all around him and he noted it all in his mind: the spectacle of fifty men hanging over the cliffs at Summit Lake, drilling holes in the rock; the sound of thunder in the pass as hundreds of tons of rock hurtled through the air; the sight of a hundred-foot Howe truss put together in a single day; the huts where the navvies slept, "huddled in like bees in a hive with little light and ventilation"; a gun battle with two men shot in a gambling den not far from the Farwell post office; and towards the end of the season, the rough pageantry of the Governor General, Lord Lansdowne himself, riding on horseback through the gap.

Each time Mallandaine made his way through Eagle Pass, that gap was shorter. By October it became clear that the road would be finished by first snow. Now, as the boy moved through the mountains, he noticed the wayside houses shut up and deserted, contractors' equipment being shifted and carted away, and hundreds of men travelling on foot with all their belongings to the east or to the west.

An oppressive silence settled on the pass – a silence broken only by the hideous shrieking of the construction locomotives echoing through the hills, as they rattled by with flatcars loaded with steel rails. Mallandaine felt a kind of chill creeping into his bones – not just the chill of the late October winds, sweeping down through the empty bunkhouses, but the chill of loneliness that comes to a man walking through a graveyard in the gloom.

"It seemed as though some scourge had swept this mountain pass. How ghostly the deserted camps would look at night! How quiet it all seemed!" The pass became so lonely that Mallandaine almost began to dread the ride between Farwell and the Landing. There was something eerie about the sight of boarded-up buildings, dump cars left by the wayside, and portions of contractors' outfits cast aside along the line of the tote road. And the silence! Not since the days of the survey parties had the mountains seemed so still. Mallandaine decided to return to Victoria. There was, however, one final piece of business which he did not want to miss: he was determined to be on hand when the last spike on the Canadian Pacific Railway was driven.

On the afternoon of November 6, the last construction train to load rails left Farwell for Eagle Pass. Mallandaine was one of several who climbed aboard and endured the "cold, cheerless, rough ride" that followed. Far into the darkness of the night the little train puffed, its passengers shivering with cold. Mallandaine, lying directly upon the piled-up rails and unable to sleep, was almost shaken to pieces as the train rattled over the unballasted roadbed. Finally it came to a stop. The youth tumbled off the flatcar in the pitch dark, found an abandoned boxcar, and managed a short sleep. At six that morning the track crews were on the job. By the time Mallandaine awoke, the rails had almost come together.

At nine o'clock, the last two rails were brought forward and measured for cutting, with wagers being laid on the exact length that would be needed: it came to twenty-five feet, five inches. A peppery little man with long white whiskers cut the final rail with a series of hard blows. This was the legendary Major Rogers. One of the short rails was then laid in place and spiked; the second was left loose for the ceremony. The crowd, which included Al Rogers, Tom Wilson, Sam Steele, and Henry Cambie, waited for the official party to appear.

It is perhaps natural that the tale of the driving of the last spike on the CPR should have become a legend in which fancy often outweighs fact; it was, after all, the great symbolic act of Canada's first century. Two days before the spike was driven, George Stephen had cabled from England: "Railway now out of danger." Nine days after the spike was driven, Louis Riel kept his rendezvous with the hangman at Regina. In more ways than one the completion of the railway signalled the end of the small, confined, comfortable nation that had been pieced together in 1867.

It is not surprising, then, that some who were present that day in the mountains should have recalled half a century later that the spike was made of gold. But there was no golden spike. The Governor General had had a silver spike prepared for the occasion; it was not used, and His Excellency, who had expected to be present, had been forced to return to Ottawa from British Columbia when weather conditions caused a delay in the completion of the line.

"The last spike," said Van Horne in his blunt way, "will be just as good an iron one as there is between Montreal and Vancouver, and anyone who wants to see it driven will have to pay full fare."

The truth was that the CPR could not afford a fancy ceremony. It had cost the Northern Pacific somewhere between $175,000 and $250,000 to drive its golden spike. The CPR had enormous expenditures facing it. Van Horne's whole purpose was to get a through line operating to the Pacific so that he could tap the Asian trade. There would be time for ceremonies later on.

The very simplicity of the scene at Eagle Pass – the lack of pomp, the absence of oratory, the plainness of the crowd, the presence of the workmen in the foreground of the picture – made the spectacle an oddly memorable one. Van Horne and a distinguished party had come out from Ottawa, Montreal, and Winnipeg for the occasion. The big names included Donald A. Smith, Sandford Fleming, John Egan, John McTavish, the land commissioner, and George Harris, a Boston financier who was a company director. Meanwhile, on the far side of the mountains, Andrew Onderdonk's private car "Eva" came up from Port Moody with Michael Haney aboard, pulling the final load of rails to the damp crevice in the mountains which the general manager, with a fine sense of drama, had decided years before to name Craigellachie.

It was a dull, murky November morning, the mountains sheathed in clouds, the evergreens dripping in a coverlet of wet snow. Up puffed the quaint engine with its polished brass boiler, its cordwood tender, its diamond-shaped smokestack, and the great square box in front containing the acetylene headlight on whose glass was painted the number 148. The ceremonial party descended and walked through the clearing of stumps and debris to the spot where Major Rogers was standing, holding the tie bar under the final rail. By common consent the honour of driving the connecting spike was assigned to the eldest of the four directors present – to Donald A. Smith, whose hair in five years of railway construction had turned a frosty white. As Fleming noted, the old fur trader represented much more than the CPR. His presence recalled that long line of Highlanders – the Mackenzies and McTavishes, Stuarts and McGillivrays, Frasers, Finlaysons, McLeods, and McLaughlins – who had first penetrated these mountains and set the transcontinental pattern of communication that the railway would continue.

Now that moment had arrived which so many Canadians had believed would never come – a moment that Fleming had been waiting for since 1862, when he placed before the government the first practical outline for a highway to the Pacific. The workmen and the officials crowded around Smith. Young Edward Mallandaine squeezed in behind him, right next to Harris, the Boston financier, and directly in front of Cambie, McTavish, and Egan. As the photographer raised his camera, Mallandaine craned forward. Fifty-nine years later, when all the rest of that great company were in their graves, Colonel Edward Mallandaine, stipendiary magistrate and reeve of the Kootenay town of Creston, would be on hand when the citizens of Revelstoke, in false beards and borrowed frock-coats, re-enacted the famous photograph on that very spot.

Smith's first blow bent the spike badly. Frank Brothers, the roadmaster, pulled it out and replaced it with another. Smith posed with the uplifted hammer. The assembly froze. The shutter clicked. Smith lowered the hammer onto the spike. The shutter clicked again. Smith began to drive the spike home. Save for the blows of the hammer and the sound of a small mountain stream there was absolute silence. Even after the spike was driven home, the stillness persisted. "It seemed," Sandford Fleming recalled, "as if the act now performed had worked a spell on all present. Each one appeared absorbed in his own reflections." The spell was broken by a cheer, "and it was no ordinary cheer. The subdued enthusiasm, the pent-up feelings of men familiar with hard work, now found vent." More cheers followed, enhanced by the shrill whistle of the locomotives.

All this time, Van Horne had stood impassively beside Fleming, his hands thrust into the side pockets of his overcoat. In less than four years, he had managed to complete a new North West Passage. Did any memories surface in that retentive mind as the echoes of Smith's hammer blows rang down the corridor of Eagle Pass? Did he think back on the previous year when, half-starved and soaking wet, he had come this way with Reed and Rogers? Did he reflect, with passing triumph, on those early days in Winnipeg when the unfriendly press had attacked him as an idle boaster and discussed his rumoured dismissal? Did he recall those desperate moments in Ottawa and Montreal when the CPR seemed about to collapse like a house of cards? Probably not, for Van Horne was not a man to brood or to gloat over the past. It is likelier that his mind was fixed on more immediate problems: the Vancouver terminus, the Pacific postal subsidy, and the Atlantic steamship service. He could not predict the future but he would help to control it, and some of the new symbols of his adopted country would be of his making: the fleet of white Empresses flying the familiar checkered flag, the turreted hotels with their green château roofs, boldly perched on promontory and lakefront; and the international slogan that would proclaim in Arabic, Hindi, Chinese, and a dozen other languages that the CPR spanned the world.

As the cheering died the crowd turned to Van Horne. "Speech! Speech!" they cried. Van Horne was not much of a speechmaker;

he was, in fact, a little shy in crowds. What he said was characteristically terse, but it went into the history books: "All I can say is that the work has been done well in every way."

Major Rogers was more emotional. This was his moment of triumph too, and he was savouring it. In spite of all the taunts of his Canadian colleagues, in spite of the scepticism of the newspapers, in spite of his own gloomy forebodings and the second thoughts of his superiors, his pass had been chosen and the rails ran directly through it to Craigellachie. For once, the stoic major did not trouble to conceal his feelings. He was "so gleeful," Edward Mallandaine observed, "that he upended a huge tie and tried to mark the spot by the side of the track by sticking it in the ground."

There were more cheers, some mutual congratulations, and a rush for souvenirs. Then the locomotive whistle sounded again and a voice was heard to cry: "All aboard for the Pacific!" It was the first time that phrase had been used by a conductor from the East, but Fleming noted that it was uttered "in the most prosaic tones, as of constant daily occurrence." The official party obediently boarded the cars and a few moments later the little train was in motion again, clattering over the newly laid rail and over the last spike and down the long incline of the mountains, off towards the gloomy canyon of the Fraser, off to the soft meadows beyond, off to the blue Pacific and into history.

Cast of Major Characters

The Politicians

Sir John A. Macdonald, Prime Minister of Canada, 1867-73, 1878-91.
Sir George Etienne Cartier, Minister of Militia and Defence, 1867-73.
Sir Charles Tupper, Cabinet minister, 1870, 1878-84.
Sir Francis Hincks, Minister of Finance, 1869-73.
Hector Louis Langevin, Minister of Public Works, 1869-73, 1879-91.
J. J. C. Abbott, legal counsel for Sir Hugh Allan, 1873; for CPR, 1880.
John Henry Pope, Minister of Railways and Canals, 1885-89.
Senator Frank Smith, Minister without Portfolio, 1882-91.
Edgar Dewdney, Lieutenant-Governor of North West Territories, 1881-88.
Alexander Mackenzie, Prime Minister of Canada, 1873-78 (Liberal).
Edward Blake, Cabinet minister; Leader of Opposition, 1880-87.
Sir Richard Cartwright, Minister of Finance, 1873-78.
Lucius Seth Huntington, M.P. for Shefford, Quebec.

The Pathfinders

Sandford Fleming, Engineer-in-Chief of CPR, 1871-80.
Marcus Smith, head of B.C. surveys, 1872-76; inspector on B.C. line.
Walter Moberly, head of mountain surveys, 1871-72.
Henry J. Cambie, head of B.C. surveys after 1876; engineer on B.C. line.
Charles Horetzky, photographer; explorer of Pine Pass region.
General Thomas L. Rosser, chief engineer of CPR, 1881-82.
J. H. E. Secretan, engineer; head of CPR survey party on prairies.
Charles Aeneas Shaw, engineer, head of prairie and mountain surveys.
Major A. B. Rogers, engineer in charge of Mountain Division of CPR.
Tom Wilson, packer and guide; friend of Major Rogers.

The Early Entrepreneurs

Sir Hugh Allan, Montreal ship owner and financier.
Jay Cooke, American banker; financier of Northern Pacific Railroad.
George S. McMullen, promoter; found American backers for Allan.
Senator D. L. Macpherson, Toronto railway builder; rival of Allan.

The CPR Syndicate

James J. Hill, St. Paul transportation merchant and railway builder.
Norman Kittson, fur trader; partner of Hill.
Donald A. Smith, Hudson's Bay Company executive; cousin of Stephen.
George Stephen, president, Bank of Montreal, 1876-81; of CPR, 1881-88.
Duncan McIntyre, Montreal merchant; president, Canada Central Railway.

Richard B. Angus, former general manager, Bank of Montreal.
John S. Kennedy, New York banker and railroad financier.

The Builders

Joseph Whitehead, contractor on Pembina Branch and Section
   Fifteen.
J. W. Sifton, politician and contractor.
Michael J. Haney, construction boss.
William Cornelius Van Horne, general manager, CPR, 1882;
   vice-president, 1884; president, 1888-99; chairman of board,
   1899-1910.
John Egan, superintendent, CPR western division after 1882.
Thomas Shaughnessy, CPR purchasing agent, 1882-85; president,
   1899-1910.
John Ross, head of Lake Superior construction, western section.
James Ross, head of construction, Mountain Division.
Andrew Onderdonk, construction contractor in B.C., 1881-85.
Collingwood Schreiber, government's engineer-in-chief after 1880.

The Native Peoples

Louis Riel, leader of uprisings in the West, 1869-70, 1885.
Gabriel Dumont, chief of buffalo hunts; Riel's adjutant general.
Crowfoot, head chief of Blackfoot tribes.
Poundmaker, Cree chief; involved in Saskatchewan Rebellion, 1885.
Big Bear, Plains Cree chief; a leader in Saskatchewan Rebellion, 1885.

The Bystanders

Lord Dufferin, Governor General of Canada, 1872-78.
George Brown, editor of Toronto *Globe*.
George Walkem, Premier of British Columbia, 1874-76, 1878-82.
George Monro Grant, minister, author; Fleming's secretary in 1872.
John Macoun, botanist, explorer; companion of Fleming and Grant.
Father Albert Lacombe, missionary to Indians; chaplain to navvies.
Sir Henry Whatley Tyler, president of Grand Trunk Railway,
   1876-95.
Joseph Hickson, general manager of Grand Trunk Railway, 1874-91.
Sir John Rose, London financier and confidant of Macdonald.
Sir Alexander T. Galt, first High Commissioner to London, 1880-83.
Charles J. Brydges, land commissioner for Hudson's Bay Company.
Arthur Wellington Ross, Winnipeg realtor; real estate adviser to CPR.
Michael Hagan, editor/publisher, Thunder Bay *Sentinel, Inland
   Sentinel*.
Nicholas Flood Davin, poet, author; editor/publisher, Regina *Leader*.
Samuel Benfield Steele, commander of NWMP detachments along CPR.

Index